OPTIONALITY

OPTIONALITY

HOW TO SURVIVE AND THRIVE IN A VOLATILE WORLD

RICHARD MEADOWS

THALES PRESS

Thales Press paperback edition: November 2020
Paperback ISBN: 978-0-473-54550-5
Kindle ISBN: 978-0-473-54552-9
Ebook ISBN: 978-0-473-54551-2

www.optionalitybook.com

CONTENTS

Book IV

RHIZIKON

Book V

KAIROS

Book VI

TELOS

PREFACE

THE APPARENTLY BATSHIT CRAZY THEORY that we're living in a simulated reality is growing on me every day. Maybe we really are trapped in some alien teenager's cosmic jam jar. They're getting bored of watching us over the millennia, so they've decided to give the jar a good old shake.

This is the only reasonable explanation for the adjectival times in which we find ourselves. This year, I personally managed to get rattled by a large earthquake, shivered and sweated through the novel coronavirus, lost my only steady income source overnight, found myself quarantined in Mexico thousands of kilometres away from home, and saw my investment accounts perform acrobatics so death-defying they would make the entire Cirque du Soleil cast quit on the spot. Possible futures flickered in and out of existence on a daily basis, and my perception of time is so warped that I'm still trying to piece together what happened.

My travails took place against the broader backdrop of a global pandemic, riots and looting in the streets, a reality TV star in the White House, jobless claims shooting up so quickly that it looked like a printing error, and California transformed into a post-apocalyptic movie set. The stockmarket crashed faster than ever before in history, and followed up with its most profitable month in 30 years. The price of oil briefly went *negative*, with traders desperately paying anyone who could take it off their hands. Money printers are still going brrr so fast that central bankers are at risk of getting a friction burn. I expect the plagues of locusts will turn up any moment now.

Welcome to the future, babies. It's not always going to be like this, but we can expect the highs to be higher, and the lows to be lower. Which brings us to the central premise of this book: how can we position ourselves to not only *survive* this kind of uncertainty, but *profit* from it?

This might sound gauche while people are dying in horrifying ways, but people are constantly dying in horrifying ways, and besides, I know you're thinking about it. Apocalypse scenarios crank up the dial on all three of the human emotions: fear, hunger, and horniness. I already ate all my emergency snacks by day two of quarantine and this is a family friendly publication, so let's go with 'fear'.

It's hard not to be scared about the future, especially if you've lost your income, are about to enter the job market, or suddenly find yourself missing tens of thousands of dollars from your retirement account. The goal of this book is to get you into a position where you don't have to worry about exactly what the future holds.

This is the position I've been working towards for some time, which means this year has been strangely vindicating. I was expecting an explosion of volatility, which means I managed to not only avoid blowing up, but end the year in my strongest position yet.

I owe my good fortune to a very old idea called 'optionality'. I first came across the concept in the writings of risk analyst Nassim Nicholas Taleb several years ago, started wondering if it might contain some kind of grand unifying theory of human flourishing, and haven't been able to stop thinking about it since.

In tumbling down the optionality rabbit hole, I found answers to several paradoxes I'd been struggling with: the intuition that more options are better vs so-called 'choice overload', the life-and-death importance of having both personal freedom and binding constraints, and most importantly, the problem of making decisions in an increasingly uncertain world.

So I started hunting for open-ended opportunities in my own life, taking simple precautions to protect against disaster, balancing my speculative projects, and rejigging my investment portfolio to get exposure to potential moonshots.

I also loaded up on cheap options: reading books and blogs written by weirdos, putting my own ideas out into the world, replying to thousands of emails from readers, and investing my social capital—and occasionally, cold hard cash—in friends and strangers whose talents had not yet been widely recognised.

This strategy has worked out nicely so far: mostly in avoiding shooting myself in the foot, but also in systematically exposing myself to serendipitous opportunities. Some of these options have landed in the money, and the future no longer looks so scary.

I'm finally ready to lay out the optionality approach in full. I've tested early versions of these ideas on my blog, Deep Dish, and in my weekly *Budget Buster* newspaper column. I've interviewed everyone from CEOs to criminals, billionaires, solo mums, entrepreneurs, polymaths, and philosophers. And I've strip-mined every relevant book and paper I could get my grubby little paws on. All this material has been ground down into its component molecules, and distilled into a set of general principles that anyone can follow. That's the book you're holding right now.

It's also a compendium of mistakes. The road I took to get here was long and winding, and honestly, kind of stupid. So you might also think of this as my journey to 'discover' age-old wisdom, in the same sense that Columbus 'discovered' the Americas, i.e. entirely by accident, driven by hubris, and 15,000 years too late.

I'm forever grateful to the people who were brave enough to strip down to their financial underwear in public, and helped me open up my own options. This is my attempt to pay it forward.

Richard Meadows
November 2020

WHAT IS OPTIONALITY?

If you have no optionality at all, life is grim. At best, you're *running in place*. Stuck in a holding pattern of boredom and frustration; capabilities forever lying dormant.

At worst, you're *trapped*. Locked into decisions that funnel you towards the abyss. Your brain stews in fear and adrenaline. Every decision is reactive, and it's a constant struggle to keep your head above water.

Optionality gives you room to breathe. You can *take it easy*. Wait, wait, wait —and then swing for the fat pitches with all your strength, using the resources you've gathered so patiently.

Optionality is the power to say "no". You can *maintain integrity*. Walk away from a bum deal, blow the whistle, refuse to do anything that conflicts with your values. Choose to fail on your own terms, rather than succeed on someone else's.

And failure is no longer so terrible, because optionality lets you *explore*. You have a safety net to take risks and chase your hubristic dreams. There's plenty of slack in the system, and no single breakage point. Tinkering and play are encouraged.

There's no need to fret about exactly what the future holds. If you have optionality, *volatility is your friend*. Instead of struggling against the chaotic randomness of the universe, you can harness it to work in your favour.

That's the poetic description. Now let's get a little more concrete.

Here's the simplest definition of optionality:

Optionality = the *right*, but not the *obligation*, to take action

Anyone who has ever taken out an insurance policy already understands the core insight here. As a semi-permanent traveler, I make small, regular payments to secure the right—but not the obligation—to call up my insurer when something goes wrong. If I get in a minor scrape, or lose my bag, I can choose to pay for it out of pocket. I am under no obligation to get the insurance company involved, and most of the time, I won't. Much better to handle it myself.

But I always maintain the *option* to call my insurer if things get really hairy: say, I accidentally T-bone someone in my rental car, or find myself in the ICU with a tropical parasite in my gut. If my hospital bills run up to a million dollars, or I have to be airlifted to another country, I want to make that someone else's problem. Maintaining this option is extremely valuable to me: far more so than the small upfront fee would suggest.

What matters here is the *asymmetry* between the cost and the potential benefit.

After all, I also have the right—but not the obligation—to go on an online shopping spree, or get McDonald's delivered to my door. I have millions of options at my fingertips at all times. The difference is that there's no positive asymmetry: the rewards are usually modest, and so are the costs.

In fact, many of these trades are asymmetrical in the wrong direction. There is such a thing as negative optionality: if you get hooked on meth or run up a gambling debt to the local mobsters, you have destroyed the right to take certain actions, and imposed an obligation in its place.

So: what we're looking for is trades that offer large, unlimited upside with small, fixed costs.

Insurance is the least-inspiring form of optionality, because it can only ever avert disaster. To get a sense of the true potential, let's look at one of the oldest and all-time-great options trades.

Thales of Miletus was the first of the Greek philosophers. All he wanted to do was pursue his ideas, but the way Aristotle tells it, everyone made fun of him for being a nerd. "If you're so smart," they asked, "why aren't you rich?"

One winter, Thales used his knowledge of astronomy—an informational edge over his detractors—to observe that there was going to be a large crop of olives. So he raised a little money, and bought advance rights to every olive press in Miletus, at a large discount. When the season arrived, the bumper crop triggered a rush of demand. Thales let out the presses on his own terms, getting good and rich, and forcing the haters to admit that, OK, fine, there might be something to this whole philosophy business.

Thales of Miletus, circa 580 BC.

As Aristotle noted, Thales' prediction didn't even have to be correct: the scheme would have been successful even if there was a modest harvest. The downside was always limited to the small deposits he placed on the unused olive presses, while the potential upside was huge.

So the concept of optionality is nothing new. In collecting a portfolio of open-ended options—what we're going to shorthand throughout this book as 'having optionality'—we're copying a Greek philosopher who has been dead and buried for 2600 years.

But I will also make a stronger claim: that optionality is massively underrated, and far more valuable today than it was in the time of Thales.

WHAT I PROMISE YOU

Individual outcomes are always mediated by some degree of blind randomness: the bounty of this year's olive harvest, a mutating cell, the mood of the assistant producer who happens to read your spec script. That's why I can't make grand claims about how this book will give you toe-curling orgasms and make you fabulously rich and cure your persistent dandruff. Even if you do everything right, you might *still* draw the short straw.

But as the great author Terry Pratchett put it, when the floppy-eared Spaniel of Luck sniffs at your cuffs, it helps if you have a collar and piece of string in your pocket.

The optionality approach to getting lucky starts with identifying and capping the risks which might ruin your life. This gets you into the position of 'not losing', which is a major victory in and of itself: all you have to do is consistently not-lose, and you'll come out well ahead of the pack.

Moonshot-style successes are much rarer, but optionality also gives you the best possible chances of raking in a big win. You keep hunting for asymmetric opportunities wherever you can find them, and systematically putting more irons in the fire. With a little luck, one or more of them will eventually pay off in spectacular fashion.

So that's my promise to you. On the defensive side, this book will get you into the position of 'not losing'. On the aggressive side, it will maximise your chances of hitting the big one. You can never be sure if the universe will come to the party, but optionality is the best system for making your own luck.

HOW THIS BOOK IS STRUCTURED

Your time is precious. Instead of beating you over the head with six different examples of each concept, I've prepared a companion reading list to dig deeper into any topic you care to learn more about. You can access it at optionalitybook.com/resources.

Key Terms are bolded and capitalised on first mention. If you forget what something means, or skipped past the initial explanation, you'll find a glossary at the back of the book.

Every fact, figure, and study referenced is listed in the bibliography, along with hat-tips and sources which would have interrupted the flow of the text. Note that I have shamelessly begged, borrowed and stolen material from dozens of fields. In some cases I can't remember where I first encountered a certain idea, or there is no clear progenitor. If you come across a clever insight, I promise it had nothing to do with me.

Books are incredibly cheap options to take out, but we need to get past the idea that we should read them from cover to cover. To cap the downside: before you commit any further, skim the table of contents and see if anything catches your eye. If not, bail out now. And if you're not having fun by Book II —Book I lays a lot of groundwork—cut your losses and go do something else.

Finally, skim with wild abandon. I'm laying out a path a smart teenager could follow, which means you're guaranteed to come across material you already know, or that doesn't apply to you. I encourage you to skip paragraphs, chapters, and entire books as you please.

Optionality is divided into six books, each designed to more-or-less stand alone, and each taking its theme from an ancient Greek concept.

I. EUDAIMONIA

Eudaimonia is the *'why?'*. Why optionality? What's it good for? Why is it more important than money, or hedonic pleasure, or happiness? An introduction to the basic concepts, and the underlying philosophy.

II. AKRASIA

Akrasia is the *'how?'*. The art of making decisions under uncertainty, and defeating a host of internal and external saboteurs. A toolkit of high-level strategies.

III. PRAXIS

Praxis is the *'what?'*. What are the specific asymmetries we might use to cap the downside and open the upside? A compendium of attractive options for building health, wealth, skills, and social capital.

IV. RHIZIKON

Rhizikon is the *'what if?'*. Protecting against ruin, taking calculated risks to open upside, and investing strategies through the optionality lens. A deep dive on risk and opportunity.

V. KAIROS

Kairos is the *'when?'*. The art of opportune timing, and in particular, when to open up our options, and when to deliberately close them off. A higher-level set of constraints for choosing our own chains.

VI. TELOS

Telos is the *'what next?'*. The endgame; what it's all about; the project of mean-ing-making in a meaningless universe. On the hard limits of optionality, and on which altars we might choose to sacrifice it.

I

EUDAIMONIA

EUDAIMONIA. (noun) from the ancient Greek εὐδαιμονία: *The ideal state of human flourishing. To go beyond happiness, health, and prosperity, to living a meaningful and virtuous life.*

INTRODUCTION

"Every morning I roll out of bed and ask myself: what should I do today?"

I WROTE THIS SENTENCE IN AUGUST 2016, looking out over a beautiful beach on a tropical island in Southeast Asia.

For the first time in my life, I had absolute freedom. The previous two decades were an uninterrupted freight train of schooling and work, which made this new state of existence feel surreal. There were moments of pure elation, and the occasional pang of guilt. Did I cheat, somehow? I kept waiting for a giant skyhook to descend from the heavens, hoist me up by the seat of my elephant pants, and jerk me back to reality.

It took a long time to realise that this sort of lifestyle was even possible. In 2013, I was working as a business reporter for Fairfax Media, where I was tasked with writing a regular feature article on personal finance. One fateful week, I chose the topic of 'net worth', which is defined as everything you own, minus everything you owe. I was curious what my own number was, so I did the math.

After tallying it all up, I found myself staring at a negative figure. Not even a big fat zero, but worse. My savings and other assets were entirely wiped out by my debts, and then some. It's kind of depressing to discover you're somehow even poorer as a grown adult than when you entered the world as a screaming naked infant.

I knew that plenty of other twenty-somethings were in the same boat, but it wasn't much consolation. Unlike them, I made my living lecturing other people on how to be good with money. It was time to get my shit together.

Journalism is not known for lucrative salaries, but the savings started trickling into my bank account. I kept tweaking my spending habits, and the trickle became a steady flow, then a torrent. I built a spreadsheet to keep track of my net worth, and got a kick out of watching the number climb higher each month. My student loan shrank, and then disappeared altogether. I needed somewhere to put all the spare cash, so I started messing around with investing.

By early 2015 I was living on half my income. I had a good job, but I felt like I was spinning my wheels. I saw the future rolling out in front of me like a great grey swatch of flannel, comfortable but dull.

I was desperate to escape my parochial island home on the ass-end of the world, so I made a promise to myself: when my net worth hit NZ$100,000, I'd quit my job, get rid of everything I owned, and move overseas.[1]

As soon as I cracked the ninety thousands, I handed in my notice and bought a one-way ticket to Bangkok. I was walking on air by this point, and probably could have saved myself the fare by floating across the Pacific.

A few months after hitting my goal, I wrote a coming-out essay on the virtues of frugality—a longer version of the words you've just read. It was called 'How to Save $100,000 by Age 25', and it became the single most popular article I'd ever written. I received a torrent of emails and messages from friends and strangers, requests for TV and radio interviews, and the dubious honour of a profile in *The Daily Mail*.

I was very proud of myself for having hacked life. But as it started to become clear—and this will shock you!—my 25-year-old self did not in fact possess the keys to the universe.

Those heady early months involved a lot of lounging on tropical islands, barely moving from the hammock except to skin up a joint or get another bottle of wine. The only sign of life came from the geckos on the ceiling. Occasionally they licked their eyeballs or caught a moth; this being a source of enormous excitement to me and my English friend, who insisted on narrating every scene like a low-rent David Attenborough.

It was around this time that I decided that maybe total unconstrained freedom wasn't all it was cracked up to be. So I stumbled out of the haze of ennui and Cambodian sativa and back into some semblance of a useful human being.

I spent the rest of my mini-retirement reading books and meeting smart people, which rubbed my face in a puddle of my own ignorance. I stopped being so critical of other people's lifestyle choices, and realised my beloved minimalism and frugality were also tribal identity movements—and in the worst case, masochistic pissing matches.

I'm sharing my character development arc upfront because it mirrors the arc of the book: starting with the popular conceptions of the good life, how and where they go wrong, and what we might replace them with.

This first book aims to answer the question 'why optionality, exactly?', and by extension, 'why *not* happiness, or money, or hedonism, or transcendental bliss?'

It's crucial to choose what to pursue upfront, because it determines the particular set of trade-offs we will face: you can have *anything* you want, but you can't have *everything* you want.

Of course, not-choosing is also a choice. The very first step towards making better trade-offs is noticing that you're making them in the first place.

1

THE POSSIBILITY TREE

I saw my life branching out before me like the green fig tree in the story. From the tip of every branch, like a fat purple fig, a wonderful future beckoned and winked.

— SYLVIA PLATH, 'THE BELL JAR'

WHAT DID YOU HAVE for breakfast this morning? A bowl of cereal? What kind? Granola? Which brand? Did you take it with milk? Full-fat or 1 per cent? After breakfast, how did you get to work? Bus, car, bicycle? What route did you take? What did you listen to on the way? Who did you have lunch with? Which emails did you read? Did you help your boss with his dumb request, or subtly make fun of him? What websites did you browse while you were pretending to work?

If you visualise all the potential actions available to you at any given moment, it's a sprawling decision tree of branching possibilities (Fig 1.1).

Unfortunately, most branches of the possibility tree are deadwood. If your crippling student loan debt condemns you to a life of indentured servitude, the fact that you can choose between 43 brands of breakfast cereal doesn't give you much in the way of optionality. If the prison guards sometimes let you choose what to watch on the telly, same again. The *quality* of choices matter.

Figure 1.1. The tangled branches of the Possibility Tree.

The overwhelming array of choices we're presented with in daily life don't display the asymmetric rewards we're hunting for—in fact, they're often asymmetric in the wrong direction. And there's no way to win: our possibility trees have grown so tangled that it's impossible to make an 'optimal' decision.

This is no accident. Consumer capitalism is designed to give us *the illusion* of great choice, even while it traps us within one narrow sector of possibility-space. Its branching confusopolies ensnare our monkey minds, and steal our most precious resources: money, time, and attention.

The end result is that we spend almost all of our efforts deliberating over a predetermined range of cookie-cutter choices, instead of generating a better set of options to choose from.

The only way to 'solve' an intractable problem is to reject its assumptions. Alexander the Great, faced with the impossible task of untangling the Gordian knot, pulled out his sword and chopped it in half. And so, instead of getting lost in the labyrinthine branches of the possibility tree, we can draw our pruning saws and hack them off at the trunk.

Finally, all the years I spent as a part-time orchard labourer are about to pay off! It turns out that pruning trees is not about making them look stylish and sophisticated, but improving the quality of the fruit they bear. Unless you ruthlessly lop off most of the branches, come harvest time, you'll end up with a million misshapen nubs.

And so, if we want to build optionality, perversely, we first have to deliberately *constrain* our choices. Here are some ways I have pruned my own possibility tree at various points:

- Banishing junk food from the house
- Blocking distracting websites
- Refusing to own a car
- Not keeping up with fashions
- Foregoing overdrafts and credit cards

These are variations on a very old idea: that constraints can be liberating. By restricting your choices along one dimension, you can create more freedom along a dimension that's more important to you. Almost every life philosophy —minimalism, Christianity, the Paleo diet, whatever—boils down to this kind of trade-off. Do *this* and not *that*, and you get to retire early, or lose weight, or ascend to heaven.

The initial round of pruning dramatically improves the quality of choices on the possibility tree. Instead of misshapen nubs, a fat purple fig sprouts from the tip of each branch. These are the juicy options that we want to collect (Fig 1.2).

Figure 1.2. The Possibility Tree after a vigorous pruning.

Generating better options is much more important than being a perfect decision-maker. But if we never picked any of those figs, they'd wither and rot on the branch. We'd keep hoarding more and more 'maybes', forever and ever, until we died. So we need a second set of constraints to *exercise* our options. These are the tools of risk management and opportune timing, as described later in the book.

CURRENCIES OF LIFE

The single most powerful way to open up your options in life is to a) have more money, or b) require less of it in the first place. The combination of simple tastes and a healthy bank balance buys you a whole lot of freedom. This is why the second running theme of this book is the practice of frugality; smuggled in like spinach in the optionality lasagne.

Now, don't pull that face!

While frugality conjures up associations of stealing ketchup packets from Burger King, it was once considered the noblest of virtues. The modern version of what the Romans called *frugalitas* is dogged by misconceptions. Frugality not only has nothing to do with being a miserly tight-ass—it's not even strictly about *money*.

Money is just one of many precious **Currencies of Life**: time, health, mental bandwidth, energy, social status, hedonic pleasure, meaning.

Figure 1.3. The Currencies of Life.

All of these things can be exchanged with one another to a greater or lesser degree. If I smoke a cigarette, I've decided to trade $1 and a small amount of health capital for a few minutes of stimulation. If I do it behind the bike sheds in high school, I might also gain social status among my fellow edgy teens. If I puff smoke in the face of diners at a restaurant, I become a social pariah.

The art of frugality starts with paying attention to the exchange rates between these currencies. Some deals are better than others. But frugality is *not* about explicitly calculating every decision. There are so many dimensions to weigh up that trying to run the numbers on every life choice quickly becomes overwhelming—the same mistake as trying to untangle the possibility tree.

Instead, we should think of trade-offs as *the enemy*: they are massively time-consuming, and they make us unhappy, because they force us to consider what we're giving up. We want to be more thoughtful about the trade-offs we make, but we also want to make as few as we can get away with.

Making perfect decisions is overrated. The information we need to make the 'correct' choice always costs us something to acquire—say, the time and energy wasted in trying to model some hopelessly thorny trade-off. When information costs more than it's worth, the rational move is to remain blissfully ignorant. Frugality requires us to decide what is actually worth deliberating over in the first place—*to choose what to choose.*

MIN-MAXING

Amongst players of role-playing games, there is a very annoying tactic in which someone ignores almost all of their character's development, and puts all their points into one branch of the skill tree. They end up with some souped-up druid who displays an embarrassing ignorance of the arcane arts, except for that one attack that can kill you with a single roll of the dice.

This is called **Min-Maxing**, and it's what frugality should look like, done correctly. Rather than delicately snipping away at the possibility tree, we have to go at it with all the enthusiasm of Edward Scissorhands on a PCP-fuelled rampage.

The idea is to ignore, ignore, ignore all the alluring 'deals' that are constantly dangled in our direction, then load up heavily on the rare attractive trades. This is not about self-denial: in ruthlessly pruning all the bum deals that aren't even worth considering, we're greedily optimising to get more of the things we actually want.

So the question is not what to cut. Our starting point is that *everything* gets cut, and has to earn its way back into consideration. The question is: what to load up on?

Some people choose to min-max on money: they're single-mindedly focused on stacking up cash, and are willing to do whatever it takes to get more of it. Others jump on every trade-off that increases their health, no matter how much it costs them in time, money, and effort. Some people pour everything into social connection, or optimise for pleasure-seeking above all else.

The argument of this book is that we should instead load up on optionality, as a kind of derivative that buys us the *right* to all the precious currencies of life, and let the trade-offs between them emerge accordingly.

Money is valuable so long as it continues to open up our options—and after that point, it isn't. Same goes for health, or social capital, or anything else. We're going to see examples of how all of these things run into the point of diminishing returns, and sometimes end up restricting our choices.

Frugality is the best framework I know of for systematically making better trade-offs, including the kind of asymmetries that build optionality.

But only if we value optionality highly enough in the first place. See, frugality also has a dark side: if you don't understand the importance of having options, you might accidentally end up closing them off.

CATCHING FIRE

Around the time I first calculated my net worth, I interviewed an eccentric online personality called 'Mr Money Mustache'. On his blog, he shared the strategies he'd used to save up enough cash to quit his job by age 30, start a family, and live off the passive income from his investments forever. By embracing a frugal lifestyle, he'd cut his entire working career down to *nine years*.

After doing my homework, I found out that Mr Money Mustache was the rambunctious alter-ego of a Canadian engineer named Pete Adeney. Not only was he the real deal, Adeney was the unofficial leader of an underground movement championing financial independence and retiring early (**FIRE**). It turned out there were cadres of rebels around the world who rejected mindless consumerism. They laughed mightily at the thought of 40 years tilling the cubicle farm, and retired decades earlier than their co-workers.

By the time the interview ran, I was a card-carrying member of the Mustachian cult. The biggest revelation to me was what Adeney calls the 'shockingly simple math of early retirement'. As he pointed out, the only number that matters is the proportion of your take-home pay that you save. The conventional advice is that you're doing great if you manage to stash 15 per cent of your after-tax pay. Follow the standard advice and you'll get a standard outcome—which is to say, 40 to 50 years of toil.

Early retirement enthusiasts manage to save as much as *half* their pay, which puts them on track to retire after 17 years. A few push the low-cost lifestyle to the extreme, and manage to retire even sooner.

The beauty of the math is that after a point, it really doesn't matter how much you earn. It's all about the proportion saved: if you manage to stash away half of your $50,000 annual salary, you'll retire a full 20 years earlier than someone who blows 90 per cent of their $150,000 pay packet. Fig. 1.4 shows how various saving rates translate into retirement outcomes, independently of how much income you earn.

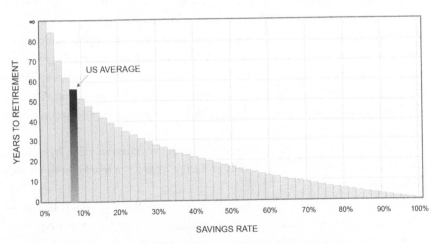

Figure 1.4. Saving rates vs retirement timeframes, starting from a net worth of zero.

This simple little chart has the power to level the playing field between the high-powered executives and average schmucks like me, and it seared through my brain like a bolt of lightning.

If I stuck it out at my full-time job, I calculated it would take me another 10 years to reach a spartan 'retirement'. There were all sorts of variables that might get thrown in the mix—a partner, kids, retirement location—but you get the general idea. Who wouldn't want to quit work at the ripe old age of 35?

FIRE enthusiasts tend to describe non-adherents in unflattering terms: they are lazy car-clowns, they are consumerist suckers, they are herd animals, they are so bad with money that they need a good punch in the face, and so on. This is mostly a joke: the froth-flecked preacher of the Mr Money Mustache persona is a much more entertaining writer than mild-mannered Pete Adeney.

But there's also a grain of truth to it. Humans are pretty smart, as individuals. In groups, we're capable of breathtaking feats of stupidity.

We're going to examine some of these herd dynamics in Book II. For now, it's enough to know that there are strong cultural, social, and biological forces that conspire to make it really hard to make good trade-offs.

The FIRE folks point out that some of these choices are so ridiculously compelling you'd have to be crazy to follow the herd. For example, you've heard the aphorism 'a penny saved is a penny earned'. I'd like to coin a more accurate replacement: *a dollar saved is ten dollars earned.*

Say you grab a $1 candy bar at the gas station. Once you've stuffed it down your maw, both it and the dollar are gone forever. What else could you have done with that dollar? This is what economists call the 'opportunity cost'. Dollars are randy little buggers. When you put them together and give them plenty of alone time, they go at it: after 10 years, that dollar coin has split into two shiny new dollars. After 20 years, the two have become four. After 40 years, there are eight dollars getting freaky in your investment account, and so on.

That original dollar you stashed away has appreciated in value by 700 per cent. Meanwhile, the candy bar's only enduring legacy is a few fat cells on your left butt cheek.

How do we get from $8 to $10? Well, every dollar you spend had to be earned through some sort of income-producing activity in the first place. Assuming floating libertarian utopias haven't taken over by the time you read this, you had to pay tax on that income. Depending on your personal tax rate and country of origin, you probably have to earn about $1.25 in order to be able to spend a buck. In other words: to match the future buying power of that single invested dollar, you'd have to go out and earn $10.

We could quibble over inflation and capital gains—maybe we only end up with a 7-8x return—but the general point stands. The central insight of the FIRE movement is that you can buy back your own freedom, one slice at a time. You won't find it in the shopping mall or the glossy catalogues, but it's always up for sale. Here's Pete Adeney:

> "Would I rather have my freedom sooner, or this big-ass television? Sometimes you still choose the big-ass television, but at least you've thought about what you're giving up."

ACTING DEAD

Most people make the mistake of trying to maximise everything at once: they want the candy bar and the big-ass TV, but they also like the idea of retiring early, and wonder why they end up with a slurry of mediocrity.

But the equal and opposite mistake is to relentlessly minimise *everything* in pursuit of some distant happiness. Did the eight-year-old version of me waste his pocket money buying Lego sets, instead of diligently investing it for retirement? I don't think so.

Some FIRE adherents fall into the trap of putting too much weight on distant future outcomes at the expense of in-the-moment experiences. They have escaped the narrow prescribed choices of consumer capitalism, only to be trapped by the narrow prescribed choices of their own ideological movement.

Old-school frugality didn't have this problem, because it wasn't an inherently subtractive philosophy. The Roman *frugalitas* was considered the mother of all virtues, standing on the same pantheon as justice, honesty, and mercy. The point of living economically and simply was to be able to better perform one's civic duty and be more fruitful in the world—not to lie around on chaise longues eating grapes. Over the intervening centuries, this noble ideal somehow degenerated into the misconception that no frugal person should own more than one teaspoon, and single-ply toilet paper is the only way to get in touch with your inner self.

The modern practice of frugality is degenerate, insofar as it doesn't have a positive impetus beyond escapism—it is all 'min' and no 'max'.

To borrow a term from sci-fi writer Bruce Sterling, joining the FIRE movement comes with a risk of **Acting Dead**. Sterling's rule of thumb is that this is any behaviour that your dead great-grandpa could do better than you. Do you spend as little money as possible? Well, your grandpa already got you licked in that department. Dreaming of escaping work? You cannot possibly escape further than great-grandpa. Do you want to be the ultimate minimalist? Yeah, great-grandpa owns three rusty buttons and a rotten shroud. That's gonna be hard to beat.

One trick to find out if you or someone you know is acting dead is to invert their advice and see if it still sounds wise, or if they're just fetishising non-existence:

Oh, every extra minute in the shower adds $20 to the electricity bill a year? Well, that means I can spend $20 to buy an extra 365 minutes of shower-time. That's like... three bucks an hour. Wow! What a bargain. Guess I'm gonna start taking longer showers.

I parroted plenty of tips of this nature during my time in the FIRE cult, and it took a long time after joining before I noticed I was constraining my own options and capabilities.

The prospect of checking out early was so electrifying that I couldn't think about anything else. I spent countless feverish hours calculating how many years I had left to go, running the numbers over and over again—just in case they'd changed overnight—and reading every case study and blog post I could get my hands on.

And then, ever so slowly, it started to lose its thrill.

I felt like the cartoon prisoner, carving a series of notches on the wall to mark each passing day. I had dreams to pursue *right now*, and I couldn't bear the thought of putting them off for another 10 years.

So I quit my comfortable job, and walked away from the FIRE club. This would turn out to be one of the best decisions I've ever made.

LEAP OF FAITH

It's eerie to think that I might still be faithfully shuffling along with one eye on the clock right now. No doubt that pathway would have led to a good life, but some options would have closed to me forever: the chance to travel unencumbered, to work on ventures with uncertain payoffs, to develop new skills and interests, and to take advantage of my youth and mobility.

What was meant to be a mini-retirement has morphed into a multi-year sabbatical with no end in sight. I still do some paid work, but only on my own terms. I barely pay attention to my net worth, but it's ticking along nicely. I've used this time to pen a couple of hundred finance columns, publish some of my best freelance journalism, start a blog, help out with startups, and write this book. I've also lived on three different continents, met some of my best friends and collaborators, and had all sorts of experiences unavailable to my counterfactual self.

Henry David Thoreau, 1856.

My inspiration for making this leap came from Henry David Thoreau, the poet-philosopher who built a cabin on the shores of Walden Pond. Thoreau is one of my personal heroes, and you'll see his influence throughout these pages. But he was also kind of a dick. He tut-tutted about the masses leading "lives of quiet desperation", while he ate his umpteenth meal of camp bread in his bare shack, and penned self-righteous sermons on the evils of gossip, railroads, and fancy hats.

Worse; Thoreau was a big old hypocrite. He could only live out his cabin-porn fantasy because he was squatting on land owned by his mate Ralph Waldo Emerson. Our famously rugged individualist also forgot to mention that his mum did his laundry and baked him cookies. He had a Harvard education, rich friends, and was only ever a 20 minute stroll away from his family home.

Thoreau said he went into the woods to live deliberately: "To front only the essential facts of life, and see if I could not learn what it had to teach, and not, when I came to die, discover that I had not lived."

The etymology of deliberate is the Latin *de libra*, which means 'scales' or 'balance'. No doubt Thoreau chose this wording very... deliberately. Yes, he was a pompous windbag, perched atop what may well be the most magnificent neckbeard of all time. His sneers were world-class. But he was also the first to poke fun at himself. Much of his preachiness was put on for dramatic effect, and often with tongue firmly in cheek: he wouldn't accept a doormat for his cabin, because, he solemnly explained, "it is best to avoid the beginnings of evil."

While Thoreau's critics always seem to miss this point, he specifically urged readers *not* to blindly imitate his mode of living: "I desire that there may be as many different persons in the world as possible; but I would have each one be very careful to find out and pursue his own way."

I want to not only copy this disclaimer, but put it up in giant flashing neon lights. If at any point you notice spittle flying from my chin, please get out of the splash zone. Everything I write is inevitably shaped by my own experience and preferences. I can pass on general principles, but you have to choose your own adventure.

The real beauty of being a minimal little wisp is the sense of *possibility* it creates. It's as if you're a little kid again, surveying the world from that long-forgotten perspective where everything is bursting with intrigue and wonder. Old skins are sloughed off at will, and you can remake yourself however you please. There you stand, gazing out across a Lego-set kingdom, while the flutter-kick of excitement rises in your chest, and you can't quite believe it: you can build whatever kind of life you want.

Frugality isn't about hoarding money indefinitely, or being an ascetic, or trying to escape from reality. That's acting dead, and great-grandpa will beat you every single time. Frugality is about *opening your options*.

2

OPEN YOUR OPTIONS

"You are fettered," said Scrooge, trembling. "Tell me why?"

"I wear the chain I forged in life," replied the Ghost. "I made it link by link, and yard by yard; I girded it on of my own free will, and of my own free will I wore it."

— CHARLES DICKENS, 'A CHRISTMAS CAROL'

WAKE UP. You're lying in a small room, surrounded by closed doors. Don't bother trying the handles; you already know they're locked. As you pace back and forth, the irons clapped around your ankle drag on the bare concrete. You're not going anywhere. This looks exactly like the room you woke up in yesterday, and the day before that, and the week before that, and the month before that, and the year before that. The only difference is, it keeps getting smaller. Every night the walls close in on you another fraction, and every morning you wake up with the panic rising in your chest.

If you're heavily in debt, you have negative optionality. Keeping up with the payments is struggle enough. Quitting your job, starting a business, or early retirement might as well be fairytales from another dimension.

About the only way you're getting out of that dingy cell is by slashing every expense to the bone, and putting every last dollar towards clearing the ledger. You will have to sell your car, wear secondhand clothes, and become intimately familiar with beans and rice, but at least the walls will stop closing in on you.

Now you have options—not a whole lot, but things are looking up. First off, you've got the skills that will keep you from waking up in that nightmare room again. You know how to save money, so you can cut up your credit cards and cancel your overdraft.

As long as you spend everything you earn and no more, this is the room you'll stay in. It's liveable in here, but still cramped and claustrophobic. Maybe you're curious about what lies behind the other doors, so you start to put something aside from each pay packet. As your discipline grows, the doors start swinging open.

This increase in optionality happens along two dimensions at once. As your desires become simpler, less work is required to meet your expenses, which gives you more time and freedom for other pursuits. At the same time, your growing stash of cash is opening doors. With enough money, you can walk right out of a crappy job. You can seize an unexpected opportunity that comes your way. You can build up enough seed capital to start a business. You can earn passive investment income. You can begin to redesign your life in a manner that pleases you.

Having more money unlocks a lot of doors, but not all of them. Some pathways are only open to those who have built up enough social capital, or health and fitness, or skills and knowledge, on which, more later. But the doors are creaking open. Which ones to step through?

ASYMMETRIC OPPORTUNITIES

Systematically collecting high-quality options is the equivalent of unlocking doors that might lead to **Treasure Chests**: say, a financial windfall, a new friend or loved one, a job offer, a successful business, an excellent investment opportunity, a life-changing idea or epiphany, and all the things we generally associate with 'good luck'.

Unfortunately, most of our time and attention is consumed by endless variations of low-quality options. Consumer capitalism presents us with doors and passages which only lead us deeper into the labyrinth, distracting us from making the decisions that really matter. These low-quality options are **Dead Ends**. They sometimes lead to modest rewards, but it's a lot of effort for not much loot.

If you hit a dead end, at least you can retrace your steps. But sometimes you open a door that you'll never walk back out of. These are the high-risk options which have a small chance of sending us tumbling into a **Bottomless Pit of Doom**: addiction, financial ruin, ideological death spirals, disease or disability, accidents, investments that blow up, and all the things we generally associate with 'bad luck'.

Dead Ends, Treasure Chests, and Bottomless Pits of Doom each have their own distinct attributes, which means we have a good chance of identifying them before we step through the door. Like Thales and his olive press scheme, what we're looking for in each case is an *asymmetry*.

I first came across this framework in Nassim Taleb's *Incerto* series. Taleb began his career in the financial markets, where he traded in options—contracts which give you the right (but not the obligation) to buy or sell an asset at a certain price, within a certain timeframe.

Taleb made his fortune by purchasing options that had a limited downside if they didn't work out in his favour, but a large, open-ended upside if they did. He was happy to accumulate a lot of small, manageable losses most of the time, then make the occasional killing from rare but high-magnitude events.

These sort of options display a major asymmetry between risk and reward. The downside is always capped—there's no chance of blowing up—while the potential upside is unlimited.

The Thales/Taleb model suggests that we should be perfectly happy to wander through doors which quickly turn out to be Dead Ends, if there's even a small chance they lead to a Treasure Chest. But we shouldn't waste precious resources on the 'safer', well-travelled doors which only hint at a modest return on investment: we're looking for a big, uneven payoff, or nothing at all.

Most importantly, we have to resist the allure of the doors that sometimes lead to a Treasure Chest, but occasionally cast adventurers into a Bottomless Pit of Doom. Let's look at a few concrete examples.

BOTTOMLESS PITS OF DOOM

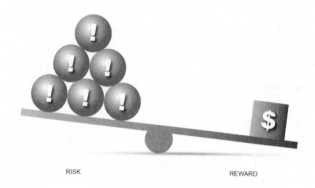

RISK   REWARD

Figure 1.5. Capped upside + unbounded downside = Bottomless Pit of Doom.

Bottomless Pits display an asymmetry between risk and reward in the wrong direction: the upside is fixed, and the downside is unbounded. There's no guarantee we'll tumble into the pit: it's enough that there's any risk of total ruin, no matter how slim.

The canonical example is a game of Russian Roulette. You have a good chance of winning a few hundred dollars, but you also have a one-in-six chance of blowing your brains out. The potential rewards are capped, and the potential loss is infinite.

I don't know anyone crazy enough to play literal Russian Roulette, but we make choices with this kind of asymmetry all the time.

Motorcycles: The upside of riding motorcycles is that it's fun, maybe you can lane-split, and save some money on gas. But the risk of ruin is astronomical: on a per-kilometre basis, the fatality rate is 29 times higher than traveling by car, and more than 3000 times higher than a commercial flight.

Addictive drugs: Some recreational drugs have a reasonably attractive risk-reward payoff. The ones to steer clear of are those with any prospect of overdose, psychotic break, or addiction. No doubt these drugs are fun, but they're not *infinitely* fun.

Cybersecurity: You'd have to be the unluckiest schmuck on the planet to have your data stolen the first time you connect to a public WiFi network without protection, or leave your laptop unattended. Probably nothing bad will happen the first hundred times, or even the first 1000 times. But if there's even a small chance of losing your money, your files, your livelihood, your accounts, your identity, that is an unacceptable risk. There are simple precautions that massively reduce the chances of getting hacked, and anyone who fails to take out these cheap options will eventually fall into a Bottomless Pit with near 100 per cent certainty.

DEAD ENDS

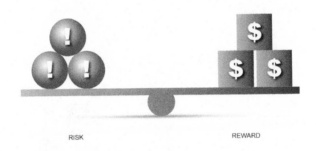

RISK   REWARD

Figure 1.6. Capped downside + capped upside = Dead End.

Most options don't display a major asymmetry in either direction. There's no prospect of horrible losses, but you also don't get any exposure to life-changing opportunities.

Moonlighting for Uber: You gain a modest source of extra income in exchange for your time and initial investment. There's essentially no chance that driving for Uber will make you a millionaire, and essentially no chance that it will bankrupt you (assuming you have insurance). Any side hustle which boils down to 'doing more hourly work' fits into this category.

Buying stocks: Most publicly traded companies are mature businesses. There's very little chance that you're going to get a 10x return on investment, and almost no chance of a 100x. Instead, you'll probably earn modest returns, in exchange for taking modest risks.

Watching TV: The upside of America's number one pastime is limited: you get to enjoy some light entertainment, but it's unlikely to change your world. The downside is also limited: it's a huge time-suck, and interferes with sleep quality, but it doesn't literally rot your brain.

There's nothing inherently wrong with options that fall in this middle ground. Driving for Uber might be a good choice for some people, investing in boring index funds is probably the right strategy for most of us, and watching TV is fun.

'Dead Ends' might be too harsh a name for this class of options, but it does point at something important—the danger of these middling paths is that they lead us away from making the kind of decisions that open up life-changing opportunities.

TREASURE CHESTS

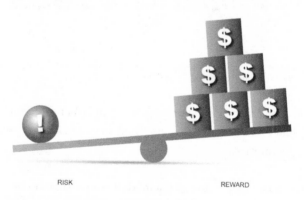

Figure 1.7. Capped downside + unbounded upside = Treasure Chest.

These are the sexy asymmetries that lead to the big wins. There's no guarantee they'll actually pay off, and most of the time, they won't. But if we systematically collect these open-ended options, we maximise our chances of getting lucky.

Scalable side-hustles: If you can sell a product or service over and over again with no marginal costs—say, software, music, art, books, or digital products—you're no longer bound by the linear returns of driving for Uber. This is really frickin' hard, and the rewards are unevenly distributed: a tiny proportion of artists and entrepreneurs capture almost all the value. But it does open an opportunity for unbounded upside.

Venture capital-style bets: Some of my investment portfolio is in early-stage startups with huge potential upside. They're unlikely to succeed, but if even one of them takes off, it will be life-changing. If they fail, I've structured my portfolio in such a way that my downside is protected (more on this in Book IV, including important caveats).

Reading books: Most books aren't worth reading. But the downside is capped: you can bail out as soon you realise it's a dud, and you've only wasted ten bucks. This is an incredibly cheap option to take out, because every once in a while, you find a 'view quake' book which turns your whole world upside down.

Messaging strangers: If you email someone you admire to introduce yourself or ask for a piece of advice, the worst that happens is you don't get a reply. The potential upside is connecting with someone who might eventually become a friend or collaborator, and change the course of your life.

This is not an exhaustive list; only a taste of what is to come. Book III is a compendium of attractive asymmetries, and Book IV is all about risk management through the optionality lens.

Crucially, these are all *exploitable* asymmetries—we know they exist, and we know we can take advantage of them. Building optionality is mostly a matter of plucking the low-hanging fruit. A savvy reader will be skeptical of this, but for those who are willing to entertain unusual ideas, conditions have never been so promising.

A BIG FAT EXPLOITABLE OPPORTUNITY

We live in an age of incredible abundance. Many essential products and services are ridiculously cheap by historical standards, and sometimes even free. It's possible to enjoy a lavish lifestyle, while still skimming a large surplus off the top to pursue other goals.

We also have an unprecedented degree of autonomy over the direction of our lives. Our ancestors died in the exact same town they were born, married whoever they were told to, did the same job as their parents, and had no choice but to follow whatever customs and ideas were peculiar to their tiny corner of the world. It's only in the last few centuries that technology and globalisation have served up the piping hot smorgasbord of options we're able to casually choose from today.

As the psychologist Daniel Gilbert points out, overcoming physical boundaries—oceans, mountains, deserts—is now as simple as buying a plane ticket. As for cultural boundaries—traditions, castes, religions—they're being forced to compete in an increasingly open marketplace of ideas, which has introduced strange and heretical new concepts: 'marrying for love', 'lady doctors', and 'early retirement', to name a few.

We live at the epicentre of this unprecedented explosion in personal freedom, abundance, and knowledge.

Our remarkable good fortune is not immediately obvious, because every single person we know just so happens to live in the same improbable bubble as us. To grasp the scale of the opportunity, lets take a quick excursion beyond the walls of the bubble, and try to catch a glimpse of the world from a slightly different viewpoint.

3

_____

ABUNDANCE

In general, life is better than it ever has been, and if you think that, in the past, there was some golden age of pleasure and plenty to which you would, if you were able, transport yourself, let me say one single word: dentistry.

— P.J. O'ROURKE

THE BURLY VILLAGERS HOLD each of your legs firmly in the stirrup position, while the physician's assistant sits on your torso. The metal catheter has already been forced into your urethra, ensuring your bladder is empty. Now the physician, nails trimmed and digits oiled, inserts first one, then two fingers into your rectum. With his other hand, he pushes your belly until he finds the telltale hard bulge of a kidney stone, and guides it downwards to the neck of the bladder. Thus suitably positioned, he makes several cuts into the bladder, while the strength and empathy of the villagers is put to the test, and pushes the stone out using the fingers in your rectum. If the stone is too large, he slides a crochet hook into your bladder, and wiggles it back and forwards until it can be drawn out. To stem the bleeding and inflammation, you must now lower your tortured nether regions into a bath of vinegar and salt—assuming you're still alive.

Surgery circa 1300 in Rome. Wellcome Library (CC BY 4.0).

This was the standard procedure for removing kidney stones for several centuries. Until the discovery of ether in 1846, all surgeries were performed on patients who were wide awake, held down on whatever flat surface was handy, and wracked with excruciating pain. Before the acceptance of germ theory, many of them died. The scenes were so horrific that friends and observers frequently fainted, and even the surgeons' assistants sometimes ran away. There was no special treatment available for the rich: a king could expect nothing more than a stiff drink and a wooden dowel to bite down on, just like anyone else.

I confess that the mere act of researching this vignette was almost enough to make me lose my lunch. I can't begin to imagine living in a world this terrifying: in the 21st century, even the poorest amongst us have standards of living that are vastly superior to our forebears. Of Americans living below the poverty line today, 99 per cent have electricity, water, toilets and a fridge, 95 per cent have a TV, 88 per cent have a phone, 71 per cent have a car, and 70 per cent have air conditioning. Even within living memory, some of these basic amenities used to be inconceivable luxuries, out of reach of the world's richest men and women.

Throughout most of history, the few elites that did enjoy a relatively high standard of living were only able to do so at the expense of everyone else, with the vast majority of the population enslaved to do their bidding. As technology advanced, human labour was replaced by animals, and then by combustion engines, and then by the full range of energy sources we use today.

The average person on the planet now consumes about 2500 kilojoules of energy every second. As Matt Ridley points out in *The Rational Optimist*, in human-power terms, that's the equivalent of having 150 slaves pedalling on bicycles for eight hour shifts. And that's the *average*: if you're an American, you have the equivalent of 660 slaves constantly working to sustain your lifestyle. Only a mighty Emperor could have dreamed of that sort of power and affluence, but we wield it unthinkingly every single day.

The point is that anyone reading this is part of the richest and most fortunate cohort that has ever existed, right back to when we crawled out of the primordial goop. Each of us has the equivalent of a personal army of invisible slaves sweating and grinding away to make our lives comfortable. The accumulated wisdom of the human race is accessible from a glass rectangle that fits in our pocket, has more computing power than the machines that put man on the Moon, and would make any ancient scholar's eyeballs pop out of their heads, but we're worried about whether it's the *latest* glass rectangle with the dancing poop emoji.

Yet some people will argue—and perhaps rightly so—that it's not particularly instructive to compare ourselves with old dead people. Maybe these horrible surgical anecdotes are only a sleight-of-hand to distract us from the state of affairs right now. By the standards of today, in a world stricken by inequality and controlled by the elite, are plebs like you and I *really* that lucky?

YOU ARE THE ONE PERCENT

It's a lazy afternoon in Jakarta. The Big Durian! An enormous, foul-smelling fruit, oozing nectar and rot, swarming with 10 million souls. There's nothing to do other than get lost in the anthill, so our driver drops me and some other off-duty reporters on the outskirts of a random kampong.

Despite being in the middle of a megalopolis, this part of town rarely receives foreign visitors. Grandmas' faces crinkle into smiles as they invite us into their homes. Boisterous children crowd around for high-fives, pull their most obscene hand gestures, and show off their counterfeit football shirts.

Soon we've attracted an entourage of barefoot little ones, following us up the street like the Pied Piper.

No-one tries to sell us anything or ask for so much as a single rupiah, although the women keep making jokes. One of my friends speaks Bahasa: they're asking you to marry them, he grins. He doesn't translate the cruder offers. I've never been proposed to before, but it's not exactly an ego-boost. The women want out, and it's not hard to understand why.

Inside one of the houses, four people sleep sardined together in a dark concrete-slab room. Mounds of rubbish spill down the banks of the river where people bathe.

It's one hell of a hard cut from earlier that morning. Leaning over the balcony of the opulent apartments on the top floors of the 50-storey Ciputra World development, we took in a breathtaking view of the Jakarta skyline. It's so high up that at first you don't notice the shanty towns around the bases of the skyscrapers. There I am, being shown around a hotel room with an $800 rack rate, looking out over folks who don't earn that much in an entire year. In cities like this, these sort of jarring juxtapositions are on every corner.

That day in Jakarta is seared into my memory, because it was the first time I'd ever been walloped over the head with my own incredible privilege—a point driven home over and over during my subsequent travels.

Maybe you don't feel particularly lucky. But if you're reading this book, you have enough education to understand these words, some leisure time, and a few dollars to spend on information and entertainment—rather than, say, a sack of rice that will make up the bulk of your meals for the next month.

The uncomfortable truth is that I am the 1 percent. If you earn more than $58,000 after tax, you're in that top percentile of much-maligned fat-cat too. If you earn at least $34,000—the typical income for many Americans—you're in the richest 5 per cent of the world's population. Even someone living at the US poverty line is still richer than 85 per cent of the people in the world, and 99 per cent of people who have ever lived.

Most of the people we happen to be surrounded with—our friends, family, colleagues, neighbours, shopkeepers, celebrities we follow on social media— are completely unrepresentative of humanity at large.

When that bubble bursts, perspective comes flooding in. You realise how insane it is to insist on having the latest iPhone, or to engage in petty status-signalling games with your fellow bubble residents.

If we want to skim some surplus off the opulent life we already enjoy, the opportunity is there for the taking. This existence might seem marginally less lavish to the residents of our bubble, but to the masses outside in the cold with their noses pressed to the window, and the billions of ancestors who came before, it's a standard of living so incomprehensibly splendid that it could only seem like a fantastic dream.

PARADISE LOST

During the early years of the Great Depression, the economist John Maynard Keynes wrote a remarkable essay. In defiance of the general air of doom and gloom, Keynes predicted that accelerating progress in science and technology would bring about a new age of abundance. By 2030, he suggested that the 'economic problem' would be all but solved, our standard of living would have increased as much as eight times over, and we'd be putting in lazy 15 hour work weeks. In this glorious land of milk and honey, Keynes' biggest concern was that we wouldn't know what to do with ourselves, and might suffer a society-wide nervous breakdown at *not* having to worry about making a living.

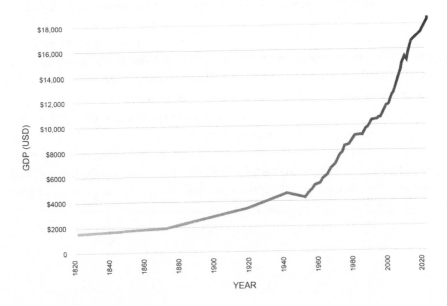

Figure 1.8. World GDP per capita 1820 - 2020.

Here we are with the deadline almost upon us, and the crazy thing is that Keynes *was right*: the wealth of developed countries really has increased eight-fold, smack bang on the most optimistic end of his prediction, and the rest of the world is catching up fast (Fig. 1.8).

Consumer capitalism has lifted billions of people out of poverty, and enriched our lives in a myriad of ways. While this is surely the greatest achievement of our age, the side effects of the upheaval have not been pretty.

The 15-hour work weeks failed to materialise, but we did get the society-wide nervous breakdown. One in 10 adults in the US is currently taking anti-depressants. My home country of New Zealand, which markets itself as a slice of paradise, has the highest suicide rate in history. The obesity and diabetes epidemics are ticking timebombs. For all our incredible progress, life expectancy in some parts of the developed world has started going backwards.

We were supposed to be the chosen ones. Why didn't we fulfil the prophecy?

Keynes was only half right, because he was only holding half the pieces of the puzzle. He knew human nature involved striving for more and better, but he didn't appreciate just how strange the roots of our behaviour were. After all, what kind of madness would possess us to squander our incredible abundance?

The Romantic view of nature is that everything is part of a grand narrative —the circle of life, complete with song-and-dance numbers. In real life, the cellist would be chewing on the third violin's intestines before the end of the first act. Our musical is a terrifying, never-ending cacophony, absent script or resolution. Up in the loft, the genes tugging on our strings couldn't care less about the happiness of their dangling puppets.

There's no benevolent director running this show. As the artificial intelligence researcher Eliezer Yudkowsky puts it, evolution is more like "a blind idiot god, burbling chaotically at the center of everything". If we want to fulfil Keynes' prophecy, we have to go and meet our maker.

4

THE BLIND IDIOT GOD OF EVOLUTION

What a book a devil's chaplain might write on the clumsy, wasteful, blundering low and horridly cruel works of nature!

— CHARLES DARWIN

"ORANGE JUICE OR CHAMPAGNE, SIR? A hot towel?"

Flying business class for the first time is quite the revelation. Never one to turn down free stuff, I gorge myself on pastries and mixed nuts in the members lounge. When the gate opens for boarding, I waltz past everyone else to the priority lane behind the red velvet rope. By the time the ordinary schmucks file onto the plane, I'm already ensconced in my marginally more comfortable seat, flute of bubbles in hand, and newspaper at the ready.

A hot streak of corporate hospitality means I end up taking half a dozen business class flights in a row, all within a relatively short period of time. By the fourth or fifth flight, it's all become humdrum. I skip the welcome bubbles, which make me feel like death. No matter how many French words they cram into the menu, airline food is still airline food. At the same time, I start looking down my nose at the peasants filing their way to the back of the plane, and half-believing I really am a very important business person, rather than a hack in a cheap suit. In no time at all, business class has become the new normal.

Apparently, soaring through the stratosphere in a metal bird with a God's eye view of oceans and mountains that would have previously taken months to traverse was somehow not marvellous enough. Now I deserve an extra inch of legroom, complimentary nuts, and a glass of fermented grape juice sourced from an exclusive province in the northeast of France.

I do have a pretty good defence for being such a monumentally ungrateful asshole: millions of years of evolution made me do it. We are slaves to our own biology; programmed at the cellular level to strive and strain for more and better, to never be content with 'good enough'. Our default setting is to try and improve our lives by adding things: more possessions, more money, more Facebook friends, a nicer house, a trendy diet, a cool new hobby, an exciting romantic partner, the latest fitness fad. We're all pounding away on the **Hedonic Treadmill**. As soon as we reach the object of our desires, panting with exertion, it cranks up to a steeper incline, shifting the goalposts further away. Contentment dangles tantalisingly in front of us, forever just out of reach.

The historian Yuval Noah Harari describes hedonic adaptation as one of history's few iron laws: "Once people get used to a certain luxury, they take it for granted. Then they begin to count on it. Finally, they reach the point where they can't live without it."

To understand why adaptation is such a crucial survival trait, it helps to look at it from the opposite direction. Try to imagine how you would rate your quality of life one year after being paralysed from the neck down in a terrible car crash. No doubt you would be cast into the deepest pits of despair. Perhaps you would even pray for death. At the very least, you'd know that life would never be the same.

But our intuition here is wrong: some people who suffer such an accident are in an OK mood as early as one month later, and continue to return close to their baseline level of happiness. Negative events certainly weigh on us, but not as much as we might expect. Our brains weave narratives to rationalise the situation, and wrap the whole thing up in meaning and purpose. As time passes, we think less and less about whatever misfortunes have befallen us. The show must go on: with the exception of chronic pain and ongoing misfortune, humans have a remarkable ability to bounce back from the brink of despair.

The pesky thing about hedonic adaptation is that it cuts both ways. How would your quality of life change if you won the lottery? That first night, you'd be dancing around the house swigging Moët straight from the bottle. But after a year or two, you'd only be a little happier than you were before the big win, on average. It doesn't matter if it's business class flights, a designer handbag, or gourmet meals—there's always the same creeping reversion to the mean. When pleasant things come into our life, we inevitably start taking them for granted, and turning our appetites toward the next bigger and better thrill.

This only makes sense when you remember that the blind driving forces of evolution care not one whit about your happiness, except insofar as it relates to your chances of passing on your genes. If humans didn't experience hedonic adaptation, we'd be dead in the water. After the first taste of a fruit, we'd never bother striving for the more delicious and calorie-dense fruit on the higher branches. After mating with one partner, we'd sit there marinating in post-orgasmic bliss forever, without feeling the slightest compulsion to sow our wild oats any further.

On the savannah, there was no abundance of calories to fuel an obesity crisis, or one-click online shopping and credit cards to ensnare us in debt. Constantly striving for more was critical to survival, while practising gratitude and temperance was a surefire way to lop off the branch of the evolutionary tree you were standing on. While we now live in an age of abundance, our reward systems are still wired up for the Hobbesian state of nature, in which life was nasty, brutish and short. Hedonic adaptation misfires constantly in modernity, leading us into what are often comically absurd situations.

KEEPING UP WITH THE KARDASHIANS

Kanye West is "the greatest living rock star on the planet"—at least, according to Kanye West. Personally, I will die in a ditch defending this claim, and I'm not the only one: the man has sold more than 32 million albums, and God knows how many stupendously overpriced plain white t-shirts. But at the height of his success, Kanye was also $53 million in debt.

"Please pray we overcome," he wrote to his fans.

After recovering from the initial shock, I started gathering candles and incense for a vigil. Then he let us know he still had enough petty cash to buy "furs and houses" for his family. Phew! Just to be on the safe side, he also hit up Mark Zuckerberg to invest a billion dollars into his ideas, instead of using that money to open schools in Africa.

When someone puts out the begging bowl while earning more than the GDP of a small developing nation, there's something strange going on. Let's speculate as to where Kanye's money troubles come from. It might have something to do with the 150 Christmas presents he bought for his wife, Kim Kardashian, or the fur coats, or the armoured cars, made by a manufacturer that upholsters its deluxe models with whale foreskins. Barack Obama once said the fact that the Kardashian-Wests' lifestyle is seen as a mark of success is everything that's wrong with American culture. He's also called Kanye a "jack-ass" on two separate occasions. As much as I love the guy, I can't help but agree with the former President on this one.

And yet, there's nothing all that unusual about Kanye's plight. Every week some incredibly high-earning athlete, musician or businessperson is revealed to be bankrupt or heavily in debt. If they'd salted away just a small fraction of their fortune, they'd be able to live in the lap of luxury by any reasonable standard, for the rest of their lives. So why don't they?

If we're honest, there's a little bit of Yeezy in all of us. All comparisons to the messiah aside, Mr West is a mortal man, subject to the usual human frailties. His predilections are not so very different to yours and mine—it's just that they're blown up by several orders of magnitude. Have you ever splashed out on a new wardrobe or car after getting a raise or a promotion? If so, you've been swept off your feet by the very same force.

Our spending habits tend to dance in lockstep with our incomes: a phenomenon known as **Lifestyle Inflation**. As soon as we start earning more, we move into a bigger house, buy fancier food, and upgrade our car. After all, we're working so hard that we surely deserve to enjoy the fruits of our labours.

Lifestyle inflation really starts to get out of hand when spending skips a beat ahead of the dance. Eventually, consumption decouples from income altogether, and whirls off to find a ready and willing queue of sexier dance partners —credit cards, overdrafts, personal loans—who are only too happy to grind away into the small hours. When the music finally stops and the lights come on, it's never a pretty sight.

Hedonic adaptation is one of the main driving forces behind lifestyle inflation, but it's not the only way in which our biology conspires against us. Evolution has also wired us to show off our attractiveness and social standing to our peers, even if it comes at great personal cost. Never mind keeping up with the Kardashians—it's the Joneses that most people struggle with.

THE BEAUTIFUL, MAGNIFICENT, COMPLETELY STUPID PEACOCK'S TAIL

The sight of a feather in a peacock's tail, whenever I gaze at it, makes me sick.

— CHARLES DARWIN

Two men pull into a parking lot. Driver number one steps out of a European sports car, looking sharp in an Armani suit and designer sunglasses. Driver number two swings his battered Birkenstock-clad feet out of a beat-up Toyota Corolla. Which of the two is more financially successful?

At face value, driver number one wins hands-down.

Here's what you don't see: our flashy friend is three payments behind on the car, which is about to be repossessed. The fine garments were bought on credit. His shades hide his red-rimmed eyes, swollen from crying because his girlfriend left him after one money fight too many. His whole precarious house of (credit) cards is about to come tumbling down.

Here's what you don't see about scruffy sandals guy: he doesn't owe anyone a dime, is a self-made millionaire, and has his own lifestyle business. His Birkenstocks are worn out from all the excellent adventures he takes with his beautiful family.

Keeping up with the Joneses is smoke and mirrors, which is why it's such a dangerous game to play. The latest and greatest gadget, glamorous holidays, carefully curated social media feeds—none of it means squat. It's often the people most desperate to appear successful who are actually miserable and drowning in debt.

It's exactly this sort of behaviour that Darwin found so nauseating when he was studying the mystery of the peacock. Our feathered friends strut and show off appendages that are undeniably gorgeous—a riot of iridescent colours, fanning out over five feet—but wildly impractical. The peacock's tail is heavy and cumbersome, making it harder to fly or escape predators, and takes a lot of precious energy to grow in the first place. It's nice to look at, but it's ridiculously *inefficient*. Surely it flies in the face of the theory of natural selection?

Darwin's breakthrough was the realisation that this inefficiency was, in fact, the entire point of the exercise. A massive spray of plumage was the male's way to signal to potential mates that it was such a fine specimen it could *afford to waste valuable resources* on costly and ornamental plumage. The more ridiculous the expenditure, the stronger the signal.

This performance of cavalier wastefulness is common across many species, but only *homo sapiens* has developed it into a true art form. The peacock has its tail, and we have our Hummers and Louis Vuitton bags and mansions and endless cycle of disposable fashions and trends, with countless companies and multi-trillion dollar industries all fanning the flames of **Conspicuous Consumption**.

As social apes, we have evolved to signal our worth not only to prospective mates, but to our peers and tribe members too. Economist Robin Hanson, co-author of the *Elephant in the Brain*, estimates that as much as 80 per cent of human behaviour boils down to signalling. Whatever pure and noble intentions we may claim to be motivated by, we're almost always trying to make ourselves look good in front of the group. This explains a great deal about why the consequences of our actions rarely match up with our stated goals. It's not that we intentionally lie about our true intentions, so much as we are highly skilled at deceiving ourselves.[1]

In the animal kingdom, where resources are scarce, there are hard limits on signalling behaviour. Throughout much of human history, this was also true of our species. The total pool of wealth was fixed and unchanging, and luxuries were the exclusive domain of the rich. If you owned a cloak dyed purple with the mucus of rare sea-snails, it really would set you apart from the lower classes—you couldn't just saunter down to the market and pick up a Chinese-made knock-off for a couple of sestertii.

While fancy possessions are still the default way to show off today, the signal is losing its reliability. The twin forces of globalisation and easy credit have eroded the exclusivity of material goods, to the point where any prole with a pulse can get a loan. It's unremarkable to buy a car on finance, a house with almost no down payment, and put a trip to the Bahamas on the credit card. As we saw in our earlier example, you can't tell anything in particular about someone's financial standing just by looking at them. Showy wealth is becoming the tell-tale sign of the insecure middle classes, while the true elite have already moved on to more sophisticated signals.

This is an uncomfortable truth, with some disturbing implications. Not only are we spending a lot of time and resources on signalling behaviours; we're spending them on signalling behaviours that *don't even work very well*. Our gaudy tails grow ever-larger, ever-more pointless, and ever-more inefficient. It's exactly this sort of one-upmanship that pushes people to bankruptcy, or spending their brief lives toiling away to buy things in a futile attempt at impressing people—like the peacock struggling to free its magnificent tail from the bushes, while the wild dogs tear it to pieces. Needless to say, continuing to engage in this negative-sum game is, in my opinion, completely bird-brained.

The all-consuming nature of lifestyle inflation underscores the importance of first ruthlessly min-maxing for the things that are actually worth having. If we try to maximise everything at once, we're doomed to pound along on the hedonic treadmill forever, and end up going nowhere fast.

I've made my best case for using frameworks like frugality to deliberately constrain your choices, skim off a healthy surplus, and divert it to more fruitful opportunities. But what if those hedonists living the high life know something we don't? Perhaps this entire chapter was nothing more than a series of elaborate rationalisations to justify my own shabby existence. To put these concerns to bed, we have to tackle the age-old question: does money make us happy?

5

HEDONISM AND HAPPINESS

I can understand wanting to have millions of dollars... but once you get much beyond that, I have to tell you, it's the same hamburger.

— BILL GATES

ACCORDING TO THE DENIZENS of news website comment sections, anyone living frugally must be a smelly, communist, cheapskate, dumpster-diving hermit. I resent that. I always wear deodorant; if only to mask the garbage juice smell.

Living simply doesn't mean being some sort of miserable tightwad. My experience has been the opposite: once you have the basics of life covered, money doesn't really correlate with happiness. The best things in life really are free, or at the very least, dirt-cheap.

I feel like I have a fairly unusual vantage point in having straddled both sides of the hedonistic divide. In my former life as a business reporter, I enjoyed a great deal of schmoozing at other people's expense. The CEO of a major airline personally served me Dom Pérignon as we took delivery of his first Dreamliner. There were many long lunches at fine restaurants, fancy hotels, and corporate boxes at the sportsball. And after I quit my job, I spent a lot of time lounging on tropical islands, doing as little as possible.

I would be lying if I denied that all of these things are tremendous fun. On the other hand, they don't tend to lead to much lasting satisfaction, losing their flavour as quickly as an old piece of gum.

Every now and again, I do an outrageous rich person activity to make sure I'm constraining myself along the right dimensions. The most recent test involved sneaking into a trendy Bombay nightclub with a door charge more than most locals earn in a week. French literary agents and Bollywood glitterati posed for photos, and a very successful Canadian stock broker bought round after round of drinks until, swaying on his feet, he mournfully admitted to having no friends. It was interesting, but approximately 100x less fun and more expensive than your typical dive bar full of rickshaw drivers. I've noticed the same general theme over and over during my time abroad: extremely well-paid young banker and lawyer-types, who are miserable and trying to 'find themselves' in the spiritual East, or using their two weeks' vacation to escape as far as they can from reality.

And so, while I've had a little taste of the baller life, it's not something I think is worth pursuing full-time. Of course, my own anecdotal experience doesn't mean anything in particular. Fortunately, you don't have to take my word for it—there's a wealth of research on the topic.

BILLIONAIRES AND BACKPACKERS

Does money make us happy? In the annals of pointlessly inane questions, this is right up there with the defecation habits of bears. The short answer is: 'yes'. Thank goodness we've had generations of scientists applying their considerable funding and big brains to this important problem. Next up: is the Pope a Catholic?

The long answer is... longer.

The relationship between income and happiness starts out very strong indeed. If you can't afford to heat your home, or buy shoes for your kids, or put food on the table, that will probably make you sad. There is a simple solution for cheering up people in this situation, and it is called 'more money'.

Once you've fulfilled the most basic needs of survival, the next step up is security. A struggling family might not actually be starving or homeless, but teetering on the brink of the financial abyss is not fun. Anyone with mounting debts or precarious work hours will know this feeling all too well. Again, simply getting more money into the hands of poor people is incredibly useful.

It makes sense that a certain amount of money is needed to survive, and to feel some degree of security. Think of this as the amount you need to pay the bills, put some simple but healthy food on the table, enjoy a few little luxuries, and sleep through the night without waking up in a cold sweat. The surprising part is that from this point on, the relationship between income and happiness starts to break down.

Until recently, the conventional wisdom was that there was *no* extra benefit after a certain point—$70,000 being the magic number most often bandied about. Now we have a ton more research, spanning hundreds of thousands of people across more than 140 countries, this turns out to be wrong.

In fact, if you chart a graph of income and happiness, you find a near-perfect relationship between the two—at least, so long as the x-axis is scaled logarithmically, with a doubling of income at each increment (Fig. 1.9).[1]

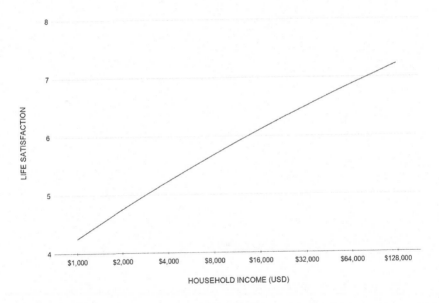

Figure 1.9. The relationship between happiness and income (log scale).

If there's a point at which earning more money stops correlating with higher happiness, we haven't discovered it yet.

Here's the catch: the richer you are, the more money is required to eke out any further gains in happiness. Each doubling of income only improves your life satisfaction by about half a point on a scale of 1 to 10. The counterintuitive conclusion is that there's very little difference in happiness between earning $75,000 and $150,000. Even someone pulling in a whopping half-million dollar pay packet is only going to score one more point of life satisfaction compared to the typical American salary earner.

We can see this problem much more clearly by plotting it on a graph with a more familiar linear x-axis (Fig. 1.10). Happiness never stops rising in line with income, but it does rise increasingly slowly, to the point where it more or less starts flat-lining.

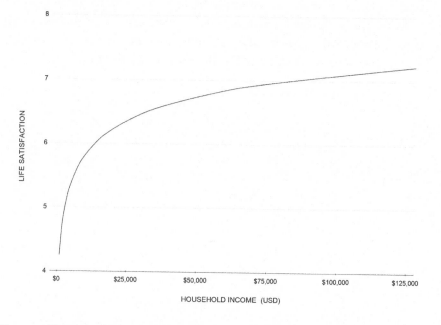

Figure 1.10. The relationship between happiness and income (linear scale).

This shouldn't be all that surprising. Receiving an extra $1000 might be life-changing for someone on the breadline. By the time you earn a six-figure income, an extra thousand bucks is a nice windfall, but not a big deal. If you're on a seven-figure income, that extra $1000 is the equivalent of a 0.1 per cent pay rise—it's barely even going to register, let alone have any noticeable effect on your life satisfaction.

This is the law of **Diminishing Marginal Returns**: if you hold every-thing else steady, ratcheting up one input (in this case, money) has less and less impact on the desired output (happiness), to the point where it becomes ineffective, and sometimes even does more harm than good.

If you don't believe the research, go ask your friendly neighbourhood billionaire. Ray Dalio is the founder of Bridgewater Associates, the largest hedge fund in the world. For his efforts, he has accumulated a net worth of $17 billion. But in his book *Principles*, Dalio says he never actually set out to make a lot of money: "If I had, I would have stopped ages ago because of the law of diminishing returns."

Why does Dalio still turn up to work each day, despite being stupendously rich and comfortably past retirement age? The money clearly doesn't matter—it's just an accidental byproduct of doing what he loves. If he had to choose, Dalio says he'd rather be a backpacking bum exploring the world than earning a fat pay packet in a job he didn't like:

> "For me, having more money isn't a lot better than having enough to cover the basics. That's because, for me, the best things in life—meaningful work, meaningful experiences, good food, sleep, music, ideas, sex, and other basic needs and pleasures—are not, past a certain point, materially improved upon by having a lot of money."

What we've described so far is the *relationship* between income and happiness. That's not the same thing as saying that having more money *causes* greater happiness.

It's possible that we have it backwards to some degree: everyone likes having optimistic and sunny colleagues and employees around, so it wouldn't be surprising if naturally cheerful people were more likely to earn more money. It also seems likely there are other underlying factors that boost happiness and income at the same time—perhaps health, or attractiveness, or social skills. It's difficult to untangle the web of causality, but if you accept that any of these other effects exist, the impact of income on happiness is even weaker than the research suggests.

Where does this leave us? Some wag once observed that anyone who thinks money can't buy happiness must be shopping in the wrong places. I couldn't agree more—although I think we might have very different destinations in mind.

STEPPING OFF THE HEDONIC TREADMILL

Forget furs and jet-skis: it's the mushy stuff that matters the most. Once you earn enough to comfortably pay the bills, non-financial factors such as good health, relationships, and a sense of purpose become far more important than money.

It's no coincidence that these areas of life also tend to be most resistant to hedonic adaptation. While we bounce back from many health issues, it's much harder to get used to chronic pain and degenerative conditions. Each successive stage of decline or fresh wave of pain provides enough 'novelty' to prevent habituation. In a similar fashion, we never adapt to a lack of control. Loud noises, long commutes, and overbearing bosses are about as bad on the 1000th day as they are on the first.

Avoiding negative things goes a long way towards improving our lives, but the positive side of the ledger also holds plenty of promise. The key is to look for what adaptation researcher Sonja Lyubomirsky calls "intentional activities".

As Lyubomirsky points out, a beautiful new sofa is a joy to behold. But after a few days, it becomes, quite literally, part of the furniture. A sofa offers no surprises or novelty, except the assortment of lint and spare change you might find while rummaging behind the cushions. It requires no effort, and presents no challenge—in fact, its entire existence is designed to make you more comfortable sitting on your ass. In the happiness stakes, even the most resplendent chaise longue quickly becomes shabby and threadbare.

The same cannot be said of work, or love, or learning. These intentional activities involve effort and engagement, and in return, generate continual fascination and challenge. The best kind of work, study, or play involves a 'flow' state of concentration, at the perfect juncture between challenge and resistance. So long as our pursuits are sufficiently varied, self-directed, and engaging, we never get bored of them.

As for human interaction and relationships, these are the richest tapestries of all—woven through with enough novelty, complexity and nuance to last a lifetime.[2] Lyubomirsky says the happiest participants in her studies devote a great deal of time to relationships. The great psychologist Daniel Kahneman concluded that it is "only a slight exaggeration to say that happiness is the experience of spending time with people you love and who love you". Freud said the cornerstones of humanity were "love and work… work and love, that's all there is."

Does this mean we should abandon the pursuit of money?

Every prophet from Jesus Christ to Paul McCartney has told us that these sacred things—love, community, meaning—are not for sale, to the point where it's become ingrained as folk wisdom. This might be *technically* true, but it seems a little unimaginative.

BUYING HAPPINESS

There's no guarantee that money can buy you love and health and happiness, but spent wisely, it gives you a pretty great shot at it. Think of it like a game of poker: there's an inescapable element of blind luck involved, but a skilled player almost always does well for herself in the long run.

And so, after hitting the point of diminishing returns from material wealth, it would be insane to keep following the same strategy. Instead, a savvy player will start looking for games with a higher return on investment. This tipping point comes about halfway up Abraham Maslow's hierarchy of needs—the famous model of human fulfilment proposed in 1943 (Fig. 1.11).

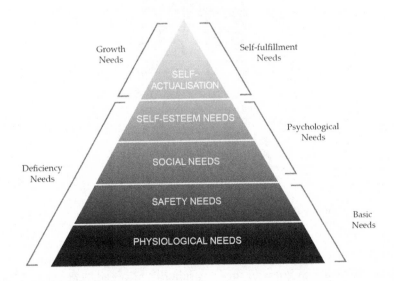

Figure 1.11. The Hierarchy of Needs, as it is usually presented.

Maslow's theory has largely held up. Cross-cultural studies have found that happiness does indeed correlate with meeting five broad categories of needs: physiological, safety and security, love and belonging, status, and self-actualisation. However, the pyramid-shaped hierarchy (which was made up by business consultants, and has nothing to do with Maslow) is wrong: the exact order doesn't matter. We know for sure that money is pretty great for fulfilling at least two of the five needs—survival, and security. Beyond that point, it depends entirely on how you spend it.

To get a sense of how we might 'buy' happiness, let's track a family as they move through the five categories.

Meet Mr and Mrs Jones—all four of them! After a rent in the fabric of the universe, which probably has something to do with the word 'quantum', parallel versions of the couple tumble down different legs of the Trousers of Time (Fig 1.12).

UNIVERSE A   UNIVERSE B

Figure 1.12. The Joneses emerge in alternate realities after tumbling down different legs of the Trousers of Time.

In Universe A, Mr and Mrs Jones use their middle-class salaries to buy middle-class stuff—a house in the leafy suburbs, high-end electronics, a couple of late-model cars.

In Universe B, the Joneses buy a secondhand car, cook at home, and live in a smaller house within cycling distance of work. The lower cost of living allows Mrs Jones to cut back her hours to part-time, even while the couple continue to save and invest.

In both universes, the families have comfortably fulfilled the basic physiological/survival needs. There's food on the table, a roof over their heads, a safe neighbourhood, and some level of financial security.

The third universal need—love and belonging—is where the couples start to diverge. In Universe A, the Joneses have a huge mortgage and piles of credit card debt, so they have no choice but to work long hours in demanding positions. They don't see much of each other, or of their kids, who are mostly raised by a succession of babysitters and nannies. When they get home from work, they're too tired to do much of anything.

The Universe B Joneses have plenty of time for each other, for their kids, their friends, and their community. They host block party cookouts and regular family get-togethers. Mrs Jones coaches the school soccer team, and Mr Jones volunteers at the local library.

The fourth universal need is status. The Joneses from Universe A work hard to get a bigger house, nicer cars, and fancier job titles. They spend hours applying to enroll their children in the most exclusive preschool in the district. Each new lifestyle upgrade brings a momentary thrill, then subsides to a dull unease as the hedonic treadmill cranks up another gear.

The Joneses in Universe B are just as thirsty for status, but they choose to play different games. Instead of trying to compete through conspicuous consumption, they take a quiet pride in their children—who are doing very well at the local public school—their home-grown vegetables, their toned thigh muscles, and their roles in community organisations.

The fifth universal need is self-actualisation. The Universe A Joneses don't have the autonomy required to live life on their own terms, or the mental bandwidth required to define those terms in the first place. Their full range of capabilities lie dormant.

Over in Universe B, the Joneses are unlocking their full potential. They've examined their own values and preferences, and have the time to explore widely. Mr Jones is learning jazz guitar, and Mrs Jones is launching an online business venture. They volunteer their time to help in the community, give to charity, have many interesting friends, and are the best parents they can be.

The Universe B Joneses managed to buy their way to the good life—it's just that they spent their money in a different way to their counterparts. You might say they're shopping in the right places.

Two important caveats. First, these are exaggerated caricatures to demonstrate that it's possible to 'buy' happiness. We could easily create another scenario in which the Joneses from Universe A gain status and self-actualisation by working hard in fulfilling careers, while the flaky dilettantes in Universe B spiral towards acting dead.

And the Joneses from Universe B didn't have it all their own way. They spent hours tending the vegetable garden, until their necks were sunburned and the creases of their palms were packed with soil. Mrs Jones could crack a walnut between her thighs, but the first time she commuted by bicycle, she thought she'd die from the lactic acid. Mr Jones' effortless jazz licks bely countless hours of frustration, which left his fingers in almost as much pain as his wife's eardrums. The couple endured long sleepless nights raising their children, which put a dent in their social life for years. Mrs Jones put in 60-hour weeks to launch her online business, wrangling developers and ironing out bugs into the wee hours of the morning.

It all sounds suspiciously like hard work. If money can buy happiness, why don't lottery winners and trust-fund kids skip all those exhausting steps, and charter a helicopter straight to the top of the pyramid? After all, they have all the spare time in the world, and no stressful jobs or responsibilities.

The naive conception of happiness is that it's a destination you arrive at. As we'll see in the final section, there's one last piece to the puzzle.

JEREMY BENTHAM'S SEVERED HEAD IS STARTING TO STINK

In the world there are only two tragedies. One is not getting what one wants, and the other is getting it.

— OSCAR WILDE

The rat's paw moves constantly, sometimes becoming a blur as it depresses the lever over and over. Once, twice, ten times, a hundred times, *five thousand times* in the space of an hour. With each push, an electrode sends a jolt of electricity coursing through its tiny rodent brain. The rat will push the lever for as long as 24 hours without stopping. It won't eat, or sleep, or make any effort to leave the confines of its stainless steel cage. Unless the men in white lab coats cut off the current, it will stimulate itself to death.

It's 1954, and science has just stumbled upon the brain's pleasure centre. Heady days! The excited researchers repeat the experiment on monkeys, and find, again, they can reach right into the hypothalamus and light it up like a Christmas tree, transforming their subjects into blissed-out automatons. The seminal paper concludes that these results could "very likely be generalised eventually to human beings—with modifications, of course".

Of course. I hope they wheeled out Jeremy Bentham's corpse for the occasion, so his mummified head could gaze upon his legacy. Bentham, a boyish, eccentric Englishman, was the granddaddy of the modern science of happiness. Having observed that suffering was 'bad' and pleasure was 'good', Bentham came up with a formula for maximising pleasure and minimising pain. This was the kind of moral philosophy everyone could get behind, and his hedonic calculus soon became a central pillar of ethics and human development.

But if you take Bentham's prescription to its logical conclusion—perfect pleasure, no pain—you end up with the rats in the cage. This rapturous state of existence is known as **Wireheading**, and it's a recurring theme in dystopian fiction. Imagine if you were offered a pill that would flood your brain with pleasure to the exclusion of any other activity—the equivalent of a permanent heroin rush, or an endless orgasm. If you're anything like me, you not only wouldn't take this pill, but it feels repellent on some deep level. Why?

The French have a delightful euphemism for orgasm, *la petite mort*. The 'little death' is a reprieve from existence, a moment to step outside of consciousness, perhaps catch a glimpse of nirvana. But the dose makes the poison. Somewhere along the way, the sacred becomes profane. Wireheading is a trip with no end, a permanent paroxysm of bliss that leaves its host mindless, drifting through the cosmos as an indeterminate blob. To wirehead is no different to killing yourself: this is the bullet that Benthamites must bite.

It's telling that Bentham was often described as boyish, because his definition of happiness is exactly the sort of thing a child might come up with: scraped knees are bad, candy is good.[3] The tragedy is that we already had a grown-up definition of happiness, 2000 years before Bentham started fiddling with his slipstick. In the *Nicomachean Ethics*, Aristotle warned against identifying the good with pleasure—which he described as a slavish life, suitable only for beasts. The ancient Greek conception of happiness from which Book I takes its name, **Eudaimonia**, is usually translated as 'flourishing', which encompasses not just pleasure, but purpose, and growth, and striving.

Eudaimonia plays merry hell with the instruments of the happiness researchers. Paradoxically, the good life often involves the denial of pleasure, or deliberate suffering. If you ask parents how they feel in the moment—up to their ankles in dirty diapers, sleep-deprived, social life obliterated, forced to endure torturous violin recitals—they're invariably miserable compared to their childless peers. And yet, many describe having children as one of the happiest and most satisfying experiences of their lives.

This will come as no surprise to anyone who has ever climbed a mountain, or fought for a cause, or run a marathon, or started a business, or even just opened a really stubborn pickle jar. Anything worth doing is likely to be painful, dangerous or unpleasant at least some of the time, but it provides a lot more lasting satisfaction than sitting safely in a padded room, eating candy.

SLAYING THE HAPPINESS CHIMERA

In Greek mythology, the Chimera was a fantastic creature made up of incongruous parts: the body of a lion, the head of a fire-breathing goat, the tail of a serpent. The popular conception of happiness is also a chimera—a cluster of loosely related traits stitched together, some of them contradictory, which doesn't exist in any coherent way. This fantastic beast is a shapeshifter which adapts to its environment, and never stands in one place for long: it only exists relative to our expectations, to our peers, and to our past experience.

The Greeks believed that laying eyes upon the chimera was an omen for disaster.

Imagine if you could take a helicopter directly to its lair. As soon as you reached the top of the mountain, you'd have nowhere left to climb. This is why the most vicious of the three Chinese curses is disguised as a polite pleasantry: "May the gods give you everything you ask for."[4]

The great irony is that those who dedicate their lives to hunting the chimera are the least likely to find it. As the psychiatrist Viktor Frankl warned, you can't pursue happiness head-on. It will find you, but only as an unintentional byproduct of some worthier goal. Instead of chasing a mirage, eyes forever fixed on the destination, all we can do is create the right conditions for it to arise.

The two modern-day heroes who have come closest to slaying the happiness chimera are the Nobel Prize-winning economist Amartya Sen, and the philosopher Martha Nussbaum.

Sen is the father of the **Capability Approach**, a critical contribution to welfare economics which has been hugely influential since the 1980s. Instead of crude financial measures or naive hedonism, Sen argued that the highest good was the freedom to choose a life one has reason to value—to have *options*, and thus be able to live deliberately.

Happiness is a terrible yardstick, because people adapt to the most appalling circumstances, and shrug off objective improvements in their standard of living. It would not be surprising to learn that we aren't dramatically happier than our peasant ancestors, but it also wouldn't mean anything. Our lives are vastly improved by vaccination, clean water, and education, even if our stupid biology refuses to acknowledge it.

It's crucially important to understand this point, so here are a few hypotheticals to hammer it home:

1. What if it were true that our peasant ancestors were roughly as happy as we are? If happiness is the desired outcome, we ought to be ambivalent about switching places with our great-great-grandparents. If optionality is the desired outcome, not so much.

2. What if it were true that making a country richer doesn't make its citizens any happier, because it's all relative?[5] If happiness is the desired outcome, it wouldn't matter if Bangladesh never escapes its current state of poverty. If optionality is the desired outcome, we should want every Bangladeshi to become as rich as Americans.

3. What if it were true that paraplegics bounced all the way back to their baseline level of happiness? (it's not, but this is the dumbed-down version that usually does the rounds). If happiness is the desired outcome, we would react to every accident or acute illness with a shrug of our shoulders. If optionality is the desired outcome, then we should feel extremely bad when people get hit by trucks, or are otherwise unable to use their full range of capabilities.[6]

4. What if it were true that the residents of World A, in which most people don't make it past childhood, were just as happy as those in World B, in which everyone lives to the ripe old age of 103? From a happiness perspective, it's a wash. From an optionality perspective, World B is vastly superior: one of the many problems with happiness surveys is that the dead don't get to fill them out.

If death is the ultimate destroyer of optionality, it's no surprise that 'life' is the first of the core capabilities valued across cultures, as determined by Sen's collaborator Martha Nussbaum. The other core capabilities include health, security, freedom of association, control over one's environment, learning and thinking, emotional attachment, and play. While these are all broadly appealing options, the capability approach is entirely agnostic about what we actually do with them.

Anyone who has spent more than five minutes in certain corners of the Internet will be aware that human preferences come in a truly startling variety of colours, sizes, fabrics, frills, bells, whistles, and mysterious wobbly rubber things. One person's pain is another person's pleasure, and vice versa.

The counterintuitive insight is that having options is valuable in and of itself, *regardless of whether or not we exercise them*. For example, I deliberately go several days without eating a couple of times a year. It's not very much fun, but I believe that fasting improves my life.[7] Under the naive hedonic calculus, my self-imposed 'hardship' is equivalent to someone who is genuinely starving, because they couldn't afford food that week. Clearly, the ability to choose makes all the difference in the world. I have the *right* to exercise the myriad alluring options in my well-stocked refrigerator, but no *obligation* to do so. If those options weren't available to me, my experience would take on a radically different meaning.

In short: Jeremy Bentham's severed head is starting to stink. Much to the annoyance of the measurement fetishists, flourishing cannot be flayed and pinned to the page. True human wellbeing is a slippery little beast: if you pursue it head-on, it only slides further from your grasp.[8]

Most moral philosophers have abandoned Bentham's hedonic calculus for models that give weight to the full spectrum of human values, in all their glorious weirdness. In economics, the capability approach has been hugely influential in moving beyond blunt output-based metrics like GDP per capita, which are blind to leisure time, child-rearing, volunteer work, study, self-improvement, environmental costs, and social freedoms.

The best known of the new capabilities-based metrics is the Human Development Index, created by Sen and adopted by the United Nations, which gives equal weighting to a whopping *three* variables: education, life expectancy and income. To be fair, even this was a major breakthrough. It's impossible to create an accurate index for flourishing, because you'd have to somehow measure every single conceivable human value, and then figure out how much weight to assign to each of them, and then it'd *still* be wrong for any given individual.

I don't envy the economists this task. The good news is that this is much, much easier to do at the level of the individual. If we want to create the conditions for flourishing in our own lives, we'll have to take matters into our own hands.

We've demonstrated that having more money is a useful tool for unlocking the good life, but not sufficient. We've seen that simple hedonism is a dystopian dead end, that the popular version of happiness is a chimera, and that Sen and Nussbaum were right: the highest good is the freedom to choose a life one has reason to value—to have options.

Now it's time to put some flesh on the bones of the optionality model: what might the capability approach look like if we implemented it in our own lives?

6

THE FOUR FACTORS OF OPTIONALITY

Wealth is not about having a lot of money; it's about having a lot of options.

— CHRIS ROCK

THE FIRST STEP in making better trade-offs is being aware that you're making them in the first place. On a trading floor, option contracts are as plain as the nose on your face. They're right there on the screen, in neat rows of constantly-updating prices. You run your model over the numbers, and then choose to buy the option, or not.

Wall Street-types love optionality, for very good reason. Unfortunately, they tend to make the mistake of hanging it up on the coat rack when they step out the door into the real world. As Nassim Taleb points out, explicit financial options are often expensive. We will briefly look at options trading and employee stock options in Book IV, but it's hard to find low-hanging fruit in these domains.

The reality is that all of life is a gigantic trading floor. The difference is the exchange rates are illegible, or not considered the topic of polite conversation. What price do you put on a pair of functioning kidneys? Unless you're hanging around some very shady people, the question has probably never crossed your mind. But these are your most valuable assets![1] Most people will only consider the price when it's too late—the equivalent of waking up in a tub of ice with the sickening realisation that the attractive stranger at the bar last night was a little too good to be true.

To their credit, finance guys often apply the optionality model to education: what doors might an Ivy League degree open, and is it worth the tuition? This is a good start, but the framework applies to all skills and knowledge, no matter how mundane. If you learn how to do basic maintenance on your car, you don't have to pay someone else to do it. That option is worth something. How much? What does it cost to obtain? Run the numbers, and you can decide if it's worth taking out.

Then there's social capital. Your friends, family, and connections open doors in life, and provide a safety net in bad times. How much would you pay to make sure you don't die alone? To have certain names in your contact book, with the option to call in a favour any time? All of these assets are near-priceless, to the point where it feels vulgar to even talk about them in monetary terms.

The curious thing is that this isn't borne out in our behaviour at all. If the most valuable assets are non-financial, so are the most crippling liabilities. Consider how much stress the typical executive accumulates to earn her bonus, how little time she spends with her family and friends, and how her body deteriorates during the prime of her life. She's building optionality in one narrow domain, and destroying it in every other.

As often as not, our supposedly sacred values end up in the clearance sale bin. This is kind of depressing, but the corollary is that there are many bargains to be found, if we choose to allocate our resources a little differently.

Broadly speaking, we might say there are four types of capital that make up the raw materials of optionality:

1. Financial Capital
Your assets minus your debts, which is strongly influenced by the simplicity of your tastes (how *little* money you require).

2. Social Capital
The strength and number of your relationships with friends, family, colleagues, and communities.

3. Knowledge Capital

All your skills, education, credentials, and experience—work, or otherwise.

4. Health Capital

Your physical fitness, mental health, mobility, and energy.

Remember the kind of asymmetries we're looking for. An attractive option has a fixed downside, and potentially unlimited upside. Each of these four classes of capital operates on both sides of the equation at once, simultaneously capping downside risk (resilience) and opening up opportunities (growth).

	RESILIENCE (CAPPING DOWNSIDE)	GROWTH (OPENING UPSIDE)
FINANCIAL CAPITAL	Safety buffer against economic shocks Archetype: "*Frugal little cockroach*"	Investing or starting a business Archetype: "*Black swan hunter*"
SOCIAL CAPITAL	Reliable support when life gets tough Archetype: "*Always a couch to crash on*"	Network effect of expanding social circles Archetype: "*Finding a tribe*"
KNOWLEDGE CAPITAL	Prosaic skills e.g. cooking and fixing things Archetype: "*Resourceful prepper*"	Marketable skills and credentials Archetype: "*Renaissance man/woman*"
HEALTH CAPITAL	Protection against disease and accidents Archetype: "*A walk in the park vs a broken hip*"	Force multiplier in every domain Archetype: "Strong, sexy, recreational athlete"

Table 1.1. The resilience and growth sides of the four factors of optionality.

The growth side of the equation is sexier: this is what generates the successful startup, the podium finish, the hot dates. But the resilience side is much, much more important. Why?

In every one of these domains, bad is stronger than good.

BAD IS STRONGER THAN GOOD

The psychologist Paul Rozin observed that a single cockroach will completely wreck the appeal of a bowl of cherries, but a cherry will do nothing at all for a bowl of cockroaches.

— DANIEL KAHNEMAN

The cockroach-and-cherry asymmetry is a recurring motif in investing, health, and relationships. Losing $100,000 feels much worse than winning the same amount feels good. If you say one nasty thing to your partner, it'll take five good deeds before you're allowed out of the dogbox. Staying alive has more to do with avoiding death than diligently eating your vegetables.

This asymmetry explains why we're more likely to fully adapt to positive events than negative ones. The lottery winners from Chapter 5 reverted closer to their baseline happiness than the paraplegics. From an evolutionary perspective, this makes perfect sense: one lovely windfall can make your day; one nasty surprise can end your life. It also makes sense mathematically, as we'll see in Book IV.

The principle was pithily summed up in a famous psychology paper by Roy Baumeister and colleagues, called 'Bad is Stronger Than Good'. The implication is that rather than adding ever-more cherries to the bowl, our initial focus should be on systematically exterminating life's cockroaches.[2]

Merely striving for a cockroach-free existence does not fit with the popular conception of success. Self-help gurus will tell you that you can achieve your wildest dreams, if you work hard enough and scrunch your face up just right while you do your affirmations in the mirror. This is a fiction designed to sell motivational tapes. Not everyone can be the next J.K. Rowling, or solve a major scientific problem, or win the Boston marathon. The optionality framework tells you how to maximise your *chances* of landing one of these rare successes, but there's no guarantee your number will come up.

The mundane reality is that winning is mostly about not-losing. Think of a counterintelligence agency which works tirelessly behind the scenes to foil terrorist plots: if it's doing its job well, we'll never notice anything at all. Most risk accumulates silently in the background, and is attenuated just as silently. 'Winning' is making it to 40 without tumbling into a Bottomless Pit of Doom.

All you have to do is consistently not-lose, and you'll come out well ahead of the pack. While protecting the downside always comes first, each of the four factors also opens up plenty of upside.

EVERYTHING COMPOUNDS

The first $100,000 is a bitch, but you gotta do it. I don't care what you have to do—if it means walking everywhere and not eating anything that wasn't purchased with a coupon, find a way to get your hands on $100,000. After that, you can ease off the gas a little bit.

— CHARLIE MUNGER

It took me just over three years to hit the savings goal that triggered my mini-retirement. It's been another three years since then, but this second period has been very different. For one thing, I haven't done much paid work. At the same time, I've loosened my purse-strings considerably. I was prepared to dip into my savings, but my net worth has grown substantially, with no great effort on my part.

What's the difference? Nowadays, I've got *momentum* on my side.

. . .

Book IV is full of strategies to get exposure to non-linear returns on financial capital, and position yourself for unbounded upside. But money is not the only thing that compounds: so do health, and habits, and knowledge, and popularity, and, as it turns out, just about everything.

Again: finance guys understand the importance of compounding better than anyone, but often fail to apply the concept outside their narrow field of expertise.

In Book III, I'll fill you in on the dirty little secret of fit and muscular people, explain how to get compound interest on your ideas, and why the most popular brands and experiences are the aesthetic equivalent of herpes.

For now, consider the strange outcome of compounding: in each domain of life, the greatest advantages accrue to those who need them *the least*.

This phenomenon is known as the **Matthew Effect** of cumulative advantage, after the conclusion to the parable of the talents in the Gospel of Matthew: "For to every one who has, more will be given, and he will have an abundance. But from the one who has not, even what he has will be taken away."

The Matthew effect is a law of nature, responsible for everything from the towering trunks of sequoias, to income inequality, to the arrangement of stars in the night sky. On the broad, macro scale, it's awe-inspiring: this is how our sun was born, how complex life was bootstrapped out of the clay. For the briefest candle-flicker, we get to resist the relentless march of entropy, and create defiant bastions of order and beauty amongst the chaos of the universe.

On the micro scale of human affairs—wealth, waistlines, popularity, power —the Matthew effect is terrifying. The 1 per cent control half of all wealth, a small number of startups succeed astronomically, and most albums are sold by the Justin Biebers of the world. But that's not the scariest part.

The Matthew effect can make us, but it can also *break* us.

If fit people have muscle memory, then we might say overweight people have 'fat memory'. Even after successfully slimming down, it can take *years* for the endocrine system and metabolism to recalibrate to a new set point.

The big guy slogging away on the treadmill is engaged in a heroic struggle worthy of Sisyphus. He has to push the boulder up the mountain every day. If he makes the smallest misstep, he slips backwards faster and faster, until he's right back at the bottom again. Momentum is constantly working against him.

. . .

In the same fashion:

- Debt tends to breed more debt, until the bank forecloses on you (or the mobster breaks your kneecaps)
- A few seductive untruths, left to colonise an impressionable mind, lead to a death spiral of ever-more-harmful beliefs
- Being in a toxic relationship isn't merely unpleasant; it actively drags you down further and further

It's crucially important to get some momentum on your side, or if it's working against you, to fight your way back to neutral ground. The gains or losses don't just compound on themselves. They also compound on *each other*.

For the sake of convenience, our model divides optionality into four components. But the Matthew effect refuses to stay in its lane! Everything is hopelessly entangled with everything else, which is why life doesn't tend to deteriorate in an orderly fashion: you spiral downwards faster and faster, until you fall off a cliff.

One of the lowest points in my life began when I was prescribed an immune suppressant drug. It made me depressed, which made me less inclined to exercise, which affected my sleep, which sapped my energy, which meant my productivity suffered, which exacerbated the original health problem even further, and so on. The only thing that pulled me out of this downward spiral was having previously 'banked' a good amount of health capital, social capital, and ingrained habits.

This entanglement also explains why the debt trap is so crushing. It's not just compounding interest on the balance of the loan, but the spillover effects on health, mental bandwidth, and cognitive capacity making it harder to keep up with payments, until the debtor is trapped in an escalating feedback loop of misery.

If we have momentum on our side, this interdependence works to our advantage. Having a buffer of cash in the bank means I don't have to stress, which improves my health, which makes me happier, which makes me more fun to be around, which makes me more productive, and so on. It's a virtuous cycle: as you collect optionality in each of the four domains, they help to fill the other buckets too.

If we add a modest compounding effect to the growth curve of our financial/health/social/knowledge capital, and then add this synergistic effect on top, we get a trajectory shooting towards the sky.

But nobody can maintain this kind of growth rate forever. There's a reason we don't live in a universe where there's only one enormous sequoia tree blotting out the sun, or an infinitely-muscular athlete who wins every competition. Like anything else, optionality is subject to the law of diminishing returns.

DIMINISHING RETURNS

The laws of physics are non-negotiable. A sequoia can only grow so tall before it takes more energy to pump water up from its roots than its new needles can harvest in sunlight. Pro athletes have to grind to eke out tiny incremental gains, and the equation gets less and less compelling with every advance.

Even where there are no hard physical limits, the advantages gained always start to level off. The most famous people are deluged with more offers than they could use in several lifetimes, and we've already discussed how each additional dollar earned is subject to diminishing returns—once you're already rich, as Bill Gates points out, it's the same hamburger.

The same is true of all the other components of optionality. Anthropologists put the maximum number of social relationships we can sustain around 150: after that point, we're at risk of becoming fake friends. Being in shape makes it easier to stay in shape, but it gets harder and harder to improve after tapping out the initial 'newbie' gains. As for knowledge capital, we could spend every waking moment accumulating diplomas and hoovering up information, but it wouldn't be much help if we never actually applied any of it.

So the pursuit of optionality looks like an S-shaped (sigmoid) curve: there's a slow take-off with lots of concerted effort, then an increasingly rapid ascent as momentum kicks in, followed by a gradual levelling-off as we run into diminishing returns (Fig. 1.14).

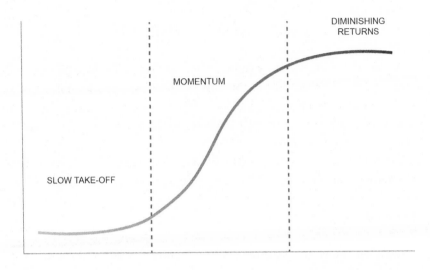

Figure 1.14. The sigmoid curve trajectory of optionality.

What does this mean? Each of the four factors of optionality offers a different marginal return, depending on our point along the S-curve. We know each bucket has a synergistic effect on the others. If we fuel them strategically, we can apply our efforts to whichever yields the most thrust at any given point in time.

At one point, it might make sense to focus on learning and acquiring skills. At another point, it might be best to accumulate cold hard cash. At another point, you might prioritise new experiences, or building social connections, or working on mental or physical health. Perhaps you notice a major liability dragging you down in one domain, or early signs of neglect that ought to be nipped in the bud. You can strategically divert effort from one bucket to another, secure in the knowledge that your overall optionality index is always on the rise.

Which brings us to the final common attribute of the four factors of optionality: they're all based on exploitable asymmetries.

EXPLOITABLE ASYMMETRIES

A pair of economists are walking down the street. The younger one looks down, and spots a $20 bill on the pavement. "Hey, a twenty-dollar bill!" he says. Without so much as a glance, his older and wiser colleague replies, "Nonsense. If there was a twenty-dollar bill lying on the street, someone would have already picked it up by now."

The takeaway of this old joke is that a) economists are deeply unfunny, and b) sometimes there really are $20 notes lying on the pavement.

Financial Capital

Every middle-class Westerner is extravagantly wealthy, by any historical or geographical standard. We just have to be a tiny bit less profligate than our fellow bubble residents, and we can skim a big old surplus off the top.

And yet... almost nobody does this. Instead, spending inevitably rises in lockstep with income, many people are hopelessly indebted, and almost everyone is stuck playing the conspicuous consumption game.

Social Capital

For the first time in history, we're no longer confined to associating with a handful of people who grew up in the same village. We have an array of near-magical tools to meet and communicate with people around the world. We can find a group for any niche interest or hobby under the sun. We can email almost anyone in the world, and they might even email us back.

And yet... a great many people don't have the time or capacity to invest in relationships, and the average American hasn't made a new friend in five years.

Health Capital

Food has become so cheap that our main problem is having *too much* of it. We understand the basics of how to exercise, eat well, and prevent disease, and have an unprecedented amount of leisure time to put it into practice.

And yet...many people struggle with poor health. Longevity has started to go backwards in the US and UK, and it's exceptional to make it into adult-hood without some kind of physical or mental affliction.

Knowledge Capital

Public libraries have millions of titles on loan. YouTube has tutorials for every subject you can imagine, and some you can't. There are free courses online, many of them offered by prestigious universities. The sum total of humanity's accumulated knowledge is available at the push of a button.

And yet... one quarter of American adults didn't read a single book in the last year. TV and social media consumes vast swathes of our lives, and attention is hopelessly fragmented. As the computer scientist Cal Newport points out, the ability to do deep work is becoming increasingly rare at exactly the same time it is becoming increasingly valuable.

These are truly astounding asymmetries. What the heck is going on?

One explanation is that the low-hanging fruit are only visible if you're willing to look at the world in a different way, like one of those Magic Eye puzzles which hides a secret image in plain sight. Like the senior economist, most people don't even bother to look. It's hard enough to spot the $20 bills in the first place, let alone ignore our older and 'wiser' peers and actually pick them up.

I've tried to trigger this shift in perspective by dragging the currencies of life and their trade-offs into plain sight. But even if you find yourself nodding along with all of this, you might also have to contend with weakness of will: you see the $20 bill lying there, you want it with all your heart, but you still can't bring yourself to pick it up.

This is the problem of akrasia—the state of acting against one's own best judgement. Akrasia is partly rooted in conflicts between the competing subagents in our brains, but our struggle to pick up those $20 notes also has to do with our wiring as ultrasocial primates.

Imagine an alien anthropologist visited Earth, and took notes on the things we compete for. It would conclude that the most valuable treasures in human society were glitzy carry-sacks made of skinned cattle by some guy called 'Louis Vuitton', and that lesser prizes, like our freedom and our wellbeing, were of no great importance.

If the French critic René Girard was still above ground, he'd explain to the confused anthropologist that among our species, the intensity of competition tells you very little about underlying value. Instead, we borrow our desires from others: a toddler will try to seize a toy which held no interest to him until his playmate wanted it—and *we never fully grow out of this tendency*. It sounds tautological, but many popular things are popular merely because they are popular.

Girard called this process **Mimesis**. As his student Peter Thiel put it, competitors often become obsessed with their rivals at the expense of their self-proclaimed goals: "People will compete fiercely for things that don't matter, and once they're fighting, they'll fight harder and harder."

If you've ever watched six year olds playing soccer, you've seen how these herding behaviours play out. While the entire mob is running after the ball, jostling and elbowing each other for position, the rest of the field is wide open. If a single individual was able to stop blindly following the pack, they'd be much better positioned to score.

This, then, is the final rule for building optionality: you have to ignore what everyone else is doing, and think carefully about what is worth competing for.

THE JOURNEY IS THE DESTINATION

This brings us to the end of Book I. We started with a bare-bones definition of optionality: the right, but not the obligation, to take a given action. We fleshed it out with a model for evaluating which options are worth pursuing: those with a small, fixed downside, and large or unlimited upside. Then we broke optionality down into its raw materials: financial, social, health, and knowledge capital, and looked at their common characteristics.

Of the four factors, financial capital has the least intrinsic value, but the most utility. It's far more liquid and fungible than its companions: you can't slice off a chunk of your health capital and exchange it for something else, except in the loosest metaphorical sense. By contrast, it's relatively easy to convert money into the other currencies of life—either directly or indirectly, by buying back your own time.

We are told that money is the 'root of all evil', but this hoary old chestnut has been garbled over the centuries: the original scripture says *the love* of money is the root of all evil. This seemingly trivial distinction captures the essence of this book: money is nothing more than a lump of shiny metal, or zeros and ones on a computer server. It only takes on meaning once you exchange it for something.

So, what are you going to exchange it for?

Those who pursue wealth as an end unto itself are doomed to spend their lives slaving away on the hedonic treadmill. Money is much better thought of as *an option* on the good life: it can be used to buy back freedom, to spend time with loved ones, to lever us into more fulfilling work, to eliminate stress and negative influences, to broaden our skills and interests, and to change the lives of the less fortunate. In short, it gives us a pretty great shot at buying happiness, in the true eudaimonic sense—but only if we shop in the right places.

To a surprisingly large degree, we are our own jailers. Continuing to play negative-sum status games and stacking up material possessions past the point of diminishing returns makes about as much sense as banging your head against a brick wall.

I've put forward frugality as a useful framework for escaping this particular prison, and for opening our options more broadly. The process of min-maxing forces us to examine the unconscious trade-offs we're making, and ruthlessly prune the deadwood from the possibility tree.

This initial round of pruning generates higher-quality options. But there's another reason why it's important to start with a principled set of constraints. The tools we use to build optionality aren't merely means to an end, or short-term hardships that must be endured in the pursuit of some grand prize. They *are* the prize.

Accidental millionaires and the rich kids of Instagram didn't get to choose their lifestyle. They were robbed of the opportunity to instil the virtues of temperance, or hard work, or striving towards difficult goals. Those doors remain forever closed to them.

The same stunted fate befalls those who think that striving and struggling should be excised from the human condition. A life spent sitting on a mountaintop in meditative bliss is no different to floating in a vat with electrodes wired to your skull, except as a matter of aesthetics. This becomes just another way of acting dead: you'll never be more equanimous or detached from the wheel of suffering than your great-grandpa.

Instead, *the journey is the destination*. Rather than looking for shortcuts to the top of the mountain, we have to plan the route ourselves, and make some wrong turns, and pick up a few scars.

That doesn't mean we should go out of our way to make the journey more difficult than it has to be. We're already in the comically absurd position of being self-aware apes born into the weirdest bubble in history, which bears increasingly little resemblance to the ancestral environment. As often as not, we're our own worst enemies.

Attempting to resist the social pressures and adaptive forces ingrained over millions of years of evolution might sound like an exercise in futility to rival King Canute himself. That's because it is.

We're not even going *to try* to confront our primal instincts head-on. Instead, we'll use a bunch of sneaky tricks to sidestep them altogether, and harness them to work in our favour. Rather than kid ourselves that we can rise above petty status-signalling games, we'll find better games to play.

This is the subject of Book II. All aboard, the Ship of Fools!

II

AKRASIA

AKRASIA. (noun) from the ancient Greek ἀκρασία. *The state of acting against one's better judgment, a lack of self-control, weakness of will.*

INTRODUCTION

Do I contradict myself? Very well, then I contradict myself, I am large, I contain multitudes.

— WALT WHITMAN

ABOARD THE SHIP OF FOOLS: *It's a fine day for sailing. In the midst of the vast blue yonder, a ship is merrily going nowhere in particular. A babble of excited voices carry across the water, punctuated by the occasional scream. The vessel drifts close enough to read the name crudely scrawled across the bow: the Ship of Fools.*

On board, all is chaos. Some of the crew are jousting with oars. A monkey swings through the rigging, untying knots at random. An ancient, leathery mariner suns himself on the deck. The crew steer clear of his terrible claws. The hapless Captain stands at the helm, wrestling for control over the wheel. Whenever his noble senses are dulled with drink or narcotics, the crew mutiny and seize control of the ship. Behind the Captain, an old man who looks like his father whispers harsh words in his ear, reminding him of his failures.

And so, the fools proceed on their voyage in such a manner as might be expected of them...

'The ship of fools', 1494. Wellcome Library (CC BY 4.0).

There is no single 'you'. Psychologists have been telling us this for the last century, but we still tend to imagine a homunculus perched inside our skulls, pulling on the levers as it peers out through our eyes. Instead, each of us is a loose assemblage of competing desires and traits, many of them ancient and animalistic, sometimes operating on different planes of consciousness.

As the satirist Terry Pratchett put it, every human is a committee:

"Some of the other members of the committee were dark and red and entirely uncivilised. They had joined the brain before civilisation; some of them had got aboard even before humanity. And the bit that did the joined-up thinking had to fight, in the darkness of the brain, to get the casting vote!"

The part doing the joined-up thinking is the Captain—the part of you that feels most like 'you'. The Captain likes to think they're in charge, but they're mostly an impotent narrator, limited to watching events unfold. When they write up the day's events in the ship's log, they convince themself it was part of the plan all along.

The Captain's long-suffering adviser is the Old Timer, standing behind them at the wheel. This is the older and wiser self—a time-traveler from the future—who's always encouraging us to plan ahead and save for a rainy day.

The Monkey swinging through the rigging is a natural mimic and a shameless show-off. This is the ultrasocial part of us that loves to compete and cooperate, and is obsessed with winning the affection of its peers.

But even the Monkey steers clear of the Reptile. This ancient mariner climbed aboard long before humanity. It doesn't think about the future, or trying to impress anyone—it doesn't think, period. The Reptile has a terrible hunger, and when the red mist descends, it takes control.

These characters are not meant to carve reality at its joints. They're just caricatures of some of the subagents swirling around our grey matter; similar to the Freudian concepts of *id*, *ego*, and *superego*. However you choose to break down your society of mind, you will always find factions with different desires, strengths, and weaknesses. The internal conflict that arises from our squabbling subagents is what the Greeks called *akrasia*—a lack of self-control, and resistance against doing the things we want to do.

Getting these subagents aligned to a common cause is a hard enough problem. But we also have to align them with the interests of other selves: our friends, our family, our tribe members, and our societies. Some of these external agents can make our journey much easier, while others actively sabotage our efforts.

Even when basic material deprivation is a solved problem—as it is for increasingly large swathes of humanity—akrasia remains the single biggest obstacle to opening high-quality options.

In trying to overcome problems of akrasia, we hear a lot about 'willpower' and 'grit'. I say these are dirty words, suitable only for masochists. Trying to do anything through sheer strength of will is like rowing into a headwind: exhausting, and largely futile. The purpose of this book is to set up systems that keep the wind at our backs, marshal all our various selves into pulling in the same direction, and give a wide berth to saboteurs and wreckers. Then, and only then, we can start rowing in earnest.

7

CHARTING A COURSE

The cost of a thing is the amount of what I call life which is required to be exchanged for it, immediately or in the long run.

— THOREAU

E VERY TASK WE DO TODAY instead of tomorrow, and every time we defer gratification, we're doing the Old Timer proud. But, of course, their wise counsel often falls on deaf ears. "That's a problem for *future* Homer," says America's everyman, pouring a bottle of vodka into a tub of mayonnaise. "Man, I don't envy that guy!"

This tendency to screw over your future self is called 'hyperbolic discounting'. The value we place on a reward or punishment depends very much on when we're going to experience it. If we're asked to make a decision that involves some trade-off taking place in the distant future, no problem—we'll almost always take the option with the highest expected value. But if it involves trading something off *right now*, we'll often blow off the delayed reward and go for the short-term fix.

Deferring gratification doesn't come naturally. If you're a four-year old child, you might be incapable of making even the simplest trade-offs (although I am impressed that you're reading this book). In the famous Stanford marshmallow tests, young children were left alone in a room with a small treat. They were told they could eat it now, but if they waited 15 minutes for the researcher to come back, they'd get *two* treats instead. Some kids went the distance, some folded after a few agonising minutes, and some gobbled the marshmallow the moment the researcher's back was turned.

The researchers followed the kids throughout life, and found that those who could defer gratification had much better outcomes in every domain of life. But the famous findings have recently come into question: as it turns out, the kids who didn't wait often came from backgrounds where adults were not exactly paragons of reliability. They weren't about to trust some stranger to stick to their word. When you grow up in a competitive and risky environment, you take what you can get, when you can get it. Those kids were no suckers.[1]

The chaotic mess of real life bears little resemblance to sterile lab conditions. In the real world, you have to adjust for the probability of actually *receiving* some distant reward. How do you know you'll be around to enjoy your retirement? Maybe you get hit by a bus tomorrow, or your preferences change over the years, in which case you're better off living it up right now.

And so, discounting the future is perfectly rational. But the reason it's called 'hyperbolic' is that we apply the discount rate inconsistently over time. For example, if I offered you $5 tomorrow, or $10 one year from now, you'd probably take the money now. But if I offered you $5 in five years, or $10 in six years, you'd almost certainly be happy to wait. It's the exact same trade-off—wait one additional year, double your money—but our minds don't process it that way.

As per usual, the blame lies squarely with the blind idiot god of evolution. Your ancestors didn't have to choose how much to contribute to their 401k, or think about the long-term implications of their high-fructose corn syrup intake. Consuming *now* was almost always the optimal strategy. If you had a glut of food, you feasted for the lean times ahead. Body fat was a crucial survival mechanism, not something to be ashamed of. As for the concept of 'debt', to the reptilian part of your mind which has no concept of the future, it might as well be manna from heaven.

The net effect is that most of us err on the side of discounting too heavily, and hold our future selves hostage to our present desires. The Old Timer sits in the corner, tearing their hair out, while the crew roll out the barrels of rum and tick it up on American Express.

Learning how to bargain with your future self pays off handsomely. The

Matthew effect of cumulative advantage makes these kind of temporal trade-offs especially compelling: if every dollar you save now is the equivalent of $10 your future self doesn't have to earn, a small initial effort can pay dividends for the rest of your life.

If you ever wished you could go back in time and do things differently, well, that's the position you're in right now. Every moment is an opportunity to change the future. You just have to cultivate the very unnatural tendency of being kind to some strange old geezer who shares the same name as you.

This is the skill of mental time-travel. While our meatsack bodies slavishly plod along at the precise rate of one second per second, our minds are unconstrained by the bounds of time or space. Our ability to create vast, hyper-detailed simulations of the past and future is the closest thing we have to a superpower, because it lets us do the following:

- Relive past experiences, and learn from the things that happen to us
- Use these lessons to run simulations with some predictive power
- Having simulated a desirable future, take steps to steer the universe in that direction

Or as we usually call it, 'goal setting'.

GOALS GONE WILD

There's a huge body of evidence behind the practice of goal setting, which is why every LinkedIn influencer and self-help writer refuses to shut up about it. In the delightfully-titled paper 'Goals Gone Wild', Lisa Ordóñez and her Harvard Business School co-authors take a slightly different tack. They're not worried that goals don't work. They're worried that they *work too well*.

As Ordóñez et al point out, goal-setting is marketed as a benign, over-the-counter treatment for motivation. But it really ought to be a prescription-strength medication "that requires careful dosing, consideration of harmful side effects, and close supervision".

Here are the main ways in which goals can lead us astray:

1. Tunnel Vision

The fact that goals narrow our focus is a big part of what makes them so powerful. The unhappy corollary is that they blind us to everything else; like those horses that are heavily into BDSM headgear. We can make good progress trotting along straight ahead. But with the blinkers on, we might be missing out on piles of delicious hay outside our line of sight, or interesting horses, or quicker routes to our destination.

It's not just potential opportunities passing us by. We're also blinded to threats. Without peripheral vision, we'll never see the pickup truck that smashes into us, consigning our fate to the glue factory.

This is not a problem if we only have one goal to maximise, and everything else can go to hell. But humans (and horses) are not wired up like that. We have a range of values to pursue, which are often in tension with one another. Do we want to run fast, or eat hay, or avoid getting hit by pickup trucks? The correct answer is 'all of the above'. It makes no sense to focus myopically on pursuing one goal if it comes at the expense of other valuable outcomes. But that's exactly what happens in real life.

The classic mistake is a narrow focus on building wealth and climbing the career ladder, while neglecting the other components of optionality. Psychologists have found that the stronger the drive for financial success, the lower the satisfaction with family life, for example. We trot along making a lot of money, then get blindsided by the divorce papers or the heart attack at 40.

The poet Ralph Waldo Emerson said "a foolish consistency is the hobgoblin of little minds". When circumstances change, we have to be able to change with them, rather than slavishly sticking to our prior beliefs. If an inflexible goal locks us into a zombie-like path dependency, we'll shuffle along until our brains fall out our noses.

2. Goodhart's Law

The government of colonial India was worried about the number of venomous snakes in Delhi, so they offered a bounty for every dead cobra. The program was wildly successful in bringing in snakes—*too* successful.

As it turned out, the entrepreneurial locals had started a thriving cobra-breeding industry. The juiciest part is that when the Brits scrapped the program, the breeders released their slithery charges into the wild, making the original problem even worse.[2]

This is an example of Goodhart's Law: when a measure becomes a target, it's no longer a good measure. It's hardly surprising that people use sneaky strategies to try and game the system for personal benefit. What *is* surprising is that it's all too easy to Goodhart ourselves.

Again, we have to be especially careful of this in the financial domain. Money is a lump of shiny metal, or ones and zeros on a computer server. It's very handy stuff to accumulate, but it should only ever be a means to an end. If you spend most of your life trying to reach an arbitrary net worth without having thought about what that number represents, you are confusing the measure with the target.

3. Onanism

A clearly visualised goal works wonders for those who lack confidence. It's an exploit of a vulnerability in the brain, which struggles to tell the difference between our inner simulations and real life. Once we have a concrete vision firmly in our mind's eye, it seems achievable in the world *outside* our skull, which subtly affects all our other behaviors.

This failure to distinguish between imagination and reality explains why it's so pleasurable to fantasise about all the cool stuff we're going to do. The danger is that we start to get a little hit of pleasure every time we think about our goal, which substitutes for actually doing the work. We're already patting ourselves on the back, without having so much as lifted a finger. This is masturbation. It's fun in the moment. But as the saying goes, at the end of the day, you're only screwing yourself.

When we share our noble ambitions with the world, the problem is compounded even further: now we're getting social adulation, too. You probably know someone who confidently talks up all the amazing things they're going to do. Their eyes light up with pride as they announce their ambitions, but they almost never follow through. As a general rule, talking about what you're going to do seems to be inversely correlated with actually doing the thing.

Again: visualisation is a brilliant tool for forcing our brains to move a seemingly impossible task into the 'possible' bucket. It's only when we're already confident we can achieve something that it might sap our motivation to act upon it.

4. Prediction errors

All of the other mistakes can happen when we're actually running the simulation correctly, i.e. we really have conjured up a desirable future to bring into existence.

But what if our starting simulation is *wrong*?

Mental time travel is much more of an art than a science. This is not for lack of raw compute: the human brain is ridiculously powerful for a few pounds of grey goo you'd hurry to scrape off your shoe if you stepped in it. Our simulations rarely lag or freeze: in fact, it's the remarkable clarity and vividness which makes them so seductive. The problem is that we have to run simulations with imperfect information—in the language of computer science, 'garbage in, garbage out'.

This is not an issue when we're running simple simulations of what would happen if, say, we jumped off that big cliff over there without a parachute. In an uncertain world, the laws of physics and the squishiness of human bodies are reassuring constants.

But there are two unstable variables which consistently lead our inner simulators to produce garbage-in-garbage-out results.

A DYNAMIC SELF IN AN UNSTABLE WORLD

"What's your 10 year plan?" is a strange question. I sure as hell wouldn't trust the 18-year-old me to decide what I should be doing right now. That guy was a dumbass. So why should I assume my current self has any right to decide what's best for the older version of me?

Future-Rich might as well be a complete stranger. I'm sure his preferences and desires will be foreign to me, in the same way that it now seems inexplicable there was a time in my life I used to like eating dirt, or Hoobastank.

There is no fixed, stable 'you'—only a collection of related mental imprints over time. The continuity between these states is more tenuous than it appears: our memories are generated afresh each time we access them, with most of the fine details fabricated. Outside of the worst cases of arrested development, we're much more like a series of different people inhabiting the same body than a constant 'me'.

Maybe you don't buy the argument that personal identity is a matter of degrees. Even so, the planning problem persists. As Harvard psychology professor Daniel Gilbert explains in *Stumbling on Happiness*, we just plain suck at predicting how we'll feel in any given situation: it's hard enough to guess in the moment, much less several years or decades in the future. Everything tends to look especially sexy from a distance, because time smears a generous film of Vaseline over the lens of our mind's eye. Once we get close enough to see the wrinkles and pores, it no longer seems quite so appealing.

The mismatch between what we *think* will make us feel good and what will *actually* make us feel good goes a long way towards explaining why we make such bizarre trade-offs. Here's Gilbert:

> "We toil and sweat to give [our futures selves] just what we think they will like, and they quit their jobs, grow their hair, move to or from San Francisco, and wonder how we could ever have been stupid enough to think they'd like that. We fail to achieve the accolades and rewards that we consider crucial to their well-being, and they end up thanking God that things didn't work out according to our shortsighted, misguided plan."

The ability to mentally time-travel—to imagine some far-off land called 'the future', and take steps to change it—is a recent development in our evolutionary history. It's not surprising that we make some rookie mistakes, but it does put us in a bit of a bind. Why bother striving for anything, if you can't be sure you'll want it once you get there?

That would be bad enough—but the 'there' to which we are trying to get is also a moving target.

For most of history, there was no history. You're a swineherd; your father is a swineherd; your grandfather was a swineherd. This makes it easy enough to make predictions about the future prospects of, say, swine herding: you're guaranteed to be as happy as a pig in muck, which is to say, not very.

It wasn't until a few hundred years ago—the last 0.1 per cent of our species' existence—that the pace of change started to really accelerate. Now history is being foisted upon us at an extremely obnoxious rate.

Book V lays out the best strategies for navigating an increasingly volatile world. These are seriously hard problems: every young person has to somehow decide on a job or career path, which will typically involve locking themselves into a rigid path, while having vanishingly little information about a) what their future selves will want, and b) the future state of the world.

Entire industries are innovated out of existence before our eyes, while new ones rise in their place. There are people working in jobs that didn't even *exist* at the time they visited their high school careers counsellor. Imagine trying to explain Instagram influencers to your great-grandma.

Which is why venture capitalist Marc Andreessen's first rule of career planning is so counterintuitive: *don't.*

As Andreessen explains, you have no idea what industries you'll enter, what companies you'll work for, what roles you'll have, where you'll live, what your preferences will be, or what you will ultimately contribute:

> "The world is an incredibly complex place and everything is changing all the time... trying to plan your career is an exercise in futility that will only serve to frustrate you, and to blind you to the really significant opportunities that life will throw your way."

It's a head-scratcher. What's a time-traveler to do?

ROUGHLY RIGHT BEATS PRECISELY WRONG

To restate the problem of goal setting: we have to generate the best possible set of outcomes for *all* of our present and future selves, on the basis of extremely unreliable information about what our future holds.

Thankfully, there is a systematic approach for doing exactly this, and it's called 'having optionality'. It's impossible to know *exactly* what your future self will want, but you can predict with near 100 per cent certainty they'll be grateful you've set them up with high-quality options: financial capital, good health, valuable relationships, and useful skills and experiences. With broad capabilities and resources at their disposal, they can execute on whatever makes sense at any given moment.

The naive view of optionality is that it involves drifting aimlessly through life, refusing to set goals, make predictions, or commit to anything, and generally embodying a sort of eternal ¯_(ツ)_/¯.

The reality is that we can move strategically between phases of opening options, and phases of exercising them. We'll get into the opportune timing for 'exploring' and 'exploiting' in Book V. For now, think of option value as a function of the level of volatility in a given area of life, and the remaining time available to us. Trying to plan your entire career when you're 17 years old is like buying a highly personalised gift for some distant cousin you've never met: for the love of sweet baby Jesus, just get them a well-stuffed envelope.

Having options is not an excuse to avoid taking action. I prefer Nassim Taleb's framing, which is that optionality serves as a stand-in for *intelligence*. You don't have to try and make complicated predictions, or have any special insights, or even be right all that often:

> "All you need is the wisdom to not do unintelligent things to hurt yourself...and recognise favourable outcomes when they occur."

The Goals Gone Wild authors warn us that goals are prescription medicine: powerful, and often dangerous. Optionality is more like an all-purpose pep tonic that keeps us in rude good health, and ready to leap on whatever opportunities present themselves. There are no side effects, no overdoses, and no misdiagnoses.

The optionality approach to planning is summarised in the popular aphorism 'better to be vaguely right than exactly wrong'.[3]

Most predictions are garbage, and some are actively harmful. But that doesn't mean we should abandon goals altogether. We just have to use them as sparingly as possible: only one, or two at the outside.

TERMINAL VS INSTRUMENTAL

Some goals are **Terminal**; we want them because we want them. Other goals are **Instrumental**; we want them because they move us closer to the thing we really want. While we often act like 'get money!' is a terminal value, it's almost purely instrumental: collecting scraps of paper with some dead guy's face only makes sense if we can swap them for things with intrinsic value. You can tell a goal is instrumental if it only prompts another question. You want to reach a certain net worth? OK, why? You want to retire early? Cool, but what exactly are you optimising for? If money wasn't an issue, how would you spend your time?

The ultimate terminal goal is something like 'flourishing' or 'the good life', as described in Book I, but we're shifting down one level of abstraction here. 'I want to buy a house' counts as a terminal goal. So does 'I want to visit Italy', or 'I want to make humans an interplanetary species'.

The defining attribute of terminal goals is that they're concrete and inherently rewarding. When I was working towards my initial savings goal, I wasn't visualising a bunch of zeroes on a spreadsheet. Instead, I was daydreaming about:

- Countries I wanted to visit
- Projects I was going to work on
- Lazy days of total freedom

As it turned out, I got all the specific details wrong—that inner simulator screwed up again!—but it still got the job done. The temporal trade-offs I made during that accumulation phase were not only painless, but *rewarding*: each time I deferred some item of spending, I'd experience a tiny shiver of excitement in anticipation of my future plans.

Terminal goals are a fantastic source of motivation, but thinking really hard about what you want isn't enough to move you towards the destination. This is where instrumental goals come in. If we're competing in the Amazing Race, these are the various flights, buses and trains we catch to try and get to the next checkpoint. Unlike the terminal goal—winning the prize money—these can be measured and tracked. There are timetables to scrutinise, and

GPS coordinates to consult. Riding on buses and trains is not the point of the exercise, but it is instrumental in getting us where we want to go.

You can use a succession of instrumental goals to get to the terminus, but I wouldn't recommend pursuing too many at once. For example: I've always felt mildly embarrassed about writing a finance column called 'Budget Buster', because I've never budgeted a day in my life. A budget is a complicated tangle of instrumental goals, all of which require time and effort to monitor and enforce. Worse, they lead to cobra-breeding situations: who cares if you blow your petrol allocation by $50 if you're $100 under budget in the groceries category? You might be tempted to spend up to the limit to compensate, which would make sense in the narrow context of the 'goal', while being antithetical to the actual point of the exercise. Having a rigid budget is another example of Emerson's foolish consistency. It's like catching a bus that takes you further away from your desired destination, just because you already bought a ticket.[4]

If you think you can juggle several instrumental goals, go for it. Plenty of people swear by budgeting. Just remember that financial capital is only one of the four factors of optionality: setting more than one or two goals in each domain adds up fast, and risks spreading your efforts too thinly.

Terminal and instrumental goals complement one another. A terminal goal supplies the *motivation*, and an instrumental goal gives you something to *measure*.

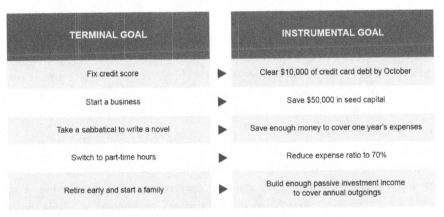

TERMINAL GOAL	INSTRUMENTAL GOAL
Fix credit score	Clear $10,000 of credit card debt by October
Start a business	Save $50,000 in seed capital
Take a sabbatical to write a novel	Save enough money to cover one year's expenses
Switch to part-time hours	Reduce expense ratio to 70%
Retire early and start a family	Build enough passive investment income to cover annual outgoings

Table 2.1. Reverse-engineering terminal goals into instrumental goals.

Once you have a destination in mind, it's easy enough to work backwards and figure out the corresponding instrumental goal (Table 2.1).

If you *don't* have a specific vision in mind, it's perfectly sensible to optimise for 'building optionality'. In one sense, optionality is the mother of all instrumental values: it's literally an instrument that we purchase in order to unlock many possible desirable pathways. But having optionality is also a terminal good, even if we prefer not to exercise our options—remember the all-important difference between fasting and starving.

The main problem with 'build optionality' as a terminus is that it's way too abstract to get the juices flowing. I suggest picking a terminal goal that has the side effect of increasing optionality in one or more of the four domains. If you happen to nail the prediction about what your future self will want, great! If you get it wrong, you still end up in a better position—no harm, no foul.

This is what happened to me. My terminal goal was 'save enough money to quit job and go traveling'. But I wasn't exactly sure how I would use my newfound freedom, and most of the half-baked ideas I left home with I abandoned altogether. Every project I ended up working on naturally emerged once I had the room to explore, and wander through some interesting doorways. There is a lot to be said for moseying along running lots of small experiments, and creating space for serendipity to strike.

When in doubt, there are two instrumental goals which are excellent for building optionality, and which I recommend to just about anyone. These are net worth, and expense ratio.

NET WORTH: THE GREAT BULLSHIT DETECTOR

In a world of cheap signalling, net worth is the great bullshit detector. It cuts through all the preening, posturing, and peacocking, and lays bare your real financial situation. Let others strut and fret as much as they want, but you can't afford to fool yourself.

If you don't know your number, let's figure it out right now. You can get a copy of my net worth spreadsheet at optionalitybook.com/resources, or grab a pen and paper. First off, make a list of everything you own of value. That means cash, bank account balances, investments, retirement accounts, property, vehicles, and any other assets worth mentioning.

Next, dig out your credit card statements, your student debt, mortgage balance, auto loan, overdrafts, unpaid library fines, the $50 you owe your cousin from last Christmas, and add them all up in a separate column. You should now have two subtotals. Subtract the debt from the assets, and you've got your net worth.

This exercise can be uncomfortable. The first time I ran the numbers, I found I had less than a cent to my name, which was like having a bucket of ice water tipped down my neck. But it was a useful wake-up call.

If your number does come out in the red, there's no need to panic. The starting point is irrelevant: what matters is getting the number moving in the right direction. Clawing your way out of debt to achieve a net worth of $0 is much more impressive than saving the equivalent sum, because you don't have compound interest helping you out.

Once you've calculated your net worth, you can set an instrumental goal to increase it by a specific amount within a specific timeframe. That might involve repaying debt, saving, investing, selling stuff you don't need, or finding another income stream—whatever makes the most sense at any given point in time, according to your circumstances. Any of these activities move the all-important number higher.

Net worth is easy to track on an ongoing basis, and kind of fun. I've kept up the practice even after reaching my target, because it only takes 15 minutes and it gives me an instant snapshot of my finances. But there's a major short-coming: once you start investing in a serious way, fluctuations in the values of your assets will start to drown out the impact of your saving habits.[5] An upswing in the markets can lull you into a false sense of security, masking the fact that your contributions are slipping. Conversely, you might beat yourself up when your net worth appears to be falling, even though you've been saving diligently.

If this starts to be an issue, you're already doing pretty great. At that point, you might consider setting an instrumental goal that gives you more of a challenge, and responds more closely to your actual efforts.

EXPENSE RATIO: THE GREAT RESILIENCE BUILDER

The ultimate measure of financial resilience is the proportion of your income you can live on. I managed to get by on half my pay check during my accumulation phase, and early retirement enthusiasts regularly pare this number down even further.

As a benchmark, most people spend close to 100 per cent of their pay packets (or more, by taking on consumer debt), and an expense ratio of 85 per cent is considered 'good'. Note that if you manage to hold your expenses steady as your income rises—i.e. resist the lockstep dance of lifestyle inflation —you'll automatically bring the ratio down over time.

The simplest way to measure your expense ratio is to have all your income paid into a checking account, see what's left over at the end of each month, then shift it across to a savings or investment account. Divide the balance by the original income, multiply by 100, and you've got your number:

- $2000 income earned throughout the month
- $423 left over at the end of the month
- $2000 - $423 = $1577
- $1577 / $2000 = 0.79
- 0.79 * 100 = 79%

If you want to get granular, there are all sorts of software tools for categorising spending, some of which automatically scrape and categorise data from your bank account.

I prefer to manually note down my expenses in a spreadsheet, and have done so religiously for the last few years. When my spending starts to get out of hand, the cells blaze a furious red, and when I'm on track again, they fade to a soothing forest-green.[6]

This daily monitoring doesn't feel like a chore to me, but I'm the kind of weirdo who gets weak-kneed at the sight of a well-formatted pivot table. Well-adjusted folks will have better things to do than collect and categorise every last receipt, but I recommend trying this as an exercise for a month or two. It lets you see exactly where all your money is going, and quickly eyeball any areas that might need reining in. Note that expense tracking is *not* the same thing as having a budget, because there are no goals for each category—the only thing that matters is getting that total expense ratio down, by any means necessary.

When in doubt, net worth and expense ratios are the best financial metrics to focus on. They build optionality in a complementary way: a higher net worth positions you to take advantage of opportunities, while a lower expense ratio keeps you streamlined and resilient to unexpected events.

Some people prefer to set more specific instrumental goals, like clearing a credit card debt, or reaching a certain balance in a saving account. The neat thing about net worth and expense ratios is that they automatically take all of those factors into account, and give you the flexibility to take whatever action has the highest impact at any point in time. But if you get more motivation out of, say, clearing your student loan—even if it's not strictly speaking the best strategy—you should absolutely do that. As always, the question to ask isn't 'is it optimal?' but 'does it work?'

WHAT GETS MEASURED GETS DONE

A more positive formulation of Goodhart's Law is the aphorism 'what gets measured gets done'. The defining feature of an instrumental goal is that it's *measurable*. Whatever you choose, make sure it has the following three attributes:

1. Trackable

Whether it's calories, weight on a barbell, or net worth, you have to be able to measure and track the mother-loving heck out of it. It doesn't matter if you use a spreadsheet, or fancy software, or a used napkin taped to the fridge. Choose a system, and stick to it.

2. Tight feedback loop

Put a timeframe on your goal, and chunk it down to shorter-term milestones. Then you can create a recurring event in your calendar that prompts you to check in regularly and make sure you're on track. You'll have to experiment to find the right interval: checking annual progress is far too slow for most goals, whereas daily monitoring would be far too often.

Once you've got the habit bedded in, you can start to loosen the feedback loop. I still update my net worth at the end of every month, but only through force of habit—now I have a good handle on my finances, I'll probably switch to quarterly or annual updates instead.

3. Rewarding

It's fine to celebrate milestones with some kind of treat, but be careful: external rewards risk eroding your internal motivation. Boring and repetitive tasks are an exception, because they're never going to be rewarding anyway. If you find that it helps, by all means bribe yourself into soldiering through them.

The Ship of Fools is turning about. The Captain has struck a deal that everyone is happy with. The Old Timer is no longer tearing his hair out. For the first time, the crew has a common destination in mind. Better still, they have a map for how to get there, and instruments to chart their progress. The ship glides across a calm sea...

....but what's this? An island of sloping meadows appears on the horizon, filled with wildflowers. Gorgeous creatures sit on the sunny shores, combing their golden hair and singing.

"I'm loving it!" croons one. "Because you're worth it!" warbles another. "Buy now, pay later!" sings a third. The honeyed voices are maddening to the senses. The Monkey hoots and beats his chest with excitement. The Reptile has already clambered overboard and is lashing his way through the water. The crew is so enraptured that they fail to notice the spear-sharp rocks surrounding the island. Could the journey be over before it has begun?

The ship drifts closer to the jagged reef...

8

THE SIREN SONG

I can resist everything except temptation.

— OSCAR WILDE

I F THERE'S A CARTON OF ICE-CREAM in the house, I will methodically shovel it into my mouth until the spoon scrapes the bottom of the container. If I start watching Netflix or YouTube before bed, the auto-rolling algorithms will keep me up until I'm a bleary-eyed zombie. It doesn't even feel pleasurable, exactly. It's more like I'm a passive observer, watching from inside the bony prison of my own skull. This is the same helpless compulsion that drives me to check my phone every fourteen seconds, cycling between social networks that only stress me out. The Siren song strips away my thin veneer of self-control faster than tooth enamel bathed in Coca-Cola.

My pathologies are not necessarily yours. But if you've ever felt like someone is tugging on your strings, know that you're not being paranoid. The evolutionary psychologist Geoffrey Miller divides the products of consumer capitalism into two broad categories: the self-stimulating, and the status-seeking. Self-stimulating products are designed to push the hot buttons in the most ancient part of our brains—bypassing the higher functions, and making a direct appeal to the Reptile.

Why do we crave fat, salt, and sugar? For millions of years, these were a reliable signal of nutrient-dense foods: ripe, non-poisonous fruit and vegetables, animal protein, seafood. It's only over the last hundred years or so—the blink of an eye in evolutionary time—that the signal has been amplified and distorted beyond recognition. An apple contains 90 calories, a decent serving of fibre, and various vitamins and minerals. A MegaThirstyGulp soda cup packs 900 calories with no nutritional value whatsoever, but our brains can't tell the difference.[1]

These products are **Superstimuli**—sensations we're biologically hard-wired to pursue, with the dial cranked up to 11. If the signal is distorted enough, like the rats from Chapter 5, we will literally stimulate ourselves to death. Drugs are the most obvious example of primitive wireheading, but mutant members of the extended family include fast food, porn, reality TV, airbrushed magazine covers, online gambling, virtual reality, and immersive video games.

The iron law of history is that hedonic adaptation always marches forward. The Siren song only ever becomes louder and more hypnotising, which means we'll always crave a stronger dose, more 'likes', new depths of depravity, and an ever-more-comically-oversized soda cup (Fig. 2.1).

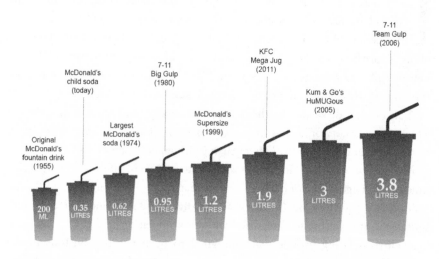

Figure 2.1. The evolution of soda cups over time.

American snack food is already converging on the most fattening diet possible, to the point where rats gain more weight eating at a buffet of the likes of Oreos and Doritos than they do when offered unlimited access to straight sugar and fat. Teams of chemists are employed in figuring out how to make food as palatable as possible, right down to the molecular level. There's some guy out there whose whole job is analysing the perfect crunch of a potato chip.

This same relentless optimisation process is underway in every domain. Behind the innocent user interface of your favourite app, game, or online streaming service, every last pixel has been A/B tested to capture your attention. Google tested 41 different shades of blue to figure out which would attract the most clicks, Facebook's algorithm knows your preferences better than your best friends do, and tech companies borrow design principles from slot machines to dispense hits of dopamine to their users at perfectly-timed intervals. The finest minds of a generation are using their formidable brainpower to exploit the very peculiarities that make us human.

The Reptile is a simple creature, with simple desires. The only things that light up its lizard brain are the four Fs: fighting, fleeing, feeding, and mating. But the Reptile isn't the only crew member in thrall to the Siren song.

The Monkey is right up there on the bulwarks, gibbering with excitement. Unlike its reptilian shipmate, the Monkey is a social mammal, and cares very much what the other monkeys think about it.[2] The Sirens' second category of temptations, status-seeking products, are directly targeted at this impulse. They're designed to help the Monkey show off its desirable traits and gain status amongst its peers—or at least, that's the promise.

CONSPICUOUS CONSUMPTION

In *Spent*, Geoffrey Miller calculates the 'cost density' of various products and commodities, and finds that the basic necessities of life—food, water, air, clothing, shelter—typically cost less than $5 per kilogram. His conclusion is that "living doesn't cost much, but showing off does".

Once we get above the cost density of silver bullion (~$500 per kilogram) we enter what Miller calls "the magical realm of consumer narcissism". This is where we find the self-stimulating products, along with those designed for flaunting or faking fitness: cosmetics, weight loss pills, branded electronics.

Above the cost density of gold, you have diamond jewellery, Ivy League diplomas, and designer sunglasses. For the people who buy these positional goods, the eye-watering expense is not a cost, but a *benefit*: the whole point of the exercise is to set themselves apart from the masses.

It's not so much about signalling wealth, but drawing attention to the desirable traits that make for a good mate or ally. Like the peacock's tail, a showy display of conspicuous consumption suggests you have resources to burn. And it works! All things held equal, rolling up to a party in a Lamborghini will improve your prospects of taking someone home, especially if the alternative is dubbing them on the back of your razor scooter. You can also use money to signal taste and sophistication: a visitor to your condo will surely be impressed by your many leather-bound books, and marvel at the smell of rich mahogany.

Unfortunately, the most sought-after traits—attractiveness, physical and mental health, intelligence—are difficult to fake in the long term. As soon as your admiring visitor asks which translation of Virgil you prefer, the careful image presented by your well-stocked bookcase starts to flicker. Similarly, your date may be disappointed to discover that the Lamborghini's muscular horse-power does not necessarily correlate with performance between the sheets. As Miller points out, we've spent countless generations honing our ability to judge fitness through the mundane means of merely spending time in each other's company. Trait-displaying products and services can project a glamorous illusion, but it doesn't hold up to any serious scrutiny.

Take pity on the poor alien anthropologist, who must be hopelessly confused by now. Why do these monkeys think wearing *this* T-shirt will make everyone want to have sex with them, but not *this* one? Or that becoming a pro athlete has something to do with drinking a particular brand of neon-coloured sugar-water? We'd fall about laughing at any sucker who fell for such an obvious scam, if it weren't for the mass hypnosis of the Siren song.

Marketers spend vast sums of money maintaining the fantasy that products and services are an effective way of displaying desirable traits. They deliberately advertise luxury goods to audiences who can't afford them, to reinforce the positional status of the brand. These names and logos are pure abstractions: a handful of letters, a cluster of pixels, a specific shade of purple. You can't hold them or eat them, but they're worth billions of dollars, and defended with great ferocity by copyright lawyers. Once the initial seeds are sown in consumers' minds, social contagion starts to take over: it's monkey see, monkey do.

Like superstimuli, conspicuous consumption only ever ratchets in one direction. Buying a gigantic blocky cellphone was a power move for the swinging dicks of Wall Street in the 80s; nowadays the homeless guy on the corner has a better model.

And the trade-offs only get worse over time. Buying a quality pair of shoes is genuinely liberating and life-improving. Buying a pair of shoes with a certain logo doesn't improve on the comfort or function, but it does cost 10x as much. By the time we're adding the 47th pair to our walk-in shoe wardrobe, we're so far past the point of diminishing returns that it's not funny.

Conspicuous consumption is a bad status game to play, because it's negative-sum: we have no choice but to spend our money in ever more ridiculous ways, locking us into a competitive spiral of ratcheting expenditure which impoverishes everyone.

Of course, no-one's forcing a MegaThirstyGulp soda down anyone's throat, or holding a gun to the head of those who queue around the block for the latest iPhone. We're in the business of building optionality. Surely it doesn't *hurt* to have more choices?

FAUX OPTIONALITY

In economics-speak, MTV and Mountain Dew Arctic Burst and prescription painkillers are 'revealed preferences'. The idea is that people know their own minds best, and it's patronising to assume everyone ought to be building rustic cabins in the mountains and reading Aristotle.

There is definitely an element of finger-wagging here: cultural elites have always sneered at the lower classes' preference for bread and circuses. But that's not the only thing going on.

In recent years, economists have puzzled over research suggesting that more options are not always better. The 'paradox of choice' clashes with our intuition: if someone offers you Option B, and it's a better fit for your preferences than Option A, great! If you prefer to stick with Option A, no worries— you're in the same position you were before. How could it be wrong to have more choices?

The simple answer: most of the time, it's not. The fact that some people experience mild anxiety when choosing between flavours of jam tells us exactly nothing about the value of pursuing high-quality options. The paradox might not even have all that much to say about the low-level choices: the headline-grabbing studies failed to replicate, and a meta-analysis averaged out the effects of the various studies to a big fat zero. Researchers have recently made some progress in figuring out the specific factors which make a larger choice set more or less appealing, but honestly—who cares? Studies designed to help marketers figure out how many brands of laundry detergent to stock are just not that interesting.

The paradox of choice does get at something important, even if it doesn't show up in the consumer psychology research. In the bad old days of *homo economicus*, people were assumed to be perfect rational actors who had stepped out of the pages of an Ayn Rand novel. Now we know rationality is 'bounded'—by the information we have available, the processing power of our minds, and the time we can dedicate to making decisions.

This creates serious problems for revealed preferences. First, it undermines the assumption that every choice is freely made: the Reptile's preferences might be best fulfilled by smoking a delicious bowl of crystal meth, and it might even manage to wrest control over our brains during some spectacular moment of weakness, but all the other subagents would really, really not be on board with this. If you've never felt powerless in the face of temptation, or addicted to some unsavoury behaviour you've 'freely' entered into, your society of mind is much better integrated than mine.

The second problem with revealed preference is that it assumes we actually consider the alternatives. Having more choices comes with a cost: we have to spend our precious time and mental energy searching through them. If you use most of your brain juice choosing between the huge array of products offered up by consumer capitalism, there's not much left over for making the decisions that actually matter.

The first time I noticed this trade-off, I was standing in a supermarket aisle after a long day at work, puzzling over jars of marinara sauce. I checked to see which were on special, studied the nutrition labels, the recipe variations. I weighed them in my hands, put one back on the shelf, picked it back up again. In a detached corner of my mind, I observed myself reduced to a shambling idiot. Even though I was fully aware of the absurdity of the situation, I couldn't bring myself to just pick one already.

I'm glad there's more than one marinara sauce to choose from. But after the first few variations, presenting me with another 20 is not going to rock my world. There's essentially no chance that the additional options will be a game-changer for my pasta bake, but every new consideration does impose an additional search cost. God forbid I make a dumb mistake on my tax return because I used the last dregs of my mental energy debating the relative merits of chunky tomato vs Italian herbs.

This is the part that's hard to capture in the paradox of choice studies: the relevant reference class here isn't 'marinara sauce'—it's the *entire space* of interesting or high-impact decisions, all of which draw upon limited attentional resources.

We can choose between thousands of different types of breakfast cereal. But why eat cereal? Maybe simple carbs aren't the best way to start the day. It took me a long time to discover that I not only perform better when I fast in the morning, but the 'breakfast is the most important meal of the day!' thing was literally a marketing slogan invented by one Dr Kellogg.[3]

The point is not that you should skip breakfast. It's that this is a more interesting choice to consider than 'cornflakes or ricies'.

When we're buying a car, we can choose from hundreds of brands and several thousand models, each of which has its own slew of customisable features. Four doors or five? Walnut paneling or bamboo? Prospective buyers spend hours doing research, taking test drives, visiting car lots, and mulling over their decision. But how many have done the math on how much healthier and wealthier they'd be if they walked or cycled instead? How many calculated the depreciation cost of buying new compared to secondhand? Or figured out how many hours of life they'd have to sacrifice to keep up with the payments on the finance plan?

Consumer capitalism creates the illusion of great choice, but the branches of the possibility tree are almost all minor variations on the same core theme. This is **Faux Optionality**: an overwhelming array designed to keep us confined in one narrow sector of possibility-space, and obscure the decisions that actually matter.

The relatively few options worth pursuing are those with a positive asymmetry: is the downside capped? Is the upside large or unbounded?

The self-stimulating and status-seeking products of consumer capitalism almost invariably fail this test. In the worst-case scenario, they cast us into Bottomless Pits of Doom: superstimuli, addiction, and signalling games that ratchet towards financial ruin. Even at their most innocuous, they're Dead Ends that steal our time and attention, drawing us into a labyrinth that leads us further away from the doors that are worth opening.

When information costs more than it's worth, the only winning move is to carefully steward your ignorance—to strike at the root of the possibility tree, and refuse to engage with its branching confusopolies. Rationality is not about making perfect decisions. It's about *choosing what to choose*. Nowhere on Martha Nussbaum's list of core human capabilities will you find 43 brands of laundry detergent.

ASYMMETRIC WARFARE

The Sirens' sunny meadow is filled with skeletons. Some of the grislier deaths make the headlines—the occasional gamer so absorbed in a virtual world that they forget to eat or sleep. But the victims are rarely dashed on the rocks so dramatically. Mostly, it's an insidious creep of slow-motion suicides: the preteens anxiously checking their Instagram following, the hardening arteries, the spiralling credit card debt.

In spite of this, it's a mistake to think of the Sirens as 'evil'. They are souls who sing to souls; harnessing the machinery of consumer capitalism to the blind idiot god of evolution. These impartial and relentless optimisers create everything that is beautiful in the world, along with everything that is foul.

Consumer capitalism is *awesome*—but only if we bend it to our will, instead of the other way around. In practice, this is not a fair fight. We're naked apes parachuted into an alien environment we weren't designed for, up against not only the best scientists, marketers, and billion-dollar corporations, but the DNA coiled through every cell in our body. The principle of momentum means we only have to make a few false moves before we're locked into a path that's increasingly difficult to escape from.

Every day, the algorithms improve, and the molecules get purer, and the games are more addictive, and the companies capture another slice of our attention. Every day, the bar for resisting gets higher and higher. Every day, the full force of technology is brought to bear on the great project of modernity: transforming human beings into passive blobs.

Once the wire is lighting up our reward circuits, we can hardly pull it out, any more than the rats in the cage could. Those of us in the developed world already have the means to anaesthetise ourselves around the clock. It's never been easier to obtain short-term pleasure, or to obviate short-term suffering: everything is available on demand, at the click of a button, delivered to the door, and beamed out across a million channels in HD clarity.

As the Siren song becomes louder and more all-consuming, the future will be divided between those in thrall to self-stimulation and conspicuous consumption, and those who resist its pull.

Attempting to lever a society out of this sticky equilibrium is a near-impossible task, and morally fraught: perhaps my wireheading nightmare is someone else's utopia.

It's much more tenable to decide to extract yourself as an individual. I've chosen which side of the divide I want to be on: I've quit smoking, don't have drug problems, rarely consume media mindlessly, keep myself in good shape, only own things that bring me joy, and carefully steward my finances. It's always a work-in-progress, but I generally feel like I'm in control of my life.

This is not to suggest any moral superiority on my part, or superhuman willpower. In fact, I have all the impulse control of a four year old. The truth is that I have never, ever managed to brute-force my way into changing my behaviour.

When you're fighting an asymmetric war, direct resistance is futile. Instead, it's time to bring out the guerrilla tactics. For every assault, there's a counterassault. For every sneaky saboteur, we can set cunning traps of our own.

Trying to be a hero is a good way to get yourself killed. But there are heroes; and then there are 'heroes'. For inspiration, we turn to Odysseus: the dirtiest brawler of all the Greeks.

9

TIED TO THE MAST

Weather this danger and you are safe, for the rest of the way is downhill. With unrelaxed nerves, with morning vigour, sail by it, looking another way, tied to the mast like Odysseus.

— THOREAU

ODYSSEUS WAS THE FIRST MAN to hear the Siren song and live to tell the tale. He was a fearsome warrior, but it was his devious, rat-bastard cunning—his *metis*—that elevated him to greatness. Instead of facing his enemies head-on, Odysseus used sneaky tricks to outwit them at every turn.

As his ship approached the Siren's islands, Odysseus plugged the sailors' ears with beeswax, and instructed them to lash him to the mast. When the melody drifted across the water, he strained so hard against the bonds that they cut into his flesh, and frantically begged his men to free him. But his ear-plugged crew only rowed harder, until the water turned white with spray, and the danger had passed.

While Odysseus' much-bemoaned misfortunes were usually the direct result of his own monstrous hubris, he did show flashes of impressive self-awareness. Most of us sail merrily towards the Sirens with the utmost confidence we'll be able to resist the call once we get there, but that steely sense of conviction is a dangerous illusion.

In a low state of physiological 'arousal', we underestimate how much our desires will change when our blood is running hot. When I tell myself I'm going to have a quiet night, I am quite certain of this fact, and cannot be moved from it. Next thing I know, it's 3am, my wallet is empty, and I have half a kebab smeared over my face.

Even when our plans are perfectly formulated, and avoid all the pitfalls of Goals Gone Wild, they're just plain *hard* to achieve. Rather than relying on willpower, we have to set up effortless systems that move us smoothly in the direction of our goals—and prevent our impulsive, hot-blooded future selves from sabotaging our efforts.

A GENTLE NUDGING

In their book *Nudge*, the economist Richard Thaler and the legal scholar Cass Sunstein argue that sometimes, we really do need to be saved from ourselves. Being good libertarians, they don't want to impose these decisions by force. Instead, they suggest the government can 'nudge' us into making better choices, without taking away our freedom to choose.

While we should be extremely wary of others trying to nudge us, especially the government,[1] there's nothing wrong with giving ourselves a gentle nudging. There are five main classes of interventions worth considering:

1. Screen out harmful stimuli

I don't keep ice cream or other junk food in the house, because experience has taught me I'll eat the whole carton in one sitting. But I *do* keep plenty of fruit and nuts on hand, so I always have something to snack on. This is what Thaler and Sunstein call changing your 'choice architecture'—redesigning the way in which options are presented to you.

Screening out unwanted stimuli is the equivalent of plugging your ears with beeswax. *La la la, can't hear you!* Other examples include removing your email address from promotional lists, using ad blockers online, deleting distracting apps, not watching the news, and generally muffling the Siren song wherever you can. It's not necessarily going to save you from temptation, but it's a good start.

2. Trivial inconveniences

I *could* still gorge myself on ice cream whenever I want, but I'd have to put pants on, leave my apartment, and walk to the 7-Eleven. That trivial inconvenience is almost always enough to put me off.

Unfortunately, consumer capitalism is constantly coming up with brilliant ways to make self-stimulation as frictionless as possible. Tap-and-go 'contactless' cards, auto-filled credit card forms, and one-click purchases save us time, but they also mean we don't have any opportunity to back out of the purchase. As soon as there's a drone that delivers ice cream to my door, I'm screwed.

The idea of a trivial inconvenience is to deliberately add some friction back into the process. The classic trick is freezing your credit card in a block of ice, forcing you to wait several hours for it to thaw before you can use it. This is a cute idea, but your card details are already scattered to the four corners of the Internet, and if you're a hardened online shopping addict, you've long since committed them to memory anyway.

Instead of trying to scour your saved payment methods from every single website, I suggest cancelling your existing card, order a replacement with a different number, and try not to memorise it. Every time you're shopping online, you'll have to climb out of your warm bed, find your new card, and punch in the details by hand. That brief reprieve is often enough to pour cold water on an impulse buy.

3. Tie your hands

Our drunk, emotional, or hot-blooded future selves can be amazingly single-minded. If you give your bong to a friend for safekeeping, you'll immediately develop the MacGyver-like ability to fashion a functioning piece out of half an avocado and a ballpoint pen. Block a certain website, and you'll devise an elaborate hack to circumnavigate your own defences.

If you feel like you're stuck in an endless arms race against your internal saboteurs, it's time to go nuclear on their asses. While you're in a state of low-arousal, take advantage of that clarity of mind to tie yourself to the mast. This type of nudge is known as a precommitment device, or **Ulysses Contract** (the Latin name for Odysseus). Once you push the big red button, there's no going back.

For example, I wouldn't have finished this book if it weren't for a piece of software called Freedom. It's programmed to ban me from accessing distracting websites, except during allotted hours. Every time I idly open a new tab, it redirects me to the message: 'You are free. Do what matters.' No matter how much I want to procrastinate, it won't let me.

Going out with a fixed amount of spending money is another example of tying yourself to the mast. You might feel compelled to buy a round for the entire bar, but when your cash runs out, you're done. If you don't leave any money for a cab, you're walking home.

A friend uses a personal lockbox to tie his hands. He puts in his phone/weed/credit card/video game, and sets the timer—say, for 5pm on Friday. No matter how much he wants to distract himself, it won't open again until the appointed hour.

4. Set and forget

Not all nudges are designed to prevent you from doing dumb shit. In fact, Thaler and Sunstein's most famous result involved nudging people into doing something *nice* for their future selves. By shifting retirement saving plans from being 'opt-in' to 'opt-out', early enrolment soared from 20 per cent to 90 per cent.

The set-and-forget approach is perhaps the most powerful financial strategy for effortlessly making better temporal trade-offs, to the point where I strongly recommend nudging yourself in at least one of the following ways:

- Increase your retirement savings contribution rate. It comes out of your salary before you see it, so you won't 'feel' the loss.
- Ask your bank to increase your mortgage repayment rate. Even on a fixed rate loan, you can usually make some level of voluntary repayments without being penalised.
- Set up an automatic payment to transfer money into an untouchable savings account every payday.
- Set up a direct debit with an investment provider to automatically drip-feed a certain sum into the market each month.

In all these scenarios, you only have to make a decision once, then you're done. This kind of nudge falls somewhere between a trivial inconvenience and a Ulysses contract. Sure, you could untie yourself from the mast any time you want, but that would involve *paperwork*.

5. Increase the cost of failure

It's hard to make good trade-offs when the consequences are either abstract, or distant in time. We can abuse our bodies for decades and accumulate all sorts of silent risk before it finally catches up with us. Sometimes, there are no negative consequences at all: if you can't bring yourself to finish writing your screenplay, literally nobody cares.

In these sort of scenarios, it might help to make the consequences more immediate, more painful, or both. One way to up the stakes is to make a bet with a friend. If you don't have a finished draft by the end of the month, you have to pay up. If your friends are too soft to hold you accountable, there are third-party services that specialise in this sort of thing. Some of them will give your money to an 'anti-charity' of your choice; if you fail to reach your goal, you have to donate $100 to the Nazi party.

This is my least-favourite type of nudge, not only because you probably end up on some FBI watchlist, but because it doesn't really change your choice architecture. You still have the exact same options surrounding you, even if the punishment for making bad choices is more immediate. My personal experience is that these commitment contracts don't work very well, but they might be worth a try as a last resort.

THE VIRTUE OF SLOTH

The great thing about nudges is they take the very natural inclination to sit on one's ass, and turn it into a *strength*. We're all biased towards the status quo. That means we can bind our hands in such a way that it takes more effort to untie ourselves than it does to just shrug and stick with the program. Once you sign yourself up for a monthly savings plan, or cancel an ongoing subscription, you never have to give it another moment's thought. If you've got the right systems in place, kicking back and doing nothing isn't just a good strategy—it's the *best* strategy.

Nudges present a happy middle ground between self-flagellating asceticism and being a self-indulgent slob. They give us an easy way to let the Old Timer win every now and again, without sparking a mutiny amongst the rest of the crew.

Whenever you're making trade-offs over time, let nudges do most of the heavy lifting. You'll still have to make the hard initial decisions—choosing what to choose—but there won't be any ongoing expenditure of willpower. Once you've set up the right choice architecture, the behavioural change takes care of itself.

There's one more type of system that's a little harder to put in place. Nudges streamline and automate your environment, which removes the friction between you and your goals. But you can also streamline and automate *your own brain.*

———

The Reptile has been plucked from the water, limbs thrashing, and locked in the brig. The Captain plugs the sailors' ears with wax. This has the added benefit of blocking out the outraged hoots and howls of the Monkey, who is currently lashed to the mast. As the Sirens' hypnotic spell loses its hold, the crew become keenly aware of the skeletons scattered through the sunlit meadow.

Everyone scrambles to the banks of oars. But the strokes are all over the place! The hapless sailors have no idea how to pull together. Some of them are facing the wrong way. Their hands are soft, and their backs are weak.

And so, the Ship of Fools drifts closer to the spear-sharp rocks...

CREATURES OF HABIT

I must Create a System, or be enslav'd by another Man's.

— WILLIAM BLAKE

T HERE'S A POPULAR TROPE in the world of personal finance which goes something like this: if you cut out a single $4 latte from your daily spending, the cumulative compounding effect adds up to a small fortune.

On paper, this really does look incredible—a small change which is worth tens of thousands of dollars over a lifetime.

Out in the real world, in which actual human beings live, it's hard to come up with a more stupid example than 'ditching the daily latte'. Want to get your finances in order? Great! All you have to do is wean yourself off an addictive, stimulatory drug, which you've been using all your adult life, will cause withdrawal symptoms and impair your performance when you try to quit, is universally available, woven into the very fabric of social life, is the only addiction that carries no stigma whatsoever, and helped bring about the Enlightenment. Oh, and it's also *really frickin' delicious*.

Now, maybe you really should stop buying those daily lattes. That's what this chapter is about: changing habits. But it's as far down the priority list as you can get.

The low-hanging fruit are the nudges, and the one-and-done decisions. You cut cable. You sell an extra vehicle. You review every utility provider, and make sure you're getting the best deal. You move closer to work so you can walk or cycle. If you manage to downsize your accommodation, maybe you save $500 a month, *every month*, without lifting a finger. That's a whole lot of lattes. Seriously. Don't major in the minors.

As far as I can tell, I've never managed to change a habit in my life, except insofar as it happened as a natural consequence of reshaping my identity, values, environment, peer group, or some other aspect of my choice architecture.

The deluge of popular books about habits in recent years tells a different story. The promise is that by following a certain formula—three simple steps to a new you!—you can reach your fingers into your brain and squidge your basal ganglia around until you've programmed yourself into some kind of robotic Terminator god.

I have read way too many of these books, and in my opinion they are useful to the extent they *don't* talk about the three-step trick. Since other people swear by this kind of thing, I'll try to condense them into a couple of pages.

CUE, ROUTINE, REWARD

Most habits resemble a simple two-step 'if this, then that' algorithm:

IF eyes='open' THEN meditate
IF meditation='complete' THEN shower
IF body='dry' THEN brush teeth

And so on. Find an 'IF' somewhere along your chain of existing habits, and you can trigger a 'THEN' to insert into the routine. You'll have to experiment a little to figure out which cue works best, but it shouldn't be that hard to chain things together, because your brain does it unconsciously all the time— think of all the turns and lane changes you make on your way to work without giving it any thought.

Charles Duhigg, author of *The Power of Habit*, adds a third element. Once the cue has triggered the routine, there's also a *reward* which reinforces the cycle. Over time, we're conditioned to feel a craving of anticipation as soon as we receive the initial cue.

For tooth-brushing, the cue could be the film of gunk all up on your gnashers, or stepping out of the shower in the morning. The routine is the brushing. And the reward is the sensation of minty freshness. As Duhigg suggests, there's no benefit to the flavour or the lather: it just makes it feel good to brush your teeth.

To create a new habit, you have to figure out the right cue and reward. If opening my laptop in the morning is my cue to start writing, my reward is brewing the first cup of coffee for the day.

Bad habits almost always involve some kind of reward, which is what makes the feedback loop so sticky. Duhigg's golden rule of habit change is that you have to keep both the old cue *and* the old reward, while sandwiching a new routine in the middle.

The first step is to reverse-engineer the bad habit: what's the existing cue, and what's the reward? Let's say that around 3pm, you always find yourself heading to the vending machine. Is the habit prompted by the time of day? Low blood sugar? Feeling stressed? Needing a break? Boredom?

Chances are, you have no idea. It's unconscious, after all. So take your best guess, and experiment with switching the routine out with something that provides the same reward. If you suspect you're really craving a break, go talk to a coworker, or stretch, or walk around the block, and see if that does the trick. If it's because you're hungry, you can try stocking your desk drawer with healthy snacks. And so on.

If you've formed an unsavoury habit, it's probably for a good reason, which is why you can't replace it without finding a different way to meet the same need. Nature abhors a vacuum. If your life is empty of activities and positive intent, that void is going to fill up with something else.

KEYSTONE HABITS

For some reason, the go-to example for changing habits is always 'flossing'. Did my dentist write these articles? If the single worst thing about you is that you don't floss on the regular, I'm putting your name forward for canonisation. Imagine being the 12-car-pileup of problems that most people are, and deciding that what you really ought to do is start rubbing a waxy bit of string between your teeth.

Anyway, Duhigg's suggestion is to prioritise 'keystone' habits. In a stone archway, there's one wedge-shaped piece at the top that locks the other stones together, so the arch can bear weight. If you remove the keystone, everything comes tumbling down. Same with habits: some behaviours have a ripple effect that carries over into other areas of life.

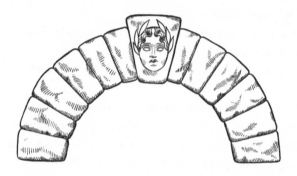

I've already suggested two keystone contenders in the realm of finance: tracking net worth, and expense ratio. The mere act of writing this stuff down day after day is often enough to change your behaviour.

Keystones can be hard to budge. Another approach is to work on an easier stone near the bottom of the arch, then work your way up to the big stuff. You might start with something completely trivial, like making your bed every morning, or OK, fine—flossing. The idea is that you get some easy wins on the board, and build up confidence. By fixing trivial bugs in your life, you start to develop some control over your environment. Instead of the frustration of failure, you create a success spiral in which competence begins to compound on itself.

At first glance, success spirals and keystones seem like opposites. Should you start with the most important thing, or the most mundane thing? For the best of both worlds, try combining them together: start with the most trivial *version* of the most important thing.

For example: I'm interested in the benefits of meditation, but have never managed to keep up the practice. I was granted an audience with a senior monk, who told me to meditate for no more than 30 seconds. If I managed to do that every morning, I could move up to a whole minute. Then two minutes. And so on. At no point was I allowed to get to any point where it was a struggle, or I'd risk losing the momentum.

The idea is that instead of trying to heave the keystone into place in one go, you build up to it. First you set your mind to moving grains of mortar. Then small flakes of stone. Then bigger and bigger chunks.

Success spirals probably don't 'increase' your willpower, so much as rewire your expectations.[1] Your brain is a giant prediction machine which constantly makes guesses about the state of the world, compares it against the raw data coming in, and then recalibrates itself accordingly. If you consistently follow through on your intentions, your brain revises its predictions of success upwards. Over time, this becomes a self-fulfilling prophecy: if you start to believe you're capable of doing hard things, that's half the battle won.

Many of my favourite asymmetries for building optionality—the contents of Book III—involve changes to ongoing behaviour. While I'm skeptical of the value of the cue-routine-reward stuff, I'm totally sold on the importance of focusing on keystone behaviours, building a success spiral of competence, and generally becoming a creature of habit.

Sometimes we have no choice but to venture forth into the tangled branches of the possibility tree. On these unavoidable excursions into low-reward domains, how can we protect our precious resources?

AUTOMATE EVERYTHING

The more of the details of our daily life we can hand over to the effortless custody of automatism, the more our higher powers of mind will be set free for their own proper work.

— WILLIAM JAMES

Probably you've read articles about how Obama wears the same suit every day, or Mark Zuckerberg has seventeen identical grey t-shirts in his wardrobe. The idea is to deliberately eliminate inconsequential daily choices and free up mental bandwidth for more important decisions; like ordering drone strikes or strip-mining billions of people's information to sell to advertisers.

Personally, I've decided that food is not interesting enough to hijack my attention three times every day. And so, I felt extremely seen by an article in *The Atlantic* on the substantial minority of Britons who eat the exact same lunches for months or years on end.

Here's the meal template I'm using at the moment, which I've repeated 500+ times in the last few years:

1. Big-ass salad with olive oil and avocado
Prep time: ~5 minutes per serving (batched, twice a week)

2. Muesli or oats with fruit, seeds, yogurt
Prep time: ~3 minutes per serving

3. Smoothie with greens, berries, protein
Prep time: ~2 minutes per serving

4. One of a revolving cast of go-to meals/random
Prep time: varies

None of this is carved in stone. The ingredients drift over time, and I'll happily abandon my packed lunch to eat out with friends. But the net effect is that I end up eating the exact same thing ~80 per cent of the time.

I've noticed five main benefits to taking this approach:

1. Mental bandwidth

During the working day, when I really don't want to think about anything else, I operate on autopilot. There's no hemming and hawwing about which food cart to visit, scrolling through delivery apps, or staring hopefully into the fridge, then coming back 10 minutes later to see if the contents have magically changed.

2. Nutrition

If you wear the same outfit over and over, nothing bad happens. Maybe you don't get invited to Fashion Week. What about meals?

The nutritionists quoted in the *The Atlantic* article say this is pretty much fine (and also how humans have eaten since forever). If the repetitive meals are nutritious, we never again have to remember which one is the bad fat, or scrutinise menus and nutritional labels.

Of course, that's a big 'if'. I'm a fan of counting calories and macronutrients, at least as a one-off exercise: it forces you to learn the basics of nutrition and get a sense of what you're actually eating, in the same way that tracking your spending turns up all sorts of patterns you might have otherwise missed.

But the aim should be to dispense with tracking as soon as possible—either by developing an intuitive sense of how to eat, or by making a template that you can more-or-less follow forever.

Meal plans are not infallible. A varied diet is a natural hedge against imperfect planning: maybe there's some mineral or vitamin that we haven't accounted for (or that science doesn't know about yet). This is another reason to take an 80/20 approach that maintains some exposure to randomness, as well as low-level variation amongst the repetitive meals.

3. Batching

When I worked full-time, I used to prepare a week's worth of meals on Sunday night, then divide them up into containers. Sometimes I'd make enough for two weeks, and freeze half for later.

Now I do the same thing with the big-ass salads: it only takes 20 minutes to throw together a few lunches' worth. My freezer is full of bags of pre-cut greens and fruit ready to be tossed into smoothies, which take all of two minutes to whizz up with a stick blender. Muesli is as simple as pouring stuff into a bowl.

Everything is batched together as much as possible, including grocery shopping: I don't need a list, and my feet carry me through the aisles on autopilot while I daydream or listen to a podcast. The fewer decisions I have to make, the less likely I'll buy a bunch of crap I didn't actually want. The other advantage is that I get a good sense for the prices of recurring ingredients, which means I can bulk-buy them when they're on special.

4. Pleasure

Folks in the San Francisco Bay area take these kind of ideas to the next level. During a recent visit, I sublet a room from the CEO of Mealsquares, which is a meal replacement concept similar to Soylent. The squares weren't as bad as I was expecting—kind of like a dense scone—but I don't think there's any possible universe in which I'd describe them as 'delicious'.

I wouldn't use these products for all/most of my meals, partly for reasons that boil down to 'we don't know what we don't know'. But mostly, it's because I'd rather just spend the extra ~25 minutes a day to prepare tastier food.

So now we have a spectrum of preferences: the Soylent-swilling entrepreneurs and programmers who don't want to look away from their monitors for more than a millisecond, right through to the gourmands who luxuriate in choosing every last ingredient. My preference is to get *close* to the Soylent end, without sacrificing too much gustatory pleasure.

Fortunately, 'cheap', 'tasty', and 'nutritious' are not always mutually exclusive. For instance: green smoothies look gross, but the flavour of the spinach or kale is masked by the frozen fruit and other ingredients, and the texture comes out like ice cream. Everything I eat is delicious to my tastes, or I wouldn't keep it on the menu.

5. Novelty

When I was a kid, we ate non-home-cooked meals exactly seven times a year —on each family member's birthday. I made up for lost time in adulthood, until restaurant meals and takeaways had completely lost their thrill. Now I prefer to eat out a couple of times a week. I don't want to deny myself, but I also don't want the experience of going out to dinner or the arrival of the UberEats delivery guy to become a humdrum part of daily existence.

While the 80/20 approach sounds boring, I think it might *increase* my net experience of novelty. Even if it doesn't bring the hedonic treadmill to a dead stop, it sure slows it down.

There are other psychological benefits: when it comes to the novel 20 per cent, there's no counting calories, no poring over ingredient lists, and no guilt whatsoever. I order whatever I want, secure in the knowledge that I'm eating well ~80 per cent of the time. Experience has taught me that striving for perfection is a recipe for eternal dissatisfaction and self-flagellation. It's much better to get to the point of 'good enough', and leave it at that.

I am not suggesting you should follow the 80/20 diet. If you are a foodie or a chef, that would be especially dumb. But I am suggesting you do *something* like this. Domains that are good candidates for automation have two defining features: they don't benefit from variety (habituation is the whole point) and they're stable over time—there's no benefit to constant tinkering and exploration.

There's nothing to be gained from going to bed at 9pm one day, at 3am on another, the next lying on the floor, the next hanging upside down from the ceiling, etc. The same goes for things like work habits, writing, appearance, exercise, and all of the bodily functions. In these domains, it's better to experiment just enough to find what works for you, then become a creature of habit at the earliest possible opportunity.

While systems like this are usually presented as productivity hacks, there's a much deeper significance to choosing your own constraints. If you're *forced* to eat the same things over and over, or to wear a uniform every day, that's called 'being in prison'. See also: school, childhood, compulsory military service, or the 9 to 5, which are rarely a font of pleasant memories.

The meaning of life is something like '*to trade the constraints imposed upon you by others for constraints you impose upon yourself*'.

If you fail to design your own choice architecture, one will be assigned to you. The brain loves efficiency; the brain wants to preserve bandwidth; but the brain is agnostic as to who installs the routines. When every other bastard is trying to run their own malicious scripts to automate your behaviour, the only way to fight back is to beat them to the punch. As William Blake said, we must create a system, or be enslaved by someone else's.

We can use nudges to streamline our environment, and habits and routine to streamline our brains. There's one last systemic factor that moves us smoothly in the direction of our goals—but if we're not careful, it can also steer us towards disaster.

———————

The Ship of Fools glides effortlessly over the sea's broad back. The Captain calls the beat, and the water turns white as the oars rise and fall in unison. It is a beautiful thing to see.

But what's this?

A flotilla of ships appears over the horizon. The sailors call out to the crew, throwing off their carefully timed strokes. Some of them swing aboard with grappling hooks, and untie the Monkey from the mast. They try to convince the Captain that his map is wrong, and insist they have a better destination in mind. The Monkey is desperate to go along with them.

The Ship of Fools, rudderless once more, turns to follow in their wake...

11

SOCIAL CONTAGION

Men, it has been well said, think in herds; it will be seen that they go mad in herds, while they only recover their senses slowly, and one by one.

— CHARLES MACKAY

YOU'RE SITTING IN A WAITING ROOM, filling out a form. It smells like something's burning. You look around, and see a tendril of smoke coiling out of a vent in the wall. A few people notice the smoke, and go back to their paperwork. A couple of minutes go by. The room is now filling up with smoke, to the point where it's obscuring your vision. Amazingly, no-one else seems to be worried. You ask the guy across from you what's going on. "Dunno," he mumbles, and returns to his paperwork. You're starting to panic now, but no-one else is showing any sign of concern. So you sit there, and try to fill out the form, as the smoke burns your eyes and fills your lungs.

If you think you'd march out and report a fire instead of sitting around with the other gormless idiots, don't be so sure. This was a real experiment, conducted by John Darley and Bibb Latané in the 1960s, using Columbia University students as subjects. The other people in the waiting room were stooges, under instruction to shrug and do nothing. Of the 10 times they ran the experiment, only *one person* took action:

"The other nine subjects stayed in the waiting room for the full six minutes while it continued to fill up with smoke, doggedly working on their questionnaires and waving the fumes away from their faces. They coughed, rubbed their eyes, and opened the window—but they did not report the smoke."

When the students were alone, they promptly took action. When they were in a group, they took their cues from others, no matter how nonsensical. This experiment was a variant of the conformity tests developed by the psychologist Solomon Asch, which have been replicated over and over in ever-more-ridiculous ways. As Asch discovered, the pressure to conform is so strong that people will ignore the evidence of their own eyes.

My favourite variant of these experiments is the elevator test. You're facing the doors, like a normal person, but every other passenger is a stooge who has been instructed to face the wrong way. There's a palpable sense of unease as they stare at you. The poor chimpanzee stapled to your frontal cortex is having a full-blown meltdown. As if it wasn't bad enough being trapped in a tiny box, there's a breakdown in one of the established norms that allows strange apes to be in close proximity without tearing each other limb from limb. Every fibre of your being is screaming at you to turn around and face the back of the lift, no matter how absurd it is. And sure enough, some people do —to the point of obediently shuffling backwards out of the elevator doors. Anything to relieve the hair-raising discomfort of going against the group.

SOCIAL REALITY

Reality is a hallucination. Your eyes are lying to you right now: as they dart around the page, you should be seeing jerky still-frames of distorted clusters of pixels, with a gaping hole in the middle of your vision. Instead, your brain strongly *suggests* that you see a smoothly rendered, 3D world, with no retinal blind spot and a full spectrum of colour—and so you do.

The brain is a prediction machine, imposing a readable map over the mind-melting mandala of reality. The question it constantly asks is not 'is this true?' but 'does this work?'.[1]

While sense-making takes place at the level of each individual brain, the crazy thing about *homo sapiens* is that our hallucinations are not confined to our own skulls. As the only ultrasocial primates, we're also wired up to make sense of the world collectively, and inhabit a giant, shared hallucination called **Social Reality**.

The fabric of social reality is woven from stories. We all have roles to play in upholding the dominant narrative, and being genre-savvy and able to hit all the right tropes is much more adaptive than sneaking glances beyond the veil where boring old 'real' reality intrudes.

The consequence of living in a socially constructed reality is that in almost every domain, we borrow our behavioural cues from those around us. This gives us a huge advantage over non-social animals: mimesis lets us copy the consensus position on what we should desire and fear without costly trial-and-error, and with far more flexibility than hardwired instincts.

Social contagion is a force of nature, and like anything in nature, perfectly amoral. We describe laughter and yawning as 'infectious', but we can also be infected with ambition, or happiness, or stupidity, or bloodlust. Researchers now suggest obesity should be classified as a 'contagious' disease, given the extent to which it spreads through social networks: if all your friends are overweight, eventually, so are you.

Social contagion is summarised by the folk wisdom that you are 'the average of the five people you spend the most time with'—the implication being that we better choose the people around us very carefully.

The most obvious example is your choice of romantic partner. When you weigh up a prospective mate, probably you sneak a few glances at their physical assets. But if you're going to do some inappropriate staring, it really ought to be at their credit card statement. Studies have consistently found the number one factor for relationship breakdown isn't infidelity, or whose turn it is to wash the dishes—it's arguments about money. Going by the current divorce rate, there's a ~40 per cent chance the whole thing will end in tears; many of them shed after receiving the lawyers' bills.

If your values conflict with the people closest to you, they can become more like you, you can become more like them, or you can each go your separate ways. The Stoic philosopher Epictetus uses the metaphor of a live coal and a dead coal lying side by side. Either the live coal will light up the other, or the dead coal will extinguish its companion.

The natural inclination is to try and bring other people around to your point of view—to light them up with the same fire that burns within you. But as Epictetus warned, few of us have the silver tongue of Socrates, who could win anyone over to his position: "Rather, it is you who are sure to be talked over by the laymen."

Even if you're confident no-one's going to dampen your spark, trying to change the norms in your local instance of social reality is fraught. It's almost always a bad idea to give well-meaning advice to the people around you, unless they ask for it—and even then, tread carefully. Instead, all you can do is shut up and live your best life. If the results are compelling enough, people will get curious, and voluntarily start rewriting their own stories.

We can't 'rescue' anyone from the hallucination of social reality: this is the water in which we swim. And in most cases, nor should we want to: different people prefer this story or that one, and they're not always compatible.

But sometimes, our herding instincts really do lead to disastrous outcomes. It's possible for large swathes of society to get stuck in a bad equilibrium, like the negative-sum game of conspicuous consumption. Having friends or loved ones trapped in a downward spiral of harmful behaviour is heartbreaking. To make matters worse, there's a good chance they'll drag you down with them.

In either case, we wind up at the same conclusion. If you can't *change* the people around you, change the *people* around you.

FINDING YOUR TRIBE

Odysseus was the first to hear the Siren song and live to tell the tale, but he wasn't the first to make it past their graveyard unscathed. That honor goes to the star-studded crew of Jason and the Argonauts, who sailed past the islands on their quest for the Golden Fleece.

As the band of heroes approached the rocks, they decided to settle things in time-honoured fashion: with a karaoke battle. As the Sirens began to sing, the legendary musician Orpheus pulled out his golden lyre and played a song so sweet that he drowned out their enchanting spell.

Rather than trying to force new behaviours on ourself or others, it's much, much easier to parachute into a group which already shares our aspirational values. If we can surround ourselves with a crew of heroes like Orpheus, their infectious ballads will make the call of the Sirens fade to a dull squawking.

My attempts to get my high school buddies to work out with me never went anywhere. One of the best moves I ever made was joining a barbell club for Olympic weightlifters and powerlifters, and making friends with a bunch of meatheads. The camaraderie, knowledge on hand, and work ethic were second-to-none. When there's a 75-year-old bus driver warming up with your max, it's hard not to be inspired.

Thankfully, social reality is not a monoculture. If we don't like the dominant narrative, we can seek out pockets of people who share a different hallucination, and deliberately 'infect' ourselves with the norms and behaviours we want to mimic.

Chapter 15 is all about asymmetric strategies for finding a tribe: cheap options that help us recruit fellow travellers, create a beautiful little bubble, and generally harness the power of social capital.

But how can we know if we're joining an uplifting community, or a dangerous cult?

Before we round off Book II, it's worth looking at some general rules of thumb for following or flaunting social convention. Are there certain areas of life where we should be more inclined to step off the beaten path? And when is it better to go with the herd?

NEVER GO FULL CONTRARIAN

There's a certain type of precocious adolescent who, upon striking upon the idea that God might not exist, refuses to shut up about it. While most of us grow out of the pompous teen atheist phase, some are trapped in the bodies of 14-year-old edgelords forever. These ghouls are the living embodiment of a raised index finger, and the word 'actually' hovers on their lips at all times. They not only mock social norms, but take great delight in running over them roughshod.

Being a contrarian for the sake of it is kind of obnoxious. But the thing that makes it unforgivable is that it's *stupid*. Because—of course—contrarians are almost always wrong. The edgiest take on any subject has no correlation with the truth of the matter, or we'd have to take the anti-vaxxers and Flat Earth Society a whole lot more seriously.

On the other hand, it's not good enough to just go with the status quo, either. On the rare occasions when contrarians are right, they're right *in really important ways*.

Praise be to rabble-rousing free-thinkers like Thoreau, irritating as he might have been, who campaigned for the abolition of slavery. Or Martin

Luther King Jr., whose dream of equality for all was so dangerous that he was murdered in cold blood. Or Emmeline Pankhurst and the suffragettes, who fought to extend the franchise to women. Or animal rights advocates like Peter Singer, who speak for those who have no voice.

The uncomfortable lesson of history is that upstanding citizens happily condone practices that will later be considered unconscionable. In the aftermath of World War II, researchers and cultural critics were consumed by the question of how ordinary people could participate in such atrocities—a problem described by political scientist Hannah Arendt as the 'banality of evil'.

Inspired by the Asch conformity tests, Stanley Milgram conducted a famous series of experiments designed to find out how far people would go in obeying authority figures. The answer was: *all the way*. Milgram's test subjects would torture people to death if someone in a white lab coat told them to, while the actors being 'electrocuted' screamed and begged for mercy.

Lest you think human nature has changed for the better in the last few decades, the British illusionist Derren Brown recently riffed on the Milgram experiments in disturbing fashion—this time, convincing ordinary people to rob a security van at gunpoint, and push someone off a roof to their death. The herd mentality runs so deep in us that we will quite literally do murder on command. If you and I happened to be born in Nazi Germany, no doubt we'd be goose-stepping along with the best of them.

This gives us the first rule of thumb for contrarianism: if your society engages in practices which cause harm to others, and offers elaborate reasons as to why this is justifiable, that's where you might investigate the claims of the fringe weirdos. Hurting yourself because you went along with the crowd is bad, but hurting others might make you a moral monster.[2]

The second rule of thumb is that when there are no consequences for being wrong, or there is no 'wrong', don't be embarrassed to follow the crowd. The reason we dance in unison, or sing together, or march in line, or wear uniform-like fashions, or swap in-jokes and memes, is that it feels pretty great to be a part of the hivemind.

In the domains of sports and aesthetics, it makes perfect sense to indulge in some (mostly) harmless tribalism. Who cares which team is 'actually' better, or whether *Game of Thrones* is any good? These are arbitrary focal points for bonding with your fellow apes, and satisfying that impulse to be one with the group. You get some water cooler chat, you feel closer to the people around you, and you build social capital. Go, uh, Wildcats!

Jumping on popular bandwagons is plain good fun. And in domains where you have limited information, it also makes a lot of sense. With the singular exception of the economist Tyler Cowen, no-one has the time to become an esthète in every single field. The arbitrary trend-following of social contagion means almost everything ends up overrated or underrated, but popularity is still a much better filter than guessing at random.

The second rule for contrarianism is summarised by G. K. Chesterton: "A man must be orthodox upon most things, or he will never even have time to preach his own heresy." Building social capital makes it that much easier to gracefully bow out of bad signalling games. Whenever your health, wealth, or autonomy are on the line, that's the time to be an uncompromising weirdo. In these domains, borrowing your desires from others is disastrous. It's no longer a matter of taste: now you're sitting in a crowded room filling up with smoke. You have to get the hell out of there before you asphyxiate, and never mind what everyone else is doing.

If you're a weird person, one way of conserving your social capital is to cast your lot in with a bunch of people who share your peculiarities. This is often a good idea, but be careful of letting your membership to a group define your identity. You should be able to get on just fine with normies without resorting to joining a literal cult, or for that matter, referring to people as 'normies'. As soon as you brand yourself as an 'X-er', a 'Y-ian' or a 'Z-ist', your brain starts to turn to cabbage. This is the foolish consistency that Emerson warned against: ideological path dependencies become increasingly difficult to escape from.

So: find your tribe, but don't let it define you. Indulge in some harmless fuzzy thinking in the realm of aesthetics. Don't be ashamed to enjoy pop culture. When other people zig, you should probably zig too. Save your zags for when they're really needed—and then *zag hard*.

12

MAN PLANS AND GOD LAUGHS

A man said to the universe:
"Sir, I exist!"
"However," replied the universe,
"The fact has not created in me
A sense of obligation."

— STEPHEN CRANE

B OOK II COULD BE SUMMARISED by the Yiddish proverb 'der mentsh trakht un got lakht': man plans, and God laughs. Even if we formulate and execute upon a goal perfectly, we still don't have control over the outcome. There's an inescapable element of randomness: we can train like a maniac, play our heart out, and *still* lose to a better opponent, or be derailed by a stroke of bad luck.

The *Dilbert* cartoonist Scott Adams suggests that goals are for losers—literally. If your sense of achievement is tied to hitting some distant milestone, every moment you're not there, you're a loser. If you fail to achieve the goal—say, because you're hamstrung by akrasia or blind misfortune—that impression is only solidified even further.

Even if you succeed, every goal has an endpoint. You celebrate briefly, and then what? Maybe you set another, more ambitious goal—in which case you're right back to being a 'loser' again. Or maybe you just drift back to your old habits, in which case, same outcome. This is the classic yo-yo pattern of perennial dieters. If you're trying to achieve sustainable weight loss, there's no such thing as 'going on a diet'. There's only 'finding a way to eat well for the rest of your life'.

Optionality is a systems approach. Instead of prescribing an outcome in advance, it tells us to systematically collect asymmetric options, and see what happens. Using nudges to shape your choice architecture is a *system*. Automating routines and low-level choices is a *system*. Surrounding yourself with the right people is a *system*.

As Scott Adams points out, every single day that you follow your systems, you're a winner. You're focused on the things within your control. If you want to be an athlete, as long as you train your heart out, it doesn't matter if you lose a game. If you want to be a writer, all you can do is get up at 5am every morning and pay your dues. So long as your overall optionality index is on the rise—building relationships, net worth, health, or skills—it doesn't matter if you miss any arbitrary milestone.

Switching from goals to systems that make you a winner every day sounds like some happy-clappy sophistry, but it's one of the best strategies we have for resisting the Siren song. The defining feature of modernity is that we're being pushed towards short-term hedonism, at the expense of long-term flourishing. Our feedback loops are hopelessly laggy, and we have to tighten them up.

Every choice has first-order, second-order, and nth-order consequences. The first-order effects of the Siren song are euphoric and immediate: a wave of pleasure rushes through you, and takes the pain away. The second and nth-order consequences are ugly—those fields of sun-bleached bones—but the feedback loop is too slow to adjust our behaviour. We don't get visibly fatter when we eat a Big Mac combo, or go bankrupt after one impulse purchase. It usually takes a whole lot of questionable decisions before the long-term consequences finally catch up with us. Sometimes there's no feedback loop at all: we accumulate silent risk over the years with no outward sign of danger, then we're struck down seemingly overnight.

If you want to steer clear of the Sirens, you're not going to get much motivating feedback to begin with. In fact, life will probably get worse before it gets better.

The first-order consequences of activities that lead to flourishing are often unpleasant. Most anything worth doing is hard. Running or lifting weights physically *hurts*. Starting a business can be gruelling. Serious self-reflection is destabilising. The second and nth-order consequences make these things worthwhile, but again, the feedback loop isn't tight enough to be motivating. We don't get slimmer after going for one run, or get rich after making one savvy spending decision. We have to keep doing it over and over again before we notice any results. Sometimes there's no feedback loop at all: we grind away for years with no outward sign of success, then it all happens seemingly overnight.

All the strategies we've discussed throughout this book involve either tightening the feedback loop, or making the process itself more rewarding. If our daily actions are a natural extension of our values, they no longer feel like sacrifices. If we're trying to resist temptation, screening out superstimuli makes life that much easier. If we want to achieve something difficult, it's a heck of a lot more enjoyable to do it as part of a team of like-minded people. We have to be able to cultivate a feeling of 'winning' from merely following our systems, even when actual progress is slow, invisible, or arrives in punctuated bursts.

From both a happiness point of view (i.e. achieving eudaimonia) and an effectiveness point of view (i.e. defeating akrasia), the *journey is the destination*. Life is a series of iterated games. The point isn't to win any individual match, but to find interesting games to play, and keep playing for as long as you possibly can.

THREE COMFORTING OBSERVATIONS

The problem of akrasia is only ever getting harder. But if I've done my job right, you will come away from this part of the book feeling optimistic. Let's wrap up with a few encouraging observations:

1. There's no need to fret about the future

Achieving a specific goal usually involves working through a chain of connected actions. If any one of the links fails, the entire chain breaks.

By contrast, the optionality approach is a web of loosely-coupled systems. There's no beginning, no end, and no single point of failure. If one strand breaks, the rest of the system picks up the slack. Our identity isn't wrapped up in one narrow domain, and our success or failure doesn't hinge on the outcome of any one event. So long as we stick to our systems, we'll win the next game. Or the next one. Or the one after that.

This framework relieves a lot of anxiety. It's interesting to note that the systems approach to mental health goes back millennia, and is undergoing a renaissance today. Both the Eastern tradition (Buddhism/meditation) and the Western tradition (Stoicism/cognitive behavioural therapy) involve accepting the randomness of the universe, and focusing on what is within our control. The idea is to bend with the winds of fortune, instead of being snapped in half. We're definitely going to lose sometimes: either through our own weakness of will, or because God dealt us a shitty hand. Whatever happens, we shrug our shoulders, and go back to the daily practice.

We know it's possible to make excellent trade-offs across time, without having to predict exactly what our future selves want. The flexibility of the optionality approach is especially useful in an increasingly uncertain world, on which, more in Book V. For now, it's comforting to know that we don't need a detailed 20 year plan—that, in fact, it might even be counterproductive.

2. The Sirens can always be defeated

Let's come up with the hardest akratic challenge possible—say, you're trying to kick a heroin addiction. Just to make it stupidly difficult, imagine that you also experienced a recent trauma—say, you were conscripted to fight an unjust war, and witnessed nightmarish atrocities.

This was the exact situation faced by tens of thousands of soldiers returning from the Vietnam War. One in five US servicemen were hooked on the most addictive superstimulus known to man. But after they dried out and returned to American soil, *95 per cent of them stayed clean.*

The stunning result turned the research on addiction upside down. Did the soldiers suddenly grow bulging willpower muscles on the plane home? Were they injected with moral fibre? Did they carefully visualise their goals, or use the three-step habit trick? Of course not. This was the first major piece of evidence to suggest that choice architecture is vastly more important than self-control.

Few of the veterans received any kind of drug treatment at all. But their environment, routines, social group, and identity changed overnight. Instead of living cheek-to-jowl with fellow users, they were surrounded by friends, family, and loved ones. There were inconveniences to scoring a fix. And they experienced a shift in their identity: from soldiers fighting a horrendous war, to peacetime workers and family men in civilian jobs.

These men did everything right, but it happened entirely by accident. We have the benefit of being able to *deliberately* apply these lessons to redesigning our own choice architecture. If you ever start to think your personal akrasia demons are impossible to defeat, remember the heroin-addicted Vietnam vets.

It's comforting to know we don't have to fight a constant battle against ourselves. The only thing that reliably works is to bring our various subagents, environment, and community into alignment towards a common cause. In a funny way, this is the path of *least* resistance.

3. It's OK to be a messy human

There's no need to beat ourselves up for being 'irrational', or to make-believe that we're anything other than glorified monkeys.[1] *Homo sapiens* is a pretty damn special species, but we're not special enough to get an exemption from reality. We can't transcend our biology, any more than we can decide one day to disobey the laws of physics and stroll around on the ceiling. And nor should we want to!

It's tempting to think of the animalistic parts of us as vestigial leftovers—dead weight that holds us back from reaching our true potential. But the day we become a race of neutered transhumans or blissed-out wireheads is the same day I reach for the off switch.

If you think human nature is something to be excised, take a slow walk down a busy street, and look at everything with fresh eyes. The skyscrapers. The businesses. The artwork, fashions, design. Even a discarded plastic wrapper—an artifact made out of ancient algae, printed with a riot of colours and information-rich symbols—is a perfect microcosm of human endeavour. Observe the everyday miracle of thousands of total strangers interacting with one another, and playing elaborate games to their mutual benefit. The students in the park, studying for their midterms. The kids on the playground, testing their physical boundaries and learning new social cues. Monkeys wearing pants did all of this. If you took the monkey out of the pants, none of it would exist.

Civilisation has done a remarkable job of reining in our animalistic drives, and rechanneling them toward productive ends. There's plenty more work to be done, but we didn't get this far by wishing away human nature.

Instead of engaging in a direct contest of wills, we can use clever tricks to route around any impulses that lead us astray. And that's the worst-case scenario. These are the parts of us that drive us to achieve remarkable things. By nudging them in the right direction, and aligning them to our cause, we can harness their enormous strength to work in our favour.

We return one last time to the Ship of Fools, as it skims over the sea's broad back. Most of the work is done automatically by the billowing sail. When the wind changes, the sailors tack around it, rather than facing it head-on. Occasionally the crew take to the banks of oars, but when they do, they pull together.

The Fools are surrounded by a fleet of fellow adventurers, spurring each other to greater heights, offering help to those that fall behind, and singing lusty ballads that drown out the Siren song. The Monkey chatters away with its counterparts, showing off a clever new sail design. The Reptile lazes in the sun. When the ship has to fight off pirates or steer around an obstacle, his terrible claws and sinewy strength come to the fore, and there are great feasts in his honour.

For the first time, the Captain is calm. He consults his charts, and takes his measurements, and holds the wheel steady. The Old Timer no longer whispers harsh words in his ear. Sometimes the ship drifts off course, or is buffeted by storms, or temporarily taken over by the unruly crew. The Captain just smiles, and returns to the wheel.

The Ship of Fools needs a new name.

III

PRAXIS

PRAXIS. (noun) from the ancient Greek πρᾶξις: *The process by which a theory or skill is enacted or realised. Putting ideas into practice; concrete action; doing.*

INTRODUCTION

Knowing is not enough; we must apply. Willing is not enough; we must do.

— JOHANN WOLFGANG VON GOETHE

T ALK IS CHEAP. There's only so much time you can spend plotting and scheming clever strategies, or inspecting the contents of your belly button. After a certain point, you have to *do something*.

In her essay 'Levels of Action', startup founder Alyssa Vance highlights the power of stepping away from the daily grind to focus on the meta-levels which compound your efforts. If you take some time to upgrade your skills and learn new strategies, you might be able to 10x your results. Perhaps you can step up to a higher level again, and *100x* your results. But as Vance cautions, if you don't actually put in the work on the lowest level of action, there's nothing for the force multiplier to act upon. One hundred times zero is still zero.

Book I took place on the highest meta-level: the 'why'. We moved down a level in Book II, to the 'how'. In Book III, we're shifting down to the lowest level of action: the 'what' (Fig. 3.1).

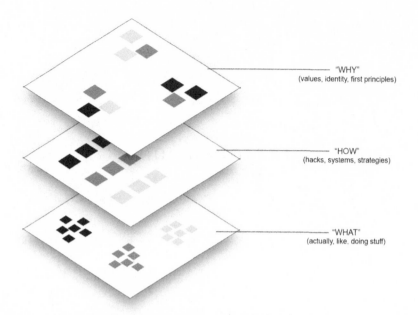

"WHY"
(values, identity, first principles)

"HOW"
(hacks, systems, strategies)

"WHAT"
(actually, like, doing stuff)

Figure 3.1: Levels of action: why, how, and what.

This is a compendium of opportunities for building optionality in each of the four domains: financial, health, social and knowledge capital. In the spirit of eating my own dog food, I've only included strategies I've used myself. If you find yourself wrinkling your nose at any of these suggestions, that's fine— don't do it. At this lowest level of action, it's impossible to give universally applicable advice.

Instead, think of this as a source of inspiration for making trade-offs with the optionality framework in mind. To paraphrase Bruce Lee: take what is useful, discard the rest, and add what is uniquely your own.

13

ASYMMETRIES IN FINANCIAL CAPITAL

I WAS BORN INTO a family of hoarders. My parents, literary magpies, never met an article they couldn't cut out and add to a pile of yellowing papers. They also accumulated art and craft supplies, building materials, exotic plants and seeds, bric-a-brac, and children. The offspring were slotted into free spaces amongst the clutter, where they soon started cultivating collections of their own.

I suspect this early exposure served as a sort of inoculation against stuff. To this day, the sight of cardboard boxes stacked up in hallways makes my skin crawl. By the time I moved overseas, I had pared my possessions down to fit within the confines of a 22-litre daypack. Every new item had to be scrutinised before I committed to adding it to the entirely non-metaphorical load on my back.

My adventures in ultralight travel taught me that it's easy for this sort of thing to cross the line into pointless masochism, like the cartoon of a pissing match between minimalists:

"Oh, I got rid of everything except my hobo bindle and jar of whispers."

"You still have *a stick* for your bindle? Ugh."

If I'm honest, much of my distaste for clutter is on aesthetic grounds—which is to say, personal preference. My family are *classy* hoarders. At least they're collecting educational materials, rather than boxes of their own toenail clippings. They have a benign relationship with their stuff, most of which cost nothing to obtain and was stashed away in the spirit of frugality.

By contrast, the minimalist movement is usually associated with design magazines filled with vintage bicycles or fine Swedish furniture. I have to confess that I kind of like this sort of thing, but it's important to note that aesthetics are never entirely divorced from underlying value systems. Unlike my parents, many people accumulate stuff through blind adherence to consumerism, manipulated by marketers who have convinced them that the key to being happy is to never let your credit card cool down. Refusing to be a part of this racket is much more than just an aesthetic choice. There are solid practical reasons for owning less stuff, and they have nothing to do with using your severe white apartment to harvest Instagram likes.

The naïve view of buying something is that you have purchased the *right*, but not the *obligation*, to enjoy it whenever you please. But ownership is much more of an obligation than is usually understood, and often ends up closing off more options than it opens.

First, there's the opportunity cost: what else could we have done with all the money we spend on stuff? The value of our new toy or trinket plummets the moment we leave the shop, and outside of a few narrow categories, continues to decline with every passing year. To add insult to injury, our depreciating assets also come saddled with ongoing costs: maintenance, insurance, and storage. But this is only the tip of the stuff iceberg.

The volume of your personal mountain of crap also dictates the size of your home, and by extension, your mortgage or rent payments, heating bill, maintenance, and insurance premiums. If you have a spare room full of junk, you no longer have the option to use it as a home office or guest bedroom, or to list it on Airbnb.

And there are subtler burdens: every single item has to be schlepped from house to house, organised and arranged, and will generally demand some small slice of your attention from the day you buy it until the day you die. If you believe the environmental psychologists, being surrounded by stuff literally makes it harder to think clearly—all that visual clutter makes for a messy mind. In light of all of this, we might reconsider the relationship between people and possessions: who owns who, exactly?

The average American home contains something like 300,000 items, supplemented by a self-storage industry so vast that every US citizen could comfortably stand beneath its canopy. As Peter Diamandis points out in *Abundance*, if everyone else took up this lifestyle, we'd need five planets' worth of resources to pull it off. Even if we colonise Mars, I think we can agree this is just not going to work out.

The low-stuff lifestyle was already looking pretty compelling, so the sustainability angle is all gravy as far as I'm concerned: not only do you have more money and flexibility, you get to feel smug and self-righteous about it too.

The mindless accumulation of vast mountains of stuff is unforgivably dumb. But *mindful curation* of meaningful possessions can be a source of great joy. As with anything else, it's a question of ruthlessly min-maxing the bloat to get more of the things worth having. These are my suggestions for making the kind of purchasing decisions that maximise optionality.

BORROW, LEASE, BEG, STEAL

...Maybe not that last one. But we should certainly jump on every trade that lets us enjoy all the upside of owning stuff while weaselling out of the obligations.

Take car ownership. In one sense, a private car is a symbol of optionality: it buys you the right to go anywhere you want, any time you want, without being obliged to follow anyone else's schedule. As someone who grew up in a country town in the middle of nowhere, I understand the importance of this kind of autonomy.

But car ownership also saddles us with a large and ongoing erosion of health and financial capital (especially if debt is involved). A private vehicle spends 97 per cent of its existence quietly rusting, punctuated by brief bursts of activity in which its two-ton metal hulk is employed to move a 75kg human and a few bags of groceries to the supermarket and back. Requiring every household to finance and maintain one or more of these behemoths is a hopelessly inefficient kludge—a one-size-fits-none solution that creates as many problems as it solves.

The market for Uber turned out to be much bigger than anyone expected, because the disruption wasn't actually 'cheap taxi fares'—it was making car ownership obsolete. We're now on the cusp of the full stack of elegant technologies required to unbundle the private car: walking and cycling for short trips, ride-sharing apps and a self-driving fleet for longer distances, and rental cars for vacations or road trips. No messy oil changes, no dodgy mechanics, no registration, no circling for parking spots, no theft, no worries. If you think owning a car is cool, wait until you have an AI chauffeur on call around the clock.

Renting is already a familiar practice for the likes of cars and homes (we'll unpick the rental vs homeownership debate in Book IV). With a little imagination, almost all of our possessions can take on this same ephemeral lightness, and be 'hired out' only as and when they're needed.

In his textbook *Early Retirement Extreme*, the Danish astrophysicist Jacob Fisker points to another transformative technology: online secondhand markets. Most people don't appreciate that you can not only *buy* stuff dirt-cheap online, you can also *store* your stuff for free. Think of eBay and Craigslist as enormous virtual storage warehouses, filled with millions of items you can borrow for next to nothing. When you need something, buy it secondhand. When you're done with it, flick it off again. Chances are you'll recover most of the price you paid, and if you understand the basics of writing ad copy, you might even come out in the black.

These decisions are easily reversible. If you flick off a generic item that you end up needing again, you'll always be able to find it for sale. This means that technically, the only items you *have* to own outright are those that are unique, or have sentimental value.

The strongest argument for owning stuff is that constantly borrowing things involves a lot of time and hassle. It would be absurd to list your fork on Craigslist the moment it hits your empty plate, which is why we need heuristics like the one-year rule: if you haven't used something in the last 12 months, kick it to the curb. You can adjust this rule in either direction according to how much you value your time, and how much capacity you have to store stuff.

This is not about being a minimalist little wisp, but avoiding the situation where your mountain of stuff grows so large that it starts to close off your options. If everyone followed even the weakest version of this heuristic—say, passing on generic items after five years of collecting dust—acres of self-storage units would be liberated overnight.

MAKE IT YOURSELF

In ye olden days, stuff was prized for its perfection: smooth surfaces, symmetrical lines, and photorealistic paintings demanded the highest price. Only rich people could afford 16-piece dining sets crafted by master artisans, while the lumpen proles made do with lumpen bowls. This state of affairs persisted more or less unchanged for millennia, until the Industrial Revolution came along and ruined everything.

With newfangled precision machinery, factories could manufacture near-flawless products en masse, priced so cheaply that even the lower classes could afford nice stuff. Rich people had to scramble to set themselves apart by shifting to a new set of status signals: brand names, antiquity, and strategic *imperfection*. In the arts, photography killed realism dead, triggering a successive chain of abstractions culminating in the literal pile of garbage sitting in the modern art museum today. And the cottage industries were back in business: this time selling organic silk, bespoke jewellery, and hand-woven single-batch kombucha.

If you take a look at the kind of people who sign up for pottery classes or start microbreweries in their garage, you can see the next step in the evolution: the middle and upper classes striving to become amateur artisans in their own right.

As Geoffrey Miller points out in *Spent*, if we owned things purely for their use value, it would rarely make sense to craft them ourselves. Imagine a corporate lawyer spending weeks learning how to knit an ugly cable-stitch, when some guy in a factory in Bangladesh can make a sweater about a million times more efficiently. From a narrow economic perspective, this is absurd: much better to use her colossal hourly earning power to send her personal assistant down to J.Crew.

But as usual, it's the narrow economic perspective that's absurd. For one thing, learning how to make things yourself is a time-honoured strategy for becoming resilient to economic shocks. As we'll see in Chapter 16, there are certain categories of skills that can't be outsourced, and others that have a payoff so large that almost everyone should practise them.

Making stuff is also an unusually wholesome signalling opportunity. Once you get to the point of not-sucking, handmade items become an effective way to display your intelligence, discernment, and other attractive traits. And the items themselves are imbued with an unusually rich source of meaning: my grandad's pottery might not be perfect, but it's worth immeasurably more to me than the smooth, perfectly symmetrical coffee mug I can pick up at Walmart for 99c.

THE BARBELL STRATEGY FOR STUFF

Imagine buying a cheap plastic laptop designed for children that can't open more than a dozen tabs without bricking itself. Now imagine you're a writer, and this hunk o' junk is the primary tool you use for several hours each and every day. Imagine how dumb you'd have to be to endure that much frustration and wasted time for the sake of a couple hundred bucks.

I don't have to imagine, because I was that guy. After hitting peak pathological penny-pinching circa 2016, I've learned which things are worth paying money for. Sometimes, a lot of money.

While I initially found it hard to reconcile my growing appreciation for fine things with the frugal ethos, that was because I was still recovering from a bad case of acting dead.

It's true that min-maxing requires us to cut out a mountain of crap, but only so we can greedily load up on the things that bring us joy. I don't see any reason to arbitrarily exclude 'material possessions' from this latter category. Personally, I want to have *more* cool stuff, not less, and I'm increasingly willing to pay top dollar for it.

There is an argument that in the long run, buying high-quality stuff actually *saves* you money. The best explanation comes from the late, great author Terry Pratchett, whose reluctant hero Sam Vimes—a grizzled, working-class cop—worked out that a really good pair of leather boots cost $50. Vimes wore $10 boots, which were sort of OK for a season or two, and then leaked like hell. He observed that a man who could afford good boots would still be wearing them in 10 years' time. Meanwhile: "The poor man who could only afford cheap boots would have spent $100 on boots in the same time—and would still have wet feet."

This is a cute and catchy parable, but... it's not really true. Sometimes it makes sense to buy the good boots. But most of the time, it's far more cost-effective to go for the equivalent of the crappy cardboard soles.

To reconcile these competing pieces of folk wisdom, we're going to borrow an old bond traders' trick called the **Barbell Strategy,** in which a portfolio is constructed with a lumpy weighting on opposite ends of a distribution, and as little as possible in the middle. Nassim Taleb extended the barbell to non-financial domains, and I want to extend it further still.

Here's the barbell strategy for stuff:

Buy the very best-in-class for a small set of items, buy the cheapest possible version of everything else, and avoid the middle ground.

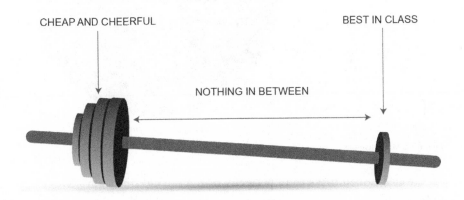

Figure 3.2. The barbell strategy for stuff.

Two categories of items cluster on the 'best in class' end of the barbell. The first are the things you use every day: laptops, desks, phones, keyboards, and tools of the trade. If you cook a lot, you might invest in quality knives and pans. You spend a third of your life in bed, so don't settle for a crappy mattress. The same goes for art, and other objects you interact with every day.

The second category includes anything with a risk of ruin. It's never advisable to pinch pennies on helmets, protective gear, bald tires, condoms, or anything else that might be ruinous to your life and liberty.

Sam Vimes' boots happen to be a great (but unrepresentative) example because they fit both categories: you probably wear shoes every day, and crappy footwear can screw up your health in all sorts of fascinating ways. If you bring the two circles together in a Venn diagram, it's worth paying special attention to the things in the middle (Fig. 3.3).

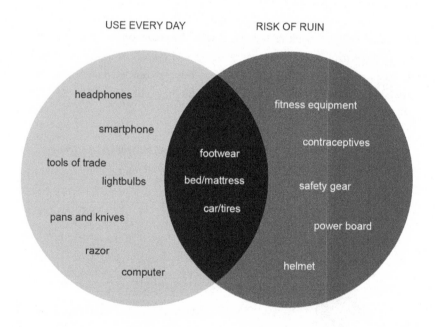

Figure 3.3. Venn diagram for buying quality stuff.

...which just so happens to perfectly match the old-timey advice to 'invest in things which come between you and the ground'. Neat!

What goes on the other end of the barbell? I'd argue 'basically everything else'. Owning expensive stuff is a pain in the butt. It's not so much the upfront cost, but all the associated *obligations* that come with it.

I once met an American backpacker who carried her $400 designer hiking boots everywhere she went, because she was too scared to leave them on the front porch of the hostel like everyone else. There's a real sense in which people with expensive stuff forge the chains that bind them. Imagine the constant stress of having to think about security, making sure the insurance policies are up to date, and the anxiety of loaning something to a friend or neighbour.

By contrast, cheap really is cheerful. When I arrive in a new city or country, I usually buy some clothes for slumming around in. Unlike my core kit of fancy technical clothing, I put very little effort or expense into this revolving cast of minor characters: I often buy them from the thrift store, then donate them back when I leave. If I spill hot sauce on them, or someone steals them off the clothesline, who cares?

The goal is to avoid the middle ground, which is the worst of both worlds. This is the realm of brand names, where price starts to decouple from quality. I'll happily spend $60 on a shirt made of merino wool, and I'll happily pay $6 for a cotton tee. But I'm never going to pay $30 for a cotton tee, because it's not going to last me 5x longer than the el cheapo version. Chances are they were both made in the same factories, with the main difference being that one of them has a swoosh logo or whatever.

If it's not obvious whether you should buy quality or el cheapo, start on the low-cost end of the barbell. If you never have any problems, great! You just saved a bunch of cash. If it breaks, or it becomes clear it's not fit for purpose, you can upgrade without having wasted much money.

This goes doubly for anything hobby-related or whimsical. It's extremely hard to predict what our future selves will want, which is why storage units and garages end up as mausoleums to long-forgotten fitness fads, cast-off musical instruments, and other lifestyle detritus. Buying cast-iron pans 'for life' is a pretty safe bet; buying a custom racing bike is not. Instead of going straight for the Tour de France equivalent, get the entry-level version, preferably secondhand, and see if the passion persists. Once you get skilled enough to actually benefit from having triple-forged titanium alloy frames or whatever, go ahead and splash out.

MANAGING EXPECTATIONS

A friend recently completed an extended tour around my home country, so I breathlessly asked her the question that every visitor, newborn baby, and occasional passing seagull is enthusiastically subjected to: *Whatdoyathinkof-NewZealand???*

"It was OK," she said.

OK? It was *OK?* You're talking about God's own country, O philistine! What about all that rugged beauty? Those 30 million fluffy sheep? The bucket fountain where Elijah Wood did a wee? Did you even *see* the quite big statue of a fizzy drink bottle?

Yes, she agreed, all that stuff was indeed very nice. Especially the quite big fizzy drink bottle. But considering how much money she spent, it bloody well better be. As a budget-conscious traveler, my friend decided she'd rather spend time in countries which are more affordable and less-hyped, even if they're objectively not as good.

New Zealand shamelessly pays Hollywood massive subsidies to ensure they keep using us as a scenic backdrop for their blockbusters. Tourism is our number one export industry. We're not exactly a well-kept secret. And so, by the time my friend visited, she was already expecting nothing short of breath-taking mountainous vistas and glistening glaciers and hairy hobbit feet.

In the *Flight of the Conchords* TV show, there's a poster on the wall of band manager Murray's office which reads: 'New Zealand: don't expect too much, you will love it.' While this slogan is unlikely to be picked up by the tourism board, it's fantastic advice.

If there's one thing that jumps out from the research on getting the most bang for your experiential buck, it's that *expectations are everything.*

If you go somewhere at the height of hype, you're already expecting the best. As soon as reality fails to measure up to your expectations, even in some trivial way, woe betide you! The only direction to go is down. But if you go into a situation with low or no expectations, there's huge potential to be surprised on the upside.

This is because of the completely stupid way in which humans are wired. Remember that 'happiness' is not a final state, but a measuring device designed to gauge our progress. It's all relative, which leads to some paradoxical situations: if you go to the fancy restaurant your friend raved about, and it doesn't quite live up to the hype, you'll be less satisfied than if you stumbled across a random hole-in-the-wall and were pleasantly surprised by the modest menu—even if, strictly speaking, the first meal was better than the second.

The psychologist Mihaly Csikszentmihalyi suggests we can do more to improve the quality of our lives by controlling our expectations than by doing almost anything else. This is the optionality approach to experiences: always keep your initial expectations low, and leave room to be surprised on the upside.

Mostly this looks like saving the good bottle for the anniversary, and leaving plenty of time between expensive vacations. If the best experiences remain occasional treats, the wheel of hedonic adaptation won't get the chance to grind them into quotidian routine.

In buying peak experiences less often, you're simultaneously preserving your financial capital and maximising what we might call 'experiential optionality'.

Besides creating artificial scarcity, the research suggests you're likely to get the most bang for your buck if you do something that:

- Brings you together with other people
- Makes a memorable story that you'll enjoy retelling
- Is tightly linked to your sense of identity—who you are, or want to be
- Is unique, and therefore hard to compare against other options

This last one presents us with another juicy asymmetry. Most people borrow their desires from others, which makes it hard to have a truly unique experience. There is much option value in exploring the under-explored, and very little in taking the path well-travelled.

GO WHERE THE TOURISTS AREN'T

During a recent trip home, my friends and I made plans to escape the Auckland metropolis over Easter weekend, and head to a beautiful peninsular several hours out of town. By some incredible coincidence, everyone else had the exact same idea at the exact same time. This meant waking up at an hour that no man should be awake, in an attempt to beat the traffic. It meant paying a substantial premium for the holiday home we rented. And it meant being surrounded by mobs of fellow city-slickers, all of whom, as the graffiti in the public toilets reminded us, "should be shot at birth".

Dutifully, we spent a day visiting one of the top 10 most beautiful beaches in the world, complete with hawkers selling T-shirts and extortionately-priced fish and chips. We spent another day visiting the must-do Hot Water Beach, circling endlessly for a park before succumbing to the hustlers selling paddock access to dumb tourists for $10 a pop, then faithfully trooped to the small section of sand heaving with holidaymakers, and scraped out trenches so that we might huddle in a few inches of gritty water that alternated between scalding and freezing cold, with a breathtaking view of the ample buttcrack belonging to the German man digging in the next hole over.

For context: New Zealand has one of the longest coastlines in the world, any given stretch of which is pretty much instant postcard material. My family home is five minutes from a remote beach, with none of the crowds, no traffic, and a complete absence of teutonic buttcracks.

This was still a great trip, because it involved friends and food and sun and sea. But I realised I had somehow become a tourist in my own country. Having finally learned my lesson, I propose this general principle:

If you skip the top-tier or 'must-do' attraction, you will usually have a much better time at a fraction of the price.

I've noticed this more times than I can count, but was too scared to say anything out loud in case I looked like an uncultured idiot. Privately, I think of these 'brand name' experiences as expensive box-checking exercises: been there, done that, bought the T-shirt. I wonder if we're trapped in an Emperor's New Clothes situation, where everyone is secretly underwhelmed, but no-one wants to defect from the agreed-upon narrative. Instead, we post up our happy snaps and loudly reassure each other how great it was.

The 'go where the tourists aren't' principle scales from restaurants, to sight-seeing, to cities, to countries. If you visit the third-best city or attraction, you will be one of the only foreigners, and relatively unmolested by touts and scammers. You'll almost certainly get a more authentic experience, at much less expense. Better still, you might put down the guidebook altogether and open up some space for serendipity to strike. Rigid itineraries are ruinous to optionality: most of my best memories have come from chance encounters and random discoveries, rather than anything found in a glossy brochure.

A caveat: I will rearrange my entire schedule to avoid having to sit in traffic, and skipping the check-in and baggage carousel lines is a large part of why I prefer to travel carry-on only. So maybe this is partly my own peculiarities talking, but I think there's also a solid general principle here—especially once you consider the blind, herpes-like contagion by which anything becomes popular in the first place.

THE MONA LISA'S MYSTERIOUS SMILE

The Matthew effect suggests popular things often become popular through what amounts to good luck, with an early breakthrough propelled into the stratosphere by social contagion. Our opinions and preferences cluster together, but it's not as if we've carefully evaluated the options on their merits and all come to the same conclusion. We just want to feel close to our fellow apes.

In other words, popularity is a lot like herpes: after catching a lucky initial break, it manages to spread to a few hosts, then rides the growth curve until it has planted its gentle, blistery kiss on 60 per cent of the population.

How do you know the Mona Lisa is the artwork most worthy of your appreciation? In theory, you'd have to:

1. Study every period and style of art and decide the Renaissance was especially noteworthy,

2. Compare Leonardo against all his contemporaries,

3. Compare the Mona Lisa against Leonardo's 15 other known paintings and hundreds of sketches,

4. Independently decide, while paying no mind to the general consensus, that *this one painting* is the best.

Unless all those fanny pack-wearing tourists queuing up at the Louvre are secretly massive art history buffs, there's something funny going on here. Why do we invest so much time and money to stroke our chins in thoughtful contemplation of what little of Leonardo's brushwork we can see behind the scrum of selfie sticks and bulletproof glass, while completely ignoring many empty galleries of equally fine paintings?

If our motive is to appreciate art, this is a real head-scratcher. But if our (hidden) motive is to signal that we are the kind of person who Appreciates Art, it makes perfect sense. Most of us don't have the time or inclination to study art history, so we've settled upon a clearly agreed narrative that the Mona Lisa = Great Art. Go see it, snap a picture for proof, and everyone will be able to see how sophisticated and well-traveled you are.

Now, imagine we designed an artificial intelligence that was immune to the social contagion of puny humans, and could evaluate and rate art in some objective fashion. After performing the many inscrutable calculations required to follow steps 1 through 4 above, it announced that the best artwork in human history was... the Mona Lisa, by one Leonardo Da Vinci.

All those fanny-pack-wearers would be feeling pretty damn vindicated. Boy, would I have egg on my face!

...Or perhaps not. As Robin Hanson and Kevin Simler point out in *The Elephant in the Brain*, even in a scenario like this, we should still be suspicious of the claim that people visit the Mona Lisa to bask in its unparalleled magnificence. In fact, we *know* this isn't the case, because you can see a thousand pictures of it online right now, for free, in a split second. If we only cared about its intrinsic merits, there would be museums filled with perfect replicas, indistinguishable from the real thing, in every city. If you wanted to unlock the secrets of that inscrutable smile, you wouldn't have to pay a dime, or stand in line, or brave the jostling elbows and body odour.

The only explanation that fits is the most awkward one. We don't really want to see the Mona Lisa. We want to be *seen* seeing the Mona Lisa.

Of course, it never pays to go full contrarian. It's true that a lot of things are basically the aesthetic equivalent of herpes: the 20x price premium on a

Louis Vuitton handbag has very little to do with intrinsic merit, and a lot to do with signalling.

But the Matthew effect is *not* an argument against merit. Some products/people/experiences rise to the top because they really are better, and a few might even be head-and-shoulders above the pack. Yes, the Mona Lisa is a 'brand name' experience. So is Paris. So is travel in general. That doesn't mean these things suck; it just means you have to think a bit more carefully about whether they're worth paying a premium for.

The happy corollary is that there must also be a ton of stuff out there which is massively *underrated*, and might be, say, 90 per cent as good for a fraction of the price or time invested. These underrated experiences not only provide more bang for buck; they're also unburdened by expectations, and leave plenty of room to be surprised on the upside.

Buying experiences is more satisfying than accumulating stuff because it defies easy comparison. Unlike a phone or a car, there's no risk of feeling deflated when your friend turns up with a newer model. The more unique your experience is, the harder it is to compare—not just against your peers, but against all the other options you could have chosen.

The problem with brand-name experiences is that they behave more like commodities: you nailed the 'holding up the Leaning Tower' photo during the 30 minute stop on your generic package tour, but so did the last million people.

Of course, that's also kind of the point. A brand-name experience is a broadly-agreed upon signal: 'holding up the Leaning Tower' = has money to vacation/appreciates culture/playful and fun.

I'm as thirsty for validation as anyone else, but I do think this trade-off deserves to be dragged out of the murky subconscious and inspected in the cold light of day. Maybe it's worth enduring a million selfie-sticks and prodding elbows and paying through the nose so you can harvest those sweet, sweet likes down at the ol' content farm. But there's an inescapable experiential divide between seeing through your eyes, and seeing through your viewfinder. You cannot possibly be in the moment while mentally composing the perfect caption for your Instagram story. Are you looking for intrinsic enjoyment, or external validation? Once you've made the trade-off explicit, you can decide how much you value each end.

RECAP

There's nothing inherently virtuous about being a minimalist, but there is a tipping point where ***owning too much stuff closes off your options***. The true costs and obligations often escape our notice, and include depreciation, maintenance, storage, insurance, security, and reduced mental bandwidth.

Never own a depreciating asset if you can rent, lease, borrow, share or otherwise get the use value of it while wriggling out of the ongoing responsibilities. If the time and search costs start to mount up, that's the point to consider permanent ownership, using a heuristic like the one-year rule.

Buy the highest-quality version of anything you use every day, that protects against the risk of ruin, or that fills you with joy. For everything else, buy the cheap and cheerful version, and upgrade as and when it's no longer fit for purpose.

The secret to psychological wellbeing lies in the gap between what we expect from the world, and what it delivers. Cap the downside by setting your expectations as low as possible, and then look for experiences that create plenty of room to be surprised on the upside.

Creating artificial scarcity prevents your internal gauge from becoming desensitised to positive experiences, and lets you maintain a constant low-level state of surprise and gratitude.

There is strong option value in seeking out experiences that are unique or under-explored. By contrast, the road well-travelled limits both the downside risk and the potential upside.

Brand-name experiences are often the result of arbitrary social contagion, which means the costs have become decoupled from the underlying merits. If you ignore the hype and take the second or third-best option, you will usually have a much better experience at a fraction of the price.

The main value of brand-name experiences is signalling. Be conscious of the trade-off between intrinsic enjoyment and external validation, and don't get sucked into status games you didn't intend to play.

14

ASYMMETRIES IN HEALTH CAPITAL

B E ATTRACTIVE; DON'T BE UNATTRACTIVE. This little gem of life advice is a favourite of the denizens of Reddit, and while it's delivered with tongue firmly in cheek, there's more than a glimmer of truth to it. Attractive people earn significantly more money, and have better prospects of finding a job in the first place. The economic disparity between 'hot' and 'not' is as glaring as the gender pay gap, and just as groundless. While some people are blessed with a heavenly visage, others fall out of the ugly tree and hit every branch on the way down.

It's curious that we don't talk about this inequality more, although I think I can guess why the cause is so unsexy. Who'd want to be the spokesperson for the Aesthetically Challenged Association? Whenever you did TV interviews, you'd have to get the makeup department to accentuate your worst features. I have a pretty good face for radio myself, but I'm not volunteering for this thankless task. All the righteous sermons in the world are never going to change the reality of human biology, in which these kinds of snap judgments happen instantly and subconsciously.

The **Halo Effect** is the most famous subtype of the Matthew effect of cumulative advantage. If a person has one positive attribute—beauty, height, charm—we automatically assume they also possess above-average generosity, intelligence, or honesty. While this applies to any positive trait, appearance just so happens to be immediately visible. And so, a study of Canadian election candidates found the attractive politicians received two and a half times as many votes as their rivals, Fortune 500 chief executives tower over the rest of the populace with an average height of 6'2", and so on.

If you think you're not as shallow as the other sheeple, consider the fact that even hot criminals get treated better. Judges are meant to be professionals at, well, judging people, and they *still* get sucked in by doe-eyed defendants, who are twice as likely to avoid jail as cons with faces that only a mother could love.

Clearly, this is unfair and arbitrary. It only starts to make a warped kind of sense from the perspective of the horny, status-seeking chimpanzee stapled to your frontal lobe, which is constantly on the lookout for potential mates and allies. A youthful appearance is an indicator of *fertility*. Good health suggests *strong genes*. On average, tall people are slightly higher in *intelligence*. Of course, none of this tells you anything useful about any given individual. There are plenty of short ugly geniuses, and towering hotties with not much going on between their very shapely ears. It's also decoupled from the things we tend to care about today, which have moved far beyond mere survival and reproduction: the young Joseph Stalin was a dreamboat, but the whole 'mass-murdered millions' thing is kind of a turn-off.

Remember that the selfish genes tugging on our puppet strings do not always have the best interests of their hosts in mind. Even if they did, these signals have become so unreliable in modernity that they constantly misfire: the young lady at the bar with the bright red lipstick is displaying peak fertility, but she's on the pill, and has no interest whatsoever in making babies. As for the ability to provide security and resources, the geeks have inherited the earth: a scrawny software engineer who gets pinned to the floor of a high-pressure shower might have 10x the earning power of a big strapping jock, and be a more sensitive partner to boot. Physical presence is increasingly irrelevant in modernity, but those ancient drives are always there, pushing and pulling beneath the surface.

Naturally, the Sirens offer an enormous range of products designed to cash in on these drives. There's a cornucopia of cosmetics, clothing, plastic surgery, exercise gadgets, herbal remedies, potions, lotions, tonics, implants, and prostheses on the market, all of which promise to enhance health, youth, and beauty. Unfortunately, most of them don't work very well, or at all. No matter how much money you spend, it's difficult to fake these kinds of traits. A fitness model could make a potato sack look like haute couture, and a beautiful person will still be beautiful when they take their brave no-makeup selfie.

If you've got a face like a smacked arse or you're too short to ride the rollercoaster, there's not a whole lot you can do about it. Even body shape is surprisingly difficult to change: as at the time of writing, there is no reliable way of losing large amounts of weight and keeping it off, short of surgery. That's not to be fatalistic: there are some promising weight loss interventions, and it is still *possible*, not to mention desirable from a health perspective.

Which brings us to the less shallow section of this chapter. Yes, attractive people have more attractive options—but not *that* much more attractive. Beauty is a leading indicator of health capital, and the defining feature of health capital is that all of our upside is bounded. Mobility, fitness, energy, and attractiveness act as a sort of force multiplier on all our other efforts, and are certainly worth having, but they're subject to hard limits. You can be 10x richer, more knowledgeable, or better-connected than the average person, but you can never be 10x healthier.

'Health' isn't defined by the presence of anything in particular, but by the *absence* of problems: if you don't have diseases, aches, pains, visible deformities, or clogged arteries, that's about the best you could hope for.

In this domain, bad is much, much stronger than good. The highest priority by far is protecting the downside, which means attenuating silent risk, and trying our best not to stumble into a Bottomless Pit of Doom.

LIVE LONG AND PROSPER

If you are dead, you do not have very many options. It doesn't matter how much money you have, or how many degrees, or how powerful your friends are. In the final counting, your choices are restricted to one unenviable decision: cremation or burial?

As any 5-year-old child could tell you, death is bad. As adults, we fool ourselves with elaborate rationalisations about its 'deeper meaning', which is a strong contender for the most absurd case of sour grapes in the history of the universe.

Life is the first and most precious option that any of us are given, and sits at the top of Martha Nussbaum's list of core capabilities. The second item on the list is 'Health'. It's really, really OK to want to preserve these things, especially given we have some tiny glimmer of hope of reversing ageing in our life-times. Imagine how silly you'd feel if you miss out on immortality by a measly few years.

If we're unlucky, God will cut us down for no reason at all. A cell divides in just such a way, and that's that. But many of the most common afflictions, and even some accidents, are *preventable*.

Anyone who makes it through their 20s without suffering from some combination of obesity, metabolic syndrome, repetitive strain injury, a bad back, high blood pressure, depression, anxiety, or insomnia—all the plagues of modernity—is a truly exceptional individual.

The fact that these diseases barely existed throughout most of human history is kind of depressing, but there is an encouraging corollary: if changes to the way we live brought these afflictions upon us, then maybe lifestyle changes can help to alleviate them. We can't put the genie all the way back in the bottle, but we can certainly try our best to cap the downside.

As far as interventions go, there's one that stands head-and-shoulders above the pack. It hits the shallow-signalling angle and the longevity angle all at once, while also being cheap, social, and highly efficient. This miracle medi-cine is called 'exercise'—more specifically, heavy resistance training.

DO YOU EVEN LIFT?

It takes a special kind of stupidity to shame people for being overweight. Even if we hold everyone forever accountable for the actions of their former selves —which are influenced by genetics, their environment, and all manner of randomness—those initial steps set us on a path which becomes increasingly difficult to deviate from (Fig 3.4).

The body doesn't like change. Once it settles into a groove, it does every-thing in its power to stay there, which means any attempt to lose weight puts you in the very unpleasant position of doing battle against your own hormones and metabolism. Like Sisyphus, you have to heave the boulder up the moun-tain every single day. All it takes is one false step, and you start sliding back-wards faster and faster, until you've tumbled right back to where you started.

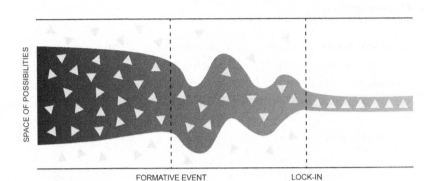

Figure 3.4. Path dependence tells us that "history matters": the decisions presented to us often depend on prior decisions or past experiences.

The reverse is also true, although the fitness folks don't exactly advertise it. If you already have momentum on your side, staying in shape is much easier than the hustle-porn #inspo posts would lead you to believe. The sculpted Greek gods who glide through a workout without breaking a sweat get all the glory, but the overweight person slogging away on the treadmill is engaged in a much more heroic pursuit.

Personally, I eat some kind of junk food pretty much every day, rarely do more than three hours of exercise a week, and haven't counted calories in years. But I've never been fitter! I would love to attribute this to some moral superiority on my part—something something 'perspiration beats inspiration'—but the truth is that I am lazy, and incapable of forcing myself to do anything I don't want to.

I say all of this not as an elaborate humblebrag, but to draw attention to two criminally neglected points:

1. Everything compounds
2. Heavy resistance training has a much higher return on investment than cardio

Lifting weights is proof that God very occasionally hides cheat codes in our simulation: just button mash up/down/up/down. If you can build up a little strength and muscle mass, you kickstart a positive feedback loop which makes life easier on every possible dimension. Let us count the ways:

1. Hormonal health

Testosterone levels in men are closely linked with body fat. Belly fat in particular harbours aromatase, an enzyme which converts the male sex hormone into oestrogen. As a general rule, the leaner you are, the easier it is to build muscle and burn fat, the better your hormonal balance, and so on.[1]

2. Metabolic rate

The more lean mass you have, the higher your metabolic rate. Muscles are expensive to maintain, and they're burning calories all the time. Even when you're sitting on your butt! My basal metabolic rate ranges as far as 400 calories from baseline, depending on how much lean weight I'm carrying. After factoring in activity levels it's close to 1000 calories, which buys me a whole lot of margin for error.

3. Flexible eating

Having a few hundred extra calories to play with means you never again have to follow a super-restrictive diet. Swedish nutrition consultant Martin Berkhan, who looks like he's carved out of marble, likes to devour entire cheesecakes in one go. As far as I can tell, there is no downside to occasionally performing these kinds of feats, apart from having your Thanksgiving invite rescinded.

4. Insulin sensitivity

After you eat a meal, your liver only has so much room for short-term sugar storage. Fortunately, your muscles are big old glucose sinks, and will happily soak up the excess. The bigger your sinks, the better your insulin sensitivity, and the lower your risk of becoming prediabetic. This is one reason why an athletic person can get away with eating the dreaded high-fructose corn syrup, or cheesecake, or whatever. Sometimes, simple sugars are *helpful*, which is why Floyd Mayweather chugs Coke during his training sessions. You can argue about whether it's 'optimal' (probably not to his face) but it sure isn't going to hurt him.

5. Vitamins and minerals

The underappreciated strategy for getting enough micronutrients is to eat more food. If you're taking in 3000 calories and aren't a total slob, you'll be over the recommended daily intake for most everything without even trying. By contrast, someone on a measly 1300 calories has to be extra careful to cover all the nutritional bases, which makes an already miserable diet even more restrictive.

6. Muscle memory

If you take a few weeks or months off from resistance training, it's not the end of the world. It takes much less time to regain muscle than it does to build it in the first place: the body remembers, and it wants to go back there.[2]

7. Enjoyment and motivation

The fitter and stronger you are, the more enjoyable exercise tends to be. This is partly because you can pull off more impressive feats; mostly because it sucks less.

8. Cruise control

Exercise is one of the few areas of life where I have no trouble whatsoever with self-discipline. It's so deeply baked into my sense of identity that it almost never requires willpower. Sure, I'll blow off a session now and again. But in the last decade, I don't think I've ever gone more than a month without consistently doing some kind of resistance training.

Notice how none of these eight factors operates in isolation. The stronger you are, the better your hormonal and metabolic health, the lower your bodyfat, the more relaxed you can be with your diet, the more motivation you have to train, the cooler feats you can perform, the more confident you feel, the more rewarding the habit becomes, and so on, in an endless feedback loop of mutual reinforcement (Fig 3.5).

Figure 3.5. The virtuous cycle of heavy resistance training.

Once the system builds up enough slack, you can *relax*. If you take a week off from the gym to clock a new video game, nothing bad happens. Any one link in the chain can seize up for a while, and the virtuous cycle keeps on turning.

Of the eight effects listed, only the two psychological factors (willpower and enjoyment) could reasonably be said to apply to cardio fitness. Aerobic exercise doesn't burn many calories, doesn't build lean mass, and comes and goes quickly—there is no such thing as 'cardio memory'.

Unfortunately, cardio is especially popular amongst the three groups who would benefit the most from stepping into the weights room: women, the elderly, and overweight folks.

This has a lot to do with the common misconception that lifting weights is 'dangerous'. Seriously, frickin' badminton causes 10x more injuries than lifting, and sports like soccer and basketball are off the charts. The reality is that *not* lifting is dangerous.

If longevity researcher Peter Attia could impart a single piece of wisdom, it would be: "To lift weights, and never stop lifting weights." Heavy resistance training protects against accidents, improves the chances of surviving surgery, and wards off almost every major cause of death and decay, from Alzheimers to zoonotic diseases. For older folks in particular, strength training is the difference between a broken hip and a walk in the park.

All these benefits are unlocked with a modest time investment and a small upfront financial cost in the form of a barbell, which happens to be one of the most beautiful technologies ever invented. The first 'barbell' I owned was a length of bamboo with a bucket on each end, filled with containers of sand. Then I saved my pennies to buy a set of crappy cement weights. Eventually I was able to afford secondhand iron plates and bars, and finally graduated to a proper Olympic bar. This will never be substantially improved upon or made obsolete, and if you buy quality, it will live longer than you do.

If you can't afford to buy equipment, or the idea of lifting doesn't appeal, fear not—there's another form of resistance training which might present an even more perfect nexus of desirable traits.

THE ANCIENT ART OF CALISTHENICS

I push the airline carry-on limit pretty far, but I suspect the cabin crew would draw the line at stuffing a barbell and a few hundred kilograms of plates into the overhead lockers. And so, when I went traveling, I started looking into calisthenics training.

My vague conception was that this had something to do with cranking out 1000 crunches before breakfast, Patrick Bateman-style. But as usual, it's a bad idea to take life advice from psychopaths.

As it turns out, calisthenics is structured strength training. The clue is in the name: *kallos* + *sthenos*, from the ancient Greek for 'beauty' and 'strength'. Just like weightlifting, you're moving through space against resistance, and reaping large benefits from small bursts of intense effort. The only difference is that instead of using lumps of iron to provide the resistance, you're using lumps of your own flesh.

You might start by doing pushups on your knees, which is a load of ~40 per cent of your bodyweight through the horizontal plane, and ultimately build up to handstand pushups, which is a load of ~90 per cent of your bodyweight through the vertical plane. In between, you can adjust the resistance with dozens of progressions that involve small changes to the plane, leverage, stability, and hand placement (visit thedeepdish.org/calisthenics for a beginner's routine).

The beauty of calisthenics is that it requires *no equipment whatsoever*. In practice, it helps to at least have a pull-up bar, but a tree branch, stairwell, or door lintel will do in a pinch.

Bodyweight training is not quite as efficient for building strength and muscle as weightlifting, but it is a much better nudge towards improving mobility and awareness of how your body moves through space (proprioception). A powerlifter is trying to shift the bar through the smallest possible range of motion while still performing a 'legal' lift. Smart lifters do a ton of stretching and supplementary exercises, but it's not actually *required*. If you want to advance in calisthenics, there's no way to fudge it—mobility is just as much of a limiting factor as brute strength.

This ancient art has been kept alive by soldiers, prisoners, and martial artists over the millennia, but it deserves to make a broader comeback. Even very poor parts of Asia and Latin America have calisthenics stations in public parks and along the beaches. In Russia, people train in the snow, because of course they do. Putting a pull-up station on every other corner would be a hugely cost-effective intervention in urban design, which I will implement when I am czar. In the meantime, it costs next to nothing to get started yourself: with a bit of imagination, the whole world becomes your gym.

(The companion reading list at optionalitybook.com/resources includes recommended programs for beginning calisthenics or weightlifting, or both—a popular combination is to work the lower body with barbells, and the upper body with bodyweight exercises.)

THE BARBELL STRATEGY FOR EXERCISE

That's the heavy lifting out of the way. What about cardio? Resistance training throws in a basic level of cardiovascular fitness as a freebie, but we also want to pair the intense stuff up with its polar opposite: large volumes of slow and unstrenuous movement, so gentle that it barely qualifies as exercise. Activities like walking, casual cycling and stretching get the blood pumping and the joints moving, and act as a kind of 'active recovery'.

This gives us the barbell strategy for barbells: short bursts of intense effort on the hyper-aggressive 'expensive' end, and lots of low-effort movement on the hyper-conservative 'cheap' end (Fig. 3.6). The distribution is highly asymmetrical, so we might aim for 2.5 hours of intense exercise each week, but 25 hours of gentle movement.

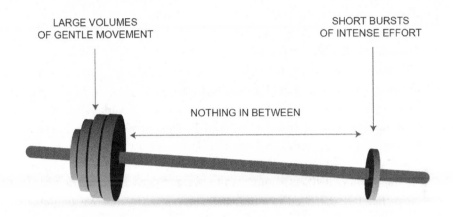

Figure 3.6. The barbell strategy for exercise.

The best way to rack up a ton of low-intensity movement is to make it part of your daily life. You shouldn't have to put on any special clothing or think of it as 'working out'.

A simple version of this strategy is to get in the habit of walking everywhere. Strolling appears to have some kind of magic juju, perhaps because humans are built to walk long distances: everyone from Nietzsche to Thoreau has raved about the powers of perambulation, and many a creative breakthrough has been attributed to a long rambling walk. Talking to a friend on the phone? Go for a walk. Getting to know a new city? Go for a walk. Run out of milk? Go for a walk. Expensive parking at the venue? Go for a walk. It's amazing how much life improves when you start thinking of everything within a ~2km radius as easy strolling distance.

Similar strategies include taking the stairs instead of the elevator, commuting by bicycle, setting an alarm to get up and stretch every hour or so, working at a standing desk, playing video games standing up, cruising on a stationary bike while watching TV, taking up active hobbies, and fidgeting with a stress ball or other doohickey.[3]

The integrated-lifestyle approach beats dedicated cardio on two fronts. First, we need lots of movement spaced throughout the day, and there's no way to 'catch up' on it with one big dose: pounding the treadmill does not compensate for 10 hours slouched over a computer. It's also more pleasant: in following the barbell strategy, I've managed to get my Vo2 max and resting heart rate (the best measures of cardiovascular health) in the 'good' to 'very good' range without doing a lick of deliberate cardio. If, like me, you find this unnatural toil boring and unpleasant, it's liberating to know that you never have to run another day in your life.

The middle ground of the barbell represents moderate-intensity exercise which you have to go out of your way to perform: jogging, treadmills, cross-trainers, serious Lycra-clad cycling. This category also includes such abominations as random circuit training and the Patrick Bateman stomach-crunch routine, which blend cardio and strength into a slurry of mediocrity. These exercises don't burn many calories, don't build much lean mass, are time-consuming, require deliberate effort, and can interfere with recovery.

Now that I've managed to annoy half the readership, let me scramble to invoke the first and only commandment of exercise science. This should really be graven in stone letters 100 feet high and trumpeted by angels, but I ran out of budget so use your imagination:

THOU SHALT DO WHATEVER EXERCISE THOU ENJOYETH ENOUGH TO KEEP DOING

The best kind of exercise is the one you can actually bring yourself to do on a regular basis. There's nothing *wrong* with the middle-ground exercises: the point is that contrary to popular belief, they're neither necessary nor sufficient. If you don't also do some kind of resistance training, you're failing to pluck the low-hanging fruit.

Of the various forms of accidental exercise we might weave into our daily lives, two are especially noteworthy. We've already mentioned walking. Now for a few words on the humble bicycle.

THE VIRTUOUS CYCLE

Commuting by cycle not only nudges us into getting a twice-daily dose of incidental cardio, it eliminates one of the single biggest sources of suckiness in the average person's life. The daily commute is relentlessly unpleasant because we don't have any *control*. If you take public transport, you're subjected to the tyranny of the timetable, the press of strange flesh, and the tinny music pumping out of your fellow passengers' phones. In a car, your fate is bound to the flow of traffic and the limited supply of parking spaces. All you can do is sit there and occasionally lean on the horn, adding your own frustrated cry to an orchestra of impotence.

By contrast, every single bike ride is a mini-adventure. There's an instant feedback loop between your effort and your results. The endorphins are pumping. You're doing battle with the elements. It's not always more *comfortable*, but comfort is a dangerous thing to optimise for.

Cycling has been my main mode of transport for the last five years. The frisson of joy that comes from whizzing past a queue of gridlocked cars would be reason enough, but the original reason I got into it was more prosaic: a bicycle is also a wealth-building machine. Running costs round to nothing— the occasional new tube, a drop of oil here and there. A cycle commute easily saves $1000 a year in petrol or bus fares, and substantially more if you usually pay for parking. You can also eliminate all the small errands: about 40 per cent of all car trips in the US are used to cover distances of less than 3 kilometres, which borders on criminal for any able-bodied person in possession of a pulse.

Owning a bicycle greatly expands your range and capacity to carry stuff compared to walking, and it's a trivially cheap option to take out. Personally, I've never owned a bike worth more than $150, or squished my bits and pieces into a Lycra flesh hammock. All you really need are some LED lights and reflective strips if you're riding at night, and you're set. Even helmets are over-rated: in countries with sophisticated bicycle cultures and dedicated infrastructure, casual riders don't bother wearing them at all.

Cycling is not much more dangerous than driving based on time spent on the road, but there are more fatalities on a per-kilometre basis. The life-extending benefits of exercise compensate for this several times over, but it's a valid concern if you care about avoiding extreme tail events. The extent to which you should factor this in depends on the infrastructure and culture in your particular part of the world: the risk profile of cycling in Amsterdam is far more attractive than the American Midwest.

If everyone took to two wheels, we'd all be better off, but no-one is incentivised to make the first move. So if you want to perform a small heroic service, join the vanguard of the cycling revolution in your town or city. The more cyclists on the roads, the more motorists learn to expect them, and the more demand there is for dedicated infrastructure. It's a virtuous cycle: every new bike lane or connection is more valuable than the last, because it makes the network greater than the sum of its parts.

Bicycles are a central part of the transport stack that is finally replacing the kludge of private car ownership, and it's not hard to see why. A car is a noisy, expensive machine that converts money into fat, atrophies health and wellbeing, belches carbon, and promotes passivity and fragility. A bicycle is a silent, near-costless machine that converts fat into money, builds health capital, helps save the planet, and promotes agency and resilience. One of these things is not like the other.

DRUGS ARE BORING

I am not a doctor; this is not medical advice. But it would be remiss not to briefly mention the vast class of substances which can improve or damage our health, and on which we spend vast sums of money.

The optionality filter suggests that 'drugs are bad, mmkay' is actually pretty good advice for any substance which might lead to addiction, overdose or psychosis. The chances of tumbling into a Bottomless Pit of Doom on any individual occasion might be small, but the asymmetric downside means it's never worth spinning the barrel (unless you're already at death's door).

The risk of ruin varies based on individual genetic factors, but some substances are universally terrible. Smoking is just Russian Roulette with slower bullets, and especially irrational now there are much cheaper and safer ways to get your nicotine fix.

Nicotine, as distinct from tobacco, is about as dangerous as caffeine, and even comes with some modest benefits. Nevertheless, I chose to go cold turkey when I quit smoking: not only because vape pens are the fedora of the mouth, but because the upside of nicotine is just not that exciting.

Which brings us to the main takeaway: drugs are boring. A handful of substances are terrible, an even smaller handful are amazing, but the vast majority don't display an asymmetry in either direction. Leaving aside medications that address specific diseases, most everything in this category is fiddling on the margin: we have to untangle a bunch of complex trade-offs with middling costs and benefits, on the basis of what is usually crappy and biased data, and the effects will still vary based on our individual physiology.

Why are drugs so boring? Well, the blind idiot god of evolution has already spent a few billion years grinding away at the optimisation problem. If there were some molecule that made us smarter or healthier with no downsides, our bodies would already synthesise it or otherwise extract it from our environment.

In other words, there's no such thing as a free lunch. Whenever someone tries to sell you a new 'smart drug' or supplement, the starting assumption should always be that you're paying for very expensive urine.

Positive asymmetries are hard to find, but they probably do exist. One example would be fixing an undiagnosed nutritional deficiency: you can get transformative quality-of-life improvements for very little cost, although this still only gets you back to a healthy baseline.

More speculatively, psychedelics like LSD and psilocybin are relatively safe and trivially cheap, and have the potential to bring about therapeutic changes or transformative insights: clinical trials are currently underway for treatment-resistant depression, addiction, and post-traumatic stress disorder.

Humans have been licking frogs and chewing cactus buds for millennia, and psychedelic rituals evolved independently across many cultures. The fact that people like getting high is not definitive proof of anything in particular, but it does fit a broader pattern: all the most promising interventions in health capital are examples of something called the 'Lindy effect'.

LINDY GUIDES OUR WAY

The central argument of this book is that volatility requires us to explore more: our preferences aren't stable over time, and neither are the activities the world rewards us for.

But this is *not* true of stable domains like human physiology. There are some occasional variations—the mutation that gave my ancestors the ability to digest milk only spread 4000 years ago—but the pace of change is extraordinarily slow.

The stability and bounded upside of health capital suggests we should get to the point of 'good enough' as soon as possible, and then happily calcify. I started out vaguely exercising, dabbled in powerlifting, moved to calisthenics, and ended up with a hybrid model. Now I'm done. I'll still tinker a little, but there's zero chance I'm going to suddenly switch to camelback polo steeplechasing or whatever. This is as good as it gets. Same goes for walking, cycling, and eating mostly the same meals.

It's important to do some experimentation early on, but only to discover your personal preferences. We already know the broad strokes of what we should do: the exact same thing our great-grandmothers did.

This is the **Lindy Effect**: the longer an idea, technology, or institution has been around, the longer we should predict it to stick around in the future. Bicycles and barbells are roughly 200 years old; we might expect by chance to be halfway through their useful lifetime. If our great-great-grandchildren are still cycling and lifting weights 200 years from now, then they will probably be useful for another four centuries, and so on. Unlike frail humans, the expected remaining lifespan of an idea or institution *increases* as it gets older.

Lindy leads us towards practices and technologies with the longest continuous history, and cautions us with a corollary: the more recent an intervention is, the more likely it is to be a fad, a scam, or a boring 'fiddling on the margins' Dead End that distracts us from the things that actually matter.

Everything recommended in this chapter is Lindy-approved. There are three other ancient practices which I don't have the expertise or time to tackle in this book, but are also worthy of consideration: we briefly touched on psychedelics, which are finally starting to be validated by modern science, as are fasting, and sauna bathing. I've included pointers on these more speculative interventions in the companion reading list.

The two reassuring constants in the domain of health capital are the solidity of human physiology, and the vast oceans of snake oil constantly crashing against it. When in doubt, Lindy parts the seas of bullshit and guides our way.

RECAP

Good health is defined by the absence of problems. The upside of this domain is bounded: we can have more energy, a better mood, more mobility, and a halo effect of attractiveness, but we can't be 'super healthy'.

Death is the ultimate destroyer of optionality, closely followed by disease and disability. We might tumble into a Bottomless Pit of Doom through blind bad luck, but most lifestyle diseases are caused by the accumulation of silent risk.

Almost all health interventions, including drugs, supplements, fad diets, and exercise gimmicks, are distracting Dead Ends. These complex trade-offs may or may not offer some modest benefits on the margin, but they don't display a positive asymmetry.

It is very dangerous to not lift weights. Resistance training is massively protective against the risk of ruin, and creates a positive feedback loop that acts as a force multiplier in every area of life.

If you follow the barbell strategy for exercise, you never have to run another day in your life. Resistance training is best paired up with lots of low-level movement integrated into daily life.

Health capital is an unusually stable domain. Experiment long enough to find out what works for you, then become a creature of habit at the earliest opportunity.

When in doubt, Lindy guides our way. Walking, calisthenics, barbells, and bicycles are time-tested technologies. Other ancient practices that show promise are fasting, sauna bathing, and psychedelic therapy.

ASYMMETRIES IN SOCIAL CAPITAL

I USED TO WORRY THAT SOCIETY was in the grips of a 'loneliness epidemic'. Thousands of think-pieces have been published on this gripping story—spoiled only by the pesky data, which tell us that loneliness levels haven't changed in generations.

Worse than this widespread journalistic malpractice is the misunderstanding of what it actually means to be lonely. You can be alone in a room full of people. You can be lonely in a marriage. And you can live by yourself and have a rich social life. Merely being in the vicinity of people is not the same thing as feeling connected.

A second, related myth is that true friendship is unconditional. I was taught that the highest form of love is to accept someone with all their flaws; that trying to change someone is a red flag; that it's cruel and mercenary to deliberately distance people or cut them out of our lives.

The third myth I fell for was the social norm that relationships should either happen naturally, or not at all—that it's cold and calculating to 'curate' the people in our lives, and strategically cultivating new connections is downright creepy.

The final myth I swallowed is that if we succeed in this unnatural endeavour, we risk ending up surrounded by like-minded people. This, too, is shameful: it's anti-egalitarian to live in a 'bubble' that doesn't reflect broader society.

The taboo at the heart of these myths is a belief that social capital has been handed down by God in his heaven, and it's wrong to strategically accumulate or allocate it. It might be OK if you change your social position by accident, as a consequence of something else, but it mustn't be pursued as a goal in and of itself.

This is the single most limiting set of beliefs I have ever personally had to overcome. No-one in their right minds would think that financial capital accumulates effortlessly, or knowledge, or health. You can improve *anything* when you a) learn how it works and b) apply targeted effort, and it should have been obvious to me that relationships are not some magical exception.

Unfortunately, I uncritically swallowed these myths for most of my adult life. I am not especially outgoing by nature, and as a result, social capital ended up being the weakest quadrant in my own optionality index.

But I also got lucky: both in having rarely encountered sociopaths and other categories of abusers, who could easily have made my life unpleasant, and in making some moves which boosted my stocks of social capital entirely by accident.

I make no pretence of being an expert in this domain. Take this chapter in the spirit of someone who is still deprogramming from bad social norms, and sharing some remedies that may be useful for others.

CRABS IN THE BUCKET

The author Steven Pressfield has a famous parable about a bucket full of crabs. When one enterprising crustacean scrambles to escape the plastic prison, its peers latch onto it and pull it back down again: "The highest treason a crab can commit is to make a leap for the rim of the bucket."

If you're unlucky, you have people like this in your life. When you share some small win or achievement, their eyes glaze over while they wait for an opportunity to one-up you. They actively try to diminish your success, and make you feel small. If they don't do it to your face, they do it behind your back. When you fail, they can barely conceal their pleasure, and take every opportunity to remind you of your shortcomings.

These people are stuck playing some kind of warped zero-sum status game. In their eyes, any success you might have is a threat to their own position on the totem pole.

Individual strength of character is no match for social contagion. If you are surrounded by people like this, they will drag you down with 100 per cent probability. The first step in building optionality is to protect the downside, which means the most important action you can take is to get rid of fake friends and toxic relationships.

The Romantics have a lot to answer for—New Age spirituality, nationalism, Hegel—but the myth of unconditional love has to be their worst legacy. This regressive norm traps us in abusive relationships, absolves us of the need to change and grow, and shifts the blame onto the person who only seeks to evade the grasping claws. How cold-blooded! How mercenary!

Once again, we've somehow managed to backslide from the more sophisticated understanding of the ancient Greeks: to truly love someone is to help them grow, to teach and be taught, to avoid stagnation and ruin. This means pointing out uncomfortable truths rather than sweeping them beneath the rug, and if someone is not willing to grow with us, the kindest thing we might do for both parties is to get some distance.

My friendship *is* conditional. It is an enormous relief to realise that just because you have a shared history with someone, that doesn't mean you're bound to them forever. I am lucky in almost never having had to actually cut anyone out of my life, and merely having this insight is enough—it has given me the courage to let people know when they were failing to clear my (very low) bar, and that we would be taking a hiatus if they didn't cut the bullshit.

I like Kevin Simler's definition of friendship as a pact in which two people agree to dispense with all the usual fine-grained accounting of status transactions. That way you can play freely—including taking the piss out of yourself and each other—purely for fun, with nothing at stake. This also gives us a heuristic for figuring out who your real friends are: if there's any undercurrent of posturing or manoeuvring in their interactions, or you wouldn't expose your soft underbelly to them, you know they're still playing games for keeps.

That's the unpleasant side of the equation. But hopefully you also have some genuine friends in your life. When you share some small achievement, their eyes light up with excitement. They love to celebrate your good fortune. When you fail, their commiseration is genuine, and they lift you back up with words of encouragement.

The next defensive step is to identify and invest heavily in these people, because they are the ones who will be there for you if things fall apart.

THE COUCH-CRASHING NUMBER

The usual heuristic for a true friend is someone who would always pick up if you called at 3am, and vice versa. My phone is permanently on silent, so I prefer to count the friends who would let me crash on their couch for some mildly uncomfortable length of time—say, a few weeks—without resenting the intrusion.

This is your couch-crashing number, and it's no exaggeration to say that it's a matter of life-and-death importance. Even the most self-reliant and competent person is only ever a few strokes of misfortune away from the abyss. Instead of deteriorating in an orderly fashion, we spiral downwards faster and faster until we fall off a cliff: if your girlfriend breaks up with you on your birthday and takes all the furniture, and your back also happens to be broken, and you are lying in agony on a slowly deflating air mattress, and you start self-medicating, you better hope you invested in a social support network. You don't need that many friends to protect against these kinds of tail risk scenarios, but I personally wouldn't feel secure if I had fewer than five couches to crash on at any given moment.

We are spoiled by the fact that our first couch-crashing contacts—our parents and other family—are granted to us with no effort on our part. This is not how it works later in life. Social capital can only be built up by taking every possible opportunity to help other people—say, by letting them crash on your couch. This is the equivalent of pooling insurance risk by making small payments into a common fund: if you never end up making a claim, great! That means you've been unusually lucky in the game of life. Remember that friendship is a pact to dispense with fine-grained transactions. (If this pact is being abused—one person is all take and no give, even though they have the means—that's the time to gently call it out.)

If your circumstances mean you're currently taking more than you can give, expressing gratitude is another way to build social capital. Everyone loves being recognised for their efforts, and everyone hates to feel like they're being taken for granted. Thank-you notes, letters, and other forms of gratitude are remarkably asymmetric and neglected options: they cost nothing, and benefit both the gifter and the giftee. As we'll see in the next section, even expressing gratitude to total strangers has an unexpected upside.

Social capital is stored in other people. When you're not sure where to invest, start with your oldest relationships. This is the most ancient and reliable safety net of all: governments fail and employers fold, but family and friends are always there for you.

Old friends and family are an especially good investment because they are non-fungible: you have built up a store of shared history, in-jokes, and mutual understanding that cannot be transferred to any other soul.

They're also an unusually *secure* store of social capital. An old friend is Lindy-approved: the further back you go, the further forward you will go. A one-week-old friendship might be expected to last another week. One year, another year. One decade, another decade. Some of my friendships now span more than half my lifetime, and I'm planning to keep them up until I die.

My old friends and I have taken different paths through life, and I don't talk to some of them very often. But we still love each other, we are invested in each other's stories, and our metaphorical couches are always laid out with a sleeping bag at the ready.

GETTING IN AT THE GROUND FLOOR

Social contagion creates grotesque inequalities in the distribution of attention. Famous people receive far more praise than they know what to do with, which means our adulation mostly goes unnoticed. As always, the greatest advantages accrue to those who need them the least.

There is an opportunity here to redistribute social capital to talented people who do not yet have the recognition they deserve—in investing terms, to 'get in at the ground floor'. Up-and-coming artists or students or entrepreneurs don't have armies of fans and backers behind them. Quite possibly, they are hanging on by a thread. A few well-placed words of praise and encouragement can change everything.

The economist Tyler Cowen encouraged his most talented students to skip a Masters degree and go straight for the PhD. They often didn't believe they were capable of making the leap, or realise this was even possible. Cowen suggests that raising the aspirations of other people in these critical moments is one of the most valuable things you can do with your life: "It costs you relatively little to do this, but the benefit to them, and to the broader world, may be enormous."

That would be reason enough to invest at the ground floor: virtue is its own reward. But you're also building social capital with a person who *might actually reciprocate*. Replying to every one of Elon Musk or Lady Gaga's tweets is evolutionary wasted effort. We were wired up to simp for powerful or attractive members of our tribe; not for a senpai who we will never meet and doesn't know we exist. But if you invest in people who are not yet famous, or are 'famous' in some very small niche, you might actually end up befriending them, or otherwise earn their favour.

Getting in at the ground floor is the biggest asymmetric opportunity in social capital, but it requires you to think like an investor. You will be rewarded for redistributing capital to where it can be deployed most effectively, not for blindly following the crowd. Glancing around and waiting for social proof that so-and-so is 'cool' is for cowards. Place your chips early, stand behind your friends, and shill for the unshilled.

BRYAN'S BEAUTIFUL BUBBLE

On the face of it, it sounds reasonable to warn against forming bubbles of like-minded people and insulating oneself from groups with different views. But this is just the myth of unconditional love again, except extended to society as a whole.

My society is not very lovely. I no longer feel a sense of duty to stand loyally by its side, while it continues to do bad things in my name. Instead, I've reluctantly come around to the position of the economist Bryan Caplan, who recommends an amicable divorce.

Caplan fulfilled his lifelong dream of living in a beautiful bubble around his 40th birthday. He is now surrounded by people he respects and admires. He never hears a commercial. He forgets about the existence of professional sports for months at a time. He still leaves the security of his bubble to walk the earth, but only as a tourist:

> "Like a truffle pig, I hunt for the best that "my" society has to offer. I partake. Then I go back to my Bubble and tell myself, "America's a nice place to visit, but you wouldn't want to live there."

I believe we have a responsibility to help improve the world outside our bubbles, and I'm sure Caplan would agree: he is a leading advocate for open borders, for example. But even if you feel strongly about reforming society, you still need a bubble as a base of operations for purely pragmatic reasons.

The problem of globalisation is that it has cast us into a sea of contradictory values and norms, and there is massive friction in trying to context-switch between them. If everything is permissible, nothing is.

Trying to please everyone at once is a recipe for derangement. This is the same misunderstanding at the heart of the debate around diversity: *demographic* diversity is great, but *values-based* diversity is a nightmare. If you want to actually get anything done without constantly wading through oceans of resentment and misunderstanding, you have to choose a bubble of social reality with stable norms and values, then wall yourself off so you can no longer hear the screams of the culture war being waged outside.

It's important not to confuse a values-based bubble with an *ideological* bubble. Subscribing to an ideology is genuinely bad, insofar as it destroys optionality in the space of possible ideas: your brain is always looking for evidence to confirm your position, and shuts down any opposition. Once it becomes part of your identity, you mysteriously find yourself agreeing with all the policies and positions of your team, instead of evaluating each policy on its own merits. Exploration of new or contradictory ideas gets harder and harder, until you are fully calcified and cannot be rescued from the warped hellscape in which you now reside. Politics ought to come with a warning label: the moment it becomes part of your identity, your brain starts to dribble out your nose.

By contrast, value-based bubbles can transcend politics. Back in the days when coming out as transgender was not exactly a common occurrence, a prominent member of my barbell club transitioned from male to female. Even the edgiest teens and working-class old timers picked up her new name pretty quickly, and treated her the same as before. Nobody gave much of a shit, because the common purpose of our bubble was to lift heavy stuff, and our shared set of values was to create the kind of environment that promoted the lifting of heavy stuff.

It's even possible to have value-based bubbles that explicitly tackle politics. One of my favourite blogs is frequented by Catholics, atheists, physicists, plumbers, libertarians, lefty liberals, and Trump supporters. The only reason it all hangs together is through a shared commitment to an unusual set of conversational norms that allows everyone to co-exist in (relative) harmony.

This is much easier to achieve in real life than it is on the Internet. I don't care if my friends are black, white, trans, cis, atheist, Christian, New Age meditators, social justice advocates, or even Australian. We have different ideas about how to reform the world, but we share the same aspirational values: something like openness to experience, and a desire to build things.

I offer no opinion as to which values are best, except to say that hating things is not a personality, and will not make for a pleasant bubble. I like Caplan's heuristic, which is to build your friendships on shared passions, rather than joint contempt.

It's crucial to surround yourself with the right tribe and infect yourself with wholesome and useful memes. How to actually go about doing this?

SCENIUS BEATS GENIUS

When passionate and like-minded people congregate in one place, the whole becomes much more than the sum of its parts. Contrary to the myth of the lone genius, many of the greatest achievements in history arose out of a scene of people riffing on each other's work, contributing new ideas, and supporting one another—what musician Brian Eno calls a 'scenius'. Think the Bloomsbury Group, Florence during the Renaissance, Paris in the 1920s, the innovation hothouse of Xerox Parc, or parts of Silicon Valley today.

A scenius is a beautiful bubble that only forms under special conditions: friendly competition and appreciation, rapid exchange of new ideas, mutual sharing of success, and most importantly, a buffer against the outside world that creates space for transgression and general weirdness.

For those of us who suspect we are unlikely to single-handedly put a dent in the universe, this is very encouraging. By signal-boosting good ideas, or providing support to others in the community, we help form the ecosystem that allows greatness to flourish.

I've never deliberately set out to join a scenius, but milder versions of this strategy have worked well for me. One of my lucky mistakes was accidentally joining a tribe of 'digital nomads'—knowledge workers and entrepreneurs who cluster together in hubs throughout Southeast Asia, Latin America, and Eastern Europe. The nomadic lifestyle is too ephemeral to allow a scenius to form: all it takes is a change in visa policy or an invasion of obnoxious lifestyle designers and everyone scatters to the four corners of the world. Nevertheless, I met some of my closest friends in these hubs, because they act as a selection filter for the kind of people who share my interests and values—in this case, openness to experience, and building stuff. It's not a perfect filter, but it's a hell of a lot more fruitful than if I'd never left my hometown in rural New Zealand (population: 2787).

The other advantage of relocating some place with a constant influx of fellow pilgrims is that everyone is trying to make new friends, which means you can freely rub shoulders with people whose clique you would struggle to break into if you met them on their home turf.

Being able to drop into a scene like this hinges on already having some optionality. You need a buffer of cash, a minimalist approach to stuff, and to be free of long-term commitments. This is neither practical nor desirable for many people, so let's look at some strategies for finding your tribe which don't require you to uproot your entire life.

CHEAP OPTIONS FOR SERENDIPITY

Being in the same location as potential tribe members is not enough. You also have to create space for serendipity to strike, which means saying 'yes' to any situation which might throw you together with interesting people.

One of my most fruitful and life-changing friendships arose out of a deliberate attempt to maximise my exposure to serendipity. I hosted couch surfers at my apartment, most of whom ended up being pleasant single-serving friends. But I really clicked with a pair of travellers, one of whom insisted I had to meet her boyfriend, and invited me to a retreat in India later that year.

As a minimal little wisp, I was able to jump on anything that smelled like an interesting opportunity. So I went to the retreat, and sure enough, her boyfriend and I hit it off. I ended up collaborating on a project with him, spent a summer in his group house, and was drawn into the orbit of a whole new circle of interesting people. I can think of at least three other life-changing friendships that began through similarly unlikely chains of events— and I'm unusually *bad* at this kind of thing.

Maximising exposure to serendipity doesn't require you to book a ticket to India. No matter where you are in the world, there are almost certainly meet-ups and special interest groups in your backyard, which will lead to invitations to more events and one-on-one coffees. These are cheap options: they're time-boxed, and you're not paying for some networking event full of hustlers trying to get something out of you. If you don't like the vibe of a party, you can just go home and watch Netflix like you would have done anyway. If your coffee date doesn't work out, so what? It's one hour of your time, in exchange for a small chance of meeting someone who changes the course of your life.

Once you've found the spaces and groups most likely to select for the kind of people you want to meet, it becomes a pure numbers game. If you don't put yourself out there, your chances will always and forever be zero. Some people are preternaturally bad at taking advantage of this obvious asymmetry, and I should know: every single time I have to go out and meet new people, I bitterly curse my former self for ever agreeing to it. This is despite the fact that 95 per cent of the time I come home having had fun, and very occasionally meet someone who changes my life.

Perhaps you live on the far-flung tundras of Siberia, or have interests so niche that there are no kindred spirits around you, or you're stuck in high school and don't have any mobility. If you're the only gay Inuit in your tribe, the third-best option is to look for community online.

BLOGGING AS EXTENDED PHENOTYPE

I never understood the appeal of online communities until I started a blog. This was my second lucky accident: over the years, Deep Dish has served as a fine-grained selection filter for drawing like-minded folks into my orbit. Anyone who gets in touch has already been exposed to my intimate thoughts and interests, and not only *not* clicked away in horror, but found something that connected with them. The blog expands my surface area for serendipity far beyond what I could achieve in real life. It's like permanently being at a party, meeting interesting people from all around the world.

A friend suggested that blogs are part of our extended phenotype, and the image of a digital peacock's tail that suggestively swooshes through cyberspace has stuck in my mind. Incredibly, it *works*. People write to me to share their triumphs and woes, to swap recommendations, to challenge my thinking, and to invite me into their homes for fine seafood dinners. I've met some of my closest confidants and friends as a direct result of blogging. My girlfriend was an early Deep Dish reader. So were several of the folks who helped me put together this book.

While I was lucky to have a couple of early posts go viral, the modal outcome of blogging is that you pour your heart out and get nothing but crickets in return. It takes a long time and lot of effort to build a following, which means any social capital should really be viewed as a happy byproduct of the main goal (for me, enforced writing practice and figuring out what I think).

Not everyone should start a blog. But everyone interested in building social capital should do *something* to extend their phenotype, be it a portfolio website, a Soundcloud, an open-source project, or—and I can't believe I'm about to say this—a Twitter account.

For a long time I thought Twitter was cancer, and using it straight out of the box, it is. But after watching artful users like Sonya Mann and Visakan Veerasamy draw together crews of fellow travellers, I realised I was doing it wrong: I'd never managed to get past the default setting—snark and hot takes —to customise it in a way that aligned with my aspirational values.

Social media platforms are not 'good' or 'bad'. They are just tools: good if we use them for building treehouses; not so good if we use them for bashing in the skulls of our enemies.

The low-friction microblogging format gives Twitter a much worse signal-to-noise ratio than longform blogs. But the same features that make it so obnoxious also create huge upside: everyone is accessible, the feedback loop is much tighter, and you can quickly get on the radar of anyone you find interesting. Someone said Twitter has become what LinkedIn always wanted to be, and after watching my tweet-savvy friends form communities, start businesses, make friends, and get job opportunities, I think this might be true.

One of the main obstacles to using these platforms skilfully is the misconception that 'connection' has something to do with being surrounded with people. In reality, being in close proximity to the average Twitter user is much more likely to be deranging. Meaningful connections can only be built by ruthlessly min-maxing in ways that might appear *antisocial*: don't follow celebrities or big accounts, be extremely liberal with the mute/block button, pay no attention to the latest trending outrage, and build a beautiful little bubble with the people who share your values and interests.

DUNBAR'S DIMINISHING RETURNS

Something like one in 10 people has no close friends. While the loneliness 'epidemic' is bogus—there is no evidence that modernity is actually making things worse—it still sucks that so many people are starving for connection. My guess is that this is caused by some combination of the following:

- Lack of time to invest in relationships due to a myopic focus on earning and consumption
- Harmful social norms about being a 'climber'
- Misfiring attempts to build social capital (e.g. celebrity worship)
- Failure to make use of technologies that facilitate connection (e.g. my Twitter mistake)

On the resilience side of the equation, a lack of strong relationships is disastrous, and occasionally fatal. An active social life increases longevity, strengthens the immune system, improves mood and mental health, and is the single biggest predictor of experiential happiness. We are social apes to our core, and even self-professed misanthropes benefit from regular doses of 'social medicine'.

On the growth side, being well-connected and plugged into the right scene opens a whole lot of doors. Social capital compounds through network effects: every new relationship you form opens up a whole new circle of potential friends and collaborators.

But stacking up social capital eventually runs into a point of diminishing returns, just like the other components of optionality.

You've probably heard of **Dunbar's Number**, which suggests we can only sustain 150 stable relationships, as determined by comparing the volume of our brains against other primates. But the pop science version of this idea misrepresents Robin Dunbar's research. In fact, there are *several* Dunbar numbers, forming concentric circles of connectedness (Fig. 3.7).

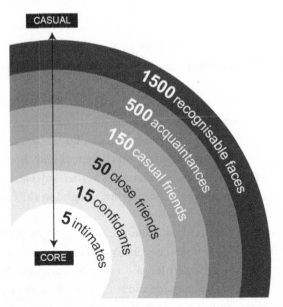

Figure 3.7. The Dunbar numbers form concentric circles of stronger and weaker connections.

The other little-known finding is that these relationships are not distributed evenly. A handful of super-socialites blow out the average, which is misleadingly high compared to the median (typical) number. Once again we see the telltale signs of the Matthew effect at work: if social capital follows a power law distribution, there will be extreme inequalities between the haves and the have-nots.

Super-connectors work in politics, entertainment, media, finance, and other industries where having the right names in your Rolodex is quite literally priceless. While their social capital compounds through network effects of new introductions, it's not an entirely passive investment: they must also devote some large proportion of their time to maintaining and cultivating relationships.

I'm not sure this is a good use of time for a typical person, and it certainly doesn't appeal to me. If Dunbar's numbers are correct, then anyone who is not a super-connector will quickly run into the point of diminishing returns. Studies have found that the likes of Twitter or Facebook don't actually increase the *capacity* of the circles, which shouldn't be all that surprising. As Dunbar pointed out, the amount of social capital at our disposal is ultimately limited by our time and attention:

> "If you garner connections with more people, you end up distributing your fixed amount of social capital more thinly so the average capital per person is lower."

My observation of Extremely Online people is that it's easy to butter your bread too thinly. Partly this is a problem of scale, but there are also inevitable trade-offs between time spent building social capital and time spent actually *deploying* it: I can't help but be suspicious whether anyone hanging out on Twitter all day is doing any kind of deep or meaningful work (I am just jealous; probably you can do both).

This suggests another barbell strategy: on the hyper-conservative end, invest in the inner circles first, and never stop investing in them. If you have 15 close friends—people who would let you crash on their couch for a slightly uncomfortable period of time—that's about 14 more than many people.

On the aggressive end of the barbell, take out cheap asymmetric options to expand your reach as far as possible, but don't get bogged down maintaining lots of tenuous middle-ground connections, or waste your valuable Dunbar's slots on celebrities or big shots who will neither benefit from your affection nor reciprocate it.

RECAP

If you have toxic people in your life, the single most important thing you can do is get out of range of their grasping claws. You don't have to cut people out altogether, but you can make it clear that your friendship is conditional.

A social support net is an insurance policy against black swans. Pay into the pool by taking every opportunity to help people. If you never end up making a 'claim', so much the better.

Invest in your oldest and most stable relationships first. Family and old friends are both Lindy-approved and non-fungible.

Giving praise and gratitude is a ridiculously cheap option with unbounded upside. Instead of shilling for famous people who don't need it and will never reciprocate, try to invest in young or talented people who are not yet well-known. Arbitraging this attentional inequality benefits you, them, and the world at large.

Soft secession is a valid form of civil disobedience. The secret to staying sane and effective is cultivating a bubble of like-minded people. Determine membership based on shared values and interests, rather than ideology or joint contempt.

Parachute into a 'scenius' and make yourself part of the ecosystem. If this is not possible, maximise your surface area to serendipity by saying 'yes' to every cheap option that might expose you to new tribe members.

Take advantage of the incredible connectivity of the Internet.

Twitter, blogging, and email are all cheap options that expand your surface area far beyond the bounds of geography.

Don't spread your social capital too thinly. Be wary of time spent cultivating a lot of weak online relationships if it comes at the expense of your core Dunbar circles.

ASYMMETRIES IN KNOWLEDGE CAPITAL

E VERY NEW TECHNOLOGY GENERATES its own moral panic: TV emits alpha waves that rot our brains, video games encourage violence, social media destroys our attention spans, news media is only making us dumber; fidget spinners are probably the equivalent of black-tar heroin.

In reality, it would be a stretch to describe any of these passive leisure activities as Bottomless Pits of Doom. They might be dangerous, but only insofar as they're dead ends that lead us away from valuable options. As with anything in the sticky middle, the real cost is the missed opportunity.

According to Nielsen, the average American soaks up 34 hours of TV each week. Over the course of a year, that adds up to a red-eyed binge of 10 straight weeks: as if you settled down in front of the set in late January, and didn't stop to eat or sleep until your zombified body finally arose from the tomb on Easter Sunday.

Extend it to a lifetime, and the average person will rack up 100,000 hours of TV-watching. What does this vast ocean of passive leisure time trade off against? Perhaps we lose some social capital: these activities don't lend themselves to creating or maintaining close ties, and encourage us to waste our precious Dunbar slots on pseudo-relationships with fictional characters and celebrities. Health capital is another minor victim: Netflix's confirmation that its real competitor is 'sleep' has to be the closest a company has come to an outright admission of evil.

But the biggest loser by far is knowledge capital—the sum total of all of our skills, qualifications, ideas, and understanding of the world. Building knowledge capital is a form of *active* leisure. What if we could repurpose even a small fraction of that great ocean of passivity towards learning stuff?

This is the **100,000 hour opportunity.** In the space of a lifetime, we might become an accomplished pianist, *and* a chess Grandmaster, *and* a competitive athlete, *and* proficient in a second or third language, *and* an amateur chef, *and* a published poet, *and* a knitting maven, *and* a skilled programmer, *and* an expert in non-violent communication, *and* a community leader.

Or we could watch a whole lot of TV.

Every skill you acquire, and every item of knowledge, is worth something. A university degree opens up your options; so does knowing how to boil an egg. In this chapter, we'll build a rough option pricing model for figuring out which skills, knowledge, and practices are worth investing in.

There is a great opportunity here that arises from the confluence of three unprecedented events: more information is freely available than at any other point in history, we have more leisure time at our disposal than ever, and accumulating broad skills and knowledge has never been so valuable.

We'll start on the mundane end of the spectrum with defensive skills that build resilience, then move through to the asymmetric opportunities for growth, including earning compound interest on our knowledge.

A FORCE FIELD OF COMPETENCE

My sparsely-populated island home was first settled in the 13th century, when the Māori made a series of extraordinary voyages across the ocean to tame a country untouched for millions of years. Europeans and Chinese began to arrive from the 18th century onwards. Each wave of settlers found themselves thousands of kilometres away from home. When problems arose, they had to improvise with whatever resources were at hand. As the legend goes, a true-blue Kiwi can fix anything using only a piece of No. 8 fencing wire—like a low-budget rural version of MacGyver, in which our hero must solve the mystery of the tractor's dodgy spark plug.

While this pioneering resourcefulness has mostly faded to a fond memory in New Zealand's cultural consciousness, it still lives on in a fringe of tinkerers and old-timers. I should know, because my dad is one of them. He built the house I grew up in, despite not being a builder. He can fix just about anything, field dress an animal, propagate a plant, program a website, write an essay, swing a sledgehammer, fell a tree, cook a decent feed, and change a nappy—not to mention work his regular day job.

People like my dad radiate a force field of competence that is extremely comforting. I imagine this ability to bend life to your will must feel pretty great. More prosaically, it also builds a safety buffer of optionality. The broader your skills, the less you have to outsource to others, and the more resilient you become: when the zombie apocalypse arrives, my dad is the kind of guy you want on your team.

In some cases, the atrophy of basic life skills borders on criminal: I once met an exchange student who didn't know how to use a microwave, having grown up with domestic servants waiting on him hand and foot. Dependency is briefly cute in pets and small children, but there's something unsettling about someone well into their 20s or 30s who proudly declares they are 'adulting' when they perform some extremely basic task.

On the other hand, forcing yourself to learn how to do something just to try to live up to some kind of 'real man' archetype is also kind of pathetic. The pioneering spirit of self-reliance was born of isolation and necessity; conditions which no longer hold true in most parts of the world. It's important to get a handle on basic life skills, but beyond that, there's nothing wrong with *strategic* incompetence. You can and should outsource non-essential tasks to your heart's content, so long as you can earn a higher return by applying your efforts elsewhere.

AN OPTION-PRICING MODEL FOR SKILLS

The first step in figuring out which skills are worth 'insourcing' (that is, paying yourself to do a task, instead of outsourcing it) is to put a dollar value on your time.

Let's say you're thinking about making your lunches at home. Maybe it takes you one hour to prepare a week's worth, for a net saving of $15. Instead of comparing this hourly rate to your salary or wages, compare it to your income *at the margin*—what additional earning opportunities do you have? Saving that $15 of lunch money is the equivalent of going out and earning ~$20 by conventional means, because any 'work' you pay yourself to do is tax-free. So if you can earn more than $20 at the margin—perhaps by insourcing some other more lucrative task—you might be better off doing that instead.

The second question to ask: what bucket is this time coming out of? Doing your own taxes drains the 'hard mental effort' bucket, which trades off against other knowledge work. But mowing the lawns or cooking might be more akin to leisure time, which you can do even when you're mentally spent.

The ideal situation is to pay yourself to do something intrinsically enjoyable or satisfying. If a task falls somewhere in the middle, you might apply a partial discount rate: mowing the lawns only feels *half* as arduous as 'real' work because it gets your heart rate up and you feel a Clint Eastwoodesque pride at maintaining your own property, so you're happy to accept half the pay.

Now we have a formula for valuing your time:

- Calculate the hourly 'pay' you could earn by insourcing a task
- Adjust that hourly rate by 33 per cent (or whatever your tax rate is)
- Apply a partial discount if the insourced task is more enjoyable than regular work
- Compare against other opportunities at the margin (leisure, work, insourcing a different task)

The next factor to consider is the upfront cost. Most skills require some kind of investment before you actually start to reap the rewards: a simple bicycle repair might take hours for a beginner, and the first batch of homebrew beer usually tastes like yeasty mud. At some point, you'll get frustrated as hell, have to start over from scratch, and wish you'd called in the professionals. And perhaps you should have!

To complete our crude option-pricing model, we need to estimate the cost of acquiring a skill—the tools, training expenses, and number of hours invested to reach proficiency. Finally, we add the potential upside: what do we stand to gain, and how many opportunities will we get to put the skill into practice?

For example, here's how my dad might have broken down the decision to learn to use a chainsaw when he was a young man (Table 3.1).

VALUE OF TIME	$25 an hour
COST OF HIRING AN ARBORIST	$75 an hour
NET UPSIDE	$50 an hour
UPFRONT COST	$300 (4 hours to learn safety and maintenance + $200 saw and safety gear)
BREAKEVEN	6 hours
EXPECTED USE	25 hours a year
OPTION VALUE:	$950 in first year

Table 3.1. Calculating the option value of acquiring a given skill.

Even if my dad's initial expectations turned out to be wrong and the option never paid off, the potential upside was so large that it was clearly a no-brainer. Sure enough, he has saved a small fortune by insourcing these kind of skills. When an urbanite like me runs the equation, the option is not only near-worthless, but comes with a risk of ruin: since I almost never get a chance to wield a chainsaw, I am much more likely to injure myself or drop a tree across my house.

Men seem to be particularly susceptible to the gung-ho 'DIY everything' failure mode. If an arcane financial event lands in my lap, my instinct is to save my accountant's fee by figuring out how to handle it myself. I'm a smart guy! I'm good with money! But forging ahead would demonstrate I am neither of these things. Running the option-pricing model reminds me that acquiring this highly specific knowledge would be unpleasant and time-consuming, I will never get an opportunity to use it again, and there's a decent chance I'll screw it up. The option value here is *negative*: much better for me to remain ignorant, and call in the professionals.

Failing to price options correctly leads to penny-wise and pound-foolish behaviour:

- If you're doing something you hate just to save a buck

- If there's a risk of ruin from straying beyond your competence (e.g. electrical wiring, complicated taxes)
- If you can earn a higher marginal return elsewhere
- If you could better use that time to level up other skills

General competence skills fall in the boring middle. They often have a positive option value, but there's no potential for unbounded upside—the only way you can 'earn' more money is by doing more work.

There's nothing wrong with that: if I can pay myself the equivalent of a tax-free $50 an hour to experience the challenges and satisfaction of building a retaining wall, you better believe I'm heading straight to the hardware store on Sunday morning.

Expanding your force-field of competence is a hedge against downside risk, and also just a plain satisfying way to live, to the point where it often makes sense to acquire these skills even when you don't have a comparative advantage (i.e. you could earn a higher return applying your efforts elsewhere). We will leave the economist David Ricardo screaming in his grave for now, and return to the 'silent risk' of specialisation in Book V.

Even if you are a brilliant person who values your time unusually highly, not everything can be outsourced. There is a second class of skills that you have no choice but to learn yourself.

NON-NEGOTIABLE SKILLS

Derek Parfit dedicated his life to unpicking some of the knottiest problems in moral philosophy, to the point where merely thinking about suffering was enough to bring him to tears. As his years ran thin and the sense of urgency increased, Parfit streamlined his entire life so he could devote every waking moment to his work. He ate the exact same spartan meals every day, drank instant coffee with water from the tap rather than waste an extra minute boiling the kettle, and kept a book on his dresser so he could read philosophy while he was putting his socks on.

In other words, Parfit was an expert at min-maxing. Thank goodness he didn't waste his precious brain juice learning how to build retaining walls. But even in the most extreme edge cases, there are limits to narrow specialisation.

And so, in Parfit's final decade of life, he took an hour every evening to furiously pedal away on a stationary bicycle.

Sport and exercise fall into a class of non-negotiable skills which can't be outsourced. I'm not going to re-litigate Chapter 14, but it's bizarre how many otherwise smart people fail to act on this glaringly obvious asymmetry.

Part of the problem seems to be the misconception that those who cultivate their physical potential are vain or stupid. I was terrified of the 180kg trainer at the first gym I joined, who looked like he might eat me alive for a light snack. But we soon became friends, and I ended up being conscripted as a test subject for his postgrad research. Having received his master's degree, Colm Woulfe now programs and coaches his own athletes, and competes in the World's Strongest Man tournament.

Even after getting to know people like Colm, I sometimes make the mistake of assuming buff movie stars and fitness models are dumb or one-dimensional—until I find out the slightest bit of actual information about them. Arnold Schwarzenegger grew up in a poor village with a violent, alcoholic father. He migrated to the US with very little English, started a series of businesses that made him a millionaire, then went on to excel at the highest possible levels in bodybuilding, movies, and politics. The whole 'robotic meathead' persona was something he *deliberately cultivated* to trick people into underestimating him.

Dolph Lundgren, the walking slab of muscle best known as Ivan Drago from *Rocky IV*, is a Fulbright scholar, speaks six languages, and has a master's degree in chemical engineering. Terry Crews, not content with being an NFL player, bodybuilder, actor, comedian, and the most wholesome person to walk God's green earth, is a brilliant visual artist. The physician Oliver Sacks penned beautiful essays on mortality, neurology, and music, while moonlighting as a record-breaking powerlifting monster nicknamed "Dr Squat". Marie Curie was an avid cyclist. Alan Turing was a good enough distance runner to be an Olympics contender. And so on.

The point is, Derek Parfit was probably onto something with his stationary bike routine. Besides cultivating physical potential, we might also put interpersonal skills in the non-negotiable category, as well as self-care skills, like cognitive behavioural therapy or meditation. No-one else can do them for us, and they improve our lives on every level.

I've invoked this pantheon of demigods because they're familiar reference points, and they show us what is possible. Obviously there are hard limits:

repeat a million affirmations and read all the self-help books in the library—there's still no way you're going to earn a chemical engineering PhD if you have a below room temperature IQ. But acquiring broad skills is a principle which scales all the way down to us lesser mortals.

Arguably, the case for generalism is much *stronger* for average Joes and Janes. Without certain blessings—genetic or otherwise—it's impossible to push to the cutting edge of most specialised fields. But if you find a way to combine your modestly competent skills, you can excel in *an entirely new niche* of your own making.

THE TALENT STACK

The Renaissance men and women of yore were only able to make six new discoveries before breakfast because the low-hanging fruit had not yet been plucked. By today's standards, these great thinkers would be surpassed by plenty of bright undergraduates. The frontier of human knowledge has expanded so far that it now takes years or decades to make an original contribution, and there will come a time when it is no longer possible to become a true polymath: it's hard enough to reach the frontier in *one* narrow domain, let alone two or more.

The good news is you don't need to be the best in the world to succeed. Heck, you don't even need to be in the top 10 per cent.

Scott Adams, creator of the *Dilbert* comic strip, describes himself as "a rich and famous cartoonist who doesn't draw well". By his own admission, his artistic skills are middling, and at social gatherings, he's rarely the funniest person in the room. When Adams was starting out, the resources at his disposal were an MBA, years of experience as an office drone, an early interest in Internet culture, and a decent sense of humour. The number of aspiring cartoonists in the centre of this unlikely Venn diagram was exactly one:

> "If you think extraordinary talent and a maniacal pursuit of excellence are necessary for success, I say that's just one approach, and probably the hardest. When it comes to skills, quantity often beats quality."

Adams calls this strategy the 'talent stack'. The idea is that you combine two or more skills you're pretty good at, until no-one else has your exact mix.

Since there are an infinite number of permutations, anyone who cultivates broad skills and interests can eventually fuse them into a unique stack.

Plenty of scientific breakthroughs have been made at the intersection of seemingly unrelated fields, as have new business ideas and innovations. As Peter Thiel argues in *Zero to One*, every successful company—be it Facebook or a family diner—is a monopoly. You don't want to *compete* with other businesses, or play the imitation game. You want to carve out a new category all of your own, and then dominate it.

A talent stack can expand the frontiers of human knowledge, but it also scales down to the humblest career ambitions. As investing legend Charlie Munger observes, most of us are never going to become pro tennis players or chess grandmasters. But we can still succeed by expanding our circle of competence, and working hard to develop an "unassailable edge". For most of us, the game of life is something like trying to become the best plumbing contractor in Bemidji.

When building a talent stack, the idea is to look for skills which will have a force-multiplier effect on your existing efforts. In 'Levels of Action', Alyssa Vance gives the example of learning to type: if you take 10 hour-long classes, each of which improves your ability by 20 per cent, you'll get 6x better at typing. This is a much better use of time than spending that same 10 hours pecking away at the keyboard.

Which brings us to the mathematical case in favour of being a generalist. You've heard of the **Pareto Principle**, or 80/20 rule: twenty per cent of your customers generate 80 per cent of your profits, and so on. While this is not actually a rule, the general idea is that in any domain governed by power laws, a small number of inputs are responsible for a large proportion of the value captured (Fig. 3.8).

Professional dilettantes like Tim Ferriss have used the Pareto principle to elevate accelerated learning to an art form. For example, practicing a handful of guitar chords in the I–IV–V progression of each key immediately unlocks thousands of songs. If you're trying to pick up a second language, focusing on a small group of keystone words and grammar rules get you to 'conversational' very quickly. Gym noobs make rapid gains in strength and muscle mass in a very short period of time by doing a few simple full-body workouts.

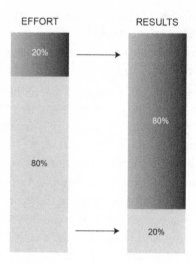

Figure 3.8. The Pareto Principle suggests that 20% of what you do leads to 80% of your results.

After you put in the initial 20 per cent of targeted effort, you start to run up against the law of diminishing returns. The further along the curve you push, the harder it is to make progress. Adding a few kilograms to an elite powerlifter's total might take an entire 12-week training cycle, while a beginner could see the same progress in the space of a single workout.

If you follow these efficient pathways, you only have to invest 20 per cent of your effort into any given field to capture most of the value. The implication is that it takes about the same amount of time and effort to truly master one skill as it does to become competent in *five* domains.

Is it better to be a highly technically skilled writer who can recite *Strunk & White* by heart, or a good one who also happens to have a solid grasp on marketing and web design, speaks Mandarin, and studies anthropology? I made up this example in five seconds; you can fill in the blanks yourself. The point is that the skills in a talent stack don't merely add value—they have the potential to *multiply* value.

Some obvious talent stack contenders include writing, time management, public speaking, sales and marketing, accounting, statistics, programming, and design, all of which can fuse with just about any core trade to give you an unassailable edge. Again, you don't have to be world-class at any of these things— you just have to be better than the other plumbing contractors in Bemidji.

Some of these skills might be planned and acquired strategically from the top down, but they can also emerge bottom-up out of your interests and inclinations—which also has the great advantage of being intrinsically motivating.

INTRINSIC INTERESTS

"Where do you get your ideas?"

This is a bewildering and depressing question, and any aspiring writer who has to ask it is doomed to failure. Every tiny facet of the world is so ridiculously fascinating that you'd have to be deaf, dumb, and blind not to notice. If you want to be interesting, *be interested*.

Lack of intrinsic interest is a big red flag for learning any skill. In the case of general competency, to the extent that something feels like a chore, the formula for deciding whether you should insource it becomes that much less attractive.

In the case of non-negotiable skills, stickability is everything. You have to find something you actually enjoy, or can bake into your overall sense of identity. This is why playing a sport—even a solo sport, where you compete against yourself—is much better than 'exercising'.

In the case of a talent stack, the ideal is to forge a career that intersects with one or more of your hobbies, and renders the notion of work-life balance obsolete.

Following your interests and hobbies won't necessarily advance your career, or even pay off in any externally measurable way. I'm not sure how I'm going to leverage my skills as an amateur guitarist who can't quite make it through a song without forgetting at least one of the chords. With that being said, playing music has helped me understand maths a little better. It has expanded the range and resonance of my writing (see what I did there). I've bonded with people who I otherwise wouldn't have. Perhaps the plasticity of my brain has improved in some small way.

Most importantly, *it's fun*.

Forget all the strategic stuff for a second. If you lived in a post-scarcity world, and the only thing that mattered was maximising your own enjoyment, how would you choose to spend your time?

A truly self-interested person would still end up acquiring a bunch of skills. This is partly because it provides a lot of life satisfaction: we don't remember how we felt in the moment—blistered fingertips, covered in grease in the belly of the engine, cursing and cramped, lungs heaving—but we do remember the sense of achievement in standing back with a beer in hand to survey our handiwork.

Active leisure is also a rich source of experiential pleasure: the endorphins of a runner's high, the joy of curling up with a fascinating book, surfing the trance-like state in the sweet spot between boredom and difficulty. The simplest argument in favour of acquiring broad skills is that it's a reliable way to get into these immersive flow states, and escape the usual trap of fixating on external outcomes.

So that's the first measure of knowledge capital: the breadth and depth of your skills. The second measure is the quality and quantity of your *ideas*.

THE CHEAPEST OPTION ON THE PLANET

A book is a pocket-sized portal through time and space that lets you crawl inside someone else's brain and try on completely different ideas, strategies, emotional states, and ways of living.

Some books are damp squibs: you waste a little time and a little money. Many more are moderately interesting. And a rare few trigger what the economist Tyler Cowen calls a "view quake". These are the ideas so wild that they set your grey matter lurching and heaving, and jolt your brain out of familiar ruts. When the tremors stop, nothing looks the same again.

Once you start this process, you can't stop: the danger of reading Ayn Rand or Karl Marx as an impressionable teen is that your foundations might begin to calcify. From this point on, the only answer is sustained creative destruction.

To anyone in possession of a library card or an Internet connection, the transformative upside of reading books is available for the low, low price of zero dollars. Even if you buy books—which you should, for reasons that will become clear—the return on investment is off the charts. I guess I have spent maybe $2000 on books so far, which has enriched me at least 100x over, and probably closer to three orders of magnitude.

Up until a few hundred years ago, books were eye-wateringly expensive options, priced out of range of all but a tiny elite. Most people were illiterate, and the largest and most famous medieval libraries had fewer than 2000 volumes. Now even the most impoverished corner bookshop can best that, and there are millions of titles available online with the push of a button.

The opportunity here is vast and unprecedented, but few people take advantage of it. The typical American finishes four books a year, allocating less than 1 per cent of their leisure time to reading. Lots of people haven't read a single book since high school. What gives?

Besides passive leisure stealing away our attention, two hurdles stand in our way. The first is our misplaced reverence for books—a hangover from the days when every volume was quite literally a precious treasure, and should be venerated as such. In a sea of $10 paperbacks and self-published screeds of varying quality, we need new norms.

The asymmetry of reading only remains juicy if we treat books like the cheap options they are. That means bailing out at the earliest possible opportunity, skimming with abandon, being promiscuous in our appetites, and abandoning the idea that it's virtuous to slog through some interminable volume for the sake of completion. Imagine how many people turn to the easy comfort of Netflix because they can't bring themselves to make eye contact with the great foreboding lump of James Joyce's *Ulysses* sitting on the nightstand.

We also need to start disrespecting books physically. Librarians, cover your ears: if you are the owner of a book, you should crack its spine and extract the marrow by any means necessary—dog-ear the pages, scribble all over it, feed it crumbs and coffee stains, sleep with it under your pillow. Reading is an *interaction* between author and reader, not a passive one-way street.

Which brings us to the second hurdle. It's often said that a reading habit generates compound interest on your knowledge. Unfortunately, this is not true. Personally, I've spent thousands of hours reading books that I have almost completely forgotten. I might be able to give you the main idea, and maybe dredge up an example, but almost everything besides the view-quake insights disappear without a trace. The knowledge not only fails to compound; it *degrades*. Passive reading is not all that much different to watching Netflix—information goes in one ear and out the other.

If we're reading purely for pleasure, that's fine. If we want to earn compound interest on our knowledge capital, we're missing a second step.

No-one is naive enough to think that merely saving money and waiting for something to happen is enough to generate compound interest. We need somewhere to put it, like a bank account, and a practice for making it grow—an investing strategy. The same is true of knowledge capital.

EARNING COMPOUND INTEREST ON IDEAS

If you asked me to choose one item to save from a fire, I don't even have to think about it. My single most valuable possession is my 'commonplace book': a big old heaving mess of several thousand interconnected ideas and confusions and open questions, and much more than the sum of its parts. Once it reached critical mass, it took on a life of its own. I am happy to anthropomorphise it, and I guess I would pay low six figures to save it from oblivion; probably in the same range as a beloved pet.

In the dark ages Before Google (B.G.) people couldn't idly search the collective fruits of human civilisation while sitting on the toilet. Instead, they had to scrapbook their own homemade internets: a patchwork of collected quotes, snippets, articles, notes, and ideas, interspersed with their own thoughts and reactions. This book served as an all-purpose repository of cool stuff, hence the 'common'—there was no specific theme, no chronological order, and no rigid structure.

While it might sound unnatural to keep your thoughts and ideas jumbled together like this, the exact opposite is true.

Every generation is doomed to model the brain after the most advanced technology of the age. Aristotle and his bros thought it was an ice-box for tempering the humours or whatever, then we had the hydraulic model of the brain pumping thoughts around, then the clockwork model, then electrical lines, and now we're stuck on the computer-as-brain model.

We've grown up storing our files in a bunch of folders neatly organised by hierarchy, and trying to taxonomise everything in discrete categories. As each new idea or nugget of information drifts along the River of Knowledge, we funnel it into progressively smaller boxes until it finds its final resting place. The boxes only have one plane open to the river, and can't overlap, which means the surface area grows in a linear fashion. This 'file-drawer' approach is very tidy, very unnatural, and completely kills the mood for the kind of freaky ideas sex we want to encourage.

By contrast, a commonplace book gives us a collection of mental models to 'hook' ideas drifting down the river from as many angles as possible. Once they're part of the structure, we can hang new ideas on them, and so on. We end up with a sprawling latticework that expands its surface area in a non-linear fashion; like beavers took a bunch of acid and built a four-dimensional dam out of coat hangers.

The psychedelic beaver dam approach not only helps new ideas stick, but creates more opportunities to combine knowledge in original ways. Whenever something juicy comes floating down the River of Knowledge, we have any number of hooks to snag it with:

"Oh! This is an example of X, except in the field of Y. I think I have a case study like this. It reminds me of Dr. Z's concept of A, except the main difference here seems to be B. I wonder how it applies to C?"

This is called 'associative knowledge', and it's a much better reflection of how the brain actually works. There are no discrete categories in your mind: only a bunch of weaker or stronger connections and patterns.

This gives us the general principle for compounding our ideas. For the specifics of how to put it into practice, we turn to a prolific German professor and his slip-box.

———

Niklas Luhmann was one of the great sociologists and systems theorists of the 20th century. He wrote more than 70 books and hundreds of articles, many of which became classics, at an almost effortless pace.

The secret to Luhmann's freakish productivity lay in his research method. When he read something interesting, he wrote it down on a notecard with a unique identifier, accompanied by his own thoughts. Then it went into his slip-box (in German, *zettelkasten*). The placement of the card was determined not by the topic, but by how it related to his own writing, thinking, and existing notes. Any one card might end up with dozens of branching threads and subthreads.

Luhmann's insight was that starting with a blank page and casting around for inspiration gets the creative process bass-ackwards. After years of building chains of thoughts and connected ideas, you will have more topics ricocheting around your skull and begging to be put on the page than you can possibly get to in a lifetime.

In the ideal case, converting the contents of your slip-box into finished prose is just a formality. This is never quite true for me—I always learn a lot during the final assembly—but I have usually done the bulk of the work months or years before I put pen to paper. As a general rule, if you need to open Google for anything other than fact-checking, you're probably not ready to write on a topic.

To the extent that I have any secret sauce, this is it. Here's my bastardised version of the Zettelkasten method:

1. Collection

Mark up interesting ideas as you read, but don't stop to second-guess yourself, or worry about which colour highlighter you should use. Most note-taking advice is useless because it focuses on this first stage, which is almost entirely personal preference.

Let your notes breathe for a few weeks, then come back with a fresh set of eyes. Dump anything that seems banal, and curate the ideas that are worthy of entering your permanent collection.

2. Deconstruction

Break each note down into its atomic components. I like to write a catchy heading that sums up the gist of the idea, then nest any subcomponents or further explanation into a few bullets as required.

I use a digital commonplace book—Roam Research—which assigns a unique ID to every bullet point. If you're using pen and paper, make sure you don't include more than one idea per card.

3. Assonance

Take the new ideas and smash them up against your existing model of the world. Hopefully you can sort of prod them into having sex with something else in your database:

- What does this 'rhyme' with?

- Is it isomorphic to this other thing (has the same form/relationship)?
- Or is it orthogonal (at right angles to it)?
- Is this a subset of a broader pattern? Or a superset?

4. Dissonance

Now do the same thing, but look for conflicts:

- How does this jive with my experience?
- What are the best criticisms?
- Does it clash with my existing model of the world?

Maybe one idea will kill the other. More likely, you'll find they're addressing different situations or use cases. Again, this helps you better understand both the old ideas and the new one.

There's no need to resolve a conflict on the spot, especially if it's some thorny issue that would require a ton of additional research. You might just have a vague hunch that something's fishy, and jot down a note to compare against other sources.

5. Remixing

We want to accumulate atomic blocks of ideas that are infinitely remixable, and can be assembled into whatever form you need. Sometimes a note will come to fruition in an unexpected context years later. But if you find you're rarely applying what you've learned in real life, something has gone wrong.

Everyone is a student at one time or another; everyone is a researcher; everyone is building something. So how is it that the commonplace book, kept by everyone from Julius Caesar to Virginia Woolf, has fallen so far from favour? Why is the Zettelkasten not a household name?

My guess is that it's partly because the tools just weren't there. The web has been a great disappointment in this sense: Google is gamed by SEO-savvy content marketers to the point of being unusable, wikis and note-taking apps are bound by the file-drawer approach, and Ted Nelson's original vision for hypertext had faded into the dusty dreams of starry-eyed fools and crackpots.

As for the original Zettelkasten method, with its arcane numbering systems and physical index cards, there's just too much friction. I don't want to lug a bunch of fireproof safes around, and I hate writing by hand; I barely earned my pen license in primary school and it's all been downhill from there.

One of my most interesting side projects in recent years has been helping out with the aforementioned Roam Research; a startup which has attracted a cult following in this field. Roam is deliberately structured as a psychedelic beaver dam: a knowledge graph of unique block-level ideas that can be endless remixed in new contexts, with bidirectional hyperlinks and references that make it effortless to draw connections between them.

Roam's initial development was backed by AI researchers, but it's now being used in so many contexts and in such creative ways that I can't keep up. Whether you use Roam, or one of the many clones which have sprung up to copy its features, I strongly suggest you take advantage of the new generation of tools to start earning compound interest on your knowledge capital.

(Visit thedeepdish.org/zettelkasten for an in-depth guide to my process, including examples of my personal Roam workflow.)

RECAP

The 100,000 hour opportunity describes the great ocean of passive leisure time that we might choose to repurpose to more active pursuits.

General competency skills build a buffer of optionality that protects against uncertainty. The broader your skills, the less you have to outsource to others, and the more resilient you become to future shocks.

We can use a crude option-pricing model to decide which skills are worth acquiring, based on the value of our time, the upfront costs, and the potential upside.

Failing to price options leads to penny-wise and pound-foolish behaviour. Even a rough sanity check will save us from investing in skills that don't pay off.

We don't have to live up to the Renaissance Man ideal, but some skills are non-negotiable: cultivating physical potential, interpersonal skills, and self-care. No-one else can do them for us, and they improve our lives on every level.

The case for generalism is much stronger for average Joes and Janes. If you cultivate broad skills and interests, you can eventually fuse them into a talent stack that gives you an unassailable edge.

Books are the cheapest options in existence, but only if we treat them as such. Skim, scribble, read multiple titles at the same time, and quit early without feeling guilty.

Compound interest in knowledge capital does not accrue through passive reading. You need a place to store your knowledge, like a commonplace book, and an investing strategy, like the Zettelkasten method.

IV

RHIZIKON

RHIZIKON. (noun) from the ancient Greek ῥιζικόν: *root, risk, hazard.*

INTRODUCTION

LONE FIGURE DANGLES from the tangled roots of a fig tree overhanging the narrow strait. Directly below, the monstrous whirlpool Charybdis sucks his raft into its maw with a horrible splintering noise. The figure slowly, agonisingly, edges along the roots towards the other side of the passage.

Suddenly, six vast heads on serpentine necks shoot out of the spray, their jaws snapping shut inches away from his face, and the stench of rotten meat on their breath. The fog swirls and lifts for a moment, revealing a glimpse of the vast bulk of Scylla, the hideous monster that guards the other side of the strait. The panicked figure scrambles back to the middle of the passage: caught between the devil and the deep blue sea.

The root gives way, then catches again, and a small avalanche of dirt tumbles off the dangling figure. We move closer, to the effort-strained face of Odysseus. Our hero has safely made it past the Sirens, only to find himself in an even worse bind. His ship has been destroyed and his entire crew drowned —vengeance for slaughtering the cattle of the Sun God—and now his own life hangs from a thread. It's been kind of a shitty week.

At least Odysseus' suffering wasn't for nothing. His misadventures gave us the very concept of risk, the etymology of which is rooted in roots: *rhiza* or *rhizikon*, as in, the trailing tendrils of the fig tree that our hero clung onto for dear life. Rhizikon also came to mean cliff, and was later used as a seafaring term for a rock or other hazard to be avoided.

Unfortunately, that's about as far as it went. For all their remarkable prescience, the Greeks did not have a sophisticated understanding of risk.[1] As far as they were concerned, there could be no regularity to earthly events, and everyone simply had to accept their fate. The Greek conception of 'risk management' went about as far as burning sacrifices before a sea voyage, and trying not to anger the gods—say, by eating their prized livestock.

Thousands of years after Odysseus made his fateful voyage, we remain bound to him across the ages by the universal human experience of risk-taking —the stomach-churning excitement of hovering on the knife edge between promise and peril. But we mustn't forget that the reason our hands tremble and adrenaline courses through our veins is that *risk can get us killed*. Odysseus might have been favoured by the gods, but he was also responsible for sending boatloads of young men to their deaths.

Our fates are no longer entirely in the hands of the gods. We understand much more about the nature of risk than Odysseus, and can make calculated decisions. Crucially, we also understand more about the limits of our knowledge—the tracts of uncertainty which cannot be tamed.

We'll start with the modest goal of 'not dying'. The first half of this book is about avoiding doing anything so stupid that you find yourself hanging from your fingertips above a ravenous monster and a raging whirlpool. When you're clinging onto the roots of the fig tree for dear life, those fat purple fruit way up in the branches don't even come into the picture. So the first step is to protect the downside: in particular, destroying debt, and eliminating the risk of ruin.

It's only once you've scrambled back to solid ground and taken steps to guard against further disasters that you might start eyeing up those juicy figs. The second half of this book is about deliberately taking calculated risks to increase your upside, and in particular, investing.

Life inevitably involves some degree of risk, whether it's falling in love, starting a business, or just getting out of bed in the morning. As we will see, taking *no* risks is the riskiest thing anyone could possibly do.

A FATE WORSE THAN DEBT

Pay every debt as if God wrote the bill.

— RALPH WALDO EMERSON

D
EBT IS SECOND ONLY to death and disease for restricting our choices in life. It's often described as a 'millstone' around our necks, a pair of 'shackles', or a form of 'slavery', and this kind of language is much less metaphorical than you might expect.

The first known written reference to the concept of freedom is the *ama-gi*, scratched into the mud in ancient Sumerian cuneiform 5000 years ago.

Ama-gi glyph, written in classical Sumerian cuneiform.

Ama-gi also translates to 'release from debt'. The symbol is made up of mother (*ama*), and to restore or return (*gi*): the only way an indentured servant could finally go home to their family was by clearing their debts.

It's important to draw a distinction between the lack of freedom that comes from being in debt, and out-and-out chattel slavery; a practice which still exists in some fetid cultural backwaters today. But this horror should only make us *more* determined not to repeat the mistakes of the past, rather than brush them off as lesser evils. Socially sanctioned versions of debt bondage and indentured servitude still exist in the 21st century, and they're causing untold suffering and misery.

To carry a debt is to be 'owned' by someone—or by multiple someones. Your creditor has the right to collect, or otherwise make your life difficult; you have an obligation to make repayments. In servicing the loan, you have to earn an income somehow. Now you have two owners: your creditor, and your employer. Don't like your job? Tough luck—the bills won't pay themselves. Ordered to do something that conflicts with your values? High-minded ideals crumble to dust when the bank is threatening you with foreclosure. Want to retrain for a lower-paid but more fulfilling career? Try explaining that to the loan officer.

As Nassim Taleb observes, corporations love nothing more than a family man with a million dollar mortgage to service, because he has little choice but to be an obedient servant. Tobacco firm lobbyists are probably not *actually* cartoon villains who rub their hands with glee at the thought of giving people cancer. Most unethical behaviour can be explained by simple pragmatism: everyone has bills to pay.

Debt is negative optionality. It removes the *right* to take certain actions, and imposes an *obligation* in its place. So why are we so awash in the stuff?

STUPID SEXY DEBT

Have you ever bought pre-sale tickets to a show, or booked a holiday several months in advance? When the big day finally rolls around, the act of payment has long since faded into memory, and it feels like you're receiving a thoughtful gift from your former self.

As behavioural scientist Elizabeth Dunn explains in *Happy Money*, the pleasure we get from goods and services is purest when it's separated from the pain of having to pay for it. Debt follows the same principle, but in the opposite direction: instead of receiving a 'gift' from your past self, you kick the can down the road and make some other bastard pay for it. In a not-entirely-metaphorical sense, it really is a different person who ends up footing the bill. The only problem is that you will eventually wake up in the body of that person, and instead of feeling a warm glow of gratitude towards your past self, you will curse them for their selfishness.

Debt is funny money. It doesn't feel *real*, and that makes us behave in stupid ways. Researchers asked a group of people to bid on tickets to a sold-out basketball game. Those who were told they'd be paying in cash offered an average of $28. Those who were told they'd be charged by credit card offered an average of $60, effectively paying twice as much for the same tickets. Where did the experimenters find this group of dullards, you ask? At a prestigious business school for MBA students. If the finest young financial minds on the planet can be tricked into paying a 100 per cent debt premium, it doesn't bode well for the rest of us.

One reason it feels so good to pay for things ahead of time is that most of the pleasure is in the anticipation. Booking a trip several months in advance provides plenty of time for daydreaming about palm-fringed beaches while you pretend to work. These fantasies rarely include the pesky details, like the superhuman lung capacity of the screaming child on your 12-hour flight, the size and persistence of the mosquitoes, or the skull-splitting hangover induced by sticky drinks with umbrellas in them. In other words, the best thing about the future is that it hasn't been spoiled by reality yet. This effect is so powerful that vacationers are happier in the weeks *before* they go away, than they are having taken the actual holiday.

A fertile imagination is a double-edged sword. If you buy something with money you don't have, the future becomes a very dark place. Instead of taking the pain upfront, you have plenty of time to ruminate on the various ways in which you're totally and irredeemably screwed. Even if you use debt to pay for something in advance, and thus reap the rewards of anticipation, it's soured by the looming spectre of your next credit card bill.

The mere ability to borrow money is enough to nudge us into making stupid decisions. Once we're in debt, the persistent feeling of doom hanging over us makes us even stupider. Researchers at Princeton found financial woes dominate our mental bandwidth, crowding out other thoughts and leaving less room for solving important problems. The net effect is that people in financial trouble temporarily lose the equivalent of 13 IQ points, which is *huge*—like losing an entire night of sleep.

It's not just cognition that suffers. Debt has been linked to higher blood pressure, and is a leading cause of stress, which weakens the immune system and makes us more susceptible to illness. It can contribute to ulcers and digestive issues, sleep problems, anxiety, depression, and broken marriages. Something like half of all adults with problem debt also have mental health problems. The causal direction isn't clear—perhaps people with mental illnesses are more likely to borrow money—but the consensus is that the effect probably goes both ways.

Everyone knows consumer debt is dumb, financially speaking. But these broader ripple effects are much less widely understood. Debt builds momentum in the wrong direction. It locks us into path dependencies, compounds on itself, and bleeds into other areas of life. In the worst case, we end up like Sisyphus, pushing the boulder up the mountain day after day, only to tumble back to the bottom and begin the grind all over again.

BREAKING THE CYCLE

Religious leaders have long understood the ugly side of debt. Pope Leo the Great condemned usury as early as 440AD, and interest payments are still banned under Islamic law today.

To see how things can get unholy, let's say you borrow $100 from a loan shark to get you through to the next payday, at a monthly interest rate of 20 per cent. That's $20, which is hardly a big deal. But when the day comes around, you've just had your car fixed, and can't quite get the money together. The lender slaps on another 20 per cent, and the hurdle gets slightly higher. Left unchecked, it would only take a little over a year before that $20 had spiralled into outstanding interest of almost $1000. If you can't get on top of repayments, you might find your kneecaps attending an unscheduled meeting with Mister Louisville Slugger.

These days, many countries have effectively outlawed both usury and creative debt collection techniques. Reputable lenders have switched to playing the long game: instead of trying to squeeze you for everything you're worth, they design their terms so you repay the original principal as slowly as possible, converting you into a docile cash cow that can be milked for interest payments indefinitely. Mortgages used to be a standard 15 or 20 years; now they're 30 years, and no doubt some genius home loan company will soon start marketing even more 'affordable' 40-year terms.

While the ideal is never to go into debt in the first place, that's not always practical or even desirable (see the following chapter on leverage). If you do have personal debt on your books, it must be smited with great and furious anger. The first step is to reduce your outgoings, and relentlessly channel the extra savings into clearing the ledger. But how to prioritise which loan to tackle first?

Broadly speaking, there are two approaches to debt repayment. The 'rational' strategy is to rank all your debts in order of interest rate, from highest to lowest. Commit to making the minimum payment on all of them, and put anything left over towards clearing the highest-interest debt, no matter how large and formidable it might be. That means the 22 per cent credit card bill takes priority over the 8 per cent auto loan, even if you only have a few hundred bucks left to pay off the minivan. Then work your way down to the next-highest interest rate, and so on.

The second approach is the 'debt snowball' method, popularised by personal finance author Dave Ramsey. This time, you ignore the interest rates, and rank all your debts in order of size. Once again, make the minimum payments on all of them, but focus all your extra efforts on clearing the *smallest* debt. Once that's gone, you roll all your repayments into the next smallest one, and so on. This gives you a sense of momentum and quick wins, as you clear each debt as fast as possible. From a strict financial perspective, the snowball method doesn't make sense, but humans are weird. Ramsey has a lot of experience in observing what actually works in the real world: if the increased motivation is enough to crank up your repayment efforts, then this really might be the 'best' strategy.[1]

The final step is to consider whether you can convert your debt into a less-terrible form. Sometimes you can transfer a credit card balance to another card with a promotional low or zero-interest rate, which gives you enough breathing room to furiously make repayments. You might also be able to wrap a bunch of different loans into one consolidated debt with a lower interest rate, or roll it into your home loan. Just be wary of the repayment conditions: for example, you'll almost certainly end up paying more interest over the course of a 30-year mortgage than you would at a higher interest rate over a shorter term.

DEBITUM DELENDA EST

The ancient north African state of Carthage was a constant thorn in Rome's side. The republic suffered several humiliating defeats to the brilliant tactician Hannibal Barca, who famously led an invasion force of war elephants across the Alps. Cato the Elder, a veteran who had fought many battles against Hannibal's forces, would not rest easy. Even after the war was won, he developed the habit of finishing all his speeches to the senate—regardless of the actual subject matter—with the phrase *ceterum censeo Carthaginem esse delendam* ("and furthermore, Carthage must be destroyed").

Sometimes you have to name a powerful and ancient enemy, and never lose sight of the importance of vanquishing it: *Debitum delenda est!* Consumer debt is the enemy, and it must be destroyed. Debt facilitates impulse buying, which strips away the pleasure of anticipation. It fools us into spending more than we otherwise would have, both upfront, and through ongoing servicing costs. It makes us stupid, stressed, and depressed. It breaks up marriages. It stifles our capabilities, and it destroys optionality.

The attempt to normalise consumer debt and market it to vulnerable people is evil. But not all debt is created equal. There are situations in which borrowing money can be a powerful strategy for *increasing* your personal wealth—so long as you tread very carefully.

18

THE PERIL AND PROMISE OF LEVERAGE

Give me a lever long enough and a fulcrum on which to place it, and I shall move the world.

— ARCHIMEDES

FTER I HIT MY savings target and published my 'coming out' essay on simple living, I received a flood of messages from like-minded people who were quietly doing the same thing. One of them was an old school mate who I hadn't seen since he joined the navy. My friend had blown my modest efforts out of the water, becoming a millionaire at the tender age of 24.

But my friend did not shy away from taking on debt—quite the opposite. We'll come back to his story throughout this chapter, with the aim of illustrating the difference between debt and leverage.

Put simply, debt is borrowing money for *consumption*, and leverage is borrowing money to *invest*. Many businesses fund their operations through debt; not because they're financially irresponsible, but because they expect to earn an outsized return on the loan. In taking someone else's money, they can *lever* themselves into a more advantageous position than they would have been able to reach with their own resources.

Leverage is usually associated with companies, but if you have a student loan, a mortgage, or an investment property, you're also borrowing to invest. These are the three most common forms of personal leverage, so let's look more closely at the promise and perils of each.

INVESTING IN EDUCATION

Knowledge capital—the sum total of all your skills, experience, education, and qualifications—dictates your earning potential, which is usually going to be your single most valuable asset. Building knowledge capital early in the game can double, triple, or 10x your lifetime earnings: on average, college graduates earn an extra $1 million over the course of their careers. Higher education also builds valuable social capital, because it lets you rub shoulders with the great and the good, and make lifelong friendships and connections. Going to college opens up a whole range of life outcomes that would otherwise be difficult to achieve. If you're looking for the archetypal example of 'good debt', you couldn't go past the student loan.

In recent years, this narrative has started to fall apart. There's no doubt that a college degree increases your optionality; partly because it makes you more skilled and useful as a worker, but *mostly* because it gives you a credential that gets you past the gatekeeper to higher-paid jobs. In other words, it's a signalling game, with all the associated herd behaviours.

In *The Case Against Education*, Bryan Caplan argues that the signalling component of formal education is much larger than we might care to admit. A college degree is a glorified test of IQ and conscientiousness: the knowledge acquired is secondary, especially in non-technical degrees, and could be learned through textbooks, free online courses, and self-directed study. Instead of receiving the broadest and most challenging education possible, the focus is on narrowly passing tests and exams. In Caplan's view, the real value is socialising you to be a good worker, ingraining the correct ideological atti-tudes, and getting a very expensive piece of sheepskin to hang on the wall of your office.

There's a scene in *Good Will Hunting* where Matt Damon's working-class character taunts a pretentious Harvard student: "You wasted $150,000 on an education you coulda got for a buck fifty in late charges at the public library." Personally, I think there's a grain of truth to this: my real education only began after I had finished my undergraduate degree, which mostly involved regurgitating the views of long-dead cultural theorists shaking their fists at clouds.

Even if formal education has a large signalling component, that doesn't mean it's not worth playing the game. The question is: does having a college degree create enough optionality to compensate for the crushing burden of debt? In the US, the average student loan balance at graduation has doubled since the 1990s, while salaries for new graduates have flatlined. In other words, the trade-off is becoming less and less compelling over time—and that's the *average* outcome. The rewards of higher education are not evenly distributed, which means that those who rack up six-figure debts without finding a matching salary end up in big trouble.

The ability to declare bankruptcy is one of the great unsung achievements of civilisation. It acts as a release valve to prevent one version of us from holding all our future selves hostage forever, in implicit recognition of the fact that there is no such thing as a stable 'you'. But in countries like the US, student loans typically can't be discharged through bankruptcy, which makes them an almost uniquely optionality-destroying form of debt. The sickening part is that it's often 17 year olds making these irreversible decisions. Teenagers are not exactly renowned for their impulse control or foresight: their frontal lobes are still a decade away from being fully developed. Imagine being in the alien anthropologist's shoes, and observing this supposedly advanced species encouraging their own children to bind themselves into a lifetime of indentured servitude.

If that wasn't bad enough, we still have to grapple with the twin dilemmas that a) we're terrible at predicting what our future selves will want, and b) we live in an increasingly volatile world. The fortunate graduates emerge with a degree that happens to be in demand, or find their way into an employable sector. If they actually like their job, that's an added bonus. But many graduates are not so lucky. They're working as baristas who happen to be extremely knowledgeable about 14th century English poetry, or running away to live in developing countries knowing they will never be able to come home. Their choices amount to indentured servitude, exile, or death: suicide is the last resort of those who feel the burden of debt has become too great to bear.

None of this is to say that borrowing money for higher education is a bad option. It's just that it requires extremely careful deliberation. As the venture capitalist Peter Thiel asks, are you making a consumption decision—a four-year party, where you get to indulge your personal interests? Or are you making an investment decision? Or are you taking out insurance? Or is it a contest to test your wits against your peers? All of these things are lumped under the word 'education', but they're not the same thing at all.

And college is certainly not the *only* option. Thiel offers paid fellowships to encourage talented young people to skip university and dive straight into entrepreneurship, following in the footsteps of dropouts like Richard Branson, Bill Gates, and Oprah Winfrey. Of course, most college dropouts do not go on to become empire-building entrepreneurs. Lower-variance pathways include coding bootcamps, where you can get hired by a growing number of companies who don't care about credentials, or the trades, or the armed forces, which pay you as you learn on the job, and sometimes cover the cost of formal qualifications, too. Plenty of plumbers, electricians and builders are pulling in six figures, which won't be a surprise to anyone who's had their kitchen remodelled lately.

My high school friend barely passed senior year, and failed every paper in economics. But by the time the rest of our cohort had finished slogging through Marxism, postmodernism, and all the other -isms, he was a fully-fledged officer of the New Zealand Defence Force. He had no student debt, almost all his expenses covered on base, and a considerable chunk of savings to his name. And so, at the ripe old age of 19, he walked into the bank and asked the manager for a home loan.

BUYING VS RENTING

It is a truth universally acknowledged that a person in possession of a good income must be in want of a house. Another truth universally acknowledged is that houses are *frickin' expensive*. Most people don't have several hundred thousand dollars lying around, so they have to borrow it from the bank. In theory, the rewards they get from homeownership are higher than the interest payments they make each month. In other words, they're using debt to lever themselves into a better position in life.

But not necessarily a better *financial* position. Imagine some shady figure sidled up to you and pitched you the following investment opportunity:

> "You're going to put everything into a single, highly illiquid investment. It takes weeks or months to buy and sell, and there are eye-watering transaction costs

each time. The asset is constantly deteriorating, so you'll also need to pay a whole raft of ongoing costs, in the form of rates, insurance, and maintenance. Oh, and you'll be up to your eyeballs in debt for decades. Questions?"

From a strict accounting perspective, homeownership is stupid. But as usual, it's the strict accounting perspective that's stupid. People buy homes because they want the right (but not the obligation) to paint the walls canary yellow, and extend the kitchen, and get a dog with urine so acidic that large patches of the lawn will never recover. They want the security and stability of having their own place, without the threat of having to uproot their lives at 30 days' notice. They want to bring up their kids in a place that feels like home, and be a part of a local community. The *utility* they get from homeownership —all of this fuzzy stuff, which has nothing to do with dollars and cents—is higher than the cost of servicing the debt. In taking out a mortgage, they get to unlock 100 per cent of these benefits, while only paying, say, 10 per cent of the sticker price.

There's no denying that a mortgage massively reduces your options in many other ways. But as we shall see in the next book, the utility of having optionality fluctuates throughout a lifetime. For a single, unattached 20 year old who has barely begun exploring life's possibilities, taking on a large mortgage is a very strange decision. It's almost certainly better to stay lightweight and nimble, and build some optionality. For a family with lots of career capital and who know exactly what they want in life, it's an entirely different proposition.

In that scenario, it might make sense to deliberately constrain your options. A mortgage is a commitment device which effectively forces you to save money for decades: after you pay the bank, you have no choice but to get by with whatever's left over. Sure, you could rent, and save and invest the difference, but many folks aren't that disciplined.

And so, the buying vs renting debate is incoherent: both because it confuses money with utility, and because it supposes there's a universally correct answer. Borrowing money to buy a house can be a perfectly valid use of leverage even if the financial case is borderline, because the financials are not what's really at stake.

Switching out 'money' and 'utility' is a bit of a departure from the traditional definition of leverage. When my friend walked into the bank, he wasn't buying a house for the warm fuzzies. Utility, schmutility! He lived on navy ships and bases, getting paid to travel all over the world. He didn't need a home. Instead, he wanted to borrow money in order to capture outsized financial gains.

Borrowing to invest in financial assets is the purest form of leverage—and also the most dangerous.

LEVERAGED INVESTING

While my friend was in the process of joining the navy, he put in long hours stacking shelves at the local supermarket. After he was accepted, he continued saving a good chunk of his salary, even though he was barely earning more than minimum wage.

And so, when he walked into the bank at 19 years old, he already had tens of thousands of dollars in his bank account—nowhere near enough to buy a house outright, but enough to scrape over the line for a home loan pre-approval. When he walked out the door that day, it was with an instant 5x increase in his buying power. And this is where leverage becomes incredibly powerful.

Let's say you put a 20 per cent down payment on a $500,000 house, and take out a loan to cover the balance. For every $1 of your own money, the bank is matching you to the tune of $4. If the value of your house increases, you get to collect all the gains: not only on the small slice of equity you own, but on the bank's much bigger share too. Your upside is effectively multiplied by *400 per cent*.

In my home city of Auckland, which experienced a house price boom between 2011 and 2017, a lot of people have become wealthy in this manner. They took a punt, like my friend, and it paid off handsomely: property prices doubled in six years, minting a whole new class of millionaires. These kinds of investment returns are hard to achieve without using leverage.

Leverage gives you exposure to major upside, but it's *not* an asymmetric opportunity. If the market falls, any losses you make are also multiplied several times over. If property prices *fall* by 20 per cent, in our scenario above, you're down $100,000, which means your deposit has been completely wiped out. All those years of sweat and toil, for nothing. If the property market continues to weaken, you'll owe more money than the house is worth. This is exactly what happened in the last US housing crash, with legions of ruined borrowers walking out the front door and mailing the keys to the bank.

Leveraged investments are much less certain than student loans or home-ownership. In those scenarios, the value of the underlying asset you're buying is relatively stable: your education can't be sucked back out of your brain, and the lifestyle benefits of owning a home don't change, regardless of how its market value might fluctuate. This is *not* the case when you borrow money to buy stocks, investment properties, or any other volatile asset. If you win, you win big. If you lose, you lose big.

In the hands of a skilled operator, leveraged debt can cut through all sorts of obstacles. But you have to know what you're doing. If you don't treat it with the respect it deserves, it'll take your fingers off.

My friend is not stupid. He was careful to only buy properties that generated enough rental income to cover the expenses, rather than relying solely on the prospect of capital gains. He hired a good lawyer and accountant, and did everything by the books. If the market had moved against him, he wouldn't be a millionaire right now—but he wouldn't be bankrupt, either.

In short, he took steps to reduce the *risk of ruin*. If you're debt-free, or have an aggressive repayment plan in place, that's a very good start. But we're not quite out of the woods yet.

19

THE RISK OF RUIN

VIZZINI: Inconceivable!

*INIGO MONTOYA: You keep using that word. I do not think it means what you think
it means.*

— THE PRINCESS BRIDE

MOST OF US GO THROUGH life with a vague sense that bad things
only happen to other people. This delusion tends to persist right
up until the moment when we discover otherwise, by which
point it's too late to do anything about it. Assuming we survive the encounter,
we tend to become more wary of whatever Bad Thing burned us, while failing
to extrapolate the lesson to other domains. If you think it's inconceivable that
you might crash your motorcycle, or lose your job, or have a rare tropical parasite set up shop in your lower intestine, then your vocabulary is just as lacking
as Vizzini's.

These kinds of catastrophic events arise from what hedge fund manager
Ray Dalio calls the 'risk of ruin'. It's okay to lose now and then. In fact, it's
inevitable. But it's not okay *to lose so badly that you can't come back*. Whatever
risks you take in life, you can never, ever expose yourself to the chance of
falling into a Bottomless Pit of Doom.

An overdue credit card bill doesn't come with a risk of ruin, because debt destroys you in a predictable manner: slowly, surely, deliberately. You can plot it on a spreadsheet, if you're feeling morbid. It's a known variable, and it usually has a capped downside. But this isn't the only kind of risk we have to contend with. For a decent taxonomy, we could do worse than former US Defense Secretary Donald Rumsfeld's famous line:

> "There are known knowns; there are things we know we know. We also know there are known unknowns; that is to say we know there are some things we do not know. But there are also unknown unknowns—the ones we don't know we don't know."

A debt is a known known. Its terms are specific and predictable, which means it can be measured and tamed. But we also have to protect ourselves against the known unknowns, which includes the likes of car accidents, messy divorces, market crashes, floods, fires, pandemics, and plagues of locusts. There's no way of knowing if any of these things will happen to us specifically. But we know they happen to people in general, or at the very least, could *conceivably* happen.

The classic strategy for dealing with known unknowns is to stick your fingers in your ears, profess your lowly mortal status, and commend your fate to the gods.

This 'pray and walk away' technique was the best the ancient Greeks could come up with. Socrates and his contemporaries were heavily into the ancient equivalent of dorm-room bull sessions, in which a bunch of toga-wearing dudes sat around ripping bongs and coming up with grand theories of the universe.[1] They were not so hot on going out in the world to look for actual *evidence*, which would probably involve some kind of vulgar labour.

If the Greeks had been more willing to dirty their hands outside the crystalline realm of pure logic, they might have noticed that these kinds of catastrophic events happen with some regularity. By gathering data on their frequency, they would have been able to figure out the chances of, say, getting struck by lightning, or dying by a certain age. Instead, we had to wait another two millennia for their Renaissance-era intellectual descendants to deliver the next great triumph of civilisation: the ability to measure risks probabilistically, and pool our collective resources to protect against them. Or as we call it today, 'insurance'.

THE ART OF SWALLOWING DEAD RATS

It's an unpleasant fact of life that every now and then, you have to swallow a dead rat. For the uninitiated, this delightful piece of New Zealand folk wisdom refers to finding yourself in a bad situation you have no choice but to accept. For an example which is especially likely to stick in your craw, take life insurance: if you live long and prosper, all those premiums you paid were for nothing. The only way to 'win' is to die young and unexpectedly, which is what you might call a pyrrhic victory.

The very concept of insurance is hard to swallow. If you run the numbers on the probability of making a claim, the expected dollar value of buying an insurance contract is negative. On average, the house always wins: insurers have to collect more in premiums than they pay out in claims, or they'd soon go out of business.

Insurance perfectly illustrates the fact that the utility (use value) of money is not the same thing as the simple dollar value. Most of us are happy to take small, steady, predictable losses in order to prevent a catastrophic loss which would wipe us out. And this is entirely right and proper! Remember that bad is stronger than good: losses hit us disproportionately hard, both psychologically and in terms of destroying optionality.

An insurance policy is very much like buying an option. It lets you pay a small, fixed cost to potentially make a large, unbounded return—or in this case, to avoid a large, unbounded loss. To figure out which type of insurance to buy, you have to decide which catastrophic events you couldn't come back from. Here are five likely candidates:

1. Loss of income
Your single biggest asset is almost certainly your ability to earn. If you lose this ability and you don't have income protection insurance, you're reliant on government assistance, support from family and friends, or saved capital.

2. Loss of life
The same concept as income protection, with the difference being that you're insuring your ability to provide for someone else. If you have

dependants who rely on you, life insurance is strongly worth considering. If you don't, it's almost certainly a waste of money.

3. Loss of health

You might be able to cover routine doctor visits and prescriptions out
of pocket, but major surgeries, accidents, chronic disease, or prescriptions for rare drugs can run into the hundreds of thousands of dollars.

4. Loss of home

A house is the most valuable physical asset many people will own.
Losing it to a fire or natural disaster would be a major setback at best,
and at worst, an irreversible financial disaster.

5. Loss of indemnity

Even if you don't own anything worth insuring, you still need to be
protected in the event that you mess up *other people's* stuff—say,
pranging a Jaguar, burning down your landlord's house, or getting sued
by a client. Auto and contents insurance often include some liability
cover, and there are entire specialist industries that provide professional indemnity insurance.

The type of cover you opt for will depend on your starting level of wealth,
your personal risk tolerance, whether you have dependents, and the social and
state support networks in your part of the world. For example, New Zealand
has a compulsory no-fault accident insurance scheme and free healthcare,
which means private health insurance is not so crucial as it might be in
the US.

No matter your individual circumstances, there are a few general principles
to keep in mind.

The first is to *self-insure as much as you're comfortable with*. Remember that an
insurance contract has a negative expected value in dollar terms. It only comes
into its own when it protects you against risks that would otherwise be
ruinous; whatever that means to you personally. If I'm driving a beat-up junker,
I'm not going to waste $400 a year on comprehensive collision insurance.
Instead, I'd save the premiums, and pay for any repairs as and when they were
needed. But if I relied on that junker to get to work and had no other savings,
it would be a different story. The sudden loss of the car would only stop being

a catastrophe once I had a few thousand dollars to my name, at which point I'd have the option of self-insuring. On the other hand, I would never venture onto the roads without being covered by third-party (liability) insurance—if I'm at fault in a crash that causes a lot of damage, it could be ruinous.

The idea is to buy as little insurance as you can get away with, but *not one cent less*. Often, this looks like removing unnecessary frills and add-ons from core policies, or taking your chances on low-value assets. Assuming you have some savings, you can ignore the Apple store salesman trying to upsell you an insurance policy for your iPhone, or the airline's attempt to scare you into buying coverage for missed flights. You might lose once or twice, but so what? A $200 replacement ticket is nothing compared to all the premiums you'll pay over a lifetime.

Another way to self-insure is to boost the co-pay or deductible as high as you're comfortable with, which reduces the premiums accordingly. For example, when I take out travel insurance, I set the deductible at $500. That means I'll never be able to make a claim for minor medical problems, or missing a short-haul flight. But I can cover all that stuff myself. The kind of thing I care about are the extreme tail risks, like ending up in the ICU of a foreign hospital with a bill running into the seven figures.

Once you commit to buying coverage, don't half-ass it. The cheapest insurance policy is highly unlikely to be the best policy, which means you can't just scroll to the bottom and blindly click 'accept'. Terms, coverage, and exclusions vary, and fish-hooks for the unwary mean you might accidentally invalidate the whole thing. Unless you hire an adviser, there is no substitute for actually sitting down and working your way through the policy document, line by line. I've read far more insurance policies than is healthy for any young man, to the point where I'm intimately familiar with the most common pitfalls, and I *still* narrowly avoided getting caught out by a confusing clause recently. So do your homework.

This is also the broader lesson for dealing with known unknowns: you have to get out there and gather data. Don't be like the Greeks, shrugging their shoulders and leaving it all up to fate. Take stock of all the risks in your life. Measure what can be measured. Run the numbers. Then take action accordingly. As Charlie Munger says: "All I want to know is where I'm going to die, so I'll never go there." Your ultimate fate will *still* be in the hands of the gods, and you'll *still* have to bend with the winds of fortune, but you'll be much better prepared to weather any storms.

Now we're two thirds of the way home. We've covered off the known knowns, and the known unknowns. But what about the unknown unknowns? How do you protect yourself against something that really *is* inconceivable?

BLACK SWANS AND UNCERTAINTY

Our knowledge of the way things work, in society or in nature, comes trailing clouds of vagueness. Vast ills have followed a belief in certainty.

— KENNETH ARROW

For most of the last 2000 years, everyone in the West knew there was no such thing as a swan with black plumage. A 'black swan' was such an outlandish idea that it became shorthand for something that was impossible. This persisted right up until Europeans arrived in Australia, and discovered they'd been wrong the entire time.

The black swan is Nassim Taleb's best-known idea, and the subject of his book of the same name. As Taleb points out, this simple little error of reasoning trips up experts every day, especially in the realm of finance. No-one can predict the inherently unpredictable. All the prior data might produce a lovely trendline that can be extrapolated out forever, but a single high-impact event makes a mockery of the whole exercise.

Taleb gives the example of a turkey on the day before Thanksgiving. It has all the grain it could wish for, lots of friends, and a warm barn to roost in. Every day brings more confirmation that life is good. When the axe comes swinging down, it has *maximum* confidence in its wildly inaccurate model of the world.

The fatalistic 'pray and walk away' approach involved a failure to go out and gather data, assess risks, and take action accordingly. The turkey problem is what happens when we overcorrect: our fancy models lull us into a false sense of security, and we forget to account for unknown unknowns.

This is not a new problem. The economist Frank Knight formalised the distinction between risk and uncertainty in his PhD thesis more than 100 years ago, with the key difference being that risk can be quantified and measured, while true uncertainty cannot.[2]

Knight was a member of the laissez-faire Chicago school of economics, but he found an unlikely ally across the aisle in John Maynard Keynes, who also despised the "mean statistical view of life". These titans disliked one another, but found common cause in condemning the hubris of those who shoehorned inherently uncertain events into tidy probability ranges. Here's Keynes, writing in 1937:

> "The game of roulette is not subject, in this sense, to uncertainty... The sense in which I am using the term is that in which the prospect of a European war is uncertain, or the price of copper and the rate of interest 20 years hence, or the obsolescence of a new invention... About these matters, there is no scientific basis on which to form any calculable probability whatsoever. We simply do not know!"

Life is not like a game of chess, where we can see every piece on the board, and trace the path of all possible moves to a set of predictable outcomes. Poker is a better analogy: we're forced to make decisions with imperfect information, and there's an element of randomness in how the cards are shuffled and dealt—a known unknown—which means we might make the best possible decision, and still lose the hand.

But poker isn't a perfect analogy either. If it were, the number of aces in the deck would change halfway through a game, some fraction of the chips would be counterfeit, mobsters might kick the door down at any second, and a small, localised hurricane would occasionally pick up your winning hand and hurl it into the ceiling fan.

We can never really know if we're turkeys on the day before Thanksgiving. We don't know whether the patterns of the past will repeat in the future. We don't know if our best-laid plans will work out. *None of this is computable.* It's monstrously difficult for physicists to calculate the motion of three simple objects—never mind the interplay of eight billion souls, with all of their innovations, triumphs, failures, wars, alliances, ideas, plans, and preferences. Next time the talking heads on TV are flapping their gums about geopolitics or stock market forecasts, remind yourself of Keynes' admonition: we simply do not know!

By definition, we can't predict a black swan event. So how are we meant to prepare for it?

At the risk of sounding like a broken record: by building optionality. Whatever surprises life throws at you, there are certain things that will never not be helpful. If you have people in your life you can rely on in a crisis, that's the difference between blowing up, and coming out the other side stronger for the experience. If you're in good physical health, that's the difference between walking away from an accident, and dying on the operating table. If you have broad skills and experience, that's the difference between seeing your livelihood automated out of existence, and pivoting to another career path.

EMERGENCY FUNDS

In the domain of financial capital, one of the most useful things you can do to prepare for unknown unknowns is to maintain a safety buffer of cash. I like to keep $10,000 in cash or checking accounts at all times. I chose this sum based on the highly unscientific 'big round number' method, but it does mean the following things to me:

- I can cover any unexpected expense on the spot (anything above this threshold will be insured)
- I can buy pretty much anything I want in cash, instead of using debt
- If all my income dries up overnight, I can go to ground and live on the bones of my ass for roughly a year

My emergency fund really came into its own during the coronavirus pandemic, when I lost my only steady income source overnight. Almost all my wealth was tied up in illiquid investments, but I didn't have to panic or even adjust my spending much: I calculated I could get by for at least six months at the same burn rate, at which point I would be able to liquidate some assets if I wasn't earning again.

There are various formulas for calculating the size of your emergency fund, but they're all missing the key variable of psychological comfort. I didn't bother with an emergency fund at all when I worked full time: I could use a credit card to manage any cashflow bumps, and if I lost my job, redundancy and accumulated leave would give me more than enough buffer to get back on my feet—especially given my low-cost lifestyle.

Maintaining simple tastes is the master strategy for building resilience to black swan events. To use a somewhat unflattering metaphor, frugal folks are hardy little cockroaches: low-slung and nimble and difficult to stamp out. We collect skills. We stash cash. We are content with a relatively lean existence. And we are always positioned to take advantage of opportunities. Come hell or high water, thermonuclear war or the second coming of Christ, we won't just survive—we will *thrive*.

We've scrambled up the roots of the fig tree, made it back to firm ground, and taken precautions to make sure we never end up in that precarious position again. We know how to protect ourselves against known knowns, known unknowns, and unknown unknowns. Now we can start eyeing up the fat purple figs high in the boughs. It's going to take a little derring-do—some of those branches are treacherous—but there is no reward without risk.

2 0

NOTHING VENTURED, NOTHING
GAINED

You come at the king, you best not miss.

— OMAR LITTLE

A FRESHMAN HOVERS on the fringes of the high school ball, lightly perspiring. He's trying to build up the nerve to approach the most popular sophomore in school, who is almost certainly called Stacey. As the various scenarios play out in his imagination, the humiliation of being publicly rejected is more crushing than the elation of successfully getting a dance. Best not to even try, he reasons. So he watches on from the relative safety of the punch bowl zone.

Losing feels worse than winning feels good. This is often presented as 'irrational' behaviour, in the sense that we respond inconsistently depending on how certain choices are framed. But even if loss aversion misfires in specific cases, it makes perfect sense as a general heuristic for survival. Missing an opportunity is not the end of the world. There will always be more chances. But if you take a shot, and you screw it up badly enough, it could be the end of you. The kid at the ball knows this instinctively. Maybe he's a coward. Or maybe he's quite sensibly preserving his limited social capital.

Wait a second. Wasn't this meant to be the chapter on boldly taking risks?

We can't escape the reality that bad is stronger than good. The first step is always to protect the downside—and once we're putting money on the line, it's not just hurt feelings at stake. Here are the rules handed down to us by the world's most famous investor, Warren Buffett:

Rule no. 1: Never lose money
Rule no. 2: Never forget rule no. 1

Losing money is much worse than gaining the equivalent sum is good. This is partly because of the diminishing marginal utility of money, as discussed in Chapter 5. But there's also a mathematical explanation, which is both extremely obvious and widely underappreciated. Let's say you start out with $1000, but fail to protect your downside:

- If you make a 20 per cent loss—so you're down to $800—you'll have to earn a 25 per cent return to get back to square one
- If you make a 50 per cent loss—so you're down to $500—you'll have to earn a 100 per cent return to get back to square one
- If you make a 90 per cent loss—so you're down to $100—you'll have to earn a *900 per cent* return to get back to square one

This asymmetry tells us two things: the sequence of losses and wins matters, and a loss hurts you more than an equivalent win helps you—hence the importance of never losing money.

And yet... Buffett's 'rules' are a load of baloney, as written. They're meant to be taken seriously, but not literally: the Oracle of Omaha has lost *billions* over the course of his career, which is more than all but a tiny handful of individuals throughout history. What matters is that the calculated risks he's taken have more than compensated for those losses (generating a net worth of $81 billion at last count). If Buffett had obeyed his own rules to the letter, he would never have made a single investment, and we wouldn't be talking about him right now. 'Don't lose money' is the equivalent of the doctor's oath to 'first do no harm'. It enshrines an important principle—it's much better to do nothing than to take an unacceptable risk—but as written, it's violated a million times every single day. And thank God for that: otherwise, no surgeon would ever be able to pick up a scalpel.

It's crucial to avoid the *risk of ruin*. Absolutely, at all costs. But avoid risk, full stop? No. In fact, *not* taking any risks is one of the riskiest things you could possibly do.

THE PARABLE OF THE TALENTS

In ye olden days, a talent was a significant sum of money—equivalent to about 36kg of silver, or 20 years' wages for a labourer. In the Gospel of Matthew, Christ tells the story of a man who entrusted his fortune to three servants while he went on a long journey, dividing it up according to their ability. The first received five talents, the second two, and the third, just one.

Upon the master's return, he found the first and second servants had doubled their talents through savvy investments, and rewarded them handsomely. But the third servant, out of fear, had buried his single talent in the ground. The master cast this wretch into the pits of hell, taking his only talent and giving it to the servant who already had 10. The Matthew effect takes its name from the conclusion of the parable: "For to every one who has will more be given, and he will have an abundance; but from him who has not, even what he has will be taken away."

The moral of the story is that you have to take risks in life, and put your talents to work—financial or otherwise.

To see how important this is, we turn to another revered source of wisdom: the cartoon sitcom *Futurama*. If you missed this gem of early noughties TV, the premise is that pizza delivery boy Fry falls into a cryogenic freezer at the turn of the new millennium, and wakes up in the year 3000. In 'A Fishful of Dollars', Fry re-discovers his old bank account. When he was frozen in the 21st century, this contained the princely sum of 93 cents. After 1000 years as a human popsicle, the balance has compounded from less than a buck to the staggering sum of $4.3 billion. Hijinks and capers ensue.

While this is a fun idea for a plotline, casual viewers might assume the numbers involved were made-up. But *Futurama* was written by a bunch of boffins who take this sort of stuff seriously. Ken Keeler, who has a PhD in applied mathematics, invented a theorem purely to resolve a plot point in another episode, which ended up being published in an academic journal. There's no way writers of this calibre would resort to using *cartoon* numbers. And so, yes, 93 cents at 2.25 per cent interest for 1000 years really does compound to $4.3 billion. If you want to get pernickety, the exact figure is $4,283,508,449.71.

If your gut is screaming that this cannot possibly be true, you're not alone. We're wired up to think about the world in simple linear terms, because that's how most of the things around us work. If you plant one seed, you get one carrot. If you produce one more dongle, you earn one more dollar. Your hair steadily grows by a fraction of a millimetre each day; you don't just wake up one morning looking like the lovechild of Tom Selleck and Wolfman.

Linear growth is intuitive, but compounding is much harder to wrap our brains around. As Mark Zuckerberg put it: "Humans don't understand exponential growth. If you fold a paper 50 times, it goes to the moon and back." This is a delicious example, not only because the imagery is so jarring—whoa, a tiny sheet of paper can do that?—but because the Zuck got it wrong. If you fold a piece of paper 50 times over, it doesn't make a paltry return trip to the moon—it goes all the way to the freakin' *sun*. Humans don't understand exponential growth, indeed.

Here's one last example, from *Abundance* author Peter Diamandis:

"If I take 30 large linear steps (say one meter) from my Santa Monica living room, I end up 30 meters away, or roughly across the street. If, alternatively, I take 30 exponential steps from the same starting point, I end up a billion meters away, or orbiting the Earth 26 times."

I like collecting these sort of wildly unintuitive examples, in the hope that if I continue to melt my brain, it might start to grudgingly give exponential growth the respect it deserves.

This is not just mathematical trivia for eggheads. It's a real-world phenomenon with the power to make us or break us. As we saw in Chapter 17: A Fate Worse Than Debt, anyone who doesn't understand compound interest risks having it used against them.

Those who *do* manage to wrap their heads around non-linear growth stand to benefit enormously. But merely doing a Fry—putting some money in the bank, and kicking back—is not good enough. The truth is, Fry *buried his talent in the ground.*

THE SILENT THIEF

The supply of money sloshing around tends to inflate over time, which means it becomes slightly less valuable every year—around 2 per cent, on average. Even at these modest levels, inflation is the silent thief in your wallet, making you a tiny bit poorer every day.

Say your grandpa saved $100 in his youth, and put it safely under his mattress where the IRS couldn't find it. Back in 1969, that was a decent chunk of change. In the short-term, he wouldn't even notice the value eroding away: one year later, his hard-earned dough would still have almost exactly the same purchasing power. But the compounding effect constantly ratchets up the magnitude of the destruction. Wind the clock forward 50 years, and inflation has run at a cumulative total of 628 per cent. Grandpa still has the same $100 note, but it's worth a pittance compared to when he stashed it away—the equivalent of about $13. This is why old people always complain about how you used to be able to buy a Buick and a bale of chickens for seventeen cents.

The reality is that every dollar you save is going to roughly halve in value 30 years from now—and that's assuming inflation behaves itself, which is no guarantee. Just ask Zimbabwe.

My sister-in-law and her family left Zimbabwe carrying suitcases full of cash to the airport— not because they were rich, but because hyperinflation had spiralled so far out of control that a loaf of bread cost trillions of dollars.

And so, unless there was a very peculiar period of monetary policy spanning 1000 years, Fry's fortune would have been wiped out by the ravages of inflation. At an average of 2 per cent a year, he'd be left with the equivalent of $11.29 when he woke up, which is somewhat less thrilling than $4.3 billion. And seeing as he didn't stash his cash under his mattress like Grandpa, the taxman would have dipped his sticky fingers in too, meaning the original 93c would have long since disappeared into the void.

Good news, everyone! Compound interest is still a wondrous and beautiful thing. The trick is to build enough momentum to break free from the opposing forces of inflation and taxation. Parking your money in the bank means you're losing money very safely. It's talent-in-the-ground behaviour. To beat inflation and tax, you have to move some of your savings into assets that pay a higher rate of return—and in doing so, take on more risk. This is the difference between saving, and *investing*.

THE MOST POWERFUL FORCE IN THE UNIVERSE

What if Fry had invested his money in the stock market? Going by the last couple hundred years of returns, he would have enjoyed a compound annual growth rate of almost 10 per cent. After accounting for inflation and tax, let's be conservative and say the 'real' rate of return was closer to 6 per cent. Now, instead of ending up with $11.29, Fry has a fortune so fantastically large I can't figure out how to say it in words, but I'm pretty sure it looks something like $18,800,000,000,000,000,000,000,000,000 (in rounding it down, I've carelessly shaved off countless trillions).

Eagle-eyed critics will proceed to ruin all the fun by pointing out that not everyone has a spare 1000 years on their hands to hang around in a cryogenic locker waiting to get rich. Nothing gets past you people! Fortunately, all is not lost. We can still reap the rewards of exponential growth in our brief candle-flicker of a lifetime.

Let's go back to Grandpa and his mattress stash. If he invested that original $100, it'd be worth $106 by the end of the first year. It's pretty hard to get excited about six bucks. But the following year, the investment returns would start accruing on that $6, as well as on the original investment. After three years, he'd be earning returns on top of returns on top of returns, and so on.

By the end of the period, he'd be earning more than $100 a year in returns alone, and his original investment would have turned into $5000.

Now we're getting somewhere. But we can't really expect to invest a chunk of cash *once*, and then kick back and do nothing for the rest of our lives. Momentum needs something to build on. The ideal is to combine the magic of compounding with the simple cumulative effect of making small contributions over time.

Instead of investing $100 and then resting on our laurels, say we sock away $100 every week—an easy target for middle-class earners. This time, we end up with a cool $1.5 million at the end of the period. If we sock away $100 a *day*, which is doable for experienced frugalistas on the higher end of the income scale, we come away with $11 million. Sweet three-toed sloth of ice planet Hoth!

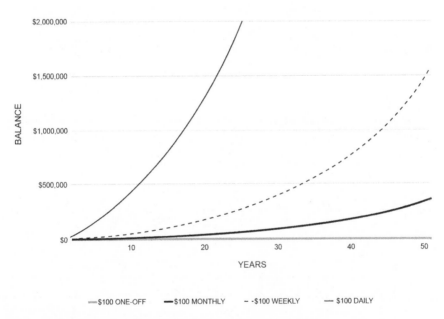

Figure 4.1. The compounding effect of saving $100 monthly, weekly, and daily, as a compared to a one-off contribution.

This savings rate is so astronomical that I had to chop most of it off of Fig. 4.1, but it's silly to extend it that far anyway—most people would switch from hardcore investing mode to spending once they'd accumulated the first million or two, which as you can see on the chart, would take 15 years or so.

Let's finish with a blatant appeal to authority: if a cartoon doesn't do anything for you, maybe you've heard of a guy called Albert Einstein? According to everyone's favourite genius, compound interest is not only "the greatest invention in human history" (take that, polio vaccine!) not only "the eighth wonder of the world" (bite me, Machu Picchu!) but, in fact, *"THE MOST POWERFUL FORCE IN THE UNIVERSE"*. Now that's what you call unequivocal.

...OK, fine, so Einstein probably didn't actually say those things, but never a truer quote has been fabricated. Compounding really is a force of nature, and you don't need to be an astrophysicist with an IQ of 160 to take advantage of it—heck, even a pizza delivery boy could manage it.

21

INVESTING FOR THE BONE IDLE

Lethargy bordering on sloth remains the cornerstone of our investment style.

— WARREN BUFFETT

A BUNCH OF LIFESTYLE TWEAKS have unleashed a firehose of savings and filled your pockets with cash, to the point where you have to employ two burly men just to hold your pants up. What to do with all that lovely money?

We know we have to avoid the risk of ruin. And we know we mustn't bury our talents in the ground. In between those two extremes, we have the entire world of investing, which covers a frankly bewildering range of asset classes, strategies, timeframes, and specialised knowledge.

While investing looks complicated from the outside, there are really only a handful of key concepts to grasp:

Risk Tolerance

We already know the utility (use value) of money is non-linear, and depends on how much of it we have already. A millionaire can go to the casino and put $10,000 on black without any change to their material circumstances, while the same punt could make or break someone on the breadline. But even with the starting level of wealth held equal, risk tolerance also varies *between individuals*.

At one end of the spectrum, you have the Nervous Nellies who pull on a hazmat suit before they venture out of their security compound to check the mail. At the opposite end, you've got the daredevils who sprinkle amphetamines on their cornflakes before a big day of free climbing, wrestling bears, and unprotected sex with strangers. Most of us fall somewhere in the middle, and it's important to figure out where.

When the next market crash comes—and it will come—can you brave a 30 per cent decline without flinching? What if it happens in the space of a couple of days? How will you sleep at night? Do you have an ulcer? No? Do you want one?

Anyone who takes on more risk than they're comfortable with is much more likely to make bad decisions. Investors often panic and sell out when the market enters a downturn, ensuring that they not only take a haircut, but miss out on all the sweet, sweet gains during the recovery.

For those with the fortitude to keep plugging away, this is where the real money is made. You're buying what will turn out to be bargain-priced stocks all the way down, and then all the way back up again, in a fire sale that only comes around once every decade or two.

The decision of which assets to invest in depends partly on your personal risk tolerance, but it also hinges on how much time you have on your side.

Investing Timeframe

The longer your investment timeframe, the more risk you can afford to take on. Someone buying and holding productive businesses for 30, 40, or 50 years has the ability to weather volatility: market prices at any given point in time are of no great consequence.

If you're planning on withdrawing your cash in the near future, it's a very different story. Let's say you want to put a deposit on a house in the next five years. If you get lucky, the market will be near a peak right as you're cashing out your investments. If you're unlucky, you'll be caught with your pants down, at which point you'll either have to put your plans on hold, or sell out and lock in a loss.

Term deposits, bonds and other fixed-interest investments are generally a better match for anyone saving for a short-term goal. The rewards are lower, but so is the volatility.

Diversification

Investments can and will go bad. You want to feel as little pain as possible when this happens, which means spreading yourself around town like a 1960s flower child.

This is the principle of diversification: by divvying up your investments between as many stocks, industries, and geographies as possible, you avoid being ruined if any one sector ends up in strife.

Expenses

The single most underappreciated factor in investing success is stopping every other bastard from dipping their fingers into your pocket. Brokers clip the ticket every time you buy or sell, which adds up fast if you're actively trading in and out of the market. Of course, trading is for chumps: while you think you're making a genius move, the person on the other side of the trade has an equal and opposite opinion. Only one of you can be right.

Don't feel bad, because the same conundrum applies to so-called professionals. Investment managers charge exorbitant fees to pick hot stocks or sectors on your behalf, but there's no evidence that they can consistently beat the average market return (most struggle to match it). To put it bluntly, they're no better than monkeys flinging poop at the business section of the newspaper.

Seemingly trivial fees have a huge impact over time. Let's say we save and invest a third of an average salary, starting from age 25. Even the cheapest investment providers, which offer fees as low as 0.05 per cent a year, will cost you about $35,000 in foregone returns by the time you retire.

Other fund managers charge like wounded bulls, with annual fees of 1.5 per cent or more—30x more expensive than the simple providers. If you go down this route, you end up with a whopping $800,000 less at retirement.

Expensive fund managers will claim that they're worth every penny, because they'll earn higher returns which more than compensate for the added costs. As we'll see in the next section, this is extremely unlikely to be true.

THE LAZY PERSON'S INVESTING STRATEGY

These four factors—risk tolerance, timeframe, diversification, expenses—will broadly determine which assets you choose to invest in. But we also have to deal with more prosaic concerns. If you're a small-time investor, some options are out of your reach: getting started in property usually requires a down payment and secure employment, and if you try to buy individual stocks, it's difficult to get enough diversification.

As it happens, there is one class of investments that is unusually accessible, is especially well-suited for new investors, and requires a bare minimum of effort.

This is one of the only specific recommendations I'm going to make in this section. Before I do, a quick bit of ass-covering:

The following section is for educational and entertainment purposes only. Any resemblance to a real financial adviser, living or dead, is purely coincidental. Do not read while operating a motor vehicle or heavy equipment.

Okay. So, which investments should you buy?

All of them! Seriously: buy a stake in every single publicly traded company on the planet.

And when should you trade in and out?

Never! Just keep steadily buying more, year after year. The losers will drop out, and the winners will keep winning.

You don't need to be a billionaire to pull this off. If you pool your savings together with my savings and a bunch of other people's savings, we can collectively buy thousands of companies, and divide the proceeds between us. This type of investment is called a 'mutual fund', and it has very low barriers to entry. You can get started with $500, or sometimes less, and build from there.

Didn't I just trash fund managers, calling them no better than poop-flinging monkeys? Yes, yes I did. All fund managers are monkeys, but some of them have the good grace to acknowledge their simian shortcomings. These 'passive' managers don't muck around trying to time the market or pick hot stocks, and they don't take outrageous performance bonuses. Instead, all they do is match an entire market or stock index, then put their feet up and take the afternoon off.

Passive mutual funds tick all the boxes: enormous diversification, different levels of risk to match your preferences, rock-bottom fees, low barriers to entry, and the ability to set up an automatic drip-feed. The biggest and best-known provider is Vanguard, a behemoth with $6.2 trillion of assets under management. Its economies of scale and member-owned structure result in extremely low expenses: the Total Stock Market Index fund's annual fee of 0.04 per cent buys you access to more than 3500 US companies.

This is fantastic news for lazy people. Investing can be as simple as finding a low-cost mutual fund that matches your risk profile, setting up regular payments, and forgetting about it for a few decades.

We could end things right here, but bitter experience has taught me that most people—myself included—are far too clever to take this simple advice.

Ever since passive investing first emerged in the 1970s, the swinging dicks of the finance industry have tried to discredit it. It's un-American! Real men pick stocks! As the decades went by, the research continued to mount up in favour of the underdogs. Now the revolution has been won: we know beyond a shadow of doubt that active stock-picking can't live up to the marketing hype. But why not?

The answer lies in a deceptively simple formula called the **Efficient-Market Hypothesis (EMH)**, which states that "asset prices reflect all available information". I have seen so many smart people lose their minds when confronted with these six little words that I am convinced that almost no-one actually understands what they mean.

The 'efficiency' of any given market and the related concept of 'edge' are so ridiculously important that the rest of the chapter is devoted to clearing up these misconceptions. (If you don't need any convincing, feel free to skip ahead to Chapter 22: Black Swan Hunting.)

UNCLE GEORGE VS THE EFFICIENT-MARKET HYPOTHESIS

Uncle George really likes his new iPhone. The dancing poop emoji is hilarious! On the strength of this insight, George speed-dials his broker and loads up on Apple stock.

The person selling the shares to George has the equal and opposite opinion. Both buyer and seller think they're getting a 'deal', and the other camp are suckers. Only one will be proven right.

By chance, Uncle George might expect to win half his trades, and lose the other half. Of course, he knows the odds doesn't apply to *him*, because he's smarter than the sucker on the other end of the deal.

Are you sure about that, George?

The offices of top investment firms are packed with Wharton School graduates. Their brains are hardwired into Reuters terminals, and their eyes glow with red and green numbers reflected on the 14 monitors surrounding each workstation. The bosses of the firm spend their Sunday mornings schmoozing top CEOs, exchanging mildly homophobic jokes as they tee off on the 18th hole. Their trading floors have the best proprietary trading software and the latest algorithms. Their bathroom stalls have the most septum-deviating stimulants.

And yet...the pros can't consistently beat the odds, either. It's not that these guys and gals aren't smart. They have brains bulging out their ears. The problem is, they don't have a *monopoly* on smarts.

Uncle George is not really competing against the professionals. It's much worse than that. Every investor—amateur or major-league—is in direct competition with the closest thing to a superintelligence that humanity has ever created: the stockmarket itself.

The market is a giant, heaving agglomeration of everyone's predictions, which constantly sucks up every new fragment of information—geopolitical events, company reports, the weather in Spain, trading activity, consumer spending reports, a billion other inputs—and then recalibrates itself in real time. The challenge for investors is to try and predict why this giant meta-prediction is wrong, and in which direction.

Let's say Apple stock goes up 15 per cent over the next year, while the broader S&P 500 only goes up 10 per cent. George becomes insufferable at family dinners as he holds forth on his stock-picking powers. Guess the market isn't so 'efficient' after all, huh!

So, did Uncle George beat the market?

In the narrowest possible sense: yes. In the sense in which we aim to string words together so that they mean things: no, of course not. The naive criticism constantly levelled against the EMH is that if the market moves in literally any direction, that must mean it was *wrong* before! By this definition, every single trade leads to one of the two parties 'beating the market'. I can flip a coin between Pepsi and Coke right now and have a 50 per cent chance of becoming a market-beating genius.

The fact that markets go through bubbles and crashes causes the same confusion. Efficiency does not imply 'goodness'. All sorts of ridiculous human behaviours are priced into the market: the fact that a junk stock with a confusingly similar ticker to Coca-Cola remains massively overvalued is not an anomaly, because the market is correctly predicting that people will continue to be idiots in the future.

Nevertheless, some people really *do* beat the market—and not in the trivial Uncle George sense. Doesn't this drive a stake through the heart of the EMH?

The second great misunderstanding is that there is no conflict between the EMH and beating the market. That's how the market gets efficient! Remember those six words: "asset prices reflect all available information". If you have access to information that *isn't* priced in yet, and you exploit the asymmetry, you move the market a little further towards efficiency.

Let's call this information asymmetry an **Edge**. If the EMH is correct, that doesn't mean the market can't be beat. It means:

> ***You shouldn't expect to beat the market without an edge, except by chance.***

This usually gets simplified down to 'you can't beat the market'. Most of the time, this simplification is good enough: you might get lucky and win like Uncle George, but over an investing lifetime, you'll almost certainly revert to the mean (and remember, that's not matching the market return—it's underperforming it).

The Uncle Georges of the world don't have an edge. All of their thoughts have already been thunk by someone else; probably by millions of someone elses. Instead, their fortunes are buffeted around by the myriad other forces that drive stock prices: everything from Tim Cook's vocal inflections on the last earning call, to the capacity of a copper mine that opened in Belarus last Thursday. The stockmarket spits out a collective signal after processing all these layers of inputs, but its inner workings remain a black box unto us mere mortals.

All Uncle George can see is that he placed his bet, and Apple stock went up. It was the poop emoji for sure! And so, he spends his days dishing out hot stock tips on online forums, oblivious to the fact that his success was perfectly random.

If we don't want to end up like Uncle George, we better learn how to tell what a real edge looks like.

FINDING AN EDGE

You versus the guy she told you not to worry about.

A century ago, investors started noticing they could consistently pick up bargains by running very simple formulas over stock prices. The most famous of these anomalies was the value investing approach developed by Ben Graham, and popularised by Warren Buffett. There was a genuine, big old inefficiency in the market, and these guys had a lovely time exploiting it.

This is the image most people have in their head when they think about 'beating the market'—diligently studying *The Intelligent Investor* and learning about PE ratios or whatever.

But this is like trying to use a stone-age axe against a fighter jet. The Ben Graham information asymmetry has long since disappeared, because—you guessed it—the market is efficient! Once the formula was widely-known, it stopped working. Investors developed more sophisticated versions, more formulas, more pricing models. Once *those* got out, they stopped working too. Now there's a great debate as to whether even the most complicated descendants of value investing might be totally dead. In which case, the anomaly has officially gone for good.

Either way, this is not how Buffett gets his edge, and it hasn't been for decades. Here's his partner, Charlie Munger:

> "The trouble with what I call the classic Ben Graham concept is that gradually the world wised up and those real obvious bargains disappeared. You could run your Geiger counter over the rubble and it wouldn't click."

Buffett's most brilliant achievement is weaving the folksy narrative that he's a cute old grandpa who beats the market by backing the best companies. Let's take a look at how market-beating investors *really* get their edge.

The Warren Buffett Halo Effect

In recent decades, Buffett has made a killing through juicy private deals which are completely out of reach of the average investor. Like, $6 billion deals with $3b in preference rights and a guaranteed dividend. Like, lobbying the government to bail out the banks, then carving off a huge piece of the action. Like, being able to play with Berkshire Hathaway's $115b insurance float.

Buffett's brand has become so powerful that at this point, his success is a self-fulfilling prophecy: when Berkshire invests in a stock, everyone else piles in after him and drives the price up. Buffett even lends out his 'halo' to companies that need it—most famously during the financial crisis—so long as they give him a generous discount to the market price.

And yet... Berkshire Hathaway has *underperformed* the S&P 500 for the last 10 years. The world's greatest investor, who has often mocked the EMH, has all but admitted defeat. When Buffett dies, he has asked that his estate be transferred into passive index funds.

Hedge Fund Drone Armies

There you are, sitting in your home office puzzling over Walmart's quarterly report, while the professionals are using an army of drones to monitor the movement of shopping carts in real time. Or sending foot soldiers out to every branch of a bakery chain at the close of business each day, because the numbered dockets start out at zero, and thus contain live sales data unavailable to the market.

The hedge fund manager Michael Steinhardt was once asked the most important thing an average investor could learn from him. "I'm their competition," he replied.

And yet...almost all hedge funds *underperform*. They're not necessarily trying to beat the market—hence the 'hedge' part—but it sure doesn't bode well for the rest of us.

Moving Mountains to Save Milliseconds

If lots of people have access to the same information, speed in bringing it to market also matters. And so, we have 'high-frequency' traders who make their fortunes trading as fast as is physically possible.

One firm spent $300 million laying a direct cable from Chicago to New Jersey. They cut straight through mountains and crossed rivers. The cable stretched 1331 kilometres. And they did this to shave *four milliseconds* off their transmission time.

And yet...the ability to transmit by microwaves came along and rendered the whole project obsolete. Whoops. Getting an edge is expensive.

Ready and Willing to Commit Felonies

Insider trading is a whole thing. Then there are the criminals who go to great lengths to hack or otherwise steal sensitive private information.

And yet...even when criminals have advance access to earnings reports, they *still* don't do all that well, which is evidence for the very strongest form of the EMH (the one that no-one believes can possibly be true).[1]

So...what was your edge again?

If you're mumbling something about having 'good intuition', or 'subscribing to the *Wall Street Journal*' then you might consider the strong possibility that you are Uncle George. If your answer involves 'fundamental analysis' or 'Fibonacci retracements', you're still in Uncle George territory. Performing a complicated ritual makes it easier to internally justify the delusion that you know a secret no-one else does, but it's still (probably) a delusion.

THE EMH REFUSES TO DIE

An edge based on personal relationships, capital investment, or proprietary technology might persist for a while, even once it's a matter of public knowledge. But most edges can't even be *spoken out loud* without disappearing. If stocks systematically rise on the third Thursday of each month but only under a waxing moon, and then someone posts this discovery online, you can kiss that anomaly goodbye. The collective intelligence of the stockmarket sucks it into its gigantic heaving maw, and it's gone forever.

The EMH has to be the only theory that grows *stronger* with every attack against it. The delicious irony is that no-one has done more to advance it than its most serious empirical critics. Every hole blasted into its hide makes the predictions it generates *more* robust. It's like some freaky shoggoth monster that Just. Won't. Die.

To be fair, the only reason the EMH can pull this stunt is because it's not real science. It's unfalsifiable. It responds to criticism by saying, 'OK, good point, but now that I've factored that in, you should believe in my theory even more.'

And...we really should?

The only way to think about the EMH without going insane is that it gives us a useful *heuristic*. It's not a stable law, like we might find in the hard sciences. At any given point in time, there are always competing models that do a better job of describing reality. But all those other models can stop working at any moment, with no warning. By the time you find out their predictive power has evaporated, it's too late, and you probably lost a bunch of money. By contrast, the EMH is reliable—reliably vague, yes, but also reliably useful.

We know that inefficiencies in the market will ultimately be absorbed into the gelatinous alien-god's hivemind. But before that happens, maybe we can make some money off of them.

So now we come to the final test. How do you know for sure if you've really found a market-beating edge, or you're fooling yourself like Uncle George?

FOOLED BY RANDOMNESS

Say we held a national coin-flipping contest. After 15 rounds, one in every ~32,800 people has managed to call every single toss correctly, perfectly predicting a sequence like this:

H T H H T T H H H H T H T T T

Pretty impressive, huh!

Well, only in a world where we don't understand basic probability. In that world, we might be silly enough to mistake randomness for skill. The lucky few winners would be hailed as the heroes of their hometowns, do interviews with breathless breakfast TV hosts, and explain that it's all about the precise flick of the wrist. Aspiring flippers would queue up to buy the inevitable best-selling book, *Flip Me Off*, and pay exorbitant sums for one-on-one coaching sessions with the master tossers.

Depressingly, this is exactly what happens in the world of investing. Past success doesn't predict future returns, but investors stampede towards managers with a market-beating aura. This pack behaviour incentivises fund managers to swing for the fences, increasing the odds they beat the market in some highly visible fashion over some short period of time. Survivorship bias ensures we only hear from those who have taken a gamble and won. They're the talk of the investing community, and do lots of important interviews with the financial press. The losers don't tend to self-promote as much—they have other things on their mind, like the mob of pitchfork-wielding investors trampling the begonias on the front lawn.

Are investing legends like Warren Buffett really just the world's luckiest coin-flippers? I'm happy to give anyone sitting atop a big mountain of cash with a long track record of outperformance the benefit of the doubt, but it's worth noting that we can never know for sure.

Instead, all we have is heuristics. If you don't know who the sucker in the room is, it's you. If you're outperforming an efficient market without any edge, you are Uncle George, and you should quit while you're ahead. If you're convinced you *do* have an edge, but you notice that you are not sitting atop an enormous pile of money, you might consider the possibility that you are wrong.

This is the one area of life where there really is no dodging that most venerable of sick burns: if you're so smart, why aren't you rich?

The EMH is widely hated and derided because it rubs against the grain of our psychology. We're conditioned to think we can win by working harder or smarter than the next guy. The reality is that the best investor is almost certainly the lazy one who commits to a low-cost fund, sets up an automatic payment, and then forgets about it for several decades.

To follow this strategy, we have to overcome a whole host of cognitive biases—overconfidence, confirmation bias, selective memory—that are working to convince us that we (or our friends) really are the Chosen Ones. Strategic self-delusion is useful when we're competing against fellow humans, but it misfires disastrously in the presence of a collective intelligence.

If you're a smart person who knows about these kind of biases, you're in the highest-risk category. Perhaps you have a track record of wandering into areas you don't know much about, and thinking you can do better than the experts who have decades of domain-specific knowledge. The consequences are usually limited to mildly annoying the people who actually know what they're talking about, and much eye-rolling when you triumphantly reinvent the wheel. Very occasionally, it might even be true: you really can breeze into a new field and exploit some obvious inefficiencies.

But it's *not* true of this particular domain, and it's not harmless either.

This is the voice of experience speaking. I've managed to fool myself in all the usual ways, and a few unusual ones. I still do clever things that contradict my own advice, and annoyingly, am rewarded for my hubris just often enough to start entertaining the thought that I'm a brilliant investing guru. Then I force myself to calculate the return on my public investments, and compare it against appropriate benchmarks, and manage to get a fingernail-hold back on boring old reality.

To the extent that I have succeeded as an investor, and I am doing very nicely thank you, it has only come through forcing myself to acknowledge the central prediction generated by the EMH: that you should not expect to be able to beat the market (in the non-trivial sense) unless you have a unique edge.

This comes with one huge and underappreciated benefit. Occasionally, I manage to divert some of my attention elsewhere, to domains where I actually *do* have an edge—and then I win.

ESCAPING THE STICKY MIDDLE

The public investment markets are boring. They're massively efficient, it's almost impossible to find an edge, and there's no potential for unbounded upside.

Buying an index fund is a roughly symmetrical option, with modest risks and modest returns. By definition, we will never do significantly better or worse than the average return. Active stock-picking opens up more potential for both upside and downside, but comes with a slight negative asymmetry.

This is just not a fruitful domain for finding open-ended options. Most publicly traded companies are mature businesses, with quarterly revenue forecasts and well-established business models. Volatility tends to hurt them, not help them: they are highly unlikely to become 100x more valuable because of some unexpected high-impact event.

The best we can do here is let the collective intelligence of public markets make our investing decisions for us, and then focus our attention elsewhere. Messing around with active strategies is not 'bad', so much as it is a quixotic and distracting quest.

If we're going to fool around, we might as well fool around in markets where we actually have some chance of hitting the big one. So let's go hunt some black swans.

22

BLACK SWAN HUNTING

When the going gets weird, the weird turn pro.

— HUNTER S. THOMPSON

ONE OF THE GREAT TIPPING POINTS in human history was learning how to generate non-linear growth: a mind-meltingly unintuitive upheaval that lifted billions out of poverty, made Fry a squillion-aire, tripped up Mark Zuckerberg, and creates vast chasms between those who ride the wave, and those left in its wake.

Exposure to non-linear growth of one form or another is at the heart of all wealth creation. The 'safest' and most reliable version is the compounding effect that comes from steadily investing over many decades, but there are many other pathways:

- Speculating in asset bubbles
- Running a pyramid or Ponzi scheme
- Working for a startup
- Investing in a company with exponential revenue growth
- A career or side-gig with scalable payoffs

Most of these strategies are risky, some are stupid or evil; all are unlikely to succeed. I'm only including this chapter because it would be hypocritical not to mention that while my retirement account is fully invested in passive index funds, I have made almost all of my money hunting black swans.

When a black swan flaps its terrible wings, great destruction and opportunity swirl out of the same chaos. Nassim Taleb made a handsome profit during the global financial crisis while everyone else was blowing up; not because he predicted the specifics of what would happen, but because he had positioned himself to benefit from any event of that nature.

Hunting black swans is a game in which there are no guaranteed prizes, the returns are unevenly distributed among a relatively tiny number of victors, and every man and his dog is trying to sell you the 'winning' strategy. So what's the difference between this style of investing, and out-and-out gambling?

In the worst case—nothing at all.

THE MADNESS OF CROWDS

One way to achieve non-linear returns is through wild speculation. Every now and then, the price of an asset starts to decouple from its underlying value, and greed and momentum take over. Buyers pay higher and higher prices in the belief that they'll always be able to find an even greater fool to offload to. Eventually the music stops, and the price comes crashing back down to earth.

These speculative bubbles are a recurring motif throughout history, from the 17th century Dutch tulip mania, to the dot-com crash of the new millennium, to the cryptocurrency boom-bust cycle today. A small number of people end up very rich, and a large number of people end up very poor. The secret to success is timing your exit right before it all comes crashing down, but of course, everyone else has the exact same idea. As Isaac Newton put it, after losing a fortune in the South Seas stock bubble: "I can calculate the movement of stars, but not the madness of men."

How do otherwise intelligent people get sucked into playing these speculative games? One answer is mimetic desire (I want my brother's toy because he wants it). Another answer is the reality-warping instinct to conform (I want to fit in with my peers, even if it means sitting calmly in a room filling with smoke). But the most disturbing answer is that bubble participants are behaving *perfectly rationally*.

Let's say you and I are at an auction house, and the contents of a mysterious black box go under the hammer. I bid $50, purely for the hell of it. You have no idea what's in that box either, but you think *I* must know something, so you bid $100. Now I think *you* know something, and raise my own bid to $200. A third person enters the gallery, sees the two of us engaged in a heated bidding war over a mysterious box, deduces that we must have information about its contents, and enthusiastically enters a bid at $400. None of us are aware that we're promising increasingly ridiculous sums for a box of old straw and mouse droppings.

This is an 'information cascade', and it's the key to explaining otherwise inexplicable crowd behaviour. It makes sense to take cues from other people's actions, and pay attention to market pricing. But if everyone's looking to their neighbour, and no-one actually has any independent information, it's all a gigantic circle-jerk. As Brian Christian and Tom Griffiths put it in their book *Algorithms to Live By*, information cascades demonstrate that "it's easily possible for any market to spike and collapse, even in the absence of irrationality, malevolence, or malfeasance". The authors give the example of a group of experienced cross-country skiers who went over a cliff. All of the skiers had private concerns about the route, but each was looking to the other for guidance; no-one said anything, and down they fell.

Bubbles are not confined to the bizarro realm of tulip bulbs, Beanie Babies, and bitcoins. They also form in the valuations of productive income-generating assets, like real estate and stocks. So it's helpful to be aware of their characteristics, and think twice if you find yourself relying solely on cues from other people, rather than on information about intrinsic value.

Speculating in asset bubbles to try to get exposure to non-linear returns is essentially the same thing as buying a lottery ticket. The defining feature here is that the expected value of the bet is negative. What does that mean?

EXPECTED VALUE AND THE MULTIVERSE

We've talked about making decisions that generate the best set of possible outcomes for all our future selves. Now we're going to add another dimension: we also have to create the best set of outcomes for all of our selves throughout the multiverse.

Parallel universes are not just a sci-fi plot device. The idea that our universe is constantly branching off into many worlds has crossed into the mainstream among physicists, and is now one of the leading interpretations of quantum mechanics.

Whether or not it turns out to be correct, the multiverse is a very useful model for thinking about investing.

Let's say you happen to buy the winning lottery ticket, or take some similarly speculative trade that hits the jackpot. It feels like an amazing 'investment', but that's such a parochial view—it only worked out in *our* universe! For every world in which you win the Powerball, you condemn 292,201,337 parallel selves to loserdom.

On the surface, a lottery ticket *looks* like the kind of asymmetric option we're interested in: the downside is small and fixed, and the upside is potentially life-changing. But we actually have to run the numbers.

If we count up all the possible outcomes across the multiverse, we see that buying the ticket had a negative **Expected Value (EV)**—the winnings don't come anywhere close to making up for all the losses. A \$2 Powerball ticket pays out an average of 85 cents under the most optimistic conditions, which means it has an EV of -\$1.15.

For an example of a bet with a positive EV, let's switch to poker. This time, we have the option to bet \$100 for a 20 per cent chance of winning \$1000. Table 4.1 shows how the various outcomes play out across the multiverse.

	PROFIT (LOSS)	CHANCES
UNIVERSE 1	(\$100)	20%
UNIVERSE 2	(\$100)	20%
UNIVERSE 3	(\$100)	20%
UNIVERSE 4	(\$100)	20%
UNIVERSE 5	\$900	20%
AVERAGE	\$100	100%

Table 4.1. The expected value of betting \$100 for a chance to win \$1000, calculated by multiplying each of the possible outcomes by the likelihood that each will occur, and then summing the values.

The EV of making the play is +$100, so you place your bet...and lose. A few hands later, the same opportunity presents itself. You lose again. Now you're frustrated. One more time. You lose!

This is the correct decision, even though it will look 'wrong' four times out of five. Every time you take this bet, you're doubling your money across the multiverse. You can hold your head up high no matter the outcome, because you just made millions of your parallel selves mad rich. This counterintuitive approach is how venture capitalists make their money: they're OK with losing almost all of the time, because the occasional investment will pay off so spectacularly that it more than makes up for all the duds.

A positive EV is necessary for an attractive investment, but it's not *sufficient*. Let's say you wager $100 that a coin toss will come up heads, with triple-or-nothing odds. In half of all possible universes, you lose your $100. In the other half, you win $300. The EV is +$200, so you take the bet.

You win! You're offered the same incredible deal again: triple or nothing. Now the EV is +$600. You win again, and the EV jumps to +$1800. In theory, you should never stop taking this bet. In practice, you'll eventually go bust *with 100 per cent probability*. Somewhere along the way, you'd have to stop and take money off the table, even though the EV will always tell you to take the deal.

This is why pros mentally separate 'house money' from their starting stakes. Expected value is an abstraction. What we really care about is the expected *utility* of our investment—how it will impact our lives. It's much better to make a bunch of your parallel selves modestly rich than to make one of you spectacularly rich while impoverishing all the others.

Remember Ray Dalio's heuristic: the risk of ruin, whatever that means to you, must always be zero. Don't bet the farm on an investment with slim chances of success, even if it has a large positive EV, because if you end up in one of the universes where it doesn't pay off, there's no coming back.

There are formulas which tell us how much we should bet to maximise our bankroll in a situation like this, but the simpler way to hedge our bets is by taking a portfolio approach.[1] We want to place several uncorrelated bets with a positive EV, and avoid staking our fortunes on any one of them, no matter how big the payoff might be.

So now we have all the questions we need to ask in evaluating an investment opportunity:

- How efficient is the market?
- Do we have an exploitable edge?
- Is there a large or unbounded upside (+EV)?
- Is it an all-in bet, or can we take a portfolio position?

Buying a lottery ticket fails every test: the market is highly efficient, no-one has an edge, and the EV is negative, which means that taking a portfolio position isn't going to help. Gambling is fun, but it's a total dud as far as black swan hunting is concerned.

Now let's ask the same questions of various other popular hunting grounds.

OUT-OF-THE-MONEY OPTIONS

In the context of risk management, option contracts are a beautiful thing. For hundreds of years they have helped us tame uncertainty: the farmer who grows potatoes and the supplier who buys them both benefit from the option to buy or sell at a given price on a certain date, because each is worried about the exact opposite risk—the farmer will be ruined if prices fall too low, and the supplier if prices rise too high. This ability to match uncertainty to whoever is best positioned to handle it is one of the great innovations of finance.

But options trading for profit is an entirely different beast. There's been an explosion in retail interest in recent years, triggered by record-breaking levels of volatility in financial markets and new platforms that make it possible for anyone to trade.

The usual noob strategy is buying cheap out-of-the-money options which have no intrinsic value at the time of purchase, but the potential for massive upside if the market gets hit by a big lump of volatility.

There is an asymmetry here, in that the downside is capped and the potential upside is unbounded, but it's *already priced in*. Unlike the other options in this book, literal options contracts are far too legible to be interesting. They are liquid, with prices updated in real-time, and scrutinised by millions of people every day. This is a highly efficient market: you are not the first person to have the brilliant idea to buy deep out-of-the-money puts on the S&P 500.

Options are 'overpriced' on average, because the seller of the contract has to be paid for the volatility they take on. This means it is theoretically better to be a net seller of options, but the risk profile is treacherous: a single unbounded loss can wipe out years of collecting small insurance premiums.

What does it take to get an edge in the options game? I defer to the judgment of Nassim Taleb, who says it might be viable as a business, but it takes 3-4 years to understand. As for individuals, he suggests they should "stay far, far away." If you think you can watch some YouTube videos and then sign up for your Robinhood account and make a killing, you are a sucker, and you are going to get pantsed.

VENTURE CAPITAL

With all the headlines about Silicon Valley unicorns, you would be forgiven for thinking that becoming a venture capitalist (VC) is a licence to print money. This is sort of true: the market is inefficient, and there really is massive upside available. But the sector as a whole is an absolute stinker—venture capital actually underperforms the S&P500, despite taking on far more risk.

Average returns have plummeted from the glory days, as the market has become more competitive. But this average is misleading: in fact, the top-tier firms are still doing extraordinarily well. They have the branding, the network effects, and the dealflow unavailable to lesser firms, which means the returns are unevenly distributed.

The bottom three-quarters of the industry is made up of earnest new firms scrabbling to get an edge, and jaded ones blatantly capitalising on rich people who want to get in on the hype train. The business model is not so much about being a savvy investor—VCs usually invest very little of their own funds —but getting paid extraordinarily well to lose investors' money.

The top firms capture almost all the profits; they are always oversubscribed, and you and I have no way of accessing them. Even if we did, these kind of opportunities are only available to accredited investors with a large net worth. So venture capital is only attractive in theory. In practice, you should be suspicious of any firm that wants to take your money.

ANGEL INVESTING

I was the first investor in a company that is currently a Silicon Valley darling. This experience has been hilarious in many ways, and totally disabused me of the notion that professional VCs are all brilliant and contrarian talent-spotters.

For a very long time, no-one would give the founder the time of day. But all the information was there! The beta product was the same as the one that would soon attract hundreds of thousands of users. Investors had the opportunity to get in at a far lower valuation, at a time when the company could have really used the help. But it was only after the first VC made a move that anyone took an interest: eventually, the biggest names were beating down the door asking for meetings. You have never seen such a bunch of lemmings as the bold contrarians of Silicon Valley.

Information cascades look silly from the outside, but I am not really criticising VCs here. Their job, in large part, is to glance from side to side and try to guess which company will be attractive *to other investors*, because access to funding is so crucial to the survival of a startup during the long, expensive years before profitability.

Being an 'angel'—an early-stage investor who backs founders before they raise money from the big guns—is an opportunity to beat VCs at their own game. There is a genuine asymmetry to exploit here: you have an informational edge about the people you know well, and there are massive inefficiencies in the distribution of attention. Everyone loves jumping on bandwagons; no-one wants to back talented people until after they have visibly 'made it'. For structural reasons, this includes most professional investors.

The founder of the company I backed was the smartest and most charismatic person I'd ever met. I knew enough about the field to be confident he was onto something, and enough about his character to be confident he would move back into a van down by the river if he had to. Yet there he was, almost broke, with no fans or users, and no chance whatsoever of getting a meeting on Sand Hill Road. The market for my friend's labour was woefully inefficient, so I began the process of arbitraging it towards its real value.

I'm three for three on this particular strategy, which means I am hopelessly biased. You should expect your friends and family members to have terrible ideas, to lose all your money, and to put a strain on your relationships. New platforms like equity crowdfunding and Angel List can give you access to deals outside of your immediate circles, but then you're competing in a much more efficient market: if you don't know the business or founder intimately, you've given up the only edge you had.

Possibly you could build up an edge by spending years devoted to the art of startup investing, but if you do go down this route, the research suggests indexing is the way to go: rather than trying to pick winners, the best you can do is take every single plausible bet that comes along.

There is a lot to be said for moseying through life and being open to the possibility of an angel opportunity that pops up in a field you know a lot about, or making a deal based on a personal relationship. But it's hard to turn this into an active strategy: if you go out *looking* for deals, you might be unlucky enough to find them.

STARTUP STOCK OPTIONS

"If you wanted to get rich, how would you do it? I think your best bet would be to start or join a startup."

So begins a famous Paul Graham essay on the rewards of entrepreneurship. This was probably true at one point in time—Microsoft minted more than 10,000 millionaires among early employees—but these days it looks more like a marketing ploy to encourage young people to exchange their labour for false hope.

Startup stock options have become increasingly unappealing over the years, with the best terms and preferred stock reserved for investors and founders. Employees need a huge exit if they want to escape the effects of dilution and liquidation preferences, and are often restricted from selling their shares. A friend has been waiting for almost a decade to access his hypothetical millions, while the company he helped build blocks his every attempt to get any liquidity.

Not every startup treats employees like second-class citizens, but even if you get good terms, this is an all-in bet. Maybe you become fabulously rich in 1 per cent of all possible universes, but in all the others, you spent the best years of your life working around the clock for the option to buy worthless stock. Assuming you could earn more money elsewhere, what you are really being sold is an overpriced lottery ticket. The rational strategy is to take the big pay check from a FAANG company instead, and then put some of it in angel investments or a side business that gives you a portfolio of open-ended options.

The one truly excellent reason to work at a startup is that you get a chance to put your own little dent in the universe. The whole 'mission-driven' schtick is also frequently abused as a hiring strategy, but if you really can work on something you love, make friends with amazing people, learn new skills, and help shape the future, that's pretty close to being the best thing in the world— at which point the financial considerations start to fall away anyway.

INVESTING IN YOURSELF

The advice to 'invest in yourself first' is as eye-rollingly banal as it is reliably underrated. This is the biggest asymmetric edge anyone has, because no-one knows you better than you do: your skills, inclinations, and character are sure as hell not priced in by the EMH, and neither are the hyper-local opportunities that you might be able to exploit. Until income-sharing agreements become a thing, literally no-one else has the ability to arbitrage any of these inefficiencies. It's entirely up to you.

Investing in yourself can take various forms:

- Skills or qualifications that open new doors
- Taking a sabbatical to try speculative side-projects
- Buying back free time to do the same (say, by shifting to part-time work)
- Buying or starting a business where you can add value

Some of these options have a clear open-ended upside: who knows what doors that coding bootcamp might open? Others don't really qualify as black swans, but are still very attractive. We'll look at strategies for the timing component of these kind of plays in the next book.

BIRDWATCHING BEATS SWAN HUNTING

Here are what I see as the most viable black swan opportunities:

- Speculation in emerging asset classes that you know a lot about and are still in the pre-hype stage
- Angel investing in people or sectors you know intimately
- Buying a growth business to which you can add value, or a portfolio of businesses
- Taking equity in a startup, *if* you don't get shafted on the terms, and *if* you're excited about the mission
- Investing in new skills, or buying back time to work on speculative side-projects

With the exception of 'invest in yourself', these pathways are inappropriate for most people, and rely on some degree of serendipity.

The truth is that actively setting out to hunt black swans is probably a bad idea. I prefer a more passive 'birdwatching' approach, in which you follow your other motivations—intrinsic talents, satisfying work, taking an interest in the world—while remaining attuned to serendipitous opportunities. Hopefully you will spot enough black swans over the course of a lifetime to put together a modest portfolio; possibly you will never come across a single one.

I realise this is not a very sexy conclusion. I deliberately *didn't* market this book around my own good fortune, or explicitly acknowledge the fact until this chapter, because it's important to be realistic about the prospects of a big win.

My options only came into the money in a serious way as I was finishing the final draft of the book. You might take confidence from the fact that I have been laying out this strategy in public for several years: I told you what I was going to do before I did it, instead of coming up with a plausible story after the fact. But it's also important not be swayed by cute anecdotes. Treat my arguments with as much or little respect as you had before reading this chapter, while we were still living in one of the universes where the strategy had only paid off in the more modest sense.

And remember that even the most braindead approach will always turn up success stories and survivors. A lottery winner will tell you 'you have to be in it to win it', or give you advice on how to pick lucky numbers. What matters is whether a strategy is *replicable*.

Some of the people hawking get-rich-quick books and courses know perfectly well they're selling false hope. But more often, they're clueless Uncle George types who are genuinely convinced that property/crypto/forex trading is the secret to getting rich, and have succumbed to the incredible internal pressure to believe they are brilliant investing gurus. If their students mysteriously fail to experience the same success, it must be because they didn't have the right growth mindset.

I am confident that at least one of my options would have paid off over a lifetime of systematically putting irons in the fire, but who knows? I have no way of checking how all my multiverse selves are getting on, I am wary of being fooled by randomness, and hyping up the hunt for black swans is not what I want anyone to take away from this book.

If you are anything like me, you will listen very carefully to caveats like this and think, 'OK, cool cool cool, but...I'm still going to go make my fortune speculating on Mongolian goat-cheese futures'. In which case, I have one last suggestion which might prevent a determined swan-hunter from discharging both barrels into their own foot.

THE BASTARD'S BARBELL

Black swan hunting is not an all-or-nothing proposition. By using our old friend the barbell strategy, we can deliberately expose ourselves to volatility while simultaneously taking risk off the table.

On one side of the barbell, a basket of risky speculative plays. On the other side, a basket of conservative investments. The weight is distributed between two extremes, with nothing in the middle: instead of taking a somewhat conservative or aggressive investment strategy, you're hyper-conservative and hyper-aggressive at the same time. This puts a fixed cap on your downside, while still giving you exposure to unbounded upside.

The ends of the barbell don't have to be equally weighted. In *Antifragile*, Nassim Taleb describes a barbell tilted 85 to 90 per cent to ultra-conservative assets, like cash or T-bills, and the remaining 10 to 15 per cent spread between small, speculative bets (Fig. 4.2).

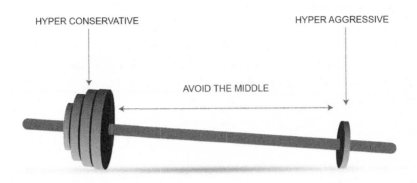

Figure 4.2. The barbell strategy for investing.

If a black swan comes along and blots out the sun, the worst-case scenario is you take a haircut of 10 to 15 per cent of your net wealth. On the flipside, if one of your bets happens to pay off, you stand to make a whole lot of money. Being in the middle gives *the illusion* of safety, but it's actually the worst of both worlds: you're still vulnerable to being wiped out by a black swan, while having no exposure to the stratospheric gains that swirl out of the chaos.

Taleb's barbell is impractical for most people. With most of your money in cash or similar, you'd be lucky to keep up with inflation. In theory, the bets on the risky side make up for the stagnant end of the barbell, but only if you can place enough of them. Someone with a net worth of $10 million can afford to spread $1.5m around a basket of highly speculative bets, which means there's a decent chance that at least one of them will hit the big time. For a small investor, that high-risk basket might only contain a measly $15,000, which is nowhere near enough money to play this game. The chances of holding the winning lottery ticket are tiny, which means you'll almost certainly end up with nothing, while the rest of your money moulders away in the bank.

I'm not saying Taleb's barbell is no good. If you walk into a gym and try to pick up the same barbell as the beefy powerlifter in the corner, you can kiss your vertebrae goodnight. Instead, you have to use the implement that suits your ability and preferences. It's not the specific weights that matter, but the general principles:

- Decide on an acceptable level of downside risk
- Make room for as much upside as your circumstances allow

- Stay the hell away from the middle

To illustrate what I mean, here's the strategy I use for my own portfolio. For reasons that will become clear, I call it the 'Bastard's Barbell'. This is a split between low-cost index funds on one side, and risky speculative bets on the other (Fig. 4.3).

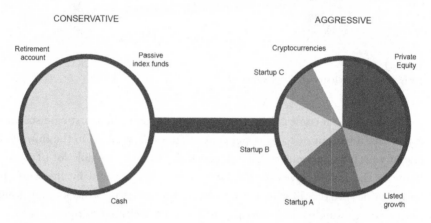

Figure 4.3. The Bastard's Barbell.

On the 'safe' side, I have some cash for liquidity and emergencies, with the rest of my portfolio invested in the cheapest, broadly diversified index funds I can buy. I don't try to pick hot stocks, and will never make more (or less) than the average market return. I'll be holding this portfolio through thick and thin for the next several decades, and investing steadily into it.

On the 'dangerous' side, I have a portfolio of privately owned startups, early-stage growth companies, and a few speculative assets like cryptocurrencies. I'll be reducing my exposure to this side of the barbell over time, in line with my waning risk tolerance.

This is a bastardisation of the barbell Taleb describes, hence the name. Personally, I'm not worried about the fact that my index funds are in the black swan danger zone. I own a stake in almost every publicly traded company in existence. The only way my portfolio could get wiped out would be an event that destroyed every single business on Earth, by which point the flesh bubbling off my charred skeleton would probably take my mind off any financial troubles.

For my purposes, a passive index fund is about as 'safe' as it gets in the long run—there's never been a 20 year period where stocks have fallen. This goes against Taleb's philosophy, which is that black swans haven't happened before by definition, but technically the same argument could be applied to fiat currencies or Treasury Bills, or anything else we might consider a safe haven.

Nevertheless, I very much doubt Taleb would approve of this approach, and I don't necessarily recommend it to others. It's not so much the violation of the 'safe' side which gives me pause: in my opinion, this is much *less* dangerous than keeping almost all your money in cash and T-bills. The problem is in finding hyper-aggressive investments that aren't garbage. There are giant gaping pitfalls associated with getting access to these deals in the first place, with valuing them accurately, and with assuming you have a genuine edge to exploit. It takes a whole lot of work and serendipity to find *one* good deal, let alone enough to build a portfolio of uncorrelated bets.

There's a sense in which it's a waste of time getting hung up on the fine details of modelling investment returns. Anyone who is sufficiently paranoid will understand that the universe can make a mockery of all our careful plans at any moment. No investment strategy is ever guaranteed to deliver the result you want—not even the 'safe' passive investing route preached by the early retirement crowd.

Now that the FIRE movement has crossed over to the mainstream, it might be worth looking more closely at the assumptions underlying it, and at buy-and-hold investing more broadly. This is a bonus chapter for my fellow paranoiacs: it's a little more technical, and can be safely skipped if you prefer to move on to the next book.

23

BEWARE OF GEEKS BEARING
FORMULAS

Investors should be skeptical of history-based models. Constructed by a nerdy-sounding priesthood using esoteric terms such as beta, gamma, sigma and the like, these models tend to look impressive. Too often, though, investors forget to examine the assumptions behind the symbols. Our advice: beware of geeks bearing formulas.

— WARREN BUFFETT

I OWN A PAIR OF GYMNASTIC RINGS, from which I like to dangle upside down above the ground. The heavy-duty straps upon which the rings are suspended are rated for 270 kilograms each. Now, gymnasts are not exactly known for being heffalumps. I'm on the heavier side at 75kg, but the straps are still almost eight times stronger than they need to be to bear my weight. I am happy with this over-the-top redundancy, because I strongly prefer the contents of my head to remain inside my skull.

Engineers, shipbuilders, and construction crews all follow this same principle. They don't design for the 99.9 per cent of the time when everything is fine, but for the edge cases in which the brown stuff hits the whirly thing: the once-in-a-century flood, earthquake, or storm.

Unfortunately, the same cannot be said of bankers, financiers and investors, who merrily dangle upside down above the concrete, with just enough strength to bear their weight—and not a fraction more.

The history of finance is a history of brains splattered on the pavement. Time and time again, we put too much faith in the predictive power of inherently flawed models. Time and time again, they break under the strain of some 'impossible' event.

Take the incredible happenings of August 2007. The great credit crunch was in full swing, and Goldman Sachs' flagship hedge fund had just lost ~30 per cent of its value in a single week. In trying to justify the huge losses, chief financial officer David Viniar told the *Financial Times* "we were seeing things that were 25-standard deviation moves, several days in a row".

If you paid attention in math class, your eyebrows just shot up so fast that they disappeared into your hairline. For those who need a quick refresher: the bell curve represents how a bunch of attributes—height, IQ, blood pressure, schlong size, the velocity of atoms in a gas—are 'normally' distributed (Fig. 4.4).

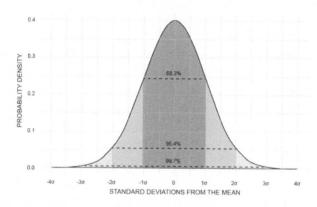

Figure 4.4. The bell curve formed by a normal probability distribution.

We can see that 68 per cent of events fall within one standard deviation of the average, which mathematicians describe with the Greek letter σ (sigma). Ninety-five per cent fall within two standard deviations, and more than 99 per cent are within three standard deviations.

Anything beyond a 3σ event becomes vanishingly rare, as the tails of the distribution drop off exponentially. The more monstrous the outlier, the more unlikely it is to occur, which means that guy on Tinder is almost certainly embellishing his attributes.

So what are the chances that a *25-sigma* event strikes your investment portfolio?

We should expect a 4σ event to happen twice in our lifetime. A 5σ event occurs about every 5000 years, or once since the beginning of recorded history. A 6σ event might have happened roughly twice in the millions of years since *homo sapiens* branched off from the other apes. A 7σ event comes along every billion years or so, or four times since our planet coalesced out of a cloud of interstellar dust. We pass the Big Bang somewhere around the 8σ mark. At 20σ, the number of years we'd have to wait is ~10x higher than the number of particles in the universe.

By the time we get all the way to 25σ, there are no comparisons that our brains can make sense of without melting into a puddle of goo.

So. Imagine the incredible bad luck of Viniar and friends! Not only struck down by a 25-sigma event, but by *several in a row*. And of course, Goldman Sachs wasn't the only company affected. Could it be that the universe served up an entire buffet of events which ought never to have happened in a million billion trillion lifetimes?

Or is it more likely that the Wall Street financiers' fancy models were... wrong?

The late, great mathematician Benoit Mandelbrot was among the first to notice that the seemingly impossible happens *all the time* in financial markets. Crashes, recessions and day-to-day turbulence are jam-packed with 'freak accidents', 'outliers', and 'billion-year' events.

One of Mandelbrot's PhD students, Eugene Fama of EMH fame, wrote his thesis on this phenomenon. Fama found that price movements of more than five deviations from the average happened *2000x* more often than the standard models would predict. A five-sigma event ought to be about as worrisome as a civilisation-threatening meteor strike, which might come along once in recorded history. In practice, these events happen every three or four years.

In other words: the chaotic world of finance cannot be tamed by the cute bell curve you learned about in eighth grade.

The models are finally starting to catch up with reality, although not before they ruined a lot of people's lives. The only small consolation is that many of the academics who lulled investors into a false sense of security also got blown up, often in spectacular fashion.[1]

And so, the fact that many people tend to be 'irrationally' wary of the markets starts to take on a new significance. The suspicious folk wisdom has often turned out to be correct, while the 'experts' have consistently been dangerously overconfident.

All we have is models of the world; all models are wrong; some are useful. The question is: how wrong are the financial models we're using today? Dangerously, *cosmologically* wrong? Or just a teensy bit wrong?

TESTED UNDER FIRE

Here's the best model we have today: instead of trying to pick hot stocks or sectors, invest in an index fund that tracks the entire market. Instead of trading in and out, buy and hold forever. This is what I've recommended for many years. It's also one of the central doctrines of the FIRE movement, which expands it into the following formula:

- Live frugally
- Pour all your savings into low-cost passive index funds
- Don't trade in and out, or try to time the market
- Retire once you accumulate 25x your annual expenses in investments
- Safely withdraw 4 per cent of your portfolio each year without running out of money

Warren Buffett urges us to be skeptical of nerdy-sounding priesthoods, and examine the assumptions behind their models. So, what are the assumptions underpinning FIRE?

1. The FIRE model works *IF* you have the intestinal fortitude to stay calm during a major market downturn
2. The FIRE model works *IF* you don't have any 'uncle points' which might force you to sell at an inopportune moment
3. The FIRE model works *IF* market timing doesn't matter for long-term investors
4. The FIRE model works *IF* historic returns are indicative of future returns

I think all four of these assumptions are a little shaky. Let's take each of them in turn.

1. Intestinal fortitude

The standard line is that for long-term investors, market crashes don't matter a damn. You ignore the headlines, and calmly ride out the volatility. Those who keep buying through the downturn get to pick up stocks in a discount sale that only comes around once every decade or two.

I have repeated the standard advice many times, including in Chapter 21. It is, as far as I know, *technically* the 'best' advice. But there's a difference between models tested under sterile laboratory conditions and what actually works out in the messy real world.

When the market crashes, it falls for more than a year on average, and loses over 30 per cent of its value. And that's *the average*. Sometimes, it's a lot worse. When this has happened in the past, many otherwise smart people have panicked and sold out with the worst possible timing—including some of those who preach the buy-and-hold approach!

So you have to be honest with yourself about how you might respond in a crisis. It's important to visualise these scenarios in as much detail as you can, and really try to 'feel' it. Maybe it makes sense to take some money off the table, or have a portfolio that isn't 100 per cent in stocks—even if it's *technically* not the best strategy.

2. Uncle points

Even if you're certain you have the intestinal fortitude to hold the line, life comes at you fast. What if you lose your job, or your marriage, or your house burns down, or a loved one gets sick? If you can provide solid answers to these kinds of questions, which ought to involve words like 'insurance' and 'emergency funds', that's great. But you can't eliminate uncertainty altogether.

FIRE assumes we're capable of behaving like Mr Spock during a crisis, and it doesn't account for what traders call 'uncle points'. When someone is twisting your arm out of its socket, there will come a point when you're in so much pain that you have no choice but to cry 'Uncle!' and close out the position, no matter how much it ruins your careful plans.

3. Market timing matters

Sure, the past returns on index funds have been good, on average. Sure, they're unlikely to go to zero, unless every productive business on Earth simultaneously melts into slag. Sure, there's never been a 20-year period in which the stock market has lost money.

But the standard advice—that timing doesn't matter—is wrong. Or to put it another way, it's right *on average*, but wrong specifically. The problem is that there is no such thing as an 'average investor'. There's just you, and me, and your auntie, and her neighbour, and a bunch of other individuals who care very much about what happens to their precious retirement fund. If *your* portfolio gets wiped out, it's not very reassuring to know 'the average investor' is doing fine.

A nifty online tool called FIREcalc hammers this point home. Let's say you retired in the early 1970s, with a portfolio of $750,000, and planned to withdraw $35,000 of spending money each year. On average, you'll do very handsomely indeed. But that average is dangerously misleading.

In Fig. 4.5, we see what happens when three friends with identical portfolios retire in quick succession: Alice retires in 1973, Bob retires in 1974, and Carol retires in 1975.

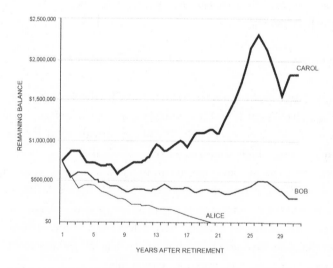

Figure 4.5. The effect of small variations in market timing on retirement outcomes.

Bob does pretty well, and Carol does *spectacularly* well, but Alice's portfolio blows up. Even the smallest variation in timing can create dramatically different outcomes.

Let's make our example a little more conservative. If we stick to the 'safe' withdrawal rate of 4 per cent, that means we can spend $30,000 a year. In Fig. 4.6, we model how this portfolio would have performed across every time period since 1871.

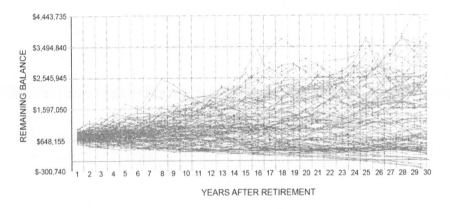

Figure 4.6. Outcomes of a retirement portfolio across a large sample of time periods.

Each path on the graph represents a different outcome. The highest portfolio balance at the end of the period is $4.25 million, and the average is $1.4m. But once again, the average is dangerously misleading. Some of the paths fall below zero, and the worst outcome is a balance of -$300,000. In 5 per cent of the cycles tested, the 'safe' withdrawal rate was anything but.

So: the assumption that market timing doesn't matter is wrong. It matters a whole lot. There's enormous variance in outcomes, purely based on luck.

One obvious takeaway is that it's important to diversify yourself across investing time windows. Unless you invest a big lump sum all at once, this happens naturally: you keep saving and investing a little more each year. If you do that for 20 years, you end up with 20 different investing windows, and 20 different lines on the graph. By spreading risk across time, we can become something much closer to the 'average investor'.

In other words, the buy-and-hold wisdom really shines during the accumulation phase. As long as you don't hit any uncle points, you're not eating into your capital during a downturn. And so long as you keep your nerve, you get to keep buying at bargain prices!

But you *can't* diversify your retirement window. It's a one-off event. From the point you stop earning, you only get one line on the graph. Instead of accumulating through good times and bad, you're burning capital through good times and bad. With a 'safe' withdrawal rate of 4 per cent, there's something like a one-in-20 chance of going bust. And even that's assuming the past has something to tell us about the future. Does it?

4. Past performance is no guarantee of future returns

Maybe we'll have an investing winter that lasts 30 years, or a crash that makes everything before it look like a minor fender-bender. Maybe the bull market will merrily rampage along for a thousand days and a thousand nights.

As Keynes put it, we simply do not know! In which case, all the meticulously-planned models and safe withdrawal rates are garbage in, garbage out.

CLOSING THOUGHTS ON RISK

Not all geeks deserve to be tarred with the same brush. The early retirement folks have nothing in common with the bankers and financiers who take other people's money, privatise the profits, and get bailed out when they go bust. If the FIRE priesthood are wrong, they will be the first to be hurt, and most of them are well aware of the nuances described in this chapter.

As far as I'm concerned, Mr Money Mustache ought to be given the Presidential Medal of Freedom. The FIRE model has worked out brilliantly for tens of thousands of people, and I hope it will work out for many more.

But it does make me cringe whenever I hear someone talk about buying and holding index funds as if it were a sure thing, or mentioning safe withdrawal rates without wrapping inverted commas around the word 'safe'.

If FIRE enthusiasts are a little careless about this—as I have been in the past—it's understandable. It's boring to include endless caveats, especially when you're trying to spark enthusiasm. What investing noob would make it through a warning about standard deviations and ensemble probabilities without their eyes glazing over?

The good news is that none of this actually changes much, in practice. As far as I can see, the best strategy is *still* to make long-term investments in cheap index funds and don't try to time the market. But it does reinforce a few important points:

1. Take steps to minimise the chances of uncle points. That means insurance policies for income, health, and catastrophic events, so you don't have to lock in a loss at an inopportune time. It also means forcing yourself to contemplate the end of a marriage, the unexpected patter of little feet, a serious disease or accident, and various other unthinkable scenarios that might cause a sudden change to your financial situation.

2. The only truly 'safe' strategy is to maintain diverse income streams, without relying on investment returns. Ideally, that means finding work you actively enjoy, and creating a life you don't need to retire from.

3. Staying streamlined is the master strategy. To repeat an unflattering metaphor from earlier, frugal folks are hardy little cockroaches. Should a black swan spread its wings and blot out the sun, those who are attempting to FIRE may have to delay their plans or return to work— but they will be among the best-positioned to not only survive, but thrive.

This brings an end to our voyage through the perilous waters of risk. We know consumer debt must be destroyed, and the risk of ruin must always be nil. Having climbed to firm ground, we know not to bury our talents in the dirt. Instead, we have to deliberately take calculated risks to get exposure to asymmetric returns, and walk the knife-edge between peril and promise.

In making these decisions, we are trailed by vast clouds of uncertainty. We have seen that the history of finance is a history of brains dashed on the pavement. We know better than to put our faith in predictive models that promise us 'safety'. Instead, we focus on what is within our control, and build optionality to position ourselves for volatility and black swanss—even if we don't know what form they will take. May all our downside be capped, and all our upside be unlimited!

But we're missing one last component: *timing*. When to be defensive with our finances, and when to bet aggressively? At what point in our careers should we take risks, and at what point should we play it safe? And what are the best models for making these temporal trade-offs? This is the subject of Book V.

V

KAIROS

KAIROS. (noun) from the ancient Greek καιϱός: *the right, critical, or opportune moment to make a decision or take action.*

INTRODUCTION

I saw myself sitting in the crotch of the fig tree, starving to death, just because I couldn't make up my mind which of the figs I would choose. I wanted each and every one of them, but choosing one meant losing all the rest, and, as I sat there, unable to decide, the figs began to wrinkle and go black, and, one by one, they plopped to the ground at my feet.

— SYLVIA PLATH, 'THE BELL JAR'

FOR A GENERATION OF YOUNG PEOPLE who have been told they can do anything, Sylvia Plath's fig tree metaphor is all too relatable. Crushing sense of indecision? Check. All-pervasive fear of missing out? Check. Creeping feelings of existential dread? Check. If the youth of the 1960s were already struggling with this malaise, imagine how much it worse it is in the age of Instagram, when the counterfactual life of the road not taken is staring you right in your stupid face.

The fig tree passage is poignant, widely-shared, and completely misunderstood.

Esther, Plath's author-insert character, experiences the dizzying vision during a tour of the United Nations. The crucial context follows on the next page, when she sits down to lunch:

"I don't know what I ate, but I felt immensely better after the first mouthful. It occurred to me that my vision of the fig tree and all the fat figs that withered and fell to earth might well have arisen from the profound void of an empty stomach."

This great soul-crushing existential angst was because... wait, no, actually she was just *hungry*. Not to make light of Esther's feelings, but this is one hell of a classy problem to have. The options she's weighing up include a happy home life with children and a husband, being a famous poet, a brilliant professor, travelling the world, taking on a pack of lovers, and becoming an Olympic champion, among others.

Sometimes we really are better off with fewer options, but this is only true in the most tangled branches of the possibility tree, where each new low-quality choice creates more downside with almost zero additional upside.

It's a grave mistake to apply this framework to high-quality options, and we should be extremely suspicious of anyone who tries to limit our capabilities 'for our own good'. Throughout most of history, Esther would have had no choice but to be a dutiful housewife and baby production line. The fact that she's in a position to choose between so many exciting and rewarding futures is nothing short of incredible. The best proxy for flourishing is having lots of juicy figs to pluck, and it's perfectly OK if we don't actually get to most of them: merely having optionality is an intrinsic good. Plenty of liberated 21st century women still choose to be housewives, but the crucial difference is that they actually have the choice.

The important insight in Esther's tummy-rumbling hallucinations is that every option has an expiry date. If we never exercise any of them, they really will wither and rot and fall to the ground. By this point in the game, all the branches have appealing outcomes—we're no longer dithering over umpteen varieties of pasta sauce. After a certain point, we have to say 'no' to most of the opportunities we've collected, commit to something, and grasp onto it with both hands.

Which figs to pluck? And when? For this second round of pruning, we need a higher-level set of constraints.

The ancient Greeks had two different words for time. The version we're familiar with, *chronos*, describes the chronological passage of time. The second word—*kairos*—doesn't have a direct translation, but the key distinction is that it's qualitative, not quantitative.

Kairos is the opportune moment to take action, or make a decision. It tells us when to *explore*: to learn new skills, meet new people, try out new ideas, hatch cunning schemes, and generally open up our options—and when to *exploit*: to deliberately constrain ourselves, and pluck those figs before they blacken and rot.

A TIME TO EXPLORE AND A TIME TO EXPLOIT

Do not be too timid and squeamish about your actions. All life is an experiment. The more experiments you make, the better.

— RALPH WALDO EMERSON

B ABIES LOVE PUTTING THINGS in their mouths: dirt, insects, bits of grass, their own poo. They have no sense of fear or self-preservation, and come up with endlessly creative ways to place themselves in mortal peril. Once they learn to talk, their constant experimentation with the world transcends the physical to the philosophical. They want to know *every-thing*. They are bottomless pits of curiosity, with very little in the way of atten- tion span or self-discipline. A typical two-year-old can only concentrate on a task for six minutes at a time. Young children are not self-aware enough to feel much in the way of shame or embarrassment. Nothing is off-limits. In a word, very young people spend almost all of their time *exploring*.

The elderly are set in their ways. The only foreign objects they put in their mouths are dentures and hard caramels; occasionally followed by a fork to extricate said caramels from said dentures. They tend to have stable routines, rituals, and social circles. They rarely try new things or experiment with new identities. They've lived long enough to know what they're about, and they intend to wring out every ounce of enjoyment before the curtains come down. In a word, very old people spend almost all of their time *exploiting*.

Exploring is analogous to opening up new options, while exploiting is analogous to executing the options you already have. Don't get hung up on the connotations—these terms are borrowed from computer science, where they're used neutrally. The important idea is that these strategies trade off against one another: time spent investigating new opportunities is time you could have spent enjoying what you already have, and vice versa. It's a real head-scratcher.

THE MULTI-ARMED BANDIT

You walk into a casino, and are faced with several banks of slot machines. Some of the machines pay out more often than others, but there's no way of finding out which ones are 'hot' without sitting down and trying them out.

Let's say the very first machine you try pays out on an average of one in every 10 pulls. If you choose to wander off and start pulling new levers, you're forsaking the opportunity to receive a tried-and-tested reward. If you stick with the tried-and-tested arm, you're forsaking the opportunity to search for a machine with a higher payoff.

This is called the 'multi-armed bandit', and it's the textbook example of the **Explore/Exploit** trade-off. The optimal solution is to start out by exploring as much as possible, and gradually move towards exploiting as your time runs out. And this is exactly how we behave throughout our lives, even if we're not consciously aware of it. *Of course* an old person isn't going to try lots of new things with uncertain payoffs: their remaining time is limited. *Of course* a young person isn't going to stick with the very first hobby, job, or lifestyle practice they try: they can almost certainly find better rewards by experimenting.

The explore vs exploit trade-off is not a binary on/off switch, but a dimmer that we adjust over time. In the formal solutions to the multi-armed bandit, it always pays to remain optimistic in the face of uncertainty, just as it does in real life.[1] Old people rarely become completely calcified and closed off to opportunities. They can, and should, remain open to a little exploring, right up until the point when they're no longer buying green bananas.

This gives us the first factor for the optimal timing of opening options: the window of opportunity available to us. The longer the timeframe, the more resources we should devote to upfront exploration, and vice versa.

In the multi-armed bandit, if you do enough exploration to find a machine with a handsome payout, you can sit there pulling the lever over and over, getting fat and happy. But in the real world, the payouts are *constantly changing*. Perhaps the machine you've settled in on goes dead on the very next pull. Meanwhile, another machine that you previously ruled out as a dud might light up and start spraying coins everywhere.

Which gives us the second timing factor: volatility. In domains where nothing ever changes, there's no point in constantly opening new options, and you can shift most of your efforts to exploitation fairly early on. But high-volatility domains reward us for constant exploration, and punish those who switch to pure exploitation too early in the piece.

Now we have our two timing factors—timeframe and volatility—let's apply them to the four main areas of optionality.

EXPLORING AND EXPLOITING IN HEALTH CAPITAL

The timeframe for being alive is (hopefully) good and long. If you have 80 years on the clock, it's well worth spending the first couple of decades doing enough exploration to discover which diet, exercise, and habits best suit your individual physiology and preferences.

But volatility is extremely low. Human biology changes on a glacial timescale irrelevant to any individual, as does the best practice for preserving health capital, which might go hundreds of years with no major developments. There is some variation in the body's needs over a lifetime, but short of an accident or unexpected health condition, these changes are predictable. The way we eat, sleep, and exercise might change between age 18 and age 80, but it's a difference of degree, not of kind. There is no world in which potato chips will suddenly start being healthy, or resistance training will become obsolete.

Fig. 5.1 shows how we can maximise the area of health capital under the curve. We start off with a lot of exploration, then steadily winnow down the options until we end up in a state of almost pure exploitation by our late twenties or thirties. After a point, there's very little to be gained in constantly trying new things, and a lot to be lost.

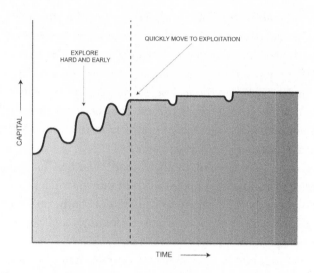

Figure 5.1. Maximising health capital under the curve.

We can also map out a couple of common failure modes. The scourge of 'Fuckarounditis' involves leaping from fad to fad, always trying new diets and pills and exercise regimes, and never committing to anything long enough to get the force of momentum on our side (Fig. 5.2).

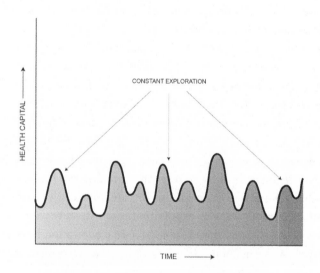

Figure 5.2. The 'Fuckarounditis' failure mode in health capital.

Then there's the 'Couch Potato', which represents a failure to launch. Without doing the initial exploration required to open up genuinely attractive pathways, there's no escaping the sticky middle of low-quality options served up by consumer capitalism. Half-hearted bursts of misapplied effort—a fad diet here, snake-oil supplements there—are too little and too late. Negative momentum has already set in, and health capital declines rapidly over time (Fig. 5.3).

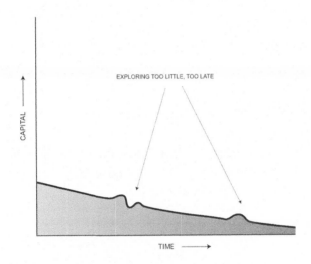

Figure 5.3. The 'Couch Potato' failure mode in health capital.

EXPLORING AND EXPLOITING IN SOCIAL CAPITAL

The timeframe for social capital is also good and long, but there is more volatility. People come in and out of your orbit as you move through different phases of life, or start over in a new city/workplace/subculture. To maximise social capital, we want an oscillating pattern of regular, small-scale exploration that contracts over time (Fig. 5.4). The older you get, the less value there is in racking up your 10,000th Twitter follower, and the more you optimise for quality of connection over quantity.

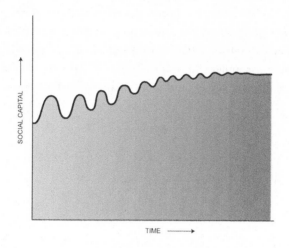

Figure 5.4. Maximising social capital under the curve.

We can also map some common failure modes. The 'Shut-in' doesn't do any exploring beyond high school or college, and ends up with very little social capital as old connections drift apart (Fig 5.5).

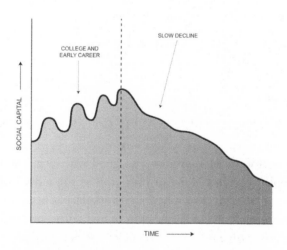

Figure 5.5. The 'Shut-in' failure mode in social capital.

The Shut-in is common among men in particular, who sometimes end up with no close friends at all, and become entirely dependent on their spouse.

By contrast, the 'Social Butterfly' spends too much time making hundreds of shallow friends, without investing enough into enduring connections (Fig 5.6). Their outer Dunbar circles are thriving, but no-one is moving into the inner circles, and close friends and family are neglected. This is a potential pitfall for influencers and other people who are driven by popularity or fame at all costs.

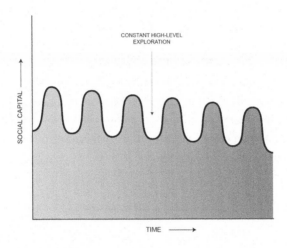

Figure 5.6. The 'Social Butterfly' failure mode in social capital.

Both health capital and social capital are relatively straightforward domains: the timeframes are long and predictable, and while volatility is increasing slightly, it's only off a very low base. Lindy rules, and many of the winning strategies here are thousands of years old.

By contrast, financial and knowledge capital have uncertain timeframes, and are subject to massive volatility. In a fast-changing world, our accumulated wisdom and tradition are increasingly leading us astray. That would be bad enough, but a host of powerful forces also conspire to nudge us into a narrow range of standardised options as soon as possible, cutting off our ability to explore widely. As a result, optionality is becoming more valuable at the exact same time as it becomes harder to obtain. This is the central argument of Kairos: *we're not exploring nearly enough.*

THE EMBARRASSING PROBLEM OF PREMATURE EXPLOITATION

You're out in the countryside, climbing a hill. You stop to rest at the top, and take in the view. The surrounding landscape is obscured by mist, and you're not sure if you're at the highest point. If you want to explore any further, you'll have to trudge all the way back to the bottom, and set off in another direction.

What you can't see is that there's a much taller peak nearby, which rises above the mist and offers a spectacular view over the entire range. You might have a map that tells you it's nearby, or hear stories from passing hikers about how great the summit is, but life is comfortable here on the small peak. If you want to do more hill-climbing, there's a huge chasm between the first-order consequences (exertion, possibility of failure) and the second-order consequences (getting to an elevated position). As we can see in Fig. 5.7, you're stuck in a local maximum.

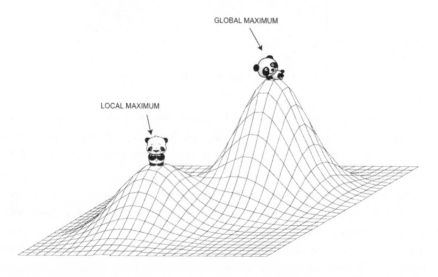

Figure 5.7. Hill climbing.

Superstimuli are examples of local maxima. A video game reliably serves up hits of achievement on cue, with a near-instant feedback loop engineered to be as 'sticky' as possible. There's a clearly defined pathway for completing quests, levelling up into a muscle-bound hero, and impressing scantily-clad elven princesses with your very big sword. The only problem is that none of your heroic endeavours carry over to real life, in which the only exercise you get is lifting cans of Mountain Dew to your face, quests don't come with convenient save points, and the scantily-clad princess is actually a big hairy Russian dude named Stanislav.

The hard thing about hill-climbing is that you have to go down before you can go up. The rewards offered by an immersive video game are a pale imitation of those available in real life, but you can get them with so much more certainty. When you're exploring unknown territory or attempting difficult things, the feedback loop between effort and reward is laggy and unpredictable. It's *doubly* hard when you're simultaneously trying to wean yourself off a reliable source of pleasure, and overcome the constant temptation to return to its mediocre but familiar embrace.

No wonder so many people end up trapped in local maxima. The argument of Book II is that the machinery of consumer capitalism is designed to keep us stuck here, that the moat is only ever getting wider, and this is compounded by the fact that we suck at making trade-offs across time—at weighing the second, third and nth-order consequences of our actions. This is the embarrassing problem of 'premature exploitation', and it affects as many as one in three men.[2]

While we often stigmatise those who overindulge in the Siren's products, in other ways, our norms and cultural beliefs push us further *towards* premature exploitation. For example, the conventional wisdom around careers is that you should work hard and climb through the ranks to specialise in your field—either the family trade, or whatever pathway your adolescent self saw fit to send you down. You draw a monthly salary, pay your dues for several decades, and eventually collect your gold watch and pension.

Working for the sake of earning a pay check early in one's career is not quite as short-sighted as playing video games all day, but it's still an example of premature exploitation. Instead of repetitively pulling the first lever you find, you're better off building knowledge, skills, and connections that open up more attractive opportunities—to keep exploring—even if it means earning less money in the short-term. You don't necessarily want to specialise until you've explored more of the possibility space.

Accumulating broad skills and options is the best way to prepare for a volatile world, but we still have to be able to make firm decisions in the face of uncertainty. The next chapter gives us a set of constraints for pointing our efforts in the right direction, without having to know exactly where we're going to end up.

25

A TIME TO IMPROVISE AND A TIME TO
MAKE PLANS

Don't try to construct the future like a building, because your current blueprint is almost certainly mistaken. Start with something you know works, and when you expand, expand westward.

— PAUL GRAHAM

IMAGINE GOING BACK IN TIME 2 million years, kidnapping your great-great-great-etc grandpa, and dropping him off in 40,000 BC. Our hairy hominin ancestor would go from banging rocks together, to... banging rocks together in a slightly more sophisticated way. No doubt he'd be impressed by the innovative new technique of pressure flaking: using a bone or antler punch to more finely shape a stone. And to think it only took 1.96 million years to figure this out!

The next big leap: 8000 years BC, when stone tools developed into early agricultural implements. The advent of farmers, crops, and cities would blow Grandpa Ugg's tiny little mind. But after the Agricultural Revolution, the daily existence of peasants settled into a new equilibrium that barely changed for millennia.

For most of our human and human-ish ancestors, life came at you slow. Nothing changed. Like, ever. Not even the rocks you banged together. You'd almost certainly be born, grow old, and die without witnessing a single advance in technology.

It's only within the last few hundred years that the rate of change started to really accelerate. If you dropped a pre-Enlightenment peasant into modern life, he'd have a mental breakdown on the spot. Flying monsters! Voices issuing from boxes! Moving pictures!

The same sort of progress that once took 2 million years now takes us all of two days. Even in the space of an individual lifetime, it's hard to keep up: dutiful children must teach their parents and grandparents how to program a VCR or sign up for Twitter. I'm still in my twenties, but I already feel ancient when trying to keep up with trends that Zoomers understand intuitively.

Back to the recurring theme of compound interest in everything: not just money, but popularity, knowledge, curiosity, and yes, technology. In the early days, there was almost nothing for momentum to work upon, so it looked like a flat line: hundreds of thousands of years of banging rocks together. Once we passed the 'knee' of the exponential curve, life got very weird, very fast (Fig. 5.8).

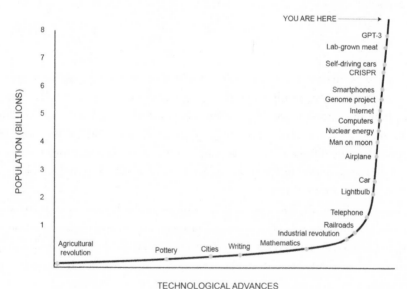

Figure 5.8. Exponential progress in innovation.

In 1975, Intel co-founder Gordon Moore made a famous prediction that the number of transistors on an integrated circuit would double every two years. Every time 'Moore's Law' looked like it was about to fail, a new innovation came along and extended the trend. Over the same half-century, we've also experienced exponential growth in computational power, hard drive capacity, the affordability of DNA sequencing, camera quality, and many other technologies.

The sheer momentum behind human innovation is notoriously difficult to grasp. Eminent scientists and engineers dismissed the airplane as impossible, right up until (and sometimes *after*) Wilbur Wright's manned flight of 0.26 kilometres—a distance which has since been improved upon 150,000 times over. This is a recurring pattern: Einstein wrote off nuclear energy as a pipe dream, and the Nobel Prize-winning economist and *New York Times* columnist Paul Krugman infamously predicted that "by 2005 or so, it will become clear that the Internet's impact on the economy has been no greater than the fax machine".

There is some evidence that the rate of progress has slowed since the 1970s, but it's still a white-knuckle ride compared to any other period in human history. As soon as a new 'enabler' technology kicks off a new round of innovation—say, a general artificial intelligence, gene editing, quantum computing, or nuclear fusion—we might expect life to get even weirder still.

Those who underestimate the force of momentum behind human innovation invariably end up looking silly. It's not that the experts are always wrong. But as the psychologist Daniel Gilbert notes, when scientists make erroneous predictions, they almost always err by predicting that the future will be too much like the present.

Computer scientists solved the multi-armed bandit problem by coming up with clever algorithms which give us the ideal strategy for exploring and exploiting. But a volatile world throws a spanner in the works. When the payoffs of each slot machine change over time, you end up with a 'restless' bandit problem, which is intractable: it's literally impossible to find the optimal solution. This is what real life is like. And our bandit is very, very restless.

THE DANGERS OF OVERSPECIALISATION

Generalists love to dunk on narrow-minded specialists, while specialists look down on scatter-brained generalists. But the generalist/specialist divide is a false dichotomy. We'd be foolish to only ever explore—to constantly acquire new skills without putting any of them to use—and we'd be just as silly to only ever exploit—to dive headfirst into the first option that presents itself, and never bother to check out the surrounding territory.

Instead, we can explore and exploit in parallel: become a jack of all trades, *and* a master of one. Or we can do it serially: lots of successful careers look like an initial period of exploration, followed by going deep on one thing for several years, then an exploration phase in an adjacent field, and so on.

There is still a trade-off between these states, but the usual arguments miss the most important factor: the winning strategy depends on the volatility of the domain in question.

In stable domains, specialisation wins hands-down. This is a solved prob-lem, and has been since 1817, when David Ricardo came up with the Law of Comparative Advantage. Even if you're a polymath freak who can beat your competitors at every task, you still ought to maximise your gains by focusing on the one area you have the highest *relative* advantage, and trade in exchange for everything else. This is a highly counterintuitive insight, but it's one of the most widely-accepted ideas in economics: each individual or country should specialise in their comparative advantage, and then single-mindedly exploit the heck out of it.

Neither of my parents ever had to switch careers, and my dad even stayed with the same government department for 40 years. The prospect of a job for life and a state pension in retirement meant it made sense to specialise. While we no longer live in that stable world, our models (and the well-meaning advice we're given by previous generations) haven't caught up with reality.

This book went to print in a year in which many countries learned a grim lesson about the dangers of overspecialisation. The world's largest economy spent *months* trying to figure out how to manufacture basic protective equip-ment, with medical personnel reduced to improvising gowns from plastic ponchos and begging the general public to donate face masks. The fragility of global supply chains left the citizens of the richest and most advanced society in the history of the world dying like flies. Ricardo really screwed the pooch on this one.

The strongest case for generalism—for countries or individuals—is the simple logic of diversification. You wouldn't put all your financial capital in one investment. So why would you concentrate all your career capital in one narrow domain? Specialising has a higher payoff in the short term, but you're constantly accumulating silent risk. When the pink slip comes out of nowhere, or your job or industry is automated out of existence, you have nothing to fall back on. All your life outcomes are tied to your one specific area of competency continuing to be valuable.

VOLATILITY CLUSTERS

The dumpster fire of a year known as 2020 was also a stark reminder of the fact that volatility *clusters*. As Lenin put it, "there are decades where nothing happens, and there are weeks where decades happen." Volatility builds up slowly in the background, like mast before a forest fire, until a stray spark sets it off—and then everything explodes at once.

This is not just a metaphor. At the time of writing, the orange-hued skies of California bear a striking resemblance to *Blade Runner*. This season's out-of-control 'megafires' are not primarily due to climate change, as the incompetent local politicians are trying to claim. California is naturally designed to burn: prehistorically, between 4.4 million and 11.8 million acres went up in flames each year. The danger comes from overzealous suppression of small fires, and layers of bureaucracy making it all but impossible to carry out controlled burns, to the point where a measly 13,000 acres were burned off in 2017. In many ways, this was the most predictable disaster ever. But its impact and timing were still ruled by randomness: it's impossible to model the exact drift of embers, or the deliberate fires set by activists and firefighters trying to score overtime, and who would have guessed that the first line of defence—I shit you not, prison inmates earning a few dollars a day—would be too sick with a novel coronavirus to work?

The same pattern repeats in financial markets, companies, and life in general: stamping out the small stressors that act as natural fire breaks only makes us more vulnerable when the Big One comes along. We would be better off letting banks fail early, refusing to protect the feelings of the over-sensitive, and taking small shocks at regular intervals. Instead, we put sticking plasters over festering wounds, and suppress volatility with a patchwork of kludges that create bigger problems down the track.

Volatility clusters, but that doesn't mean the events it unleashes are all 'bad' or 'good'. Price movements in markets can exhibit *dependence* without displaying any *correlation*: a big swing leads to the probability of more big swings, with no way of knowing which direction it will be in. The 2020 coronavirus crash sent the market into the fastest tailspin in history, with the S&P 500 tumbling 35 per cent in just over a month. This was immediately followed up by the fastest recovery of all time, to the point where, astonishingly, the market set a new all-time high in the middle of a global pandemic. The Dow Jones notched up 14 of its 17 biggest single-session point declines in its 124-year existence, and eight of its nine biggest single-day point increases. During the same period, we crowned our first $2 trillion public company, oil prices briefly went *negative*, and asset classes were generally flung around like rag dolls.

It's not always going to be like this. There will be periods of relative stability and calm. But we know that a single technological breakthrough or black swan event can trigger a chain reaction of world-changing consequences, with the shock of the impact exacerbated by our naive approaches to risk management. It's only a matter of time until the next drifting ember (or arsonist) sets everything alight.

How the heck are we meant to think about planning our lives in these kind of conditions?

FOLLOW YOUR BLISTERS

One popular and very bad piece of career advice is to 'follow your passion'. In *So Good They Can't Ignore You*, Cal Newport makes a valiant effort to kill off the passion myth for good. As he points out, when you ask college students what they're passionate about, a full 84 per cent can provide an answer. But the top five passions are dance, skiing, reading, swimming, and hockey (this being a Canadian study). Only a tiny minority of kids will actually make careers out of these things. By contrast, approximately zero teenagers have a burning passion for, say, ethnobotany, or user experience design.

It's easy to find examples of actors or athletes who became successful by pursuing a childhood dream, but that's only because these stories naturally generate headlines and inspiration-porn memes. The career trajectories of high-profile outliers are the exception to the rule, and following their well-intentioned advice typically ends in frustration.

In fact, the passion myth gets the causality backwards: most people don't identify their passion in advance, and then work hard to make it a reality. Instead, passion is something that *emerges over time* as a consequence of cycles of exploration and exploitation.

Newport cites a Q&A session with the astrobiologist Andrew Steele, who made a critical breakthrough in analysing the evidence for life on Mars. A student asks if he'd started his PhD in the hopes of changing the world:

> "No. I just wanted options. [...] If I actually sat down and said I had planned any of this, I'd be lying through my teeth."

Then the student asks if Steele knew what he was going to do from a young age:

> "No. No. I had no idea what I was going to do. I object to systems that say you should decide now what you're going to do. That's BS. Don't close doors."

After analysing the careers of successful people, Newport found that few had a grand plan to get where they ultimately ended up. Instead, they worked hard to get themselves into a position where they were exposed to possibilities, and let serendipity do its thing.

Even Apple founder Steve Jobs, who famously lectured a Stanford graduating class on the importance of doing what you love, had no special interest in technology or business. He studied history and dance, and was heavily into Eastern mysticism. It was only through leveraging a chain of unlikely events that he ended up building one of the greatest companies of all time. Newport argues we should look at what Jobs actually *did*, and ignore what he said. Instead of following your bliss, follow your blisters.

A successful business or career pathway usually emerges organically from the bottom-up, instead of being planned from the top-down. This approach *benefits* from volatility. It doesn't rely on complex multi-decade plans full of contingencies and breakage points and prediction errors. It looks a lot more like Darwinian evolution than intelligent design. This process is called 'effectuation'.

EFFECTUATION

Here's how effectuation works: first, take stock of whatever resources you already have at your disposal. Next, choose a goal based on whichever of your current options is the most promising. In the course of pursuing that goal, you open up new options, and create space for serendipity to strike. And you zigzag your way along in this manner, springboarding off whatever new opportunities present themselves.

It sounds absurd to let your goals emerge from your actions and circumstances, instead of the other way around. But the great strength of effectuation is that it works well under conditions of uncertainty, whereas classic causal planning (from A →B → C) does not.

As the leading effectuation expert Saras Sarasvathy puts it, the logic of causal reasoning is that to the extent that we can predict the future, we can control it. The logic of effectual reasoning is that to the extent that we can control the future, *we don't need to predict it.*

Here are Sarasvathy's four principles of effectuation:

Bird-in-Hand: Create solutions with the resources available here and now

Lemonade Principle: Mistakes and surprises are inevitable and can be used to look for new opportunities

Crazy Quilt: Entering into new partnerships can bring the project new funds and new directions

Affordable Loss: You should only invest as much as you are willing to lose

Sound familiar? It should, because effectuation is basically the optionality approach for entrepreneurs: the Lemonade Principle encourages us to consider how volatility might help us, Crazy Quilt highlights the importance of social capital and exploring new ideas, and Affordable Loss is what we've been calling the risk of ruin.

Like it or not, we're all 'entrepreneurs' now, even if we never start a company. The old model of stable employment for life with a government pension in retirement is no longer a safe bet. Instead, we have to increasingly think in terms of non-linear returns, protecting the downside, finding ways to profit from volatility, and creating diverse income streams.

All of which involves a whole lot more exploration than we're used to. The effectuation strategy bakes this in through alternating cycles of exploring and exploiting: you work hard towards a goal, based on the most attractive option that happens to be available to you. Then you survey your expanded range of options, see what new opportunities present themselves, and choose the best of the bunch. Rinse, and repeat. This cycle ensures you're always attuned to new opportunities, and able to adjust course based on the new information you've gathered.

The takeaway is that it's perfectly OK to let your goals emerge from your strengths and available resources, rather than try to work towards a fixed outcome. You're never entirely sure where you'll end up, but you can be confident it'll be somewhere good.

I was stunned when I came across Sarasvathy's research, because I realised I've accidentally followed effectual reasoning my whole life. Instead of choosing the best university and then planning how to get there, I made the decision on the basis of the resources at my disposal: a full-tuition scholarship to a decent but non-prestigious school. Then I enrolled in the best undergraduate course available, without having any burning interest in it. I had no idea I would major in journalism until my final year, as I explored and then winnowed down the various options. Then I used internships to get work experience, including a trial as a business reporter which turned into a job offer. Up until this point, I had *no interest whatsoever* in finance. As a little boy, I did not dream of reading company balance sheets or learning about the vagaries of the stock market. But it was the best option available to me. Now here I am, having devoted a substantial chunk of my life to writing a big-ass book about finance, purely because I find it so fascinating.

It's not as if I was lacking in passion to begin with. In my high school interview, I told the principal I was going to be a lawyer. With the benefit of hindsight, I can't think of a career I would be worse-suited for. I am extremely glad I didn't accumulate a massive debt trying to achieve my childhood dream, only to discover that I had spent several years and hundreds of thousands of dollars locking myself into a career that I hated.

You might think I'm lucky to have found my 'calling'. But this is the passion myth all over again. There are countless parallel universes in which I'm equally enthusiastic about landscape gardening or exotic skin diseases, and don't give a fig about finance. Maybe it's a coincidence that I ended up enjoying what I do, but again, the research suggests otherwise. Here are the main predictors of job satisfaction:

- Working with good people
- Having autonomy over your work
- Feeling like you're making an impact
- Finding something you're half-way good at, and
- *Sticking at it long enough to develop mastery*

I enjoy writing now, in large part because I've written almost every day for the last nine years. I only work with people I like, have plenty of autonomy, and probably had some talent to begin with. But I was never 'fated' to be a writer.[1]

With the right working conditions and enough time to develop mastery, almost anything can become interesting and rewarding. But if you're *not* enjoying your job and see no prospect of that changing, of course you should come up with an escape plan. Again, this is part of the effectuation strategy: you gather information, open up new opportunities, and pivot accordingly.

But the effectuation strategy doesn't mean buzzing around like a blue-arsed fly, either. A company that constantly chases the shiny new thing is doomed to fail. Same goes for careers. There are very real costs associated with switching, not least of which is the lost opportunity to build mastery. Have we been too hasty in dismissing traditional causal planning?

INVENTING THE FUTURE

The strongest argument against the optionality/effectuation approach comes from the serial entrepreneur and investor Peter Thiel. Thiel is not a fan of the pursuit of "many-sided mediocrity", the hoarding of indefinite options, and a lack of firm convictions. In *Zero to One*, he claims that much of the dysfunction in our world today can be blamed on our fuzzy attitude toward the future, and points us to many examples of people who changed the course of history by executing on a specific vision.

Take Elon Musk, who has been methodically working towards making humans an interplanetary species for the last 20 years. Musk perfectly embodies the Silicon Valley philosophy that the best way to predict the future is to invent it. His plan to elevate us to the stars involved a series of unlikely events and the reinvention of entire industries, but it looks like he might actually pull it off.

It's hard not to be impressed by examples of visionary planning, but there are a few alternative explanations worth considering.

Survivorship Bias

We're much more likely to hear from bold visionaries who pulled off a grand plan than we are to hear from the multitudes who crashed and burned. This is survivorship bias.

Let's rework the coin-flipping example from the last book: if 1000 entrepreneurs come up with complex 10-step plans, each stage of which has a 50 per cent chance of failure, we should expect one of them to take the plan all the way to completion, entirely by chance. From the sole survivor's point of view, it's perfectly obvious that her long-term planning and foresight was crucial to her success (and perhaps it was). But it's not as if the 999 competitors who blew up were lacking in vision.

Effectuation Under the Hood

Another explanation is that a lot of success stories presented as visionary four-dimensional chess look suspiciously like effectuation under the hood.

Peter Thiel's argument is somewhat undermined by the fact that when he co-founded PayPal, it was with modest ambitions to beam IOUs between PalmPilots and other early handheld devices. The company pivoted not once, not twice, but *six times,* before stumbling into a viable business idea. And even this happened almost by accident: one of the cofounders posted up a demo for online payments, triggering a deluge of emails (which he initially ignored). That idea turned out to be worth many billions of dollars, but it was never part of the plan.

As for Elon Musk, his detailed multi-step plans didn't survive their first encounter with reality either. SpaceX was originally going to *buy* rockets, not build them. The Russian rocket designers Musk visited literally spat on his shoes in disgust. After three failed launches of Falcon 1, he pivoted to resupply contracts with NASA. The basic design, mission scope, and funding strategy changed several times.

In fact, Musk hasn't had a formal business plan since 1995, when he launched his first company: "These things are just always wrong, so I didn't bother with business plans after that."

This chapter started with a quote from Paul Graham about the perils of trying to construct the future from a blueprint. As the cofounder of startup accelerator Y Combinator, Graham has had the chance to observe thousands of ambitious young companies. In his view, the way to do really big things is to start with deceptively *small* things. Instead of trying to identify a precise point in the future, and then figuring out how to get there, he advocates heading in a general westerly direction, like Columbus. While the popular image of a visionary is someone with a clear view of the future, "empirically, it may be better to have a blurry one."

High-Variance Pathway

A third explanation is that inventing the future is a high-variance strategy: it works well for a select few people who are unusually good at thinking from first principles and making accurate predictions, but is a bad idea for everyone else. In which case, the problem becomes knowing which group you belong to: there's a very fine line between 'visionary' and 'deluded'.

Which explanation is correct? My guess is that it's a combination of all three: inventing the future sometimes works, but only for unusually gifted planners, and only so long as they're willing to do things that look a lot like effectuation.

It's plausible that a firm vision really is a necessary ingredient for trying to achieve the impossible—the kind of 'zero to one' transformative technologies that Thiel is interested in. This is not incompatible with the evidence that most visionaries will fail, and that complicated causal planning is a bad idea for the majority of people.

In the context of careers, business, and general life planning, I believe effectuation/optionality is a much better strategy, and will only become more attractive as the world gets weirder.

Perhaps a few teenage savants know exactly what their future selves will want, and exactly how to get there. But it is generally a bad idea to let a child choose your life for you. Most of us would do better by leveraging whatever resources we have at our disposal, pursuing the best of the various options, then continuing to explore an expanded range of possibilities.

The important insight to take away from Thiel's argument is that merely drifting around collecting optionality forever doesn't make sense. After all, the whole point of exploring is to get into a better position to *exploit*.

But once again, it's not an on-off switch. If you leverage yourself into a solid position that you want to exploit, that doesn't mean all exploration is off the table. Conversely, if you want to spend time exploring, you don't necessarily have to abandon the security of a steady pay check.

As the girl in the Old El Paso commercial put it: *¿Por qué no los dos?* Why not both?

26

A TIME TO TAKE RISKS AND A TIME TO PLAY IT SAFE

The key to success lies in knowing how to both strive for a lot and fail well.

— RAY DALIO

NINETEENTH CENTURY PARISIANS have a lot to answer for. Imagine consuming nothing but water and stale baguettes. Fighting for dominance against armies of cockroaches. Living in a tiny unheated attic in the depths of winter; life-force draining away with every rattling breath.

The literary gypsies of the Bohemian movement lived in self-imposed squalor, but the 'starving artist' mythology they created somehow made the whole mess seem heroic and très chic. Now the thin veneer of romanticism overlaying the starving artist lifestyle is peeling away, laid bare by the humdrum reality of modern existence. Creative ghettos have gentrified. Being poor is not sexy.

Everyone knows someone with big dreams. I'm a dreamer! Maybe you are too. What happens to the dreamers seduced by the starving artist aesthetic?

You move back into your childhood room to save on rent. The racing car bed and N*Sync posters don't quite create the same atmosphere as the Boulevard Saint-Michel circa 1920, but that's OK. While your friends accumulate money and careers and other bourgeois trappings, you await the day you get your big break and everyone finally recognises your brilliance.

And wait. And wait. And wait...

...Until your brittle bones turn to dust and you're working shitty odd jobs to make rent and phantasms of forgotten dreams drift through your unconscious and Justin Timberlake's faded yellow nightmare visage accuses you through those 16-year-old eyes: what the fuck have you done with your life, anyway?

At the risk of sounding like an infomercial, there has to be a better way.

SCALABLE CAREERS

A normal career has one very appealing feature: your effort is roughly proportional to the reward you receive. If you're a plumber, the more taps you fix, the more cash in your pocket. No-one's labouring away unblocking toilets in obscurity, hoping that one day someone will recognise their unparalleled brilliance in U-bend gasket seals.

The flipside is there's an upper limit to how much money you can make. This is what Nassim Taleb calls a 'non-scalable' career. A plumber can only fix so many taps. A baker can only bake so many loaves. A lawyer can only represent so many clients.

Artists—which includes anyone from writers to musicians to entrepreneurs—don't face this bottleneck. Something idea-based can be sold over and over again with almost no extra time or effort. Your debut album might sell 10 copies (three of which your mum bought) or 10 *million* copies, but the amount of work that went into recording it was the same either way.

Scalable careers are highly attractive insofar as they give us exposure to unbounded upside.

But there's a catch. We're entering black swan territory, which means the relationship between effort and reward breaks down. It doesn't necessarily matter how good you are, or how hard you work: a select few people capture almost all the upside, while everyone else goes hungry.

In the publishing industry, a million new books hit the shelves every year. On average, each title will sell a paltry few hundred copies over its lifetime. Like venture capitalists, publishers rely on diversification: one of the bets they make will succeed in spectacular fashion, more than making up for all the books that sink like lead balloons. On *average*, the industry is profitable. But there is no such thing as an 'average' author. You may recognise this as another instance of our old friend, the power law distribution (Fig. 5.9).

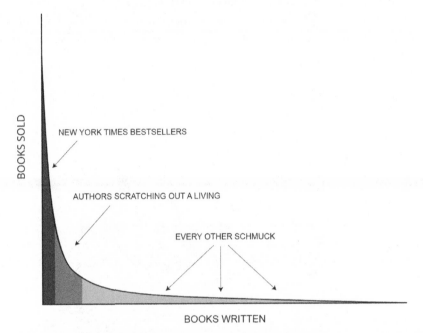

Figure 5.9. The power law distribution of sales in the publishing industry.

The left-hand side of the graph is dominated by the Dan Browns and Stephanie Meyers of the world. The peak of sales almost immediately plummets into a long, tragic tail of aspiring authors stretching to the right, which would be several kilometres long if I had drawn this to scale.

There's not much of a happy middle ground here. In the land of the black swan, taking the middle path only gives the *illusion* of safety. You're still exposed to potentially ruinous events, with no chance of tapping into the unlimited upside that swirls out of the same chaos.

THE BARBELL STRATEGY FOR CAREERS

Nassim Taleb suggests targeting the two extremes of the career spectrum at once. On one end of the barbell, you play it safe with a secure, staid job. On the other end, you take highly speculative risks. In the middle, as little as possible.

This allow you to explore and exploit in parallel, giving you two separate paths for maximising career capital over time (Fig. 5.10).

The exploration pathway starts out at rock bottom, with the hope being that it might one day climb high enough to overtake the line representing steady exploitation.

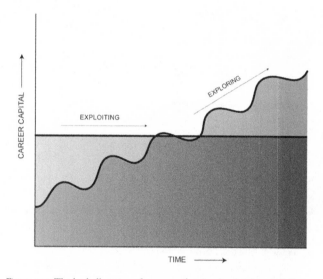

Figure 5.10. The barbell strategy for careers (explore/exploit in parallel).

Taleb describes the perfect barbell strategy job as having "few intellectual demands and high job security, the kind of low risk job that ceases to exist when you leave the office". Ideally, it should be non-political, low-profile and won't force you to bastardise your other work. You do your 9 to 5, and then you check out. All your evenings, weekends and vacation time are free for working on your speculative side-gigs. (Note that a non-scalable hustle—driving for Uber, walking dogs, nannying—is not a barbell.)

As Taleb points out, comfy sinecures have frequently been fertile ground for greatness. Vladimir Nabokov was a museum curator, T.S. Eliot worked in a bank, and Anthony Trollope resigned as a post office clerk at age 52, having generated enough income from his novels and short stories to replace the pension he forfeited by leaving.

Another classic approach to the parallel barbell is to split the roles between spouses, with one person speculating wildly, while the other plays defence. This is likely to place a strain on the relationship, but is an option for those with a strong enough bond.

In either case, if the big dreams don't work out, you still have a regular income source to keep working towards financial independence. If your side-gig *does* start bringing home the bacon, you can ease out of the day job by reducing your hours, or by taking a sabbatical—which brings us to the serial barbell.

In this model, you spend one block of time focused on accumulating financial and career capital in a regular job, then the next block single-mindedly focused on your art, in waves of serial exploration and exploitation (Fig. 5.11).

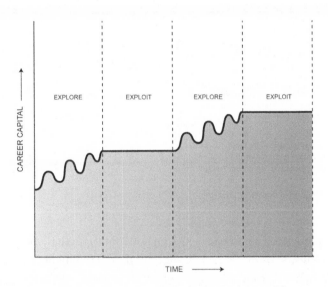

Figure 5.11. The barbell strategy for careers (explore/exploit serially).

Again, Taleb notes that this has been a successful strategy throughout history: "Many of the 'doers' turned 'thinkers' like Montaigne have done a serial barbell: pure action, then pure reflection."

With no comparisons to Montaigne intended, this is the approach I've taken. I worked intensely for almost five years in what was a fulfilling and rewarding career. Now I'm taking a sabbatical—perhaps for the same length of time—to explore some creative and entrepreneurial passion projects: helping with startups, early-stage investing, freelancing, broadening my skills, writing this book.

If my speculative gigs hadn't paid off, I could always fall back into a regular, non-scalable career. And if I hadn't got all the black swan hunting out of my system, I could always repeat the cycle.

The 'Starving Artist' failure mode is an attempt to jump straight to the high-risk end of a serial barbell without doing the hard work to begin with (Table 5.1).

STARVING ARTIST		BARBELL STRATEGY
If you fail, you have no backup plan and no financial security	▶	If you fail, you're still working towards financial independence by other means
Stretches the patience and generosity of friends, family, and society to breaking point	▶	Completely self-reliant
Requires you to do unpleasant things to pay the bills, or 'sell out'	▶	No need to compromise your integrity
If your identity is tied to your art, writing, or business idea, failure will prompt a bone-crunching existential crisis	▶	You have more than one string to your bow —you're still an accomplished insurance broker or librarian or whatever
You have no capital, which is crucial for getting anything entrepreneurial off the ground (all successful artists are entrepreneurs)	▶	You have enough capital to give yourself the best shot at making your side-gig succeed

Table 5.1. Starving Artist vs Barbell Strategy.

The advantage of a barbell—serial or horizontal—is that you can get *paid* to acquire skills, knowledge, and social capital. You're building optionality on the job. When the time comes to pivot to a more speculative gig, these resources will be invaluable for gaining traction.

Failing to pay your dues is the most common mistake I've noticed among aspiring freelancers and entrepreneurs. Digital nomad hotspots like Chiang Mai are a revolving door for naive kids with no cash, no marketable skills, and a copy of *The 4 Hour Workweek* clutched to their chests. It's not impossible to skip over the boring part, if you're especially lucky and talented. But it's a hell of a lot harder.

I don't blame these kids in the slightest. I, too, love finding ways to get ahead in life with a minimum of effort. But wherever you find gullible people chasing a dream, predators are never far behind. An entire cottage industry fuelling the lifestyle has popped up like mushrooms—i.e, in the dark, and based on bullshit.

This industry sells courses on how to live the nomadic life, make money online, and sip coconuts in sun loungers for the rest of your days. The graduates go on to shill their own e-books and courses to the next influx of wantrepreneurs, in a pyramid scheme so industrious that Ramses II is sitting up in his sarcophagus.

You might think the whole blind-leading-the-blind thing provides a bit of harmless schadenfreude. Now imagine this conga line continuously screaming in your face about their travel vlogs, and trying to enlist you in their get-rich-quick schemes. It's not pleasant, but I understand the motivation—everyone has bills to pay.

Which brings us to the other great strength of the barbell strategy: you will never again have to compromise on your integrity or artistic vision.

THE BREEZY DENIM HOTPANTS OF FREEDOM

I used to own a pair of denim cut-off shorts that were objectively hideous—stained, ragged, and holey. As the fabric disintegrated, they got shorter and shorter until public decency was perilously hanging in the balance. Successive girlfriends tried to throw them out, but I always rescued them from the trash.

Being told what to do rubs me the wrong way, to the point where I will occasionally die in a ditch over the pettiest cause. But I usually have a good reason for acting like a diva. While I've had some great editors in the course of my journalism career, I've had others who constantly introduced errors—or worse. It is an awful feeling to see a carefully-researched article splashed on the front page, stripped of nuance and sexed up beyond recognition, with your name printed above words you did not write.

The best advice I've heard for maintaining integrity comes from Derek Sivers, a musician, circus clown, author, blogger, and entrepreneur. People with high-paying jobs often ask him for advice, because they want to become full-time artists. But full-time artists ask his advice too, because they're finding it impossible to make money.

Both groups of people receive the same answer:

- Have a well-paying job
- Seriously pursue your art for love, not money

Sivers says this is the lifestyle followed by the happiest people he knows: "How nice to not expect your job to fulfil all your emotional needs. How nice to not taint something you love with the need to make money from it."

My primary creative outlet is my blog, Deep Dish. I have made approximately zero dollars from blogging, and I hope that never changes. I regularly get offers from companies who want to enter 'partnerships' with me, which basically means running thinly-veiled ads shilling their products. The legitimate offers I politely decline. If they're shady, I take great pleasure in casting them into the fiery pit of the spam folder.

If I was on the bones of my ass, these sort of offers might start to look pretty tempting. The great thing about the barbell strategy is that it clearly separates bread-and-butter work from creative pursuits. Your identity isn't solely tied up in one or the other, and you don't have to bastardise what you do in an attempt to curry commercial favour.

Instead, you can hang out in your raggedy-ass Daisy Dukes, and enjoy the gentle breeze percolating through your unmentionables. Let me tell you—it's a pretty great feeling.

A TIME TO OBEY AND A TIME TO REBEL

Better to reign in hell than serve in heaven.

— LUCIFER

J OHN MILTON'S EPIC POEM *Paradise Lost* has two redeeming features. The first is that you can look at the pretty pictures when you get tired of slogging through 10,000 lines of blank verse. The second is the character of Lucifer, who is an example to us all.

Milton depicts the God of the Old Testament as the worst boss ever: petty, vengeful, micro-managing everything, transforming Karen from HR into a pillar of salt. He probably reheats tuna casseroles in the office microwave, which would turn anyone into a being of pure evil.

And so, Lucifer rebels against God's tyranny, is cast out into the darkness as the fallen angel Satan, and utters the immortal line: "Better to reign in hell than serve in heaven."

Now, I know Satan is meant to be the bad guy. He's literally *the* Bad Guy! But honestly, I'm siding with the devil on this one.

Having autonomy—being able to set your own rules of engagement, and play games of your own making—is really important. Like, life-and-death important.

LIBERTY OR DEATH

Newborns babies have almost no autonomy. They are at the mercy of the large humans who pick them up, pinch their cheeks, and make stupid noises at them. About all they can do is flail their limbs around and turn their heads to look at interesting stuff.

But babies love exercising even the tiniest scraps of control. In a landmark study, researchers placed a group of 3-month-old infants face-up in a crib. When they turned their heads on the pillow, a mobile of dancing animals lit up. This was hugely thrilling to the babies, who soon learned how to make the animals appear at will, and never tired of the spectacle.

A second group of babies were passive observers. When their cribmates turned on the mobile, they initially enjoyed the show just as much. But without the ability to turn it on and off themselves, they quickly lost interest.

The importance of being in control starts in the cradle, and it follows us all the way to the grave. Another body of research suggests that senility is not an inevitable consequence of ageing, but may be reversed by giving older folks the ability to make independent decisions and maintain some mastery over their world.

Nursing homes usually have names like 'Paradise Lodge' or 'Eden Care', barely bothering to conceal the fact that the residents have been dumped in God's waiting room. I'm sure some of these facilities really are heaven-like: the nurses take care of everything and give you sponge baths and listen patiently to your stories about catching the ferry to Shelbyville with an onion tied to your belt, which was the style at the time.

But it's not worth it. Not if everything is predetermined, not if the days bleed together, and not if the staff won't let you do anything for yourself. No wonder so many 'stubborn' old people refuse to leave their own homes. Living independently is dangerous and difficult—but it's better to reign in hell than serve in heaven.

As the psychologist Daniel Gilbert put it, in *Stumbling on Happiness*:

"The fact is that human beings come into the world with a passion for control, they go out of the world the same way, and research suggests that if they lose their ability to control things at any point between their entrance and their exit, they become unhappy, helpless, hopeless, and depressed. And occasionally dead."

We're right back to the difference between fasting and starving, or the reason why gridlocked commutes are irredeemably miserable. It's infuriating to feel as though you're not in control of your own life, and this is a feeling we never adapt to.

The barbell strategy is one way to regain autonomy, but it's not the final word in personal freedom. Neither is the FIRE strategy. Even if your endgame is to achieve total independence, there are *degrees* to this thing. If you want to slave away for decades so you can one day retire and do whatever it is you actually want to do, that's one approach. But it's probably the hardest.

Here's the one piece of advice Peter Thiel wishes he could give his younger self: *there is no need to wait.* If you have a 10-year plan, think carefully about whether you can achieve it in the next six months. Sometimes, this exercise will reveal that you really do have to take the long way. Other times, it will reveal that you're telling yourself a story. Do you really need to retire early to improve your life? Not necessarily. Maybe all you need is a little fuck-you money.

FUCK-YOU MONEY

Humphrey Bogart used to keep a $100 bill in his dresser drawer at all times— this being a decent chunk of change in the 1920s. He called it his 'fuck-you money', because it meant he'd never be forced to take a crappy part. According to Bogie, the only good reason for making money was "so you can tell any son-of-a-bitch in the world to go to hell".

Unlike Bogart, I am not a tough guy. One time I cried in front of my boss. She gave me the rest of the day off. In fact, all my bosses have been great. I'm struggling to think of a single person I'd like to say 'fuck you' to.

But there are plenty of people who I'd like to politely say 'no thanks' to. And I say it all the time! It's great. Fuck-you money means you can walk away from a shitty situation. You can fire an annoying client. You can turn down offers that conflict with your values, or are just plain boring. You can call out shady behaviour in your company or industry, instead of being held hostage by a comfortable salary.

So, how much do you need?

Financial Samurai, a popular finance blog, asked readers for their definition of fuck-you money:

> "Based on over 2000 votes, $5m is the #1 vote-getter to feel financially free. I personally chose $10m because $10m is what's necessary to generate $250,000 in risk-free income based on today's interest rates. Somewhere between $5m–$10m seems reasonable, depending on where you live."

Somewhere between five and ten million dollars... seems... *reasonable?*

I feel like I live on a completely different planet to these finance guys. Scanning the comments under the post, there are people who already have a ton of money and are still unsatisfied. One guy who 'only' makes $100k complained that he'd never have enough to feel free, and was counting on dying young so that it wouldn't matter. And this is a blog with the tagline 'Financial freedom sooner rather than later'. What's going on?

The confusion here is that fuck-you money is *not* synonymous with the amount of money you need to hit financial independence or retire early. Unlike FIRE, this is not an all-or-nothing proposition. You can improve your life right now, rather than eat shit sandwiches for decades while you try to reach some distant number. There's no need to save $10 million. Even *$10,000* might be enough to change things up.

Let's define fuck-you money as the amount of cash you need to feel a basic sense of security. Say, a couple years of living expenses: enough to walk away from a bum situation, turn down any gig, or re-train for a new career. Now we've got a much more realistic target to aim for—but the big spenders are still facing an uphill battle.

If I were accustomed to living on $250,000 a year, my fuck-you money would have lasted about as long as a fart in a hurricane. My spending habits are just as extreme as the finance guys, except in the opposite direction: during my sabbatical, my annual expenses averaged ~$12,500. Since my outgoings are literally 20x lower, so is my threshold for freedom.

There are two ways to be free: you can either get more money, or require less of it. The first is obvious, but the second doesn't get enough love. Let's call it 'fuck-you frugality'.

FUCK-YOU FRUGALITY

Sysman (CC BY 4.0)

Whenever you need a refresher on the importance of frugality, go peel off a $100 bill, and subject yourself to the silent, brooding judgment of Benjamin Franklin. That side-eye is so doleful it traverses time and space. It's almost as if Franklin knows his face is about to be a) rolled into a tube and stuck up some degenerate's nostril, or b) used to purchase another superfluous piece of junk that will, in short order, be discarded upon a mountain of previously purchased superfluous junk.

He's not mad; he's just disappointed. One of my favourite Franklin stories is the time he was offered a lucrative sum to print a defamatory hatchet-job. Here's the process he went through to decide whether or not he should publish it:

> "I went home in the evening, purchased a twopenny loaf at the baker's, and with water from the pump made my supper; I then wrapped myself up in my great-coat, and laid down on the floor and slept until morning, when, on another loaf and a mug of water, I made my breakfast. From this regimen I feel no inconvenience whatsoever. Finding I can live in this manner, I have formed a determination never to prostitute my press to the purposes of corruption and abuse of this kind for the sake of gaining a more comfortable existence."

This is the same reason the Stoic philosopher Seneca used to deliberately practice poverty, despite being the richest man in Rome. Every now and then, he'd spend a few days sleeping on the floor, eating bread and water, and travelling roughly. The idea was that should his fortunes ever change, he would accept his fate without complaint or compromise:

"Ask yourself, is this what one used to dread?"

Lest you think Seneca was just a pretentious asshole—the old-timey equivalent of celebrities who 'sleep rough' one night to land fawning magazine profiles—the man had the courage of his convictions. When Nero sent troops to order his former tutor's death, Seneca didn't protest, or plead for his life, or flee. Instead, he calmly cut his own wrists. The blood wouldn't flow, so he did a Socrates and drank a cup of hemlock. Being a hard old bastard, he *still* wouldn't die, so he finally had to suffocate himself in the bathtub. While his friends were quite naturally upset by this grim spectacle, Seneca used his last breath to gently make fun of them for being crybabies.

By contrast, I am a little weasel. If a deranged emperor ever threatened my life, I would say, 'Yes Mr Nero sir, I'll have their head on your desk by morning.'

We petty mortals can only tiptoe between the legs of history's demigods, but at least we can tiptoe in the right direction. As a trivial example, I have deliberately maintained creative control over every detail of this book—from the title, the illustrations, the cover, the structure, right down to the typefaces. I'm not reliant on income from book sales, or trying to placate a publisher, or sexing it up with marketing sizzle in the usual manner of self-help books. Whatever will be, will be. I would much rather fail on my own terms than succeed on someone else's.

FUCK-YOU CAREER CAPITAL

The necktie is the equivalent of a slave collar for male office workers. It serves no function whatsoever, except to gently strangle you all day long and occasionally flop into your soup. It is the least subtle symbol of subservience imaginable.

And so, in December 1993, Nassim Nicholas Taleb deposited his last business tie in the garbage can at the corner of 48th St and Park Avenue.

Did Taleb quit his job? Save enough money to retire early? Nope. But he had become so successful as a trader that he was too valuable to fire:

"If you were profitable you could give managers all the crap you wanted and they ate it because they needed you and were afraid of losing their own jobs."

Taleb had what we might call 'fuck-you career capital'. If you become an extremely valuable employee, you get all the perks of being a wage slave, without having to wear the collar.

When I got my first proper job as a business reporter, I removed my earrings and wore a suit every day and ironed my shirts and shaved regularly and made sure to turn up earlier than everyone. This was a big effort for me, because I am naturally a scruffy person. But I was a nobody, with zero career capital, on a temporary contract, with no guarantee it would be renewed. I had to pay my dues.

After a year or so, I had proven myself, and started to get job offers from competitors. I slowly reverted to my natural appearance, my hours became more flexible, and no-one batted an eyelid when I took occasional long boozy lunches.

The unspoken rule is that if you deliver the goods and aren't an asshole, you can do what you want. I'm hardly claiming I was indispensable, but I was valuable enough to leverage some pay rises and get my own column and generally have a reasonable degree of autonomy over my work.

Career capital gives us the third layer of our 'fuck you' independence stack:

1. Fuck-you money
Stash enough cash to cover your expenses for a year or two, so you can walk away from a bad situation, find a better job, or retrain.

2. Fuck-you frugality
Follow Ben Franklin's lead, and commit to living simply rather than betray your principles.

3. Fuck-you career capital
Become such a useful and profitable employee—ideally, the only person who knows how to do some important thing—that you're difficult to push around.

This doesn't give you license to strut around radiating an aura of 'fuck you'. Much better to be mild and treat people kindly. But it does give you license to push back against things you don't want to do, gently ignore arbitrary rules and norms, and maintain *the option* to go nuclear.

DEGREES OF FREEDOM

"Better to rule in hell than serve in heaven" is the unofficial motto of many of the freelancers, entrepreneurs and digital nomads I've met in the last few years. They've all walked away from overbearing bosses, steady pay checks, and 9 to 5 office hours to build their own dominions—with all the risk and reward that comes with it.

Being cast out of God's light is liberating. There are no rules in hell! You can set your own hours and fire annoying clients and be your own boss and blow off work to go drinking at 11 in the morning.

But there's a price to pay. You're no longer part of a heavenly choir singing in harmony. You're one lone voice in the wilderness. You don't have the comfort of a monthly salary to draw upon. Or sick leave. Or holiday pay. Or health insurance. And there's no guarantee your new boss (you) is any less of an asshole.

In my opinion, it's all worth it. But who cares about my personal preferences? Self-reliance is not an all-or-nothing proposition. It's a broad continuum, and you can choose where to place yourself on the spectrum. In *The End of Jobs*, Taylor Pearson breaks it down into eight different positions, from most to least entrepreneurial (Fig. 5.12).

Figure 5.12. The spectrum of entrepreneurship.

At any of these levels, you can have optionality. At any of these levels, you can maintain some level of autonomy over your day-to-day existence. At any of these levels, you can decouple financial incentives from your behaviour.

Pearson argues that it's never been easier to become an entrepreneur. And as the future of work changes, even employees will have to adopt entrepreneur-like behaviours. How far you take this depends on your personal risk tolerance, which changes with time and circumstance: when you're a minimalist little wisp, you can afford to take more risks. Once you have a family to support or a mortgage to pay, maybe you don't go all in on that speculative project. If your kids are grown up, you can dive back in the deep end again.

Pushing all the way to the 'founder' end of the spectrum is really hard. I am extremely grateful to the people who create art, music, literature, and businesses, and generally take risks for the sake of the collective. They make all of us wealthier, at great personal cost: most entrepreneurs fail, most artists and musicians are doomed to obscurity, and most books go unread. Remember those grotesque inequalities in the distribution of rewards.

The distinction I would make is this. Do not rely on these things to make money. Do them because you enjoy them as an end unto themselves. Do them because this is your Art, and if you *didn't* do them, they'd claw their way out of your chest anyway.

Optionality gives you the safety buffer required to take these kinds of risks without blowing up. It lets you set your own terms of engagement, say 'fuck you' when necessary, and refuse to compromise on your values.

But optionality is subject to the law of diminishing returns, just like anything else. In the final chapter, we'll look at the limitations of the model: is it possible to have *too much* personal freedom? And what are the edge cases in which we might deliberately sacrifice our options?

A TIME TO OPEN OPTIONS AND A TIME TO GIVE THEM AWAY

Freedom is the power to choose our own chains.

— JEAN-JACQUES ROUSSEAU

SOMETIMES I WANDER THROUGH the suburbs in the evenings and peek into living rooms and fantasise about watching telly and bickering with my spouse and buying curtain rails at Home Depot.

These domestic reveries are new and disquieting. The traditional path through life—a steady job, white picket fence, two point three children, monthly mortgage payments—never held much appeal. Now, if I squint my eyes up, I'm starting to see it: not a rut as I originally thought, but a well-worn groove; like settling into an armchair moulded to the exact contours of your butt.

In Book I, I reproduced the opening lines of my viral essay on frugality: "Every morning I roll out of bed and ask myself: what should I do today?"

I'm as surprised as anyone to find that I still have this same freedom four years later. This period of my life has been transformative in many ways, which is why I'm a relentless booster for personal autonomy.

But it's time to introduce another through-line. With the benefit of hindsight, the state of existence in which you wake up with no obligations no longer sounds so appealing. Something I've learned the hard way during my extended sabbatical is that you can *absolutely* have too much of a good thing.

Here are some archetypes:

- The Peter Pan man-child who refuses to grow up
- The Trustafarian rich kid aimlessly wandering the earth
- The attractive New Yorker who constantly dates, but never settles
- The dilettante who flits from job to job without acquiring mastery
- The early retiree who triumphantly quits her job, then falls into a depressive funk

Constraints can be liberating. When you're doing creative work, the total space of all possibilities is so vast that it's unworkable. You have to carve off one tiny little sector, and think inside the box. The same is true when you zoom out to the scale of an entire life, but this is not obvious until all the constraints are *removed*: you don't know what you've got till it's gone.

And so, my twenties have largely consisted of circling back to the fusty old institutions I was originally trying to escape, with a twist.

What follows are some constraints that have stood the test of time, that I've found helpful, and that you might freely choose to implement in your own life.

CHESTERTON'S FENCE

You're strolling through a sun-dappled meadow of wildflowers when you come across a big ugly fence cutting right through the middle of the field. There are no livestock in sight, and the fence is getting in the way of your walk. The scenery would look so much better fence-free, so you boldly tear it down.

Just as you're admiring your handiwork, a bull appears over the rise, and charges straight at you. The second-to-last thing that goes through your mind is: "Whoops! Guess that fence was there for a pretty good reason." The last thing that goes through your mind is 18 inches of angry bull horn.

This is the parable of Chesterton's Fence, after the writer and critic G.K. Chesterton, and it's something I think about a lot these days.

Before I began my travels, I had a vague romantic notion of freelancing on the road. See ya later, corporate drones! No more sterile office cubicles for this guy! Instead, I'd tap away on my laptop while I sipped mimosas at the beach, or dash out brilliant missives from a hammock in the middle of the jungle.

As it turns out, hammocks are not ergonomically designed workspaces, and sand and electronics don't play nicely together. Instead, I ended up spending most of my time at shared office spaces. My younger self would be mortified that I am not only dutifully sitting down at a desk, but paying handsomely for the privilege of doing so. As much as offices might suck, they have been honed over centuries into a half-decent environment for actually getting shit done.

Then I decided I needed more daily structure, so I played around with a schedule. What it ended up looking like was working in the morning, then doing fun stuff in the evening. You know, kind of like one of those '9 to 5' things. To prevent my time from dilating into a featureless void, I also decided to insert a dedicated block of recreation at the end of the week. I'm thinking of calling it a 'week end'.

It turns out that offices and 9 to 5s probably exist for a good reason. But while Chesterton's fence is a useful constraint, it's *not* a catch-all argument for longstanding institutions and cultural practices.

The lumpy clay of human civilisation has generations of distilled wisdom baked into it; also, generations of deeply ingrained stupidity. All Chesterton was saying is that before you tear something down, you better make sure you know why it was put there in the first place.

THE WANING OF THE COMMONS

The French sociologist Émile Durkheim struck upon the importance of constraints in 1897, after gathering data on suicides from all over Europe. His groundbreaking report found that people who lived alone were most at risk of killing themselves, while those with spouses, families, tight social networks and communal obligations were the happiest and healthiest.

Many of these ties have continued to unravel since Durkheim's time. The communal structures in which we used to find meaning are crumbling, and the lonely pillar rising in their place—the atomised, self-reliant individual—is looking a little wobbly.

We live in an increasingly anxious and depressed society, subject to unprecedented psychic misery at a time of unprecedented prosperity. The psychologist Martin Seligman explains this paradox with two parallel forces, which he calls 'the waxing of the individual and the waning of the commons'. On the one hand, we have the breakdown of traditional family structures, of belief in God, and of nationalism—the things in which we have historically found a sense of purpose that transcends the self. As these collective myths break down, the void has been filled by the rise of extreme individualism. There are no gods, no objective moral truths, and no borders. Who cares what the village elders say? Be yourself! You're the captain of your own destiny—and you're all alone in the universe.

Our individualistic mythology elevates the iconoclasts and free-wheeling mavericks who march to the beat of their own drum. But did you know that a lone wolf—far from living a noble and wild existence—has to eat rats and scavenge rotting carcasses to survive? Well, humans are social animals, too. We need hierarchy, and routine, and structure.

I am happy with the life I've chosen, and extremely grateful for the opportunities I've had. But I've eaten my fair share of rats (metaphorically and literally—Cambodian cuisine is wild) and I have to say: domesticity no longer seems like such a terrible fate.

The foundations of our social wellbeing are pinned down by two broad classes of constraints. As Freud put it: "Love and work... work and love, that's all there is."

We've already discussed how happiness is mostly a function of time spent around people you love, and who love you: whether they're friends, family, romantic partners, or tight-knit communities. I hope this is uncontroversial.

Work, on the other hand, deserves a little more explanation. We tend to think of work as the opposite of 'fun' or 'play', but this tautological definition is unhelpful. I never thought I'd say this, but it's time for a few words in defence of work.

WORK IS...GOOD, ACTUALLY?

John Maynard Keynes predicted that an explosion in wealth would lead our generation to work no more than 15 hours a week. He nailed the 'explosion of wealth' part, but he got the 15-hour workweek dead wrong. As discussed in Chapter 3, Keynes' prediction failed because he didn't account for the ratcheting forces of lifestyle inflation and conspicuous consumption.

But there's another reason he got it wrong: work is good, actually.

One of the stranger arcs of my adult life is that I apparently love work now. I just checked my records, and I've spent more than 1500 hours researching and writing this book, for example. If you calculate the hourly rate, I'd almost certainly make more money flipping burgers. What's going on?

A fascinating essay in *The Atlantic* by Derek Thompson reveals that I am far from alone in this apparent madness. Certain sectors of the population are working more than ever before, in a shift that Thompson says "defies economic logic". Historically, the rich always worked less than the poor. The more money you had, the more downtime you'd have for leisure and hobnobbing with your fellow elites.

Today's rich Americans can afford vastly more leisure than ever before, but as Thompson points out, they're using their wealth "to buy the strangest of prizes: more work".

This trend only starts to make sense against the backdrop of the waning of the commons. In a world absent God or meaning, work is evolving from a means of material production to what Thompson calls a means of identity production. We've gone from 'jobs' to 'careers' to 'callings', mirroring the ascending needs of survival, status, and meaning.

While the future of work is here, it's not evenly distributed. For the poor and middle classes, work is mostly the same as it ever was: a means of putting food on the table. It would be a stretch to describe back-breaking agricultural labour or manning a factory assembly line as a 'calling'. The truth is that for many people, work really is miserable. There's nothing remotely noble or fulfilling about it, and sometimes it's dangerous or physically ruinous. As Thompson points out, no-one is under any delusions about the higher purpose of screwing bolts into a chassis all day.

I agree that it's malicious to gaslight an entire society into thinking their work ought to be a source of deep meaning, based on naive mimicry of those lucky people for whom this is actually true. But Thompson is not quite right about the nature of this distribution.

It's patronising to assume that blue-collar workers could not possibly find meaning in their labour, and anyway, it's not true: the distinction between 'jobs', 'careers', and 'callings' has little to do with vocation. As discussed in Chapter 25, the label people use to describe their work depends on time on the job, mastery, autonomy, and working alongside good people. And so, you can find doctors who view practising medicine as little more than a 'job', and cleaners in the same hospital who see their role as a 'calling'.

No doubt a lot of people really are stuck in unfulfilling jobs, because most workplaces do not create the conditions described above. If that's the case, then it makes even less sense to *denigrate* those who manage to escape from mindless drudgery, and portray the pursuit of meaningful work as if it were some kind of mental illness. This is the zero-sum crabs in the bucket mentality again: it's not about compassion for one's peers, but resentment of those who make a leap for the rim.

It is fun watching a certain class of elites squirm with this internal contradiction. Having spent several thousand words railing against "the religion of workism", Thompson comes within a hair's breadth of self-awareness, confessing that he, too, gains most of his identity and satisfaction from work:

> "And I know enough writers, tech workers, marketers, artists, and entrepreneurs to know that my affliction is common, especially within a certain tranche of the white-collar workforce."

Of course he calls it his "affliction". Cultural elites hide behind this kind of humble-bragging because it is gauche to come right out and admit that work is pretty great for those who, say, get paid to write brilliant articles for prestigious magazines. It's necessary to maintain the aw-shucks charade so they can pretend to relate to the guy at the drive-through and show some class solidarity with their oppressed brothers and sisters. We're all just workin' stiffs here!

And so, it's simultaneously true to say that work is a soulless meat grinder of misery, and that work is a deeply satisfying source of meaning. Most everyone in the first camp subscribes to the 'work is bad' position, because that's their lived experience. But those in the second camp, who are in charge of shaping the narrative, sometimes *also* pretend to be in the first camp, either out of embarrassment or for political reasons. That means the humble suggestion that work might actually be good, far from being a dominant and pervasive myth that is ruining society, sounds more like the contrarian position.

Our desks were never meant to be our altars, writes Thompson. OK, sure, but nothing was ever 'meant' to be anything. We have to work with what we're given, and what we've been given is work.

You might consider this somewhat lacking in imagination: in a post-scarcity world, no doubt we will derive our sense of meaning elsewhere. I'm looking forward to Fully Automated Luxury Gay Space Communism as much as anyone else! But in the world we *actually live in right now*, work just so happens to be a major contributor to life satisfaction, and a useful constraint. It would be short-sighted to dismiss it out of hand and close off a rich source of potential meaning, because we need every scrap we can find.

FILLING THE VOID

The modern motivation for practicing frugality might be summed up in one word: escapism. *Don't be a cog in the machine. Escape the nine-to-five grind. Retire early. Hack life. Tune in, save up, and check out.*

But we need to be running *to* something, not just *from* something. Having a void in your life in which you wake up every morning with no structure and no obligations and a yawning chasm of time... that's the Bad Thing.

Mr Money Mustache did a good job of pre-empting this problem, including redefining the concept of 'retirement' to include paid and unpaid work. Here's what he'd been getting up to when I interviewed him:

> "Since retiring myself I have built two houses from the ground up, renovated a dozen other ones, raised my boy to age seven, started a blog, volunteered on loads of projects, and learned more things and had more fun than I had in the entire time I was working. It's busy, but very satisfying work."

But Mr Money Mustache is not a prototypical early retiree, and many of his followers have failed to read between the lines here. The absence of a negative doesn't solve the problem of meaning-making. It's a tough transition for those who dreamed they would finally be content when they hit a certain number, only to find themselves steamrolled by ennui when life doesn't become perfect overnight.

Getting a taste of mini-retirement early on was the best thing that ever happened to me, because it saved me from wasting decades chasing after a phantasm. This is the Acting Dead failure mode: 20 years of grinding low-level exploitation, followed by a retirement phase of yet more subsistence-level exploitation (Fig. 5.13). There is no exploration, no growth, no taking risks, and no attempting to put a dent in the universe.

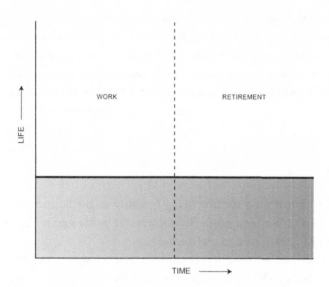

Figure 5.13. The 'Acting Dead' grind of constant low-level exploitation.

The early retirement pathway is viscerally appealing. It certainly got my attention. But I now believe an equally attractive pathway is to accumulate enough optionality to lever yourself into an enjoyable career.

It's not as if there's anything magical about work. But if we want to replace it, we at least have to acknowledge the itches it scratches:

Flow States

We need the right level of stress—not too much, not too little—to continue to grow and develop. Everyone who is not busy being born is busy dying, and all that.

The technical term is 'eustress'. In its biochemical/physical form, we call it hormesis: micro-tears to muscle fibres make them grow back stronger; periodic fasting resets metabolic systems and cleans up damaged cells.

The psychological/cognitive form of eustress is **Flow**. Deliberate practice and skill acquisition throws you up against problems that are hard enough to extend your limits, but not so hard that you give up. The best kind of work provides plenty of opportunities for entering these flow states, where time seems to melt away.

Community

The good kind of work also brings you into the orbit of exciting and interesting people. You get daily doses of gossip around the water cooler, friendships, maybe even romance. And you're part of a team, which lets you indulge the hivemind instinct in the service of something bigger than yourself.

Hierarchy

As one early retiree watched his friends and former coworkers rise through the ranks, he described feeling like a little puppy, while they were becoming the Big Dogs.

This is an apt analogy. Dogs are one of several species, including humans, that have social dominance hierarchies. Joining a hierarchy is not about getting to the top of the heap, so much as having a sense of your place in the pecking order. It gives you a clearly defined role, and a part to play in the great game of life.

One of the points we will cover in the final book is that you can't *not* play status games. They are not good or bad. They just are. And it just so happens that a job title is an unusually legible way of conveying status: it says so right there on your business card. If you walk away from this role, and you haven't sufficiently diversified your identity, you're going to need another game to play.

Impact

Convincing people to hand over money for something you produce is a reasonable proxy for the value you're creating in the world. If you believe in what you're doing—which you do, because you're no longer working passively for Evil Corp—then you're getting paid to do something intrinsically enjoyable, while also making the world a better place. That's an extremely attractive combination.

Good work provides opportunities for flow, community, status, and doing good, but it's not the only activity that ticks all the boxes. These itches might also be scratched through study, athletics, hobbies, volunteering, worship, or raising a family, for example.

As for 'workism', Derek Thompson is right about its potential pitfalls:

- If it trades off against more valuable things, like health, family, and relationships (Keynes worked himself to death)
- If your sense of identity is insufficiently diversified (Thompson mentions falling into an existential funk when he gets writer's block)
- If it encourages the myth that everyone can find meaningful work (This is simply not true, which is why we need to get to a post-scarcity world as soon as possible)

But these failings are not reason enough to damn the whole enterprise. If you *can* find a way to leverage yourself into getting paid to do something meaningful, for the love of sweet baby Jesus, do that! Take a paycut if you have to. Retrain or study. And do it *now*, not after 20 years of grinding towards FIRE.

Maybe you'll conclude that it's not a viable option. But it's worth giving some serious thought to, because of the enormous potential upside: creating a life you don't need to retire from.

CHOOSE YOUR OWN CHAINS

We've seen that autonomy is a necessary condition for human flourishing, but so are binding constraints. This apparent contradiction is pithily reconciled in an adage attributed to the Enlightenment philosopher Jean-Jacques Rousseau: "Freedom is the power to choose our own chains."

Constraints are unpleasant if they're imposed upon us from above—by fiat, by force, by threat of starvation. But they take on a completely different character if we deliberately choose to impose them upon ourselves. Once again, we're back to the simple definition of optionality: the right, but not the obligation, to take action.

We shouldn't aspire to drift through life untethered. But we can choose how and when we constrain ourselves.

Let's look back at some examples we've used throughout the book:

- Fasting is *categorically different* to starving
- Signing an employment contract with the security of a fuck-you independence stack is *categorically different* to having to do someone's bidding to survive
- Eating the same meals or wearing the same clothes every day is *categorically different* to being forced to follow a diet or wear a uniform
- Starting a family is *categorically different* to being born into one which you did not choose
- Joining a religion is *categorically different* to being trapped in a faith which punishes apostates with death or ostracism
- Frugality is *categorically different* to not having the means to spend money in the first place

Whenever a third party wants to impose constraints upon you, alarm bells should be ringing. It doesn't matter if it's the state, the Church, consumer capitalism, employers, or your own family. Throughout history, these institutions have often been deeply immoral, misery-inducing, and even murderous. It's important to cultivate a natural suspicion of rules and social norms, as described in Book II. Sometimes it will be necessary to zag hard when others are zigging, and choose your own code to live by.

With that being said, I suspect that some of the best constraints to consider are those with a strong historical precedent: family, work, marriage, membership of clubs and groups, schedules and routines, religion, children.

The great thing about imposing constraints upon yourself is that if they don't work in the way you intended, you can always change the rules. You don't have to ask anyone's permission. There's a reduction in optionality, which is the point of the exercise, but it's *reversible*. The decisions mentioned above are not permanently binding, unless your religion has a policy of murdering apostates (maybe don't join one of those).

But this is not universally true. There are a few cases in which it makes sense to not only commit hard to exercising a given option, but to ritually *sacrifice* your optionality forever.

SINK YOUR SHIPS BEHIND YOU

Hernán Cortés landed on the Yucatán Peninsula with a mere 500 men and a dozen horses, in direct violation of orders from the Governor of Cuba. The splendid city-state of Tenochtitlán lay hundreds of miles inland. If he returned to Cuba, he would face imprisonment or execution. And he now faced a rebellion of his own, with some of his men still loyal to the Governor.

So Cortés made an irreversible decision. He had the ringleaders of the mutiny killed, and sank his own ships to destroy any possibility of future defection. Cortés had trapped himself in a hostile land, but his men had no option but to follow his lead. They marched into Mexico, and history changed forever.

Cortés may have been a genocidal maniac who rained death and ruin upon an entire continent, but he was undeniably a great tactician. 'Sink your ships behind you' is the nuclear version of a Ulysses contract: in the context of akrasia, tying yourself to the mast was about limiting access to the self-stimulating and status-seeking products of consumer capitalism. The difference here is we're using it to destroy genuinely valuable options.

The classic example is marriage: a symbolic gesture that we shall explore no further. The optionality approach to relationships would be to explore a lot initially, learn about your own preferences and compatibilities, meet new people, open up opportunities, and become a more worthy and valuable partner. You end up with lots of juicy figs on the possibility tree, and while you can uh, sample widely, the long-term benefits generally come from picking *one*.

It is a mathematical certainty that there will always be someone better out there.[1] This fact is liable to drive two people mad. So, you each ritualistically sacrifice a large chunk of your optionality. You vow to stop looking, and to resist the endless drive towards more and better. Actually getting married doesn't matter, except insofar as it's a costly and public signal of your sacrifice. To commit to monogamy is to scuttle your ships, shoulder your weapons, and march into Mexico side by side.

But even marriage isn't truly irreversible. These days, most marriage contracts come with an escape clause, which more than a third of couples end up exercising. Divorce has heavy financial and social costs, but it's always there as a last resort.

There are no takesy-backsies when it comes to having a child. As a lady friend puts it, a baby sucks your identity out through your nipples. It becomes your duty to put the child's happiness ahead of your own, and apparently, that's exactly what happens: your life becomes more meaningful and satisfying, at the expense of in-the-moment happiness. This is why most parents don't regret having children, even though it's devastating to their personal freedom.

This is not so much a destruction of optionality, as a *sacrifice*. Remember that life itself is the first and most important capability any of us are given. Having a child is a transfer of optionality to a potential being plucked out of the void of nonexistence.

The final argument I want to make is that sacrificing your optionality so that others might flourish is an excellent way to improve the lives of others, and not just the small people that happen to live in your house.

It's no coincidence that the most vocal critics of optionality already have more options than they could use in a lifetime—usually finance professors, venture capitalists, and Peter Thiel-types. In pooh-poohing the value of having options, they are either targeting a very specific audience, and thus not bothering to make the necessary caveats, or clueless about the incredibly unlikely bubbles in which they live. Perhaps it is shameful to stay in your cushy Goldman Sachs job instead of boldly taking a risk, but this critique is wildly irrelevant to the vast majority of regular people. Most of us did not graduate from Stanford, or clerk for the Court of Appeals. Most of us are just trying to get some options in the first place!

But Thiel and friends are absolutely right about the narrower claim: anyone who *is* fortunate enough to accumulate a large buffer of optionality would be a coward to hoard it indefinitely.

As my final act, I ask you to consider using your expanded range of quality choices to help unlock the capabilities of others. I believe this is not an obligation, so much as an *opportunity*: a selfish decision which simultaneously benefits you, me, and everyone else.

VI

TELOS

TELOS. (noun) from the ancient Greek τέλος: *inherent purpose, the ultimate reason for being.*

INTRODUCTION

Despite the high cost of living, it remains popular.

— ANON

E'VE COME TO THE END of the book, which means it's time to contemplate the deep metaphysical questions: what is a 'book', anyway? You might describe it physically: it's made of paper, with squiggles and dots printed in ink, it's heavy, and so on. But after a while, you'd also describe what *it's for*. Hopefully by this point you'd say that the purpose is to be read and enjoyed, rather than, say, relegated to the outhouse as a handy source of paper.

This is what Aristotle called *telos*: the ultimate end, and reason for existence.

Man-made objects have a telos, but so do all natural things. An acorn's telos is to grow into a mighty oak tree; a thoroughbred foal's purpose is to become a fast runner.

This final book explores our own telos. To what end were human beings created?

According to Aristotle, our reason for existence is to be happy, in the fullest sense of the word—what the Greeks called eudaimonia. Hedonic plea-sure is not enough to reach a state of flourishing: we must also live a life of virtue, and use all of our capabilities to their fullest. To live without virtue is to fail to reach our true purpose—like a book that's only used as a doorstop, or a racehorse with a lame leg.

This is an inspiring and noble ideal, and like most noble ideals, only somewhat spoiled by not having the slightest bit of grounding in reality.

We can hardly blame Aristotle for pushing his pet theory a little too far. Humans and other natural things sure *look like* they were designed with some purpose in mind. It wasn't until that nerd Charles Darwin stuck his beak in that we learned the awful truth: evolution is an impersonal and frankly ridiculous process that involves no planning, forethought, or intention of any kind.

While creationists still cling to Aristotle's teleological argument, they should be careful what they wish for. If we were 'designed' for anything, it's only the ignoble end of replicating our genes by any means necessary. We might call this the blind idiot god of evolution's telos: have sex with anything that isn't nailed down, and try not to die in the process.

Now, this life philosophy works quite nicely up until your mid-20s. After that point, we start being confronted by some niggling questions: What's the meaning of life? What's it all *about*?

This is supposed to be a great mystery, but the answer is staring us right in the face if we can only bear to look at it: there is none. Zilch. Zip. Nada.

The universe doesn't care about a bunch of murder-monkeys on a rock hurtling through space. It's nothing personal; caring just isn't in its remit. As far as the universe is concerned—and to be clear, it's not—we're all just shuffling atoms in a cosmic game of billiards, blindly bouncing along a causal pathway that started with the Big Bang and extends all the way to the cosmic heat death.

The only thing that makes us special is that unlike every other blissfully ignorant speck unburdened by the 'gift' of self-awareness, *we have to deal with this bullshit*. As Nietzsche dramatically put it, God is dead, and we have killed him. How shall we comfort ourselves?

The usual response is to paint your fingernails black, scrawl the anarchy symbol on your school bag, and write very bad poetry about how nothing matters. Thankfully, most of us grow out of the nihilism phase by the end of high school, or at least convert to the more popular philosophy of "have sex with anything that isn't nailed down, and try not to die in the process".

Then we do what humans do best: we adapt, and get on with it.

There's no such thing as the meaning *of* life, in the cosmic sense. But there is such a thing as the meaning *in* life. If we can't find any of it floating out in the universe, we'll just have to make our own.

Again, the process of meaning-making is portrayed as some kind of great mystery, but it's a simple empirical question. We already know that many people lead meaningful lives. All we have to do is *ask them how*, and then blatantly copy their answers. Upon doing so, responses usually fall into one of the following categories:

- Family and children
- Religion
- Work or entrepreneurship
- Philanthropy
- Creation (art, music, literature)

These fonts of meaning-making have a lot in common. They all transcend individual desires, they're oriented towards the interests of a group, and they're among the best ways to leave the world a better place than you found it. Relevant to our interests, they all demand a sacrifice of personal optionality on the altar of the collective good.

The religious wording here is deliberate. Remember Émile Durkheim, who authored the groundbreaking report on the importance of constraints for preventing suicide? Durkheim believed the central characteristic of a religion was not so much its supernatural beliefs, but the dichotomy between the sacred and the profane. Something is *sacred* insofar as it represents the interests of the group, and *profane* insofar as it involves mundane individual concerns.

The wave of secularisation after the Enlightenment elevated the profane at the expense of the sacred; a trend that has accelerated in the last century. Durkheim's great concern was figuring out how societies could maintain coherence under these conditions. We have fewer and fewer cultural practices that bridge the gap between the two domains—temporarily pulling us out of our self-interested day-to-day existence, and into the higher realm of the sacred.

So this is where we get religious, although I don't expect you to take any of this on faith:

- Why care about the collective good?
- Why not look out only for you and yours?
- Why should you sacrifice optionality at all?

The short answer is that Aristotle was right all along. At the beginning of this book, I argued that money is purely instrumental to worthier goals, and not an end unto itself. Then I suggested that happiness, too, is a misguided target, and can't be pursued head-on. Instead, I claimed that the real prize is optionality: to unlock the full range of human capabilities, and strive and suffer in the manner of one's own choosing.

Now it's time for the final tweak. Even optionality is not an end unto itself. Instead, the ultimate point of the exercise is to deliberately *sacrifice* our options.

Aristotle's reasoning might have been a bit wonky, but he still arrived at the right conclusion. Flourishing really does require us to live a virtuous life: not because human beings have an intrinsic telos, but because we have to worship *something*, and choosing the profane—money, fame, beauty—is guaranteed to eat you alive.

What follows is the juiciest class of options we've encountered yet. You have the right, but not the obligation, to achieve some truly extraordinary outcomes.

If we choose to play certain games, we can simultaneously improve the lives of others, have a positive impact on the planet, and make our own lives better, too. This is the art of selfish selflessness.

29

SELFISH SELFLESSNESS

My life seemed like a glass tunnel, through which I was moving faster every year, and at the end of which there was darkness... When I changed my view, the walls of my glass tunnel disappeared. I now live in the open air. There is still a difference between my life and the lives of other people. But the difference is less.

— DEREK PARFIT

I CARE ABOUT THE ENVIRONMENT in the same way that most people do, by which I mean cooing over YouTube clips of charismatic megafauna and sagely remarking that Something Must Be Done about this whole climate change business. I'm not exactly out picketing against Evil Corp, or sailing my solar-powered yacht to Davos to berate the global elite.

So it's kind of funny that I've accidentally ended up with a 'greener' lifestyle than certain eco-warriors, despite my fondness for international travel. I wish I could say this was a result of firm and principled action, but the truth is that it happened almost entirely by accident, as a side-effect of pursuing my own self-interest.

In the course of seeking out attractive trade-offs, I ended up ditching my car, riding a bicycle, living in modest accommodation, travelling as slowly as possible, owning hardly any stuff, mostly buying secondhand, and switching to a plant-based diet. Some of these lifestyle changes are rewarding in the 'warm fuzzies' sense, but I am motivated by harder currencies: money, time, health, and pleasure.

If you can find a way to align your own self-interest with the interests of other people and the interests of the planet as a whole, you get a beautiful outcome. This is the idea of selfish selflessness: with the right incentive structure, there's no need for sermons and shaming tactics—the virtuous behaviour takes care of itself.

The classic example of this is the gift of life.

THE GIFT OF LIFE

There is a tragic but unintentionally funny Reddit forum called r/childfree, in which people who don't want to have kids come together to vent about 'breeders' and their grotesque 'crotchspawn'.

In justifying their own life decisions, these strident non-parents often make the argument that having children is an inherently selfish act. And they're right! Having kids is the archetypal example of selfish selflessness: it's a fundamentally self-centred decision that just so happens to make the world a much better place.

The first and greatest benefit goes to the new person brought into existence. It's almost impossible to maintain the requisite sense of awe for bringing life into the world, especially in a society which denigrates parenthood as somehow less worthy than other pathways, so we will have to explicitly make the case for pronatalism.

'Life' is at the very top of Martha Nussbaum's list of core capabilities, and the first and most precious option any of us are given. This seems like a good altar upon which to sacrifice optionality—maybe the greatest altar of all, or you wouldn't be reading these words, and I would never have written them. Our parents plucked us from the void and gave us this most precious of gifts. If we have the opportunity to pay it forward, we might at least consider doing so.

Certain edgy philosophers will claim this is an act of cruelty: "I exist against my will!" If they're really going to bite that bullet, they'd presumably have to bite a literal bullet. Life has an option value: if there is no prospect of future upside, we can always return to the void of non-existence. It is unspeakably sad that anyone should so much as contemplate this decision, but the fact that the vast majority of people *don't* kill themselves is pretty good evidence that existence is generally better than non-existence.

As for concerns around overpopulation, historically, these fears have been completely backwards. Every time, it's education, technology and innovation that lifts us out of poverty and saves us from imminent apocalypse, while population controls and 'de-growth' initiatives lead to stomach-churning atrocities.

A long line of Malthusians have used a veneer of academic respectability to enact the kind of policies that make Thanos look sane: deliberate starvation camps in India, granting aid to developing countries conditional on forced sterilisation, an enthusiastic eugenics program in California (which notoriously inspired some fellow travellers in Germany), and a brutal campaign of forced abortion and infanticide in China—all of which were widely praised by the authorities of the day as bold and necessary measures. Astonishingly, vaguely-genocidal views are still uncontroversial: all you have to do is compare humanity to a cancer or virus, and you'll receive sage nodding of heads from 'compassionate' people who actually think you have said something wise.

As soon as developing countries get rich, fertility rates drop close to or below replacement levels. While having children is often presented as some kind of existential threat, the truth is that we desperately need *more* people, not fewer.

Which brings us to the next great benefit: fighting the good fight against entropy. If we prefer a universe teeming with life over a sterile void of rock and ice, we should consider it our duty to fill our future light cone with as much complexity as possible.

Humans are certainly the strangest things in our corner of the universe, and possibly the only intelligent life form to make it past whatever Great Filter has caused our skies to appear so empty. If we are alone, we have one heck of a responsibility to keep the spark of consciousness alive.

Finally, the most important benefit of having children is the purely selfish reason that motivates the decision in the first place: the mega-dose of meaning bestowed upon the parents.

Having kids is a time-honoured solution to the problem of meaning-making. If you start getting anxious about your impact on the world, or lying awake at night wondering what it's all about, you throw out a hospital pass to the next generation. Now it's someone else's problem!

This is the biggest trade-off almost anyone will ever make. It requires a

costly sacrifice of our most precious resources— time, money, and happiness—
in exchange for the existential relief that comes from sublimating individual
desires, and letting the universe revolve around someone or something else.

At least, that's the theory. I am not a parent, and don't have any special
insight as to whether the trade-off is actually worth it. It's extremely hard to
find reliable studies on how many people regret having children—a taboo
subject for obvious reasons—but it's certainly a real risk. There's no *guarantee*
that having kids creates meaning, and for some people it might even destroy
it: lots of life pathways are massively constrained by having children at the
wrong time or with the wrong partner. Perhaps the best framing is Christo-
pher Hitchens' observation that there are no pain-free options: all we can do
is choose our future regrets.

Consciously or not, every single one of your ancestors made this trade: you
come from a long and unbroken line of breeders stretching back 1.2 billion
years. It's a cheap biological hack, but so what? There are no more or less
'valid' sources of meaning. If giving in to the DNA puppet-masters tugging on
your strings does the trick, so be it.

If it doesn't, don't. We don't need to invoke the anti-natalist propaganda,
because there's already a perfectly good reason not to have kids: because you
don't want to.

Maybe you already have rich sources of meaning in your life. Maybe you
don't think the trade-off is compelling, or you don't like children, or whatever.
The exact reasoning doesn't matter: it's much better to *follow your self-interest*
than to have a child that isn't wanted.

And as it happens, there's a much more efficient way to give the gift of life,
which doesn't involve squeezing a melon-sized object out of your pelvis.

SECRET SUPERHEROES

The mark of a civilised man is the ability to look at a column of numbers and weep.

— BERTRAND RUSSELL

What price can we put on a human life? The socially acceptable answer to this
question is "every life is priceless". The heartless but pragmatic answer is
"somewhere in the range of $4-10 million".

Having been primed to think of everything as a trade-off, hopefully you will sympathise with the economists and statisticians who grapple with this question every day. If we thought life was literally priceless, we would crawl along the highway in Mack trucks in full body armour at 5 kilometres per hour. Safety regulations would be so stringent that every company would be forced out of business, all sports and hobbies would be banned, and civilisation would grind to a halt.

Instead, we have to come up with a figure for calculating the costs and benefits of any given policy decision which lets us make these kinds of taboo trade-offs. The statistical value of life ranges widely, but several million dollars seems about right—I would value my own life in that range, but not much higher or lower.

The corollary is that if you save someone's life, you might consider that your good deed was worth several million dollars.

Outside of comic books, opportunities to save a life don't come along very often. Every now and then, you read a story about a bystander who saves a child from drowning, or pulls someone from a burning building. They get a plaque, and a commendation of bravery, and an aw-shucks TV interview.

But a little-known secret is that you can save a life every single year of your career, and never once have to brave the flames. You won't get a plaque, but you can be a secret superhero. Every year, another child gets to learn, and love, and dream, and grow old. And it's all because of you.

How much does it cost to become a secret superhero? As at the time of writing, about $3400. Seriously. That's not a typo. There's an exploitable asymmetry which lets us save lives for *less than 0.1 per cent* of their statistical value.

This opportunity comes to us courtesy of a movement called **Effective Altruism**. This band of calculating do-gooders ruthlessly analyse the impact of each charity in order to do the most good with each dollar, hunting for asymmetric opportunities in scope, tractability, and neglectedness.

While many of the sexiest brand-name charities are woefully inefficient, the effective altruists have found that others are massively undervalued: you can give someone a childhood free of parasitic worms for a few bucks, and a treated mosquito bed net costs less than a cup of coffee.

Mosquitoes kill more humans than any other animal on the planet, by an enormous margin. Malaria alone infects 400 million people a year, and claims half a million lives. Seventy per cent of the victims are children under five,

many are pregnant women, and most are people of colour. The extraordinary thing is that every single one of these deaths is preventable. We already know how to beat malaria—primarily, by distributing enough insecticide-treated bed nets—and on average, it only costs a few thousand dollars to save a life.

The way things are going, malaria might be vanquished in our lifetime. This is a disease that has plagued our ancestors for 20 million years, halted the army of Genghis Khan in their tracks, and killed at least seven popes. You get to tell your child or grandchild that you personally played a part in eradicating the single deadliest disease in history.

This is exciting, but it raises some gnarly moral questions. If it only costs $3400 to save a life, and the opportunity has never been more compelling, wouldn't it be outrageously negligent to spend money on luxuries? If you take an expensive vacation, does that mean you've chosen to let someone die?

This is the disturbing idea at the heart of moral philosopher Peter Singer's 'drowning child' thought experiment. You're walking through the park on your way to a meeting, when you see a figure splashing in the muddy duck pond. You realise it's a child, and they're not swimming—they're drowning. You look around, but no-one else is in sight. You're wearing an expensive suit and patent-leather shoes, which will surely be spoiled. And if you miss your meeting, you'll lose out on a new client. What do you do?

The overwhelming moral instinct is that it would be monstrous to walk away. So you jump in, save the child, and take the financial hit.

Here's the twist: this is the situation we're in all the time. There are millions of drowning children, and we *always* have the option to pay a few thousand dollars to save them from a grim death. The only difference to the duck pond scenario is that these kids don't happen to be in our direct line of sight.

I have yet to hear a satisfying counterargument to Singer's thought experiment, and to put my cards on the table, I don't think there is one. That means I'm a moral monster. So are you. So is Singer. After all, he 'only' donates 40 per cent of his income to charity, rather than living in a cardboard box and subsisting on bread and water.

Of all the rationalisations we might use to wriggle out of this, the most compelling is simple pragmatism. I believe it's much more mentally healthy to frame altruism as an *opportunity*, rather than a bottomless obligation.

A popular option amongst effective altruists is to pledge a fraction of your income to the most effective causes: say, 10 per cent. That's small enough that it doesn't materially reduce your own quality of life, but large enough to have a real impact—on an average salary, you're saving a life every year, without burning out and abandoning the whole enterprise.

This is the approach I've taken. My charity dollars go towards buying anti-malarial bed nets, and 50 per cent of the profits from this book will go towards buying more.

So that's the scale of the opportunity, and the incredible asymmetry: you can buy someone a $10 million gift for a few thousand dollars. But *why* should you care? How is it in your self-interest to help total strangers on the other side of the world?

THE BLURRY BOUNDARIES OF SELFHOOD

I've been trying to chip away at your sense of self since Book II. If you recall, defeating akrasia requires us to integrate our squabbling subagents, and create the best set of outcomes for all our current and future selves.

Once you practice being kind to your future self—who might as well be a stranger—it's no longer such a stretch to be kind to literal strangers. This is what it means to have a fully integrated self: not only internal alignment between your current and future selves, but expanding circles of concern radiating out to loved ones, to your tribe, to humanity as a whole, and to non-human beings.

Once the boundaries of personhood start to dissolve, there's no difference between being good to others and being good to yourself, except that you apply a discount rate as the circles expand across time and space. Virtue becomes its own reward, and vice becomes its own punishment. Every action you take ripples out laterally through the circles and forward through time. It's like, *totally cosmic*, man.

I know this sounds weird. But you and I are the weird ones! Or, more accurately, WEIRD: western, educated, industrialised, rich, democratic. While the sharp lines of personal identity are sacrosanct in the West, other cultures have much blurrier boundaries of personhood.

The Hindu Vedas distinguish between one's true self (Ātman) and the transcendent self (Brahman). A person can only be liberated when they realise that their true self is indistinguishable from the single binding unity of reality, and that there is no difference between 'I' and 'you' and 'her'—in other words, that Ātman and Brahman are one and the same.

If you think this is mystical hocus-pocus, you're not going to like the leading theories in modern metaphysics. These days, Tibetan monks intersperse their sutras with memorised passages from *Reasons and Persons*, the groundbreaking work of moral philosopher Derek Parfit (he of the furious stationary cycling in Chapter 16). Parfit experienced the dissolution of self, as described in the passage at the beginning of this chapter: "I now live in the open air. There is still a difference between my life and the lives of other people. But the difference is less."

Parfit did more than anyone since the Buddha to dislodge the idea that 'rationality' is synonymous with acting in one's own self-interest. With a battery of brilliant thought experiments, he demonstrated that there is no time-spanning, immutable entity—a self is always a matter of degrees. We can see this most clearly at the beginning and end of life: when does a zygote become a self, exactly? If you descend into dementia or a coma, when do you stop being 'you'? There are only ever stronger or weaker patterns of relatedness between mental states. Cryonics experts will tell you that even *death* is not a discrete event, so much as a spectrum of decay.

Until the last few years of my life, I would have dismissed all of this as a load of baloney. The illusion of selfhood is so powerful that it's extremely hard to viscerally *feel* otherwise, and I'm not sure I could be reasoned out of a position I wasn't reasoned into.

In order to fully internalise this reality, it seems like you either have to spend a lifetime practicing meditation, study moral philosophy for decades, or take a heroic dose of acid.

If you don't buy it, it doesn't matter: there are also more prosaic reasons for helping others.

TO GIVE IS TO RECEIVE

Even if we're being entirely mercenary about giving, we might make a calculated decision to spend some money on warm fuzzies. One study suggests that the proportion of your income you spend on others is a very strong predictor of happiness—in fact, it's just as powerful as the effect of income itself. If this is true, then Charles Dickens got it right in a *Christmas Carol*: the Scrooges of the world really are more miserable than big-hearted poor folks.

Of course, we know that happiness is a desperately flawed measure of human wellbeing. That cheerful tyke Tiny Tim would do pretty good on a hedonic survey; he's still going to end up in a tragically small coffin.

But there are other advantages to generosity. Spending money on others certainly builds social capital, and possibly makes you healthier. In a study of more than 1000 older adults, those who gave money and support to others—family or not—reported better health. This was true even after taking into account their income, mobility, and other factors.

Generosity seems to be especially important as you move from exploring to exploiting. Another longitudinal study found that volunteer work boosted every measure of wellbeing including health and longevity, with the elderly benefiting the most.

Honestly, it's best to take social psychology research published prior to 2016 with an enormous pinch of salt.[1] Let's assume this is all wishful thinking, and giving doesn't make you the slightest bit happier or healthier. Even in that absolute worst-case scenario, philanthropy is still an attractive proposition.

For one thing, it gives us another answer to the problem of meaning-making. You get to sacrifice some personal optionality in exchange for a large dose of satisfaction and purpose.

The related benefit is that it provides us with interesting games to play. Social status is a core human need, right up there with food and water, intimacy, security, and self-actualisation. We've previously looked at some of the status games that lead us astray, and how we might choose to play different ones. Now let's make it explicit.

30

STATUS GAMES

Finite players play within boundaries; infinite players play with boundaries.

— JAMES CARSE

TATUS IS THE SHADOW CURRENCY that makes the world go around. Of all the currencies of life, the marketplace for social status is the biggest and most bustling.

The games we play in pursuit of raw status are rarely as wholesome or legible as the strategies we use to build social capital. There are hidden micro-transactions in every instance of eye contact, an arm casually draped over a chair, the conjugation of a verb, a specific tone of voice, and every aesthetic choice from the clothes you wear to the car you drive.

While status is necessarily nebulous, it's much *less* of an abstraction than money. This is the basic currency of social animals: it can be traded, saved, invested, loaned out, or crystallised. Unlike health or knowledge capital, status is liquid—it can be readily exchanged for sex, information, money, or other favours. But it has one terrible feature that sets it apart from all the other currencies of life.

Unlike wealth, or health, or learning, status is purely *positional*. The size of the pie is fixed, and everyone's out to get a slice of it.

Maybe you gain status by leading raids on World of Warcraft. Maybe I gain status by being on the cutting edge of obscure trends. Maybe Grandma gains status from her role as the family matriarch.

Globalisation and the splintering of subcultures have massively opened up the status landscape, with more games to play than ever before. But even while everyone has the chance to occupy different positions in different contexts—you could be a lowly grunt at work, but a towering colossus of prestige to your 3 year old—it all ultimately coalesces together. Claiming that status is infinite is the same kind of wishful thinking as believing our mums' assurances that we're all special, or that we can all get rich by cranking up the money printers.

In the language of game theory, this is a zero-sum situation. We can only gain status at someone else's expense, and vice versa.

The aim of this chapter is to demonstrate that this is not nearly as depressing as it sounds, and that we have no choice but to play the game anyway. As the only ultrasocial primates, our drive to acquire social standing is a biological imperative, right up there with food and water. Anyone who doesn't possess the tiniest scrap of status will have a miserable life, and quite possibly die.

While some people claim to be status-blind, they are really saying that they are bad at picking up on status dynamics, or they're making a clumsy attempt to signal that they're high-status individuals, or both. Declarations of this nature can be taken about as seriously as the 'breatharians' who claim to subsist only on fresh air and sunlight.

We can't escape the constraints of our biology. And we can't escape the constraints of game theory. But in the centre of this Venn diagram, we have a few degrees of freedom.

See, the fixed pool of status itself is zero-sum. But the games we play in pursuit of it are not.

PLAY STUPID GAMES, WIN STUPID PRIZES

Let's run through some common scenarios in game theory. In the top-left quadrant of Fig. 6.1, we have the 'win-win' outcomes: these are positive-sum games which leave both players better off. In the two diagonal quadrants, we have the 'win-lose' outcomes: these are zero-sum games in which one player's winnings come at the expense of the others' losses. Finally, in the bottom-right quadrant we have the 'lose-lose' negative-sum games: if we add up all the players' gains and losses, everyone is collectively worse off.

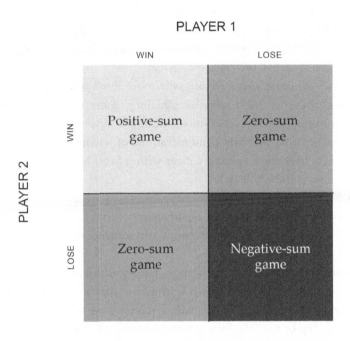

Figure 6.1. A matrix of possible outcomes in game theory.

Negative-sum games often resemble competitive spirals of ratcheting expenditure. This helps explain why the blind god of evolution's creations are so absurd and inefficient: there are constant arms races between predators and prey, parasites and hosts, competing suitors, and even different sexes of a single species. Male ducks have evolved ballistic, corkscrew-shaped penises longer than their own bodies that launch into the female's reproductive duct in a fraction of a second, which means mating doesn't require the delicate and cooperative alignment of vents seen in most other birds. In response, female ducks have evolved labyrinthine vaginas with false turns and dead ends, which allows them to regain some autonomy over their reproductive systems. There are cheaper and less gruesome ways to handle mate selection than violent assault, but both sexes are stuck in a costly equilibrium.

Arms races don't always involve aggression or coercion. As a group, male peacocks are massively impaired by their long, resource-intensive tails. They'd be much better off if they could somehow unionise, and agree to switch to competing over who has the most winning personality or whatever. But they can't, and neither can the peahen who selects for this ridiculous trait, because she wants her male offspring to have a greater chance of passing on her genes. Again, the peafowl are stuck in a bad equilibrium.

Homo sapiens—the 'wise man'—is allegedly more intelligent than the pea-brained peafowl, but our most popular signalling game is equally stupid. Conspicuous consumption locks us into spending our resources in ever-more absurd ways, culminating in literal demonstrations of having money to burn, like the trope of a billionaire lighting a cigar with a $100 bill. The pointlessness of the exercise is the whole point.

Credentialism is another example of a runaway signalling game. As discussed in Chapter 18, the costs of qualifications spiral higher and higher, and are increasingly decoupled from the actual quality of the education received.

These games trap us in a bad equilibrium. Each individual player is acting rationally in their own self-interest, but it leads to a crappy outcome for everyone. We would all be better off if we made a solemn vow to stop performatively wasting money, or to make hiring decisions in which cheap and effective tests of ability were given as much weight as Ivy League sheepskins. But we'd have to somehow coordinate to get everyone to switch at once. Since no individual player has any hope of shifting the equilibrium, the 'optimal' move is to keep defecting.

When the rules of the game force us into a bad strategy, the answer isn't to try to change strategies—it's to change the games we play.

THE SUPERWEAPON OF COORDINATION

Chasing status makes us act like idiots, but it's also responsible for all of the awesome stuff humans have ever achieved. When we flock to marvel at the wonders of the world—the Taj Mahal, the Great Pyramid of Cheops—what we're really gazing upon is our ancestors' dick-measuring contests. Once we developed the technology to build straight upwards, the symbolism became about as subtle as a brick. Nevertheless, these colossal erections are monuments to something genuinely awe-inspiring: our ability to coordinate at scale.

Unlike the unfortunate animals stuck in wasteful evolutionary arms races, human beings can coordinate to escape from 'sticky' negative-sum games. This is our secret sauce as a species: instead of constantly defecting against one another, we occasionally manage to create and capture surplus value.

Almost no other animal can do this, with the noteworthy exception of the ultrasocial insects. Once ants, bees, wasps and termites started working together in giant families, they literally took over the Earth: the social insects now make up the majority of all bugs on the planet, and have erected some of the most impressive monuments and cathedrals in the natural world.

The social psychologist Jonathan Haidt suggests that humans are "90 per cent chimp and 10 per cent bee". That last 10 per cent makes all the difference in the world: it would be unheard of to see two chimps carrying a log together, let alone cooperate at scale. Prosocial behaviour is intrinsically rewarding for us, which probably has something to do with being able to model the minds of others—a child will include someone they haven't met before in play, because they know the other will enjoy it. Our primate cousins cooperate too, but not for its own sake: they use others more like social tools to maximise their own rewards, and the evidence suggests they don't have a fully developed theory of mind.[1]

Social insects use powerful but rigid technology to become unified super-organisms—changes at the genetic level which make it impossible to distinguish between loving one's hivemate and loving oneself. Everyone is closely related, and the queen uses chemical mind-control to dictate the reproduction and other functions of her subjects. Each ant or bee is effectively a cell in a larger organism, with no agency of its own.

Our programming is much more flexible. The status-seeking behaviour that drives us to improve our social standing is hardwired, along with whatever split separated us from our less prosocial primate cousins. But we've also built a fluid layer of technology on top of our genetics, in the form of language, gossip, writing, money, contracts, laws, and courts. These tools make it easier to track reputation, allocate status, and punish defectors—in short, to coordinate at a scale so massive that it makes ants look like, uh, ants.

Coordination at scale is not always a good thing. If all the ants on the planet ganged up against us, no picnic basket would be safe, but it wouldn't be the end of the world. When *humans* weaponise coordination, we end up with literal arms races: war, empire-building, propaganda, factory farming, slavery, trafficking, and the threat of nuclear armageddon. This is a scale of destruction completely unheard of in the animal kingdom—not because humans have a special talent for cruelty, but because we're so much better at coordinating at scale.[2]

The Great Pyramid is a monument to this coercive form of coordination. Tens of thousands of labourers spent decades destroying their bodies for the vanity project of a tyrant who fooled the peasants into believing he and his family were gods.

Notice how the same cannot be said of the Eiffel Tower, or the Chrysler Building, or any of the modern wonders of the world. We're steadily moving away from coercive games by adding more layers of social technology: trade, globalisation, boycotts, human rights, ethics, and workplace safety, to name a few.

To paraphrase the great poet Homer, here's to status-seeking—the cause of, and solution to, all of life's problems. History suggests humanity is moving in the direction of becoming a truly cooperative superorganism. There's no guarantee this trend will continue, but I for one would like to maximise our chances.

We can choose to play games that allow us to jockey for position in such a way that it benefits everybody—and these games don't involve erecting phallic monuments.

Before we get there, there's one last assumption to unpack. I am claiming that status signals don't reliably point to what is good in life, and we can actively manipulate them to achieve better outcomes. But what kind of hubristic hope is this?

THE SCOURGE OF FAT PRIVILEGE

Imagine a parallel universe in which thin people are freely mocked by the overweight. Liberal magazines publish thinkpieces calling out the scourge of 'fat privilege'. Young girls are bombarded with messages encouraging them to eat more, and that big is beautiful. Unthinkable? We've just described "most of human history, prior to the 20th century".

Our cultural conditioning is so strong that it's hard to remember that body fat is not some evolutionary mistake—it's a precious survival feature. In a world where everyone is constantly at risk of starvation, love handles are a reliable signal of beauty and fertility (women) and access to resources (men).

Rather than wearing slimming stripes, 16th century fashionistas carefully styled and padded clothes to accentuate a big belly. In China, thin singletons were placed on special bulking diets so they could find marriage partners. The Connecticut Fat Man's Club, founded in 1866, barred entry to those who weighed less than 200 pounds. Adolescent girls of the Nigerian elite class spent two years in 'fattening huts', and didn't emerge until they were sufficiently thick.

It's only in the last century that the signal began to weaken, and ultimately reverse direction. As food became cheaper relative to income, love handles were no longer so impressive. Now we're awash in a sea of cheap calories, and most people will spend their entire lives in a permanently 'fed' state, without ever experiencing true hunger.[3]

As our environment changes, so do our fitness indicators. Today, being slim is considered higher-status, because it's a reliable signal of conscientiousness, free time to work out, being able to afford cocaine, etc.

This historical perspective on fatness is not meant to be an empowering story of body positivity. Ruben's voluptuous nudes were anything but enlightened: he was a privileged elite painting the *Playboy* magazine equivalent for his fat-cat patrons, with a male gaze and unrealistic beauty standards that exemplified the exuberant opulence of his social class. Same shit, different status signal.

So: on the one hand, we lock up young girls in huts and force feed them 20 litres of camel's milk. On the other hand, we bombard them with images that tell them to hate themselves if they don't have a thigh gap. What are these opposing signals meant to tell us about the 'right' body shape?

Another head-scratcher: my Victorian forebears poisoned themselves with lead makeup in the pursuit of whiteness, to signal that they didn't work in the sun with the peasants. Now I poison myself with radiation in the pursuit of a tan, to signal that I have the leisure time to escape the office and lie around in the sun. If you're still attached to the idea that there's some objective Platonic desirability in every attribute we compete to display, good luck reconciling these kind of contradictions.

It's even possible to have conflicting signals at the same point in time. In certain parts of Southeast Asia, I found it almost impossible to buy skincare products that didn't contain bleach. This fixation on whiteness goes back centuries, and has little to do with Western beauty standards: it exists because the elite want to separate themselves from the majority of the population, who are still subsistence farmers and manual labourers.

Hopefully you now have the appropriate level of ambivalence towards status signals. They are lagging indicators of fitness, they're constantly in flux, and they don't always enshrine any objectively 'good' attribute.

The mere fact that a status game exists tells us very little about its merits. Instead, we have to judge it on its *externalities*: does playing this particular game have the happy side-effect of making both of us healthier and wealthier? Or does it make us both do stupid things, like caking our faces with poison and setting fire to $100 bills?

There's nothing we can do to 'fix' runaway signalling games like conspicuous consumption or credentialism. Instead, we have to defect against the defectors: the only way to win a negative-sum game is *not to play in the first place*.

This is an immediate victory at the personal level, but it also has the effect of siphoning status and attention away from the bad equilibrium. In time, and in great enough numbers, we can steer humanity towards better games, and let the old ones crumble to dust. They will be bad up until the very end. But at least they will end.

If status is a universal human need, we can't just go cold turkey. The good news is that we've never had a more attractive array of positive-sum games to play, or more choice about who we play them with.

31

CONSPICUOUS SIMPLICITY

Our life is frittered away by detail. Simplify, simplify! A man is rich in proportion to the number of things which he can afford to let alone.

— THOREAU

C ONSPICUOUS CONSUMPTION IS A poor man's game. In a world of cheap debt, the signal is losing its reliability. At best, it shows you have the creditworthiness and income security to get a loan, but even that's imperfect: lenders of last resort will loan to anyone with a pulse.

The bigger problem—and what a problem!—is that we're getting too rich. The middle classes of the developed world are already running up against the point of diminishing returns. We have personal chariots, our own dwellings, an unlimited array of delicious foodstuffs from around the world, and a bounty of entertainment on demand. More money only provides marginal improvements on these wonders: the fact that you have a dedicated bathing room in your house with a constant source of running hot water provides 99.9 per cent of the value, as compared to the gold plating on the shower head. Money is always useful, but it's increasingly not the main bottleneck.

Conspicuous consumption is already considered tacky and low-status among certain elite groups. My bold prediction is that this trend will continue to accelerate, so we might as well get ahead of the curve.

To take it to the reductio ad absurdum, once we get to Fully Automated Luxury Gay Space Communism, setting fire to $100 bills will be a perfectly empty signal. Or maybe it *won't* be empty: it will signal that you have nothing else to offer, and people will look at you with pity or contempt.

After a certain point, the only people still playing the conspicuous consumption game will be those for whom it is still a useful signal—lower socioeconomic groups, people in developing countries—and those who don't have other dimensions on which they're able to compete. In other words, it will quite literally be a poor man's game.

We can already see the first stages of this transition taking place. Why does wearing a chunky gold chain look rich to poor people, and poor to rich people? The signal is simple: "I have enough resources that I can waste $500 on this shiny metal ornament." But rich people are *not worried* about being confused with people who don't have $500. They have to distinguish themselves from the insecure middle classes, and the way they do so is through 'countersignalling': by refraining from obvious displays of wealth, they demonstrate that they're so secure in their position that they don't need to broadcast it.

McMansions and Louis Vuitton bags are visual indicators of the kind of people who loudly tell you how great they are. If it was actually true, they wouldn't need to aggressively draw attention to themselves.

By contrast, only the elite can get away with dressing like homeless people. Mark Zuckerberg's trademark hoodie is a countersignal that he's powerful enough to ignore even the most high-class social conventions, and doesn't have to worry about being confused with your typical scruffy kid. Bill Gates rocks a $70 Casio watch. Warren Buffett still lives in the same modest house he bought in the 1950s. These are the richest men in the world, and everyone knows it. Not competing on this axis only *increases* their prestige: they've got enough going on that they don't need to engage in such transparent attempts to gain status.

We're a long way from post-scarcity, which means conspicuous consumption is still a reliable signal across many parts of the world, and in lower socioeconomic groups within rich countries.

But it is weakening relative to other signals, especially among the type of people likely to be reading this book, and this trend will continue. As money becomes less of a constraint, other fitness indicators become comparatively more attractive: knowledge, skills, generosity, discernment, and physical health.

So what games might we play that have these happy side effects?

THE 'FRUGALER THAN THOU' GAME

Frugality is an attractive status game to play, because most of the underlying practices are positive-sum. If I start riding my bike to work, it doesn't make my coworker any less healthy—in fact, the opposite is more likely to be true. If we get stuck in a competitive spiral of who can cycle the furthest, or who has the strongest thigh muscles, or who has the smallest carbon footprint, well... good?

The same goes for acquiring broad skills and knowledge. Life is not graded on a curve: if I learn something new, it doesn't suck the same amount of knowledge out of your brain. If we get into a competitive spiral of trying to ace the pub quiz, or showing off our weekend construction projects, again, that seems like a pretty great outcome.

We already see this kind of positive-sum jostling for position in the FIRE movement. Early retirement enthusiasts compete over how anti-consumerist and 'badass' they can be: they save such-and-such a proportion of their income, they cycle so many miles through the snow, they install solar panels and save so much on their energy bill.

I can see FIRE becoming an increasingly popular subculture. But I don't anticipate it going mainstream, and it's not a status game which I personally want to play.

The first major limitation is the framing of work as something to escape from. This destroys way too many opportunities to gain status: remember the early retiree who felt like a little puppy while his colleagues were becoming the Big Dogs. The leaders and evangelists of the movement are incapable of understanding this problem, because they have legions of admiring fans, thriving businesses based on selling the early retirement dream, and are gener-ally awash in status. But not everyone can have a popular early retirement blog (although God knows they're trying). The acolytes further down the pyramid will have to get their sense of status elsewhere, and strong thigh muscles and solar panels might not be enough.

The second major limitation is that outside of a few niche subcultures, frugal behaviour is anything but high-status. I used to think this was unfair, but now I can see there is nothing especially virtuous about frugality as it exists today, and in the worst case, it's become a funhouse-mirror perversion of the original virtue.

NIHILISM AND ACTING DEAD

When St Augustine described *frugalitas* as "the mother of all virtues", he was riffing on Marcus Tullius Cicero, a prolific writer and orator who made the same observation in 45 BC. It was Cicero who first translated the Greek concept of frugality into Latin, and defined it as encompassing the virtues of courage, justice, and prudence:

> "Let us allow, then, frugality itself to be another and fourth virtue; for its peculiar property seems to be, to govern and appease all tendencies to too eager a desire after anything, to restrain lust, and to preserve a decent steadiness in everything."

The aesthetic ideal of temperance was a big deal in classical antiquity. Contrary to depictions of wild orgies, the Romans considered it embarrassing and unmanly to show anything other than moderation and self-control. Frugality was so high-status that the consul Lucius Calpurnius Piso had the honorary *agnomen* 'Frugi' added to his name, beginning a family tradition that spanned hundreds of years.

Imagine this happening today: I shall henceforth be known as Richard the Frugal, and I will bestow this title upon generations of descendants, all of whom will proudly bear my name and definitely won't get shoved into lockers in high school.

Outside of niche subcultures, it would be hard to argue that frugality is high status today—and the opposite is much more likely to be true. Why?

Until recently, I assumed frugality had lost its virtuous shine because people were confusing it with being cheap. This is a common misunderstanding: for the record, frugality is about making deliberate trade-offs in such a way that it maximises your own values. It's only when you make a trade-off at *someone else's* expense—'forgetting' your wallet, hogging a common resource, monopolising someone's time—that you're being a tightwad.

But this is unlikely to be the explanation, because it turns out people have been making the same mistake since forever. St Augustine, writing in 380 AD, tells us that the word frugality is already commonly being used as if it were synonymous with 'stinginess'.

It's possible that cheapskates have become more common over the centuries, but I don't see the modern proponents of frugality behaving selfishly. Or at least, not *explicitly* selfishly. And this turns out to be an important distinction to make.

St Augustine points us back to Cicero, who traces the etymology of frugalitas to fruit (*fruge*), which is "the best thing the earth produces". To be frugal is to be fruitful. The equal and opposite vice is prodigality, or worthlessness (*nequitia*). This is a state of being without purpose (*nequiquam*), in which we are called Nihil—nothing.

So we have our paired opposites: frugality and nihilism, growth and stagnation, being and non-being.

Even Cicero admits this etymological groping is a stretch, but it does give us some insight into how things have changed. In the Greco-Roman world, the point of living simply and economically was to be able to better perform one's civic duty, and be more fruitful in the world—not to escape from work at the earliest opportunity.

The problem with the modern version of frugality is that it's a purely *subtractive* philosophy. It has a lot to say about what to avoid, but it doesn't elevate anything in its place. The point of pruning the possibility tree is to channel your resources into something fruitful; not to keep pruning until the tree is completely bare.

In the best case, frugality is a benign game that encourages various low-level positive-sum competitions. In the worst case, the movement becomes a kind of nihilistic death cult, in which otherwise talented and useful people are convinced it is 'virtuous' to lead the thinnest possible existence, and do the bare minimum required to check out: there is no risk-taking, no exploration, and no trying to put a dent in the universe.

In the same way that hating things is not a personality, a game motivated largely by escapism is not attractive to play. I am not saying frugality is 'bad', but I am saying it has stunted aesthetics.

CONSPICUOUS SIMPLICITY

Aesthetics are a leading indicator of the culture. Anyone interested in the evolution of design can see this happening in real time: **Conspicuous Simplicity** is crushing the competition.

Look at your iPhone, which combines the function of hundreds of different tools within one sleek rectangle of glass. Think about how websites have changed from the 2000s. Compare Google's homepage to Yahoo's. Negative space is high-status. Clean design is high-status. Clutter is low-status.

There's nothing impressive about a plain white gallery with no art on the walls, because negative space only works when it draws attention to a focal point. Done right, conspicuous simplicity is the opposite of subtractive: it forces us to *elevate* whatever remains.

The minimalist aesthetic reflects and reifies values that are genuinely worthy of emulation. It takes a huge amount of skill and effort to make anything complex appear simple, not to mention tasteful discernment, and a dash of courage: instead of hedging your bets, you have to stake your fortune on what you believe is worth elevating, and sacrifice everything else.

In other words, conspicuous simplicity is a *costly signal*. Only Google can afford to 'waste' the most valuable real estate on the web by letting its distinctive brand stand alone in an ocean of white space. A website covered in ads and pop-up promotions is inadvertently sending the opposite signal: it is not prestigious enough to be able to dispense with these gimmicks. It takes a lot of security in your product, brand, offering, or idea to let it stand unadorned on its own merits.

I prefer the 'conspicuous simplicity' framing over frugality, because it provides us with many more opportunities for this kind of positive discernment. There are a handful of products, services, and experiences that bring me joy: fundamentally, things that are beautifully designed. I want *more* of these things, not fewer—and if money can buy them, fantastic!

Conspicuous simplicity will no doubt create its own strange loops: say, interfaces so streamlined that they insult the intelligence of users, or a house so orderly that it can no longer be comfortably lived in. I am not saying we have reached the end of history here, but if conspicuous simplicity becomes the dominant status game, I expect the future to bring more intentionality, more curation, better design, less bloat, less inefficiency, and less ugliness.

There are two other rising games worth mentioning. Chasing clout and influence online is a huge emerging status landscape—YouTube, Twitter, member-only clubs of 'thought leaders'—but it's unclear whether this game is positive-sum, so I'll leave it to others to write about.

I am much more excited about another trend which has more in common with the Roman focus on doing one's civic duty: the reinvention of the classic game of conspicuous charity.

CONSPICUOUS DO-GOODING

Altruistic behaviour has a very obvious signalling component: you're demonstrating you have enough resources that you can afford to give them away, and showing off your caring personality to prospective allies or partners.

Sometimes the underlying status play couldn't be more blatant, like donating a gigantic building with your name on it. Men tend to give more money to pretty lady charity collectors, and most people will find a clever way to mention their good deed on social media so they can get the public adulation they deserve.

In other words, altruism is **Virtue Signalling**. This term is often used as a pejorative, but I think we should reclaim it. Signalling doesn't strip all that is good and beautiful from the world. It puts up a big neon sign pointing to it!

Does true altruism even exist? My position on this debate is 'who cares?', and I'm willing to bet the villagers whose kids get dewormed aren't lying awake at night wondering about it either. The brain is extremely good at obscuring its motivations from itself, for reasons of plausible deniability. We genuinely believe we are doing good, but most importantly, we *are* doing good.

The real problem with shallow clicktivism is that it's not a costly signal. There is nothing brave about adding the 100th dunk to the pile-on, or parroting whatever line will earn you back-slaps from your ingroup. Talk is cheap. What matters is taking action that actually requires you to sacrifice something: preferably money, but also time, or reputation.

While a costly signal is necessary, it's not sufficient. A lot of charitable giving through history has been woefully inefficient, with money often frittered away in exchange for what amounts to warm fuzzies, and sometimes doing more harm than good.

Why do I believe conspicuous do-gooding is on the rise? For one thing, the game is becoming much less ambiguously positive-sum. Thanks to the efforts of the Effective Altruism movement, we can now identify the juiciest exploitable asymmetries, and be much more confident that our money is actually having a real and positive impact.

For another thing, the fellow players are unusually awesome. This is a tribe of thoughtful and caring people who are working on very interesting problems: from animal welfare, to clean energy, to longterm economic growth, to bioterrorism, to the alignment of AI, and everything in between. There is much meaning to be mined here.

Conspicuous do-gooding is an opportunity to gain status in ways that are universally recognised: working for a prestigious organisation, being a 'known name', displaying your altruistic bent, and so on. But it's also an opportunity to join a beautiful bubble that rewards very different behaviours: you might gain status by being willing to change your mind and admit you were wrong, and lose status through displays of ostentatious wealth, or by joining in bloodlettings on the Internet. This is still an emerging game, which means you have an opportunity to be in the vanguard.

Rather than prescribe a specific path here, I am only trying to gesture in the direction of what is attractive.

The first step is to acknowledge that we all crave status on some level, and plan accordingly. Next, we have to look for positive-sum games that lead to good outcomes, or at the very least, don't make us worse off. Conspicuous consumption is distasteful not because of the signalling component, which is inevitable, but because what we're doing is *exchanging information*, and there are far more efficient ways of doing so than lighting $100 bills on fire.

Finally, we have to choose games that are aligned with our own values, or reward the specific behaviours we would like to exhibit. In short, we need games that are fun and virtuous to *play*, not just to win.

CONCLUSION

We're not in here to eat mozzarella and go to Tuscany. We're not in here to accumulate money. We're in here mostly to sacrifice, to do something. The way you do it is by taking risks.

— NASSIM TALEB

THREE SERVANTS ARE GIVEN silver talents to look after; two are rewarded for investing them wisely; another is punished for burying his talent in the ground. In Chapter 20, we took the parable's conventional reading as a lesson on putting our abilities to good use.

But this story also has a darker moral. The first servant was given 5x as many talents as his wretched friend, which means the game was rigged from the start. If he lost a talent or two through bum investments, it wouldn't matter. He had plenty of room to breathe. But the poor sap who buried his single talent in the ground was—quite sensibly—desperate to avoid the risk of ruin.

The author of the Gospel of Matthew was perfectly aware of this inequity, but it took almost 2000 years to make it into the scientific lexicon. The Matthew effect is still widely underappreciated today, not only for its strength, but its sheer pervasiveness: financial inequality, academic citations, scientific discoveries, early childhood education, investing, poverty, fame, popularity, physical fitness, market pricing, and beauty are all governed by the principle of cumulative (dis)advantage.

My guess is that the parable of the talents is meant to *describe* the harsh reality of the world, rather than suggest we should be OK with it. After all, Christ certainly wasn't.

John Wesley, the founder of Methodism, delivered a famous sermon on this topic in the 18th century. He summed up the only appropriate response in this line: "Having first gained all you can, and secondly, saved all you can, then, give all you can."

In the language of optionality: having first opened as many options as possible, and secondly, exploited those that are most useful, then, give them away.

This order is important. Without a buffer of optionality to protect against shocks in your own life and open up opportunities, you have no ability to take risks. This is the same reason the flight crew tells us to put our own oxygen masks on before helping others: unconscious people are not known for being very useful.

If you want to have an impact on the world, it helps to make yourself strong first. At the very least, your life gets better. Maybe you're nicer to your dog. If you never accumulate enough optionality to put a dent in the universe, that's OK. You can still act with dignity, and hold your head up high. But perhaps you *do* find yourself in a position to take risks.

If you agree with the case I have made—that optionality is the best proxy for human flourishing, and that many people today are still massively constrained by debt, by poverty, by disease, by lack of opportunity, by regressive cultural or social norms, by bad legislation, by 'sticky' negative-sum games —then perhaps you will use your options to help break them free of their chains, and unlock their full range of capabilities.

It's a big old world of possibility. I'm excited to see what you do.

On that note, it's time to part ways. We've met our maker in the blind idiot god of evolution, glimpsed our future in the rats stimulating themselves to death, joined (and left) an anti-consumerist cult, convinced a lunatic crew of shipmates to pull together, compared the Mona Lisa to herpes, uncovered the dirty little secret of muscular people, declared war on consumer debt, swallowed some dead rats, gained a healthy respect for the freaky shoggoth monster of the stockmarket, met the secret superheroes who saves lives for pennies on the dollar, dissolved the boundaries of selfhood, escaped thigh gaps and fattening huts, and hunted black swans through parallel universes.

It's been a weird journey, which feels appropriate.

We never know exactly what tomorrow will bring, or where we'll end up. In an uncertain world, the optionality approach is a source of great comfort. No matter what fate sends our way, we can rest easy in the knowledge that we've done everything in our power to not only survive—but to thrive.

10 LAWS OF OPTIONALITY FOR A VOLATILE WORLD

1. LIFE TRAILS VAST CLOUDS OF UNCERTAINTY

We live in a world ruled by wild uncertainty; not by the kind of tame risks that can be neatly measured and pinned to the page. The expanding frontier of human knowledge is cutting through the fog, but the clouds of uncertainty gather faster: the world is only ever becoming more dynamic and unpredictable.

2. IT'S HARD TO MAKE PREDICTIONS, ESPECIALLY ABOUT THE FUTURE

We can't even reliably predict our future preferences, despite having near-perfect knowledge about our selves. Forecasting the interplay between the markets, governments, and technologies of 8 billion people is a fool's game.

We still have to make decisions under uncertainty, but it's crucial that our choices preserve optionality, rather than lock us into path dependencies from which we cannot easily deviate. That means more bottom-up tinkering and effectuation, with less emphasis on top-down planning and long-term goals.

3. BEWARE OF GEEKS BEARING FORMULAS

One of the great longstanding follies in 'scientific' thinking is the conviction that everything can be measured and transformed into a quantifiable risk. This overconfidence has been a source of great suffering: the history of finance in particular is a history of brains splashed on the pavement.

Domains ruled by uncertainty are better navigated by simple heuristics, which often perform better than complex models, without giving us a false sense of security.

4. OPTIONALITY BECOMES MORE VALUABLE UNDER CONDITIONS OF UNCERTAINTY

As our world gets weirder, the problem of decision-making under uncertainty gets harder, which makes it more important to maintain optionality.

This is partly a defensive play: optionality acts as a stand-in for intelligence, and means we don't have to rely on flawed models and detailed forecasts. But it is also opportunistic: it positions us to benefit from violent swings in future states of the world. If you have optionality, volatility is your friend.

5. GENERATING BETTER OPTIONS IS MUCH MORE IMPORTANT THAN TRYING TO MAKE PERFECT DECISIONS

Consumer capitalism gives the illusion of great choice, even while it traps us within one small sector of the total space of possibilities, squandering our time and attention on a narrow range of standardised options.

When information costs more than it's worth, the only winning move is to carefully steward your ignorance—to strike at the root of the possibility tree, and refuse to engage with its branching confusopolies. Rationality is not about making perfect decisions, but choosing what to choose.

6. THE SIREN SONG ONLY GETS HARDER TO RESIST

The smartest minds of a generation are employed in trying to exploit us at the level of our DNA, distorting the sensations we're hardwired to pursue into powerful superstimuli.

It's increasingly difficult to escape the allure of short-term rewards, and make decisions that maximise our long-term capabilities. The result is that optionality is becoming more valuable at the exact same time as it becomes harder to obtain.

7. WINNING IS MOSTLY NOT-LOSING

In every area of life, bad is stronger than good. 'Winning' is mostly a matter of avoiding the Bottomless Pits of Doom—consumer debt, addiction, ideological path dependency, sticky status games, uninsured tail risks, hubristic investments, security exploits, and heart disease.

Anyone who can consistently refrain from shooting themselves in the foot will meet with a victory unexpected in common hours.

8. SPECTACULAR SUCCESS IS A MATTER OF PUTTING IRONS IN THE FIRE

Big wins are always mediated by some element of randomness, which means there is no guarantee of a spectacular success.

The best strategy for getting lucky is collecting open-ended options with potential for massive upside. We can never be sure if these will pay off, but by systematically putting irons in the fire, we maximise our chances of hitting the big one.

9. HAVING HIGH-QUALITY OPTIONS IS THE BEST PROXY FOR THE GOOD LIFE

Money is a useful servant but a terrible master. Naive hedonism is an equally misguided pursuit, and fails to account for the full complexity of human values.

True flourishing comes from having high-quality choices and the ability to explore one's full range of capabilities—including the right, but not the obligation, to suffer and make sacrifices.

10. HOARDING OPTIONS INDEFINITELY IS FOR COWARDS

It's always wise to maintain some level of personal optionality, but the endgame is to deliberately sacrifice it on a worthy altar. That means using our positions to unlock the capabilities of those who have been less fortunate, or to take risks on behalf of the collective.

This is not an obligation, but the natural consequence of pursuing our own self-interest: anything else will eat us alive.

ACKNOWLEDGMENTS

First, an anti-acknowledgement: some of the people whose ideas I have expounded in this book are probably assholes, and no doubt hold opinions which are Bad and Wrong. If I had to disavow each of them, starting from Aristotle, this book would be even more obnoxiously long than it already is. Instead, I leave this as an interesting exercise for the reader.

The one exception is Nassim Nicholas Taleb. No other asshole, alive or dead, has influenced my life and thinking more. It's not even close. Thank you for your work, Nassim.

I owe a huge debt of gratitude to Paul Barnes, Sonnie Bailey, Rachel Meadows, and especially to Britt Mann, who gave constant encouragement and feedback on multiple iterations of the manuscript. Any remaining mistakes are their fault.

Many thanks also to Connor Dowd, Max Bodoia, and Pedro Castilho, who gave feedback on sections of the manuscript, and to Débora Pereira for the beautiful illustrations.

My patrons and Deep Dish readers Marcus Buckland, Nathan Broadbent, Cso Horvath and Anna Frecklington all contributed to light a fire under my ass and make this thing happen.

Other people whose work has had a large impact on me: Peter Adeney, Scott Alexander, William MacAskill, Deirdre McCloskey, Benoit Mandelbrot, Sonya Mann, Geoffrey Miller, Cal Newport, Taylor Pearson, Venkatesh Rao,

Naval Ravikant, Barry Schwartz, Kevin Simler, Derek Sivers, Eliezer Yudkowsky, and the econ crew from the beautiful bubble at GMU, many of whom I have been fortunate enough to correspond with, and some of whom were generous enough to help shape or clarify specific points in this book. Even the smallest word of encouragement from someone you admire can make all the difference: you know not what you do.

To Sara and Laurie Meadows, who could not have been more gracious about their son's decision to throw in his comfy office job and become a professional bum, thanks for plucking me from the void of nonexistence. It's way more interesting out here.

Finally, huge thanks to the many readers who have sent messages of support and stories that provided the fuel to keep doing this thing. Yes, you! Your words matter. My inbox is open, and I'd love to hear from you any time.

Want to stay in the loop? Visit optionalitybook.com/resources, and get access to exclusive reader bonuses:

Net Worth Spreadsheet: Get a copy of the custom tracker that was instrumental in hitting my initial savings goal (Excel and Google Sheets).

Custom Expense Tracker: Find out how much you're spending every week, month, or year, with conditional formatting that tells you when you're hitting your targets. (Excel and Google Sheets).

Companion Reading List: A hand-picked list of 80+ of my favourite books, articles and resources, broken down by category and expanding on every theme in the book.

NOTES

INTRODUCTION

1. My savings goal was in New Zealand dollars; it took another year to reach six figures as denominated by the greenback. To avoid having to switch between currencies, all remaining figures are given in US dollars.

4. THE BLIND IDIOT GOD OF EVOLUTION

1. As Hanson explains, this is also a useful adaptive behaviour, because it gives us plausible deniability when someone questions our motives.

5. HEDONISM AND HAPPINESS

1. Technically, the rate of happiness increase is sub-logarithmic. If it were an exact fit, we'd need to define such a thing as negative happiness.
2. Once again, this cuts both ways. A loving spouse will delight you for decades; an annoying workmate will never run out of new ways to get under your skin. When relationships are good, they are very, very good, but when they are bad they are horrid.
3. Bentham was a genius, and far ahead of his time. But John Stuart Mill said his teacher was "always a boy", even as an old man, and knew "so little of human feelings... still less of the influences by which those feelings are formed".
4. Apocryphal. The first two curses are "may you live in interesting times", and "may you be recognized by people in high places".
5. This is known as the 'Easterlin paradox'. Whether it actually exists is a matter of ongoing debate.
6. After being diagnosed with an autoimmune disorder, I quickly came up with clever rationalisations as to why it was actually a blessing in disguise: it would force me to take good care of my health, reduce my stress levels, and so on. And as far as I can tell, my happiness level now is no different to the time before I had to travel around with shoe boxes full of medication, insert eye-wateringly large suppositories, and endure occasional bouts of other unpleasantness. But if I'm honest with myself, *of course* I would be better off without this condition: it already limits my options in some ways, and will increasingly do so as time goes on.
7. Another strike against naive hedonism: deliberate exposure to low-level stressors is crucial for long-term wellbeing, despite being unpleasant in the moment. Muscles grow after sustaining damage, and atrophy without it. Public speaking only becomes comfortable after a few knee-knocking experiences, while we tend to enter a downward spiral of anxiety if we deliberately avoid stressful situations. Fasting is similarly unpleasant, but it accelerates the purging of damaged cells and recalibrates hormonal and metabolic systems.
8. The fact that people refuse to be boxed into narrow experiential measures of wellbeing is one of the reasons Daniel Kahneman left the field: "They actually want to maximise their satisfaction with themselves and with their lives. And that leads in completely different directions than the maximisation of happiness."

6. THE FOUR FACTORS OF OPTIONALITY

1. As Geoffrey Miller notes in *Spent*, bodily organs are among the only physical objects with a cost density (price per pound) higher than gold bullion. If you're the owner of a healthy body, you might literally be worth your weight in gold.

2. We don't want a blanket decrease in suffering, à la Bentham—we still want to maintain the *option* to suffer in ways which are meaningful to us. Breaking one's hip, getting Type 2 diabetes, or being trapped in an abusive relationship do not fall into this category.

7. CHARTING A COURSE

1. Then there's the fact that waiting around for 15 minutes to receive one measly marshmallow is a lousy deal. One plausible alternative explanation is that the experiments actually predict something like the desire to pass tests, or win approval from adults. Even the lead researcher, Walter Mischel, said the children "might be responding to anything under the sun".

2. Possibly apocryphal. The same thing really did happen in Hanoi (except with rats) and there are lots of darker examples, from the collapse of Enron to the absurd factory targets of Soviet Russia.

3. Formulated by British logician Carveth Read, but usually misattributed to John Maynard Keynes.

4. A friend who used to run the planning department of a large corporation tells me there is a movement against budgeting in the business world: "It contends that it is better to use a rolling forecast, continually reallocating resources in response to the changing environment, and assessing performance after the fact relative to peers (so as not to award bonuses for achieving soft targets). So while you don't have a budget, you constantly have a clear understanding of the path you're on and where it will lead to without course corrections."

5. The other problem with net worth is that it doesn't include non-financial assets, which leads to some anomalous results: the people in Oxfam commercials are technically 'richer' than final-year medical students. A reminder that optionality is not synonymous with mere dollars and cents.

6. Again, you can get a copy at optionalitybook.com/resources.

8. THE SIREN SONG

1. Even fruit and vegetables have been massively distorted by thousands of years of selective breeding, and in most cases are unrecognisable from their 'natural' forms.

2. This is why self-stimulating products are often used furtively. No-one is impressed when you pass out in front of the TV, covered in a film of Doritos dust and surrounded by empty beer cans.

3. The good doctor also promoted eating cornflakes as a cure for masturbation; a piece of folk wisdom which has proven to be somewhat less enduring.

9. TIED TO THE MAST

1. A lot of the research used to justify creeping paternalism at the highest levels of policy-making turns out to be junk science, bordering on outright fraud. Here I'm only recommending common-sense nudges that you can use on yourself, not the bullshit studies that never should have been taken seriously in the first place.

10. CREATURES OF HABIT

1. The science of the mysterious substance called willpower is far from settled. It's not clear if you can build it up, like a muscle, if it's finite, or if it can be replenished. My guess is that anything that looks like an increase in raw willpower is probably the result of streamlining your environment (nudges) your brain (habits) and your identity (values) to the point where you need less of it in the first place. In which case, people who display 'grit' are not unusually heroic—they just happen to have higher conscientiousness, and/or a less tempting environment.

11. SOCIAL CONTAGION

1. Our senses are bombarded with ~11 million bits of data every second, but the conscious mind only processes an average of ~50 bits. In order to not go completely insane, we have to filter out ~99.9995 per cent of the world.
2. The psychiatrist Scott Alexander suggests the following thought experiment: what if life were a giant Asch conformity test? Think of it as *The Truman Show* on steroids. Every single person around you is an actor or computer simulation trying to lead you astray. At any given point in time, you might be hauled in front of a panel of enlightened future humans, aliens, or deities, and asked to explain your actions.

   'Well...um...everyone else did it!' is going to sound pretty feeble when you discover that in the real world outside the simulation, slavery or factory farming or conspicuous consumption had been condemned as barbaric for hundreds of years. Or that of all the test subjects, you were *the only one* who shrugged your shoulders and went along with the atrocities.

   Alexander's rule of thumb is that you should live your life so that if it *did* turn out to be some alien's Asch conformity experiment, "the debriefing won't be too humiliating".

12. MAN PLANS AND GOD LAUGHS

1. To head off the 'we're apes, not monkeys!' pedants with some meta-pedantry: contrary to popular belief, these are casual terms that are used interchangeably in most languages, in the same way I use them in this book. Insofar as they can be mapped onto clades, apes (*hominoidea*) are a subset of monkeys (*simiiformes*). This means that all apes—including humans—are monkeys, but not all monkeys are apes.

14. ASYMMETRIES IN HEALTH CAPITAL

1. The relationship is not as straightforward for women, but being overweight can cause abnormalities in sex hormones, and vice versa.
2. Muscle cells are so big that they need more than one nucleus. As they grow, the surrounding cells heroically sacrifice their own nuclei to the noble cause of getting you jacked. These 'myonuclei' each control a certain area of the muscle fibre, and stick around for *years* after the contractile proteins have atrophied. When you start training again, they ramp up protein synthesis, and expand their deflated domain to its former glory. You also benefit from the colloquial 'muscle memory' (motor learning) which takes place in the brain: once you've drilled a skill long enough, it becomes second nature.
3. Even seemingly inconsequential movements like clicking a pen or jiggling a knee can add up to several hundred calories over the course of a day—to the point where fidgeting is one of

the body's main strategies for regulating bodyweight. In one study, healthy volunteers were overfed by 1000 calories a day. Without being consciously aware of it, they started fidgeting more, readjusting their posture, and tensing their muscles throughout the day. The amount of weight each person gained was strongly predicted by their level of fidgeting, with those who moved more putting on less weight.

INTRODUCTION

1. As Peter Bernstein points out in *Against the Gods*, this is a curious oversight: the Greeks were skilled mathematicians, masters of logic, and loved gambling. Their failure to discover probability may have something to do with the unwieldiness of Greek and Roman numerals: what's MDCCLXXXVI multiplied by LXIX?

17. A FATE WORSE THAN DEBT

1. There is some research in support of Ramsey's method: Kellogg School of Management found that people juggling significant credit card balances were more likely to pay down their entire debt if they paid off the cards with the smallest balances first.

19. THE RISK OF RUIN

1. To be fair, these were unusually productive toga parties: the Greeks correctly predicted the Earth was round, and hypothesised that everything was made out of tiny particles called 'atoms'. On the other hand, Pythagoras banned his followers from eating beans because he was convinced they contained the souls of the dead. You win some, you lose some.
2. A technical aside: black swans are not defined by the distinction between Knightian risk and Knightian uncertainty, which Taleb considers to be an artificial division. He points out that *all* small probabilities are more or less incomputable, even if they fall on the 'risk' side of the divide, which means there is no such thing as Knightian risk outside of sterile laboratory conditions.

21. INVESTING FOR THE BONE IDLE

1. The weak form of efficient markets: historic data is already priced in. The semi-strong form: all public information is priced in. The strong form: all private information is priced in, too.

22. BLACK SWAN HUNTING

1. This is the Kelly criterion, or 'scientific' gambling method. It goes beyond the scope of this book, but look out for a supplementary blog post.

23. BEWARE OF GEEKS BEARING FORMULAS

1. The most notorious example is Long-Term Capital Management, a hedge fund directed by two Nobel Prize-winning economists, Myron Scholes and Robert Merton. It was bailed out

in 1998, having lost $4.6 billion and almost caused the collapse of the entire financial system. Whoops!

24. A TIME TO EXPLORE AND A TIME TO EXPLOIT

1. For a detailed explanation of the problem and solutions, see *Algorithms to Live By* by Brian Christian and Tom Griffiths.
2. Mostly kidding, but men are heavier users of almost every type of drug, are three times more likely to become alcoholics, are eight times more likely to become problem gamblers, watch more TV than women (including more amygdala-baiting news media), get more of their calories from fast food, spend 60 per cent more time playing video games, watch a heck of a lot more porn, and generally seem to be more susceptible to premature exploitation.

25. A TIME TO IMPROVISE AND A TIME TO MAKE PLANS

1. If you review this book, feel free to quote this sentence out of context as a brutal self-own.

28. A TIME TO OPEN OPTIONS AND A TIME TO GIVE THEM AWAY

1. Depending on your definition: if relationships are non-fungible, then the accumulation of years of common knowledge, in-jokes, and shared history might mean your partner is literally the best in the world.

29. SELFISH SELFLESSNESS

1. Psychology was one of the worst-hit fields in the 'replication crisis': only a third of studies published in premium journals actually yielded a significant finding when repeated, and even those had a much smaller effect size than the original papers. Almost every pop-psych book you read in the last decade, including those authored by genuine stalwarts such as Daniel Kahneman, are riddled with studies that have failed to replicate, along with various instances of outright fraud and malpractice.

30. STATUS GAMES

1. Haidt cites Michael Tomasello, a chimpanzee cognition expert who argues that even when chimps hunt in large groups, they're really just simultaneously chasing after the same prey. They might respond to each other's actions during the hunt, but there's no actual coordination going on.
2. If you're still hung up on the Disney channel bullshit about nature being 'good' and humans 'bad', and don't want to sleep tonight, go look up what sea otters like doing to baby seals.
3. It takes as long as 48 hours for your body to use up all its stores of glycogen, circulating nutrients, and partially-digested food. This activates a second metabolic system for converting fat

into energy—ketosis—which lies dormant in most people for their entire lives. It is nothing short of a miracle that we now live in a world in which we will never go two days without a meal.

GLOSSARY

Acting Dead: Any behaviour your dead great-grandpa could do better than you; a misplaced sense of virtue in leading the leanest possible existence. A trap for hardcore minimalists and frugalistas.

Akrasia: Weakness of will; the feeling of being powerless to follow one's own best judgment. Often caused by squabbling subagents, and exacerbated by saboteurs that nudge us towards short-term decisions.

Barbell Strategy: A bimodal distribution between two extremes, avoiding the middle ground. One end of the barbell is hyper-conservative, or 'cheap'; the other is hyper-aggressive, or 'expensive'.

Black Swan: A rare and unexpected high-magnitude event that cannot be forecast ahead of time.

Bottomless Pits of Doom: An option with a negative asymmetry: the potential upside is small or capped, and the potential downside is unbounded.

Capabilities Approach: An influential theory in welfare economics that argues that the highest good is not hedonism or wealth, but the freedom to choose a life one has reason to value—to have options.

Conspicuous Consumption: A status game in which we buy luxury goods and services to signal our wealth and position in society.

Conspicuous Charity/Virtue Signalling: A status game in which we signal we are so rich in resources that we afford to give them away, while demonstrating our altruism to prospective allies or partners.

Conspicuous Simplicity: A status game in which we signal our positive discernment in design, efficiency, and thoughtfulness.

Constraints: Binding limits on behaviour that close off the possibilities available to us. Dangerous when imposed by force; liberating when self-directed. One set of constraints prunes low-level choices and generates better options. A higher-level set determines which of our expanded options to exploit.

Credentialism: A runaway signalling game in which credentials are the only accepted evidence of suitability for a role, to the detriment of those forced to jump through the relevant hoops. Also known as 'degree inflation'.

Currencies of Life: Limited and precious resources that often trade off against each other: money, time, health, mental bandwidth, energy, social status, hedonic pleasure, and meaning.

Dead Ends: Options in which both the downside and upside are capped: there is no asymmetry in either direction. The vast majority of the choices presented in daily life fall into this 'sticky middle'.

Diminishing Marginal Returns: In which ratcheting up one input creates less and less of the desired output, to the point where it becomes ineffective, or starts to have the opposite of the intended effect.

Dunbar's Numbers: The suggested cognitive limit to the number of people with whom we can maintain stable relationships across various group sizes.

Edge: An informational or other asymmetry that grants an exploitable advantage in a competitive market.

Effective Altruism: A social movement focused on using evidence and reasoning to determine the most powerful ways of doing good in the world.

Effectuation: A business theory based on the observation that entrepreneurs create companies based on the resources they have at their disposal, then springboard off new opportunities that arise along the way.

Efficient-Market Hypothesis: A theory stating that asset prices reflect all available information. The implication is that it extremely hard to 'beat' an efficient market, other than through random chance, unless you have an informational edge.

Expected Value: The anticipated average payoff of an investment or decision. Calculated by multiplying each of the possible outcomes by the likelihood that each will occur, and then adding the values together.

Explore vs Exploit: A central trade-off in computer science, biology, and business. Time spent exploring new opportunities is time we could have spent exploiting the resources at our disposal, and vice versa.

Eudaimonia: An ideal state of human wellbeing that includes not only happiness and prosperity, but living a virtuous and purposeful life.

Faux Optionality: A vast array of Dead Ends based on minor variations to a core theme, with no favourable asymmetry, designed to distract from the high-quality decisions that actually matter. Related to the 'paradox of choice', which describes how we are better off with fewer of these options in certain circumstances.

Financial Capital: The financial assets and tools you have at your disposal. Strongly influenced by the simplicity of your tastes (how little money you require).

FIRE: Financial Independence/Retirement Early. An anti-consumerist movement based around frugality and passive index investing. Mostly a force for good; occasionally dogmatic in unhelpful ways.

Flow: An intrinsically enjoyable immersive state in the sweet spot between boredom and difficulty.

Frugality/Frugalitas: The art of paying attention to trade-offs between life's most precious resources, in order to better fulfil one's goals. With a positive impetus, it helps adherents become more fruitful in the world. As a subtractive philosophy, it comes with a risk of acting dead.

Fuck-You Money: The amount of cash you need to feel enough security to walk away from an unethical situation, fire a client, or re-train for a new career. Often confused with the number required to reach financial independence or early retirement.

Halo Effect: The phenomenon by which a person who is beautiful or smart or charming is assumed to also possess unrelated positive attributes. A subtype of the Matthew effect of cumulative advantage.

Health Capital: The sum total of your physical fitness, mental health, mobility, and energy.

Hedonic Treadmill: The observation that we quickly return to a relatively stable level of happiness after major positive or negative events, and that constantly pursuing more and better is unlikely to lead to lasting satisfaction.

Instrumental vs Terminal: The difference between a value or goal that we pursue purely for its own sake (terminal), and a goal we pursue because it brings us closer to the underlying ambition or desire (instrumental).

Knowledge Capital: The sum total of our skills, education, credentials, and experience.

Lindy Effect: The longer an idea, technology, or institution has been around, the longer we should predict it to stick around in the future. Named after a New York deli and restaurant called Lindy's, where Broadway artists developed a rule of thumb: if a show ran for a year, it would be last for another year. Unlike biological systems or physical objects, the expected remaining lifespan increases with age.

Matthew Effect of Cumulative Advantage: The observation that resources tend to accumulate to those who need them least, and are taken from those who need them most. Named after the conclusion to the parable of the talents.

Mimesis: The Greek word for 'imitation', used by Girard to describe the escalating feedback loop in which we borrow our desires from others, leading to rivalry and violence through scapegoating.

Min-Maxing: Deliberately ignoring all of the low-level branching paths presented to us in daily life, in order to systematically load up on the relatively few trades worth having.

Naive Hedonism: Mistaken belief that human wellbeing is a matter of seeking pleasure and avoiding suffering. Sometimes quantified by the intensity and duration of the experience, like the hedonic calculus of Jeremy Bentham.

Negative-Sum Game: A 'lose-lose' situation in which the sum of all gains and losses amongst the players is negative. Value has been destroyed, and everyone is collectively worse off than when they began.

Net Worth: Everything you own, minus everything you owe. The main component of Financial Capital, and a useful metric to track.

Nudge: A constraint that shapes our environment and the way choices are presented to us in such a way that it becomes easier to adopt certain behaviours.

Pareto Principle or 80/20 Rule: The idea that 20 per cent of effort leads to 80 per cent of the results, and vice versa. This is not a hard rule, but a description of power law distributions, in which a small number of inputs generate a large proportion of the value captured, and a large number of inputs are essentially worthless.

Passive Investing: Low-cost investing strategy that mimics the performance of an entire sector or index. Consistently proven to outperform 'active' strategies, and now accounts for the majority of new funds flowing into the investment market.

Path Dependence: Situation in which the options we're presented with are dependent on our prior decisions or past experiences. An acknowledgement that "history matters", and that the sequence of events is more important than the average.

Possibility Tree: A metaphor for the vast number of branching possibilities presented to us in daily life, almost all of which are Dead Ends. Requires vigorous pruning in order to bear fruit, in the form of high-value options.

Positive-Sum Game: A 'win-win' situation in which the sum of all gains and losses amongst the players is positive. The size of the pie grows, and everyone is collectively better-off than when they began.

Rationality: The ability to make decisions that move us towards winning/not-losing. Bounded by uncertainty, cognitive blind spots, and time and processing power available.

Risk of Ruin: The possibility of the unacceptable happening, i.e. tumbling into a Bottomless Pit of Doom from which you cannot come back. Must be avoided or mitigated at all costs.

Signalling: A behaviour that indirectly but credibly conveys information to another party about e.g. status, access to resources, virtue, or tribal allegiance. The true motive is often unconscious or obscured for reasons of plausible deniability.

Siren Song: A metaphor for the self-stimulating and status-seeking products of consumer capitalism, which are designed to directly appeal to our lower instincts.

Social Capital: The strength and number of relationships with friends, family, colleagues, and communities.

Social Contagion: The phenomenon whereby our behaviours and preferences are shaped by the people around us, and vice versa. Primarily driven by mimesis, information cascades, and conformity bias.

Social Reality: The giant, shared hallucination in which *homo sapiens* collectively make sense of the world. Almost always the victor when individual reality or 'real' physical reality threatens to intrude on the dominant narrative.

Status Games: Games that allow us to compete and cooperate to signal our worth. May be negative-sum, zero-sum, or positive-sum.

Superstimulus: An artificially distorted and amplified version of a signal we're biologically hardwired to pursue. Includes drugs, fast food, porn, reality TV, airbrushed magazine covers, online gambling, virtual reality, and immersive video games.

Survivorship Bias: Focusing on the people or things that made it past a selection process without considering the far larger number of invisible failures.

Treasure Chest: An attractive option with a small or capped potential downside, and an unbounded potential upside. Usually referred to in this book as an asymmetric or 'open-ended' option.

Ulysses Contract: An industrial-strength nudge, typically used to forcibly eliminate unattractive or dangerous options, as in the original context of Odysseus sailing past the Sirens. Can also be used to sacrifice high-level options: marriage is the nuclear version of a Ulysses contract.

Utility: The 'use value' of a given resource—how much it actually improves our lives—as opposed to its market or other value.

Volatility: Measure of the level of rapid and unpredictable changes in a given domain.

Wireheading: Artificial state of perfect pleasure and no pain; named after experiments on rats given the ability to stimulate their own pleasure centre, variously considered utopian or dystopian.

Zero-Sum Game: A 'win-lose' situation in which all gains and losses amongst the players sums to zero. Value has neither been created or destroyed, and can only be transferred between players.

REFERENCES

& HAT TIPS

INTRODUCTION

That's the poetic description... This device was inspired by 'Slack', Zvi Mowshowitz, published on Don't Worry About the Vase, 2017. The concept of slack is an example of convergent evolution, with strong parallels to what I am calling optionality.

The way Aristotle tells it... Book I, *Politics,* Aristotle, circa 350 BC, Benjamin Jowett translation.

EUDAIMONIA

I interviewed an eccentric online personality called Mr Money Mustache... 'Finding the road to early retirement', Richard Meadows, published in *Sunday Star-Times*, 2013.

As Adeney pointed out, the only number that matters... 'The Shockingly Simple Math Behind Early Retirement', Peter Adeney, published on MrMoneyMustache.com, 2012.

To borrow a term from sci-fi writer Bruce Sterling... 'Transcript of Reboot 11 speech', Bruce Sterling, published on Wired.com, 2011. Hat tip to Venkatesh Rao of Ribbonfarm.

I first came across this model in Nassim Taleb's Incerto series... The Incerto comprises *Fooled by Randomness, The Black Swan, Antifragile, The Bed of Procrustes,* and *Skin in the Game,* 2001-2018.

On a per-kilometre basis, the [motorcycle] fatality rate... 'Comparing the Fatality Risks in United States Transportation Across Modes and Over Time', Ian Savage, Northwestern University, 2013.

As the psychologist Daniel Gilbert points out... *Stumbling on Happiness,* Daniel Gilbert, 2006.

If you earn more than $58,000 after tax, you're in that top percentile... 'How Rich Am I?', Giving What We Can, last updated 2019. Based on an adjusted version of the working paper 'The Future of Worldwide Income Distribution', Tomáš Hellebrandt and Paolo Mauro. Median personal income: U.S. Census Bureau.

The economist John Maynard Keynes wrote a remarkable essay... 'Economic Possibilities for our Grandchildren', John Maynard Keynes, 1930.

One in 10 adults in the US is currently taking antidepressants... National Center for Health Statistics, 2011. The rate of antidepressant use among teens and adults increased by almost 400% between 1988–1994 and 2005–2008.

New Zealand [...] has the highest suicide rate in history... 'New Zealand suicides in 2018-19 highest since records began', *New Zealand Herald,* 2019.

As the artificial intelligence researcher Eliezer Yudkowsky puts it... 'An Alien God', Eliezer Yudkowsky, published on Less Wrong, 2007.

The historian Yuval Noah Harari describes hedonic adaptation... *Sapiens: A Brief History of Humankind,* Yuval Noah Harari, 2014 (English edition).

Some people who suffer such an accident are in an OK mood as early as one month later [...] How would your quality of life change if you won the lottery? 'Lottery winners and accident victims: Is happiness relative?', Philip Brickman, Dan Coates, Ronnie Janoff-Bulman, published in *Journal of Personality and Social Psychology*, 1978. Lottery winners (M=4.00) were only very slightly happier than controls (M=3.82), and both lottery winner and controls were slightly happier than paraplegics (M=2.96). This was a small study and numerical ratings are hard to interpret, but the surprising power of hedonic adaptation has been confirmed many times by stronger and better-designed studies.

I have to tell you—it's the same hamburger... Speech at the University of Washington, Bill Gates, 2011.

Each doubling of income only improves your life satisfaction by about half a point on a scale of 1 to 10... 'Subjective Wellbeing and Income: Is There Any Evidence of Satiation?', Betsey Stevenson and Justin Wolfers, published by National Bureau of Economic Research, 2013.

As Lyubomirsky points out... 'Hedonic Adaptation to Positive and Negative Experiences', Sonja Lyubomirsky, published in *The Oxford Handbook of Stress, Health, and Coping*, 2012 (online edition).

The great psychologist Daniel Kahneman concluded... *Thinking, Fast and Slow*, Daniel Kahneman, 2011.

Maslow's theory has largely held up... 'Needs and Subjective Wellbeing Around the World', Louis Tay and Ed Diener, published in *Journal of Personal and Social Psychology*, 2011. See also *Transcend* by Scott Barry Kaufman for a thorough treatment of how Maslow has been misinterpreted.

The seminal paper concludes that these [pleasure centre] results... 'Positive reinforcement produced by electrical stimulation of septal area and other regions of rat brain', James Olds and Peter Milner, published in *Journal of Comparative and Physiological Psychology*, 1954.

[Happiness] is an ongoing process—an instrument that measures the distance to reference points... 'Evolutionary Efficiency and Happiness', Luis Rayo and Gary Becker, published in *Journal of Political Economy*, 2007.

No surprise that 'life' is the first of the core capabilities valued across cultures... 'Creating Capabilities: The Human Development Approach', Martha Nussbaum, published in Harvard University Press, 2011.

One of the reasons Daniel Kahneman left the field... 'Daniel Kahneman on Cutting Through the Noise', Conversations With Tyler podcast, 2018.

Explicit financial options are often overhyped... *Antifragile: Things That Gain From Disorder*, Nassim Taleb, 2012.

The principle was pithily summed up in a famous psychology paper... 'Bad is Stronger Than Good', Roy Baumeister, Ellen Bratslavsky, Catrin Finkenauer and K. Vohs, published in *Review of General Psychology*, 2001.

The average American hasn't made a new friend in five years... OnePoll, 2019, sample size of 2000.

One quarter of American adults didn't read a single book in the last year... Pew Research Centre, 2019.

AKRASIA

Aboard the Ship of Fools... The device comes from Plato, in Book VI of *The Republic*. Imagery and metaphors borrowed from *The Odyssey*, Robert Fagles translation.

As the satirist Terry Pratchett put it... *Thief of Time*, Terry Pratchett, 2001.

One plausible alternative explanation is that the [marshmallow] experiments actually predict something like the desire to pass tests... 'The Stanford Marshmallow Prison Experiment', Hotel Concierge, 2015.

While our meatsack bodies slavishly plod along at the precise rate of one second per second... This framing is borrowed from 'Miswanting: Some problems in the forecasting of future affective states', Daniel Gilbert and Timothy Wilson, 2000.

In the delightfully-titled paper 'Goals Gone Wild'... 'Goals Gone Wild: The Systematic Side Effects of Over-Prescribing Goal Setting', Lisa Ordóñez, Maurice Schweitzer, Adam Galinksy and Max Bazerman, published in *Academy of Management Perspectives*, 2009.

Venture capitalist Marc Andreesen's first rule of career planning... 'Pmarca Guide to Career Planning', Marc Andreesen, 2007 (archived).

Nassim Taleb's framing [...] that optionality serves as a stand-in for intelligence... *Antifragile: Things That Gain From Disorder*, Nassim Taleb, 2012.

External rewards risk eroding your internal motivation... *Drive: The Surprising Truth About What Motivates Us*, Daniel Pink, 2009.

These products are superstimuli... Hat tip to 'Superstimuli and the Collapse of Western Civilization', Eliezer Yudkowsky, published on Less Wrong, 2007.

American snack food is already converging on the most fattening diet possible... *The Hungry Brain*, Stephan Guyenet, 2017. Scientists struggled to make rats gain weight, even with high-fat and sugar chow, until they stumbled upon the idea of feeding them palatable human food.

Facebook's algorithms know your preferences better than your best friends do... 'Computer-based personality judgments are more accurate than those made by humans', Youyou Wu, Michal Kosinski and David Stillwell, published in *Proceedings of the National Academy of Sciences*, 2015.

The headline-grabbing [paradox of choice] studies failed to replicate... a meta-analysis averaged out the effects to zero... 'Can There Ever be Too Many Options? A Meta-analytic Review of Choice Overload', Benjamin

Scheibehenne, Rainer Greifeneder and Peter Todd, published in *Journal of Consumer Research*, 2010.

Researchers have made some progress in figuring out the factors which make a larger choice set more or less appealing... 'Choice Overload: A Conceptual Review and Meta-Analysis', Alexander Chernev, Ulf Bockenholt, Joseph Goodman, published in *Journal of Consumer Psychology*, 2015.

When information costs more than it's worth, the [rational] move is to carefully steward your ignorance... *Price Theory: An Intermediate Text*, David Friedman, 1990 (online version).

An article [...] on the substantial minority of Britons who eat the exact same lunches... 'The People Who Eat the Same Meal Every Day', Joe Pinsker, published in *The Atlantic*, 2019.

My favourite variant of these tests involves standing in a crowded elevator... 'Face the Rear', Candid Camera, 1962.

Researchers now suggest obesity should be classified as a 'contagious' disease... 'The Spread of Obesity in a Large Social Network over 32 Years', Nicholas Christakis and James Fowler, published in *New England Journal of Medicine*, 2007.

The psychiatrist Scott Alexander suggests the following thought experiment... 'Don't Be An Asch-Hole', Scott Alexander, published on Slate Star Codex, 2014.

If you're a weird person, one way of conserving your social capital... Hat tip 'You have a set amount of "weirdness points". Spend them wisely', Peter Hurford, published on Less Wrong, 2014.

Scott Adams suggests that goals are literally 'for losers'... *How to Fail at Almost Everything and Still Win Big*, Scott Adams, 2013.

Life is a series of iterated games... Hat tip to *Finite and Infinite Games*, 1986. RIP James Carse.

PRAXIS

The average American home contains something like 300,000 items...'For many people, gathering possessions is just the stuff of life', Mary Macvean, published in *LA Times*, 2014.

The 'go where the tourists aren't' principle... Inspired by Kristin Hall, 'How to travel long term: Tips and tricks from a tight-arse', published on People|Places|Things, 2018.

Attractive people are paid significantly more than unattractive people and have better prospects of finding a job in the first place... 'Does it pay to be beautiful?', Eva Sierminska, published in IZA World of Labor, 2015.

Doe-eyed defendants [...] are twice as likely to avoid jail... 'Defendants' Attractiveness as a Factor in the Outcome of Trials: An Observational Study,' John E. Stewart, published in *Journal of Applied Social Psychology*, 1980. Other studies and meta-reviews have confirmed this bias, and found similar effects in jury decisions and other aspects of the legal process.

On average, tall people are slightly higher in intelligence... The correlation is about 0.2: weak, but statistically significant. 'On the sources of the height–intelligence correlation: New insights from a bivariate ACE model with assortative mating', Jonathan Beauchamp, David Cesarini, Magnus Johannesson, Erik Lindqvist, and Coren Apicella, published in *Journal of Behavior Genetics*, 2011.

Even body shape is surprisingly difficult to change... The consensus is that permanent weight loss is extremely difficult to achieve. For an explanation of relevant factors see 'Maintenance of lost weight and long-term management of obesity', Kevin Hall and Scott Kahan, published in *The Medical Clinics of North America*, 2018.

As any 5-year-old child could tell you, death is bad... Hat tip to *Harry Potter and the Methods of Rationality*, Eliezer Yudkowsky, 2010-2015.

Frickin' badminton causes 10x more injuries than lifting... 'Relative Safety of Weightlifting and Weight Training', Brian Hamill, published in *Journal of Strength and Conditioning Research*, 1994.

If longevity researcher Peter Attia could impart a single piece of wisdom... 'Live Ep.1 with Peter Attia MD', Invest Like The Best, 2018.

Cycling is not much more dangerous than driving based on time spent on the road... The number of fatalities per million hours is something like 1.3-1.7 times higher for cycling than for driving. 'Fatality rates associated with driving and cycling for all road users in Great Britain 2005–2013', Shaun Scholes, Malcolm Ward, Paulo Anciaes, Benjamin Heydecker and Jennifer Mindella, published in *Journal of Transport & Health*, 2017.

The starting assumption should always be that you're paying for very expensive urine... See 'The Algernon Argument', Gwern Branwen, published on Gwern.net, 2010.

The data suggests loneliness levels haven't changed in generations... 'Is there a loneliness epidemic?', Esteban Ortiz-Ospina, published by Our World in Data, 2019.

I like Kevin Simler's definition of friendship... 'The Economics of Social Status', published on Melting Asphalt, 2013.

Caplan fulfilled his lifelong dream of living in a beautiful bubble... 'My Beautiful Bubble', Bryan Caplan, published on Econlib.org, 2012.

As Dunbar pointed out... As told to Maria Konnikova, 'The Limits of Friendship', published in *The New Yorker*, 2014.

RHIZIKON

Researchers asked a group of people to bid on tickets to a sold-out basketball game... 'Always Leave Home Without It: A Further Investigation of the Credit-Card Effect on Willingness to Pay,' Drazen Prelec and Duncan Simester, published in *Journal of Marketing Letters*, 2001.

Vacationers are happier in the weeks before they go away... 'Vacationers Happier, but Most not Happier After a Holiday', Jeroen Nawijn, M. Marchand, Ruut Veenhoven, Ad Vingerhoets, published in *Applied Research in Quality of Life*, 2010.

People in money trouble temporarily lose the equivalent of 13 IQ points... 'Poverty Impedes Cognitive Function', Anandi Mani, Sendhil Mullainathan, Eldar Shafir and Jiaying Zhao, published in *Science*, 2013.

Debt has been linked to higher blood pressure... 'The high price of debt: Household financial debt and its impact on mental and physical health', Elizabeth Sweet, Arijit Nandi, Emma Adam and Thomas McDade, published in *Social Science & Medicine*, 2013.

Kellogg School of Management found that people juggling significant credit card balances... 'Can Small Victories Help Win the War? Evidence from Consumer Debt Management', David Gal, Blakeley McShane, published in *Journal of Marketing Research*, 2012.

Their choices amount to indentured servitude, exile, or death... One in 15 borrowers has considered suicide due to their school loans, according to a 2019 survey by debt advisory group Student Loan Planner (sample size of 829).

What hedge fund manager Ray Dalio calls the risk of ruin... *Principles: Life & Work*, Ray Dalio, 2017.

Here's Keynes, writing in 1937... 'General Theory of Employment', John Maynard Keynes, published in *Quarterly Journal of Economics*, 1937.

This is not how Buffett gets his edge, and it hasn't been for decades... *Poor Charlie's Almanack*, Charles Munger, 2005.

[Buffett's] brand has become so powerful that at this point, his success is a self-fulfilling prophecy... Hat tip to Matt Levine, 'Someone Stole Warren Buffett's Halo', published in Money Stuff, 2020.

A $2 Powerball ticket is worth about 85 cents under the best conditions...
'Should You Play Powerball? Science Solves The Mystery', Ethan Siegel, published on Forbes.com, 2016.

As for individuals, [Taleb] suggests they should "stay far, far away"... 'Ask Me Anything on Options and other Nonlinear Derivatives', Nassim Taleb, published on Reddit, 2017.

So begins a famous Paul Graham essay... 'How to Make Wealth', Paul Graham, originally published in *Hackers & Painters: Big Ideas from the Computer Age*, 2004.

In trying to justify the huge losses, chief financial officer David Viniar said... 'Goldman pays the price of being big', Peter Thal Larsen, published in *Financial Times*, 2007.

KAIROS

The scourge of 'Fuckarounditis'... Hat tip to Martin Berkhan for diagnosing this global outbreak: 'Fuckarounditis', published on Leangains.com, 2011.

We've also experienced exponential growth in [...] many other technologies... 'Technological Progress', Max Roser and Hannah Ritchie, published by Our World in Data, 2013.

There is some evidence that the rate of progress has slowed since the 1970s... See *The Great Stagnation: How America Ate All the Low-Hanging Fruit of Modern History, Got Sick, and Will (Eventually) Feel Better*, Tyler Cowen, 2011.

California is naturally designed for fires... 'They Know How to Prevent Megafires. Why Won't Anybody Listen?', Elizabeth Weil, published by Propublica, 2020.

Price swings in markets can exhibit dependence, without displaying any correlation... Hat tip to Benoit Mandelbrot. See *The (Mis)Behavior of Markets: A Fractal View of Financial Turbulence*, 2004.

As the leading effectuation expert puts it... 'What Makes Entrepreneurs Entrepreneurial?', Saras Sarasvathy, published on Effectuation.org, 2008.

The main predictors of job satisfaction... Drive: The Surprising Truth About What Motivates Us, Daniel Pink, 2009.

Musk hasn't had a formal business plan since 1995... Talk at SXSW festival, 2018.

In [Graham's] view, the way to do really big things is to start with deceptively small things... 'Frighteningly Ambitious Startup Ideas', Paul Graham, published on paulgraham.com, 2012.

On average, each title will sell a paltry few hundred copies... Finding reliable sources is extremely hard, but traditionally-published books seem to average ~2000 lifetime sales (comprising 30% of titles in 2015, according to Bowker) while self-published average ~250 sales (70% of titles). The median (typical) number is much lower.

Sivers says this is the lifestyle followed by the happiest people he knows... 'How to do what you love and make good money', Derek Sivers, published on sivers.org, 2016.

Babies love exercising even the tiniest scraps of control. In a landmark study... as cited in The Paradox of Choice: Why More is Less, Barry Schwartz, 2004.

Another body of research suggests that senility is not an inevitable result of ageing... For an overview see 'The Relevance of Control Beliefs for Health and Aging', Margie Lachman, Shevaun Neupert and Stefan Agrigoroaei, published in Handbook of the Psychology of Aging, 2011.

The one piece of advice Peter Thiel wishes he could give his younger self... As told to Tim Ferriss in Tools of Titans, 2016.

Scanning the comments under the post... 'Once You Have F You Money, It's Hard To Tell Others To F Off!', Sam Dogen, published on Financial Samurai, 2015.

In December 1993, Taleb deposited his last business tie in the garbage can... Nassim Taleb, Twitter. The quote comes from *Skin in The Game*, 2018.

The psychologist Martin Seligman explains this paradox... *Learned Optimism*, Martin Seligman, 1991.

A fascinating essay in The Atlantic... 'Workism Is Making Americans Miserable', Derek Thompson, 2019.

TELOS

According to Aristotle, our reason for existence... *Nichomachean Ethics*, circa 340 BC, translated by W. D. Ross.

There's no such thing as the meaning of life [...] but there is such a thing as the meaning in life... Hat tip to Jonathan Haidt for this framing, *The Happiness Hypothesis*, 2016.

As for concerns around overpopulation, historically, these fears have been completely wrong... Hat tip to Matt Ridley, who charts the entire gruesome history in *The Evolution of Everything: How New Ideas Emerge*, 2015.

How much does it cost to become a secret superhero? The $3400 figure comes from *Doing Good Better*, William MacAskill, 2015.

A popular option is to pledge a fraction of your income to the most effective causes... Giving What We Can has more than 5000 members who have already donated $200 million to effective charities.

Parfit experienced this very dissolution of self... *Reasons and Persons*, Derek Parfit, 1984.

One study suggests the proportion of your income you spend on others...
In a study of more than 1000 older adults... As cited in *Happy Money: The Science of Smarter Spending*, Elizabeth Dunn and Michael Norton, 2013.

This is the basic currency of social animals... Hat tip to 'The Economics of Social Status', Kevin Simler, published on Melting Asphalt, 2013.

The social psychologist Jonathan Haidt suggests... *The Righteous Mind: Why Good People are Divided by Politics and Religion*, Jonathan Haidt, 2012.

Being slim is [...] a reliable signal of conscientiousness... 'Personality and obesity across the adult life span', Angelina Sutin, Luigi Ferrucci, Alan Zonderman and Antonio Terracciano, published in *Journal of Personality and Social Psychology*, 2011.

It was Cicero who first translated the Greek concept of frugality into Latin... Book III, *Tusculan Disputations*, Marcus Tullius Cicero, circa 45 BC, translated by C. D. Yonge.

St Augustine, writing in 380 AD... Volume 2, *On the Happy Life: Cassiciacum Dialogues*, Saint Augustine, translated by Michael Foley.

Negative space is high-status... Hat tip to 'Status as Space', Kevin Simler, published on Melting Asphalt, 2012.

We need games that are fun and virtuous to play, not just to win... Hat tip to Eliezer Yudkowsky for this framing, *Rationality: From AI to Zombies*, 2015.

We're not in here to eat mozzarella and go to Tuscany... 'Nassim Nicholas Taleb on Self-Education and Doing the Math (Ep. 41)', Conversations With Tyler, 2018.